The Penguin ISCO Careers Guide

TWELFTH EDITION

Jan Widmer

PENGUIN BOOKS

PENGUIN BOOKS

Published by the Penguin Group
Penguin Books Ltd, 80 Strand, London WC2R ORL, England
Penguin Group (USA) Inc., 375 Hudson Street, New York, New York 10014, USA
Penguin Books Australia Ltd, 250 Camberwell Road, Camberwell, Victoria 3124, Australia
Penguin Books Canada Ltd, 10 Alcorn Avenue, Toronto, Ontario, Canada M4V 3B2
Penguin Books India (P) Ltd, 11 Community Centre, Panchsheel Park, New Delhi – 110 017, India
Penguin Group (NZ), cnr Airborne and Rosedale Roads, Albany, Auckland 1310, New Zealand
Penguin Books (South Africa) (Pty) Ltd, 24 Sturdee Avenue, Rosebank 2196, South Africa

Penguin Books Ltd, Registered Offices: 80 Strand, London WC2R ORL, England

www.penguin.com

First published as *The Peacock Book of Careers for Girls* 1966
Second edition published as *Careers for Girls* 1970
Third edition 1973
Fourth edition 1975
Fifth edition published as *Equal Opportunities:*
A Careers Guide for Women and Men 1978
Sixth edition 1981
Reprinted with revisions 1982
Seventh edition 1984
Reprinted with revisions 1985
Eighth edition 1987
Ninth edition published as *The Penguin Careers Guide* 1992
Reprinted with updating material 1993
Tenth edition 1996
Eleventh edition 2002
Twelfth edition 2004
This edition published exclusively for ISCO 2004
1

Copyright © Ruth Miller, 1966, 1970, 1973, 1975, 1978, 1981, 1982, 1984,
1985, 1987, 1992, 1993, 1996, 2002, 2004
Copyright © Anna Alston, 1984, 1985, 1987, 1992, 1993, 1996, 2002, 2004
Copyright © Anne Daniel, 1992, 1993, 1996, 2002, 2004
Copyright © Jan Widmer, 2002, 2004
All rights reserved

This book is intended as a general guide to careers and not a substitute for careers advice. Neither the author
nor the publisher accept any responsibility for loss suffered by any person acting or refraining from acting as
a result of material contained within this book. Careers information changes quickly and where necessary
readers should make themselves aware of recent developments and consult a professional adviser

The moral right of the author has been asserted

Set in 10/12.5 pt PostScript Adobe Minion
Typeset by Rowland Phototypesetting Ltd, Bury St Edmunds, Suffolk
Printed in England by Clays Ltd, St Ives plc

PENGUIN BOOKS

THE PENGUIN ISCO CAREERS GUIDE

Jan Widmer started her career in magazine and newspaper journalism and posts included chief sub of the British *Readers' Digest*, feature writing for the *East Anglian Daily Times* and editing the *Soil Association Journal* before she turned to freelance editing and writing while bringing up her family. She now specializes in careers and related topics and has written for a number of publications. Since 1984 she has been Editor of *Newscheck*, a leading monthly magazine for careers practitioners, formerly published by the Department for Education and Skills and now by Trotman Publishing.

The Penguin Careers Guide is one of the longest established careers directories published in the UK. This edition takes forward the work of the three previous editors. Anna Alston, although continuing to edit *CareerScope* magazine, is now focusing on her work as a university careers adviser. Anne Daniel is concentrating on her work as an admissions officer in an Oxford college. Ruth Miller, one of the pioneers of careers writing, particularly for girls, and on whose original concept the *Guide* is based, is now retired but continues to take an active interest in the book.

Contents

Contents

Part Two
Main Careers in Alphabetical Order 39

Contents

Acknowledgements

I would like to thank the many organizations who have provided the information which has made this twelfth edition of the *Guide* possible, particularly the work life balance sections. I would also like to acknowledge the help of others who gave me advice or direction in my research, and I must make special mention of my researcher, Ann Mason. I am also greatly indebted for the support and encouragement given me by the past editors, Ruth Miller, Anne Daniel and Anna Alston.

Foreword

Over the last few years there have been a number of significant changes to employment legislation. These have largely related to protecting the position of those who must or prefer to balance their time in employment with time to care for children, elderly or disabled relatives, or indeed to pursue some other interest on a regular basis. Professional bodies are also beginning to seriously consider how best to support members with domestic responsibilities, not least perhaps because in quite a few professions there are more women entrants than men.

This 12th edition of *The Penguin Careers Guide* reflects this growing emphasis on the importance of work life balance by being, as far as I know, the only careers directory which includes information on these developments. The aim is to encourage those either deciding on a first career or considering career change to give some thought to whether once having established themselves in work they would easily be able to move to part-time or flexible working or take a career break. This used to be considered a woman's issue but increasingly is being seen by both sexes as part of their life plan.

BACKGROUND TO THE GUIDE

The *Penguin Careers Guide* was first published in 1966 as *Careers for Girls*. At that time, when nursing, teaching and secretarial work were considered the main 'good' jobs for girls, it was a trailblazer, its purpose unambiguously to encourage girls to widen their career choices. When in 1976, following the passing of the Sex Discrimination

Act, the book was renamed *Equal Opportunities: A Careers Guide for Women and Men*, there remained many hurdles to equality in employment. In 1992, by which time jobs and careers, with one or two statutory exceptions such as certain roles in the Armed Forces, were open to applicants regardless of their gender, the book was given its present title. In recognition, however, that women still had different concerns in choosing or progressing their career, each chapter continued to include additional information specifically for women, under the headings 'Career-break', 'Part time' and 'Position of women'.

On the evidence of research undertaken for the last couple of editions to provide the information to appear under the 'Position of women' heading, the battle for equal career opportunities has ostensibly been won. In many professions women now outnumber men, certainly in the younger age groups, and women appointed to top jobs no longer hit the headlines. Childcare is increasingly a responsibility shared by both parents. But despite the fact that 'new man' himself is now no longer quite the novelty he once was, women remain the main carers, both of children and of elderly or sick relatives. And it is still mainly women who opt for part-time or other family-friendly working hours.

In many cases, of course, this is a considered choice – women may prefer to dedicate part of their time to their family. And men, too, are recognizing the need for more balance between work and home. It is no longer so unusual for the woman to be the main breadwinner in a family or for the male partner to choose to arrange his hours around childcare. Fathers are as increasingly concerned as mothers to have a lifestyle that allows them to be home in time to see their children before bedtime.

So the goal now is not for women to be treated as if they are men but for the different roles and responsibilities which either sex may have at different times in their lives to be recognized and valued equally.

As a result, thinking on the subject of equal opportunities is moving on. In the past there were two main ways of tackling gender inequality: equal treatment supported by legislation, in which women could expect no less but no more than men and which in effect left them discriminated against because of their domestic responsibilities; and positive action, specific initiatives to attract women into particular employment areas. These two have now been joined by a third option: gender mainstreaming. This aims to get away from the single 'male' model of working life and introduce a variety of different arrangements which are equally valued and suitable for both women and men at different stages of their lives.

A changing climate

Work life balance is an issue which is currently being given serious consideration in many areas of employment. Equal opportunity and diversity recruitment – recruiting employees from all sectors of society – are now an inbuilt feature of workforce recruitment in all responsible companies and flexible working to cater for those with caring responsibilities is a major feature of this development. Some employers, a notable example being the NHS, promote flexible working as a major recruitment inducement. A number of professional organizations have commissioned research on which to recommend future employment practices.

The government is taking work life balance very seriously and is actively promoting the economic benefits of offering flexible working – increased production, less absence through sickness and a more committed workforce – to employers. New legislation introduced in April 2003 gave parents the right to ask for flexible working and introduced paid paternity leave (see p. 27). The Department of Trade and Industry has dedicated part of its website to work life balance issues (see *www.dti.gov.uk/work-lifebalance*) and has introduced an annual work life balance week to promote flexible working.

Perhaps most crucial to most women, regulations introduced in 2000 improved the rights of part-time workers (see p. 28). They should now not be treated less favourably than comparable full-time workers and are entitled to the same hourly rate of pay, the same access to annual leave, maternity or parental leave, sick pay, training and company pension schemes. And very importantly, there is now protection for workers returning, for example after maternity leave, to part-time work in employment where they previously worked full time.

Not all rosy

Despite this progress there are still major causes of concern. Although it is now 30 years since it became illegal to pay women less than men for doing similar work, statistics published by the Equal Opportunities Commission show that overall they still earn less than their male colleagues. In 2003 the gap between the average hourly earnings of men and women working full time was 18%. Areas of work in which women predominate, such as social care, continue to be considerably less well paid than areas in which men predominate, such as engineering. The pay gap exists at all qualification levels, and is widest for managers and administrators. However, this gap widens markedly when part-time work is put into the equation – the hourly rate for women working part time is on average only 41% of that earned by a man in full-time work.

The Equal Opportunities Commission is still campaigning vigorously to rectify this and late in 2003 introduced a new code of practice on equal pay. Further information can be found on *www.eoc.org.uk*.

In 2004 the EOC also published a report revealing that women still hold less than 10% of the most senior positions. They make up only 7% of the senior judiciary and senior police officers, and 9% of top business leaders. However, 23% of Civil Service top management are now women and 36% of public appointments are given to women.

Despite working time regulations that no workers should be required to work more than 48 hours a week without their agreement, a long hours culture persists in many occupations, impacting on women's ability to combine family and career. While welcoming the new employment legislation, many women will tell you that they still fear discrimination if they opt to take a career break or work part time, although, and I have no evidence to support this, I would suggest that in many employment fields a man's career would suffer even more severely if he took up these rights.

Looking ahead

Nevertheless, while acknowledging that there are still battles to be fought before all work is considered of equal economic value to society and for fairer treatment for all those who need to tailor their work around their domestic life, any young woman today would be truly astonished to be overtly denied entry to employment on account of her gender. Indeed, the focus of concern is moving to young men who now are more likely to lose out in the job market.

As we move into the twenty-first century, many new employment patterns have emerged, from long-distance commuting to home tele-working. There are increasing choices to be made about how, when or where to work. For this reason the subsections containing information specifically for women, 'Career-break', 'Part time' and 'Position of women', have in this new edition of the *Penguin Careers Guide* been merged into one under the heading 'Work life balance', although where there are still issues regarding employment of women, such as in the Armed Forces and the construction industry, the 'Position of women' heading has been retained. It is my hope that this book will help readers of both sexes to put work life balance into the equation when considering their career or career change.

However, this has always been an aim of the *Penguin Careers Guide* and perhaps we have just come full circle. To quote from the first edition: 'Choosing a career is difficult: how best to find a suitable training and a career that will be satisfying and also fit in with domestic responsibilities after marriage.' It suggests a 'two-stage' model of career in the future, that girls will 'train and work for a few years before marriage, then devote themselves to their families for a time, and later start what is usually the longer stage of their working lives.' Now that women and men are finding that 'you can't have it all' and that postponing a family is not always an option, maybe this model should be advocated again but for either sex.

Maybe the younger generation is already moving in this direction. A survey published in January 2004 to support the DTI's work life balance campaign found that 87% of employees would like to spend more time with their family and that 47% of 16–24 years olds had already made changes to their working hours to accommodate other interests, compared to 37% aged between 55 and 65.

A tribute

But to return finally to equal opportunities for women, despite the pay gap it must be acknowledged that real progress has been made since the *Guide* was first published in 1966. And it falls to me at this point to pay tribute to the role of the previous authors of the *Guide* for their contribution to that progress. Ruth Miller, author of the first and subsequent ten editions who continues to take a keen interest in the *Guide*, still recounts her surprise when Penguin agreed to publish *Careers for Girls*. An enormous amount of perseverance was required to research the information and statistics on female employment which have distinguished the book and given it its unique value. My own strong belief is that posterity should award both Ruth, and her later co-authors Anna Alston and Anne Daniel, considerably more than a footnote in the story of the fight for equal careers opportunities for girls and women.

Jan Widmer

Introduction to the *Guide*

OPENING

Access to careers information, like access to all other information, has been revolutionized by the Internet. Universities, professional bodies and providers of qualifications all now have websites where up-to-date details can be found instantly.

So why publish a printed careers directory? The answer is, in the main, for the same reasons that it has ever been useful. This publication aims to provide unbiased information, and to bring it together so that different careers can be compared and contrasted. In addition it provides the sort of information not readily available on the Web, such as insights into the work and the sort of person likely to be good at/happy in it, based on experience and observation. This is what differentiates the information in this book from that provided by the sources mentioned above, in whatever media the information may be provided.

That said, the Internet is a most valuable tool for those researching careers information. Qualifications and education and training structures are constantly being changed and once a particular career has been identified, the Web can be used to seek out the latest information. Website addresses are provided within the text where appropriate or at the end of each chapter.

WHO IS IT FOR?

The *Guide* is likely to be used mainly by young people between 14 and 20. However, it is also valuable for the increasing number of people in their twenties, thirties or forties who want to, or have to, change their occupation. Some made the wrong choice the first time around or have developed new interests; others face lack of demand for their existing knowledge and skills, or redundancy. It is important to realize that most people could be happy in several different careers. What you enjoy at 40 may well be different from what you enjoyed at 21. Some people, in fact, take a long time to find out what they really want to do. For many occupations maturity is seen as an asset; education and training facilities may well be available; and standard entry requirements may be relaxed for older people (see individual entries, 'Late Start and Return to Work', pp. 22–25, and 'Higher Education', p. 12).

More than ever before, individuals are expected to take charge of their own careers. This applies to everyone, from those working for large organizations to unemployed people on government training schemes. From time to time we all need to assess where we are in job terms, decide what we are aiming at and what we need to achieve our aims. 'Buzz' phrases today are 'personal portfolio' – the individual's package of knowledge, skills and experience – and 'transferable skills' – those which can be put to good use in any work situation. The man or woman who is prepared to be flexible, to take advantage of (increasingly compulsory) continuing professional development (CPD), and who doesn't assume that any job is immune to change, is the one most likely to weather times of high unemployment.

HOW TO USE THIS *GUIDE*

Careers in this *Guide* are listed alphabetically. However, many if not most careers are really 'areas of work'. Look at the index and you see how many more jobs than careers sections there are. Usually one kind of training leads to jobs in a variety of settings and you can normally mould training plus experience to the kind of job you will want to do when you know more about the whole spectrum and about your own likes, dislikes, strengths and weaknesses.

We could not hope to include all occupational areas in one book, so we have had to make arbitrary choices. Since the future demand is expected to be for more highly skilled, highly trained people, we have left out jobs requiring few, if any, educational qualifications, concentrating instead on those which need formal training or which lead to the widest range of options. School-leavers needing information on other jobs and training opportunities should contact their Connexions service. Adults should consult the Jobcentre or local guidance centre. Use this *Guide* in conjunction with 'Sources of Help' (p. 33), combined with discussions with personal/careers advisers, family, friends who know you well and, if possible, with people doing the jobs you'd like to do.

Look at job advertisements. If you are a mature job-seeker you may be baffled by some of the newer or rarer job titles. Often it is only by reading the job specification that you discover it is something you know under a different name. Some are genuinely new occupations and you may need to dig more deeply to find out if your background and possible future training would make you a good candidate. Be adventurous, look at as wide a range as possible, using the 'Related careers' sections as signposts.

PROSPECTS

We do not mention prospects, for the following reasons: first, within the book's lifetime the job market is likely to change. Secondly, there are always regional variations. Thirdly, and perhaps most importantly, it is frequently a mistake for a 16-year-old choosing A levels or an 18-year-old choosing a degree subject to do so with the aim of entering a 'shortage' occupation 5 or 7 years later, as the marketplace may change dramatically meanwhile. Lastly, the term 'prospects' does not mean the same thing to all people – for some it means high salaries and/or early promotion, others link it with job security or the chance to follow the occupation anywhere in the country.

Part One

The Qualifications System

THE NATIONAL QUALIFICATIONS FRAMEWORK

Successive governments have tried to bring the academic and vocational qualifications which have grown up piecemeal over the years into some kind of logical structure, to aid equivalence and progression. The aim is to bring all qualifications, general, vocational and occupational, within the national qualifications framework. The framework has 5 levels: foundation; intermediate; advanced; level 4 at the equivalent of a first degree; and level 5 which takes in higher level and professional qualifications. There is also entry level for students not ready for level 1 qualifications.

Further information Qualifications and Curriculum Authority website: *www.qca.org.uk*

GCSE

The General Certificate of Secondary Education is the main qualification awarded at 16+ to pupils in England and Wales. Grades are on a scale from A* to G; GCSEs at grades C and above are level 2 qualifications (intermediate level) and at grades D to G level 1 (foundation level). Short course GCSEs, which cover half the content and take roughly half the time of a full award, are available in a number of subjects. Four or five GCSEs at grades A–C is a common starting point for most of the careers and courses in this book.

GNVQs and GCSEs in Vocational Subjects

General National Vocational Qualifications introduced in 1993 are now gradually being replaced by GCSEs in vocational subjects. The 3-unit or Part One GNVQ was replaced in 2002 but Foundation and Intermediate level 6-unit GNVQs will be available until at least 2005 or until there are suitable alternatives available. The new vocational GCSEs are currently available in 8 subjects: Art and Design; Applied Business; Engineering; Health and Social Care; Applied Information and Communication Technology; Leisure and Tourism; Manufacturing; and Applied Science. A GCSE in a vocational subject is the equivalent of 2 academic GCSEs and is graded A*–G in the same way.

ADVANCED LEVEL QUALIFICATIONS

The structure of advanced level qualifications changed in 2000 with the introduction of a modular unit-based curriculum designed to increase breadth of study and make it easier to mix academic and vocational programmes. All advanced level qualifications are now made up of a number of units assessed in stages or at the end of the course and awarded at grades A–E.

AS level

The new GCE AS (Advanced Subsidiary) is a 3-unit qualification designed both to provide a bridge between GCSE and A level and give students the opportunity to broaden their range of subjects. In practice the AS acts as the first half of an A level but it is a qualification in its own right.

A level

The new GCE A levels are 6-unit qualifications, and are made up of an AS plus a further 3 units called the A2, taken in a second year. Assessment is through varying combinations of course work and exams.

Vocational A levels

The vocational A level or VCE is available in 3, 6 or 12 units. The 3 unit is equivalent to the AS, the 6 unit to an A level and the 12 unit (double award) to 2 A levels. These are designed to develop knowledge, skill and understanding relevant to a broad vocational area. From September 2005 VCEs are being revised to follow the AS/A2 structure and will be called A levels.

Advanced Extension Award

The Advanced Extension Award was introduced in 2002. This is designed for the top 10% of A level students, to allow them to demonstrate their depth of understanding of a subject. It is awarded at merit and distinction grades and is currently available in 17 subjects.

Key Skills Qualification

There are 6 key skills qualifications: communication, application of numbers, IT, working with others, improving own learning and performance, and problem-solving. Introduced as part of the curriculum changes in 2000, they are available at different levels and are assessed on the basis of course work and a test.

Entry to Higher Education

The standard entry to higher education is 2/3 qualifications at advanced level and many higher education institutions now accept a combination of A/AS/VCEs. However, degree level courses differ greatly in their requirements and universities and higher education colleges are not uniform in their response to the new curriculum. Prospective students should seek advice before choosing their advanced level programme and check carefully with individual institutions.

Scottish Qualifications

The system in Scotland differs from the rest of the UK. The following is a basic guide to its structure.

Standard Grade

Standard Grade (formerly SCE Ordinary grade) is the equivalent of GCSE and is normally taken in Scottish fourth year. It is awarded on a scale of seven grades: grades 1 and 2 are known as 'credit', 3 and 4 as 'general' and 5 and 6 'foundation'. A credit pass in a certain subject may be a prerequisite for certain degree courses.

National Qualifications

This is a programme of units and courses offered in fifth and sixth year of secondary education and some schools will offer these in fourth year instead of Standard Grade.

The programme has 5 levels: Access, Intermediate 1, Intermediate 2, Higher and Advanced Higher. Students usually complete a course in 1 year but can take longer if desired. Students can progress from one level to the next or move sideways on to other subjects at the same level.

The courses taken by students in fifth year are determined by the levels achieved at Standard Grade. Students normally take 5 subjects in fifth year but may take a variety of subjects at different levels depending on how they have performed at Standard Grade level. Each course at each level is divided into three separate units and each unit has its own internal assessment. In order to get the course award a student must pass all 3 units.

At the end of the whole course – i.e. at the end of all 3 units – there is an external assessment. Its form is appropriate to the subject so it may be a traditional examination or it could be, for example, a performance. The final course grade is given on the basis of how well the student does in this external assessment/exam.

Vocational subjects such as care, hospitality and mechanics are offered in the same 5-level course pattern as more traditional subjects like English and maths. Courses taught at FE colleges – as well as those taught at school – are within the same NQ programme.

Group Awards
Pupils can do five separate subjects of their choice or, if they choose a group of subjects that go together, they can get a Scottish Group Award (SGA). For example, they might get an SGA in technology, or in languages. The SGA includes full courses, extra units and evidence of appropriate competence in five key core skills – communication, numeracy, using IT, problem-solving and working with others. There are no extra exams for the SGA – the award is made simply on the basis of having completed the necessary courses and units.

University Entrance
Universities use passes at Higher level as the basis of their offer, with some giving credit for Advanced Highers. For example, they may accept a grade at Advanced Higher as equivalent to one grade above that in the same subject at Higher level. Scottish universities may allow students with Advanced Highers direct entry on to the second year of a closely related 4-year degree course (in the same way that they may allow A level students from elsewhere in the UK to do so).

Scottish Qualifications Certificate
Students are awarded the Scottish Qualifications Certificate, which lists all educational and training achievements to date. This includes a Core Skills profile showing the level achieved in communication, working with others, numeracy, problem-solving and information technology. Those gaining Group Awards are given an additional certificate.

All Group Awards have compulsory Core Skills units. Core skills are also being developed through Highers.

Scottish Qualifications Authority (SQA), Hanover House, 24 Douglas Street, Glasgow G2 7NQ.
   Helpline: 0141 242 2214
   www.sqa.org.uk

UCAS Tariff

The University and College Admissions Service (UCAS) has developed a tariff which calculates advanced level qualifications on a points score system to evaluate achievement for entry to higher education. Additional qualifications are being added into the tariff year by year. Many institutions now use the tariff system to express their entry requirements but some still ask for specific A level grades.

Further information *www.ucas.com*

EDEXCEL (BTEC)

Edexcel offers nationally recognized BTEC qualifications in a wide range of subjects. These include: business, health and social care, art and design, media, engineering, hospitality, IT and computing, travel and tourism, sport and leisure, public services and science.

BTEC courses may be taken in schools, colleges of further and higher education, approved training centres and companies. Courses are modular, with a range of compulsory 'core' and optional subjects so students can tailor-make programmes to suit their needs and interests.

There are several levels of course and qualification.

BTEC Introductory Certificate and Diploma

Introduced in 2003, these are the first step to skills in a chosen vocational sector.

BTEC First Diploma

No minimum qualifications are required, but some colleges may set some. Programmes are usually one year and may be full or part time. The First Diploma is available in many schools.

BTEC National

A minimum of 4 GCSEs (A*–C) or GNVQ Intermediate or acceptable pass in First Diploma, or at the discretion of the college. The National Certificate takes 2 years part time, the National Diploma takes 2 years full time or 3 years part time or sandwich. They are roughly equivalent to A levels and are acceptable (at the right standard of pass) for entry to degree courses.

BTEC Higher Nationals – HND and HNC

A minimum of 1 A level plus supporting GCSEs (A*–C) or Advanced GNVQ/Vocational A level (double award) or BTEC National award. The Higher National Certificate (HNC) usually takes 2 years part time, the Higher National Diploma (HND) takes 2 years full time or 3 years part time or sandwich. They are generally accepted as equivalent to pass degree.

Continuing education

Edexcel also offers a range of individual units and programmes for adults wishing to update and acquire new skills.

Further information Edexcel, Stewart House, 32 Russell Square, London WC1B 5DN.
www.edexcel.org.uk

CITY & GUILDS

City & Guilds awards its own qualifications in over 500 different subjects in a wide range of vocational areas, including catering and hospitality, construction, engineering, printing, travel and tourism, agriculture and horticulture, media, retail and distribution, and health and social care. City & Guilds does not run courses itself; these are held in centres such as colleges of further education, adult education institutes and training centres. Courses may be part time, full time or a mixture. Some are available by distance learning or through flexible learning programmes.

In the main, no specific time limits or entry requirements are laid down for qualifications. Many certificates are awarded jointly with partners in industry. All City & Guilds awards are normally available at several levels and individuals often progress from one to the next. In addition, there are many senior awards that people can work for and which depend solely on experience and demonstrated ability, not on conventional academic study: Licentiateship (higher technician or master craftsman level); Graduateship (equivalent to first degree); Membership (equivalent to a Master's degree or full corporate membership of a professional body); Fellowship (outstanding professional achievement at the highest level).

Further information City & Guilds, 1 Giltspur Street, London EC1A 9DD. *www.city-and-guilds.co.uk*

NATIONAL VOCATIONAL QUALIFICATIONS/ SCOTTISH VOCATIONAL QUALIFICATIONS

National Vocational Qualifications (NVQs) and Scottish Vocational Qualifications (SVQs) are work-based qualifications which record the 'skills, knowledge and understanding' of an individual in relation to their work. They are based on national occupational standards developed by Sector Skills Councils. These identify the level of competence expected of people in their work.

Competence means the ability to perform tasks, and this is assessed 'on the job'. This may be as an employee, through a Modern Apprenticeship, or as a school or college student through a work placement. NVQs are unit based and a unit is achieved when the candidate is assessed as competent in the skills and knowledge specified.

NVQs are awarded at the 5 levels of the qualifications framework. Level 1 is the most basic, level 3 broadly equates to 2 A levels, while level 5 represents higher professional qualifications. Levels 1–4 are in place in most sectors. Because each NVQ fits into a framework it should now be possible to relate one vocational qualification to another, regardless of what organization has awarded it, making it easier to move up the qualifications ladder.

NVQs are awarded by established organizations, such as City & Guilds (see p. 10), Edexcel (BTEC) (see p. 8) and a host of organizations representing different industry sectors. In England the qualifications are approved by the Qualifications and Curriculum Authority; in Wales by the Qualifications, Assessment and Curriculum Authority for Wales; and in Scotland by the Scottish Qualifications Authority (the SQA differs in that it awards as well as accredits qualifications). These qualifications are not graded, since candidates are either competent or not yet competent.

MODERN APPRENTICESHIPS

Modern Apprenticeships are a national initiative designed to equip young people with the range of flexible skills needed in today's changing employment market and 150 are available in 14 different sectors within industry and commerce. The aim is to ensure that more young people obtain higher level vocational skills. They differ from old-style apprenticeships in three main ways:

1. they are not 'time-serving';
2. they are not male-dominated;

3. they are available not only in traditional industries but in occupational areas which never had apprenticeships.

A Modern Apprenticeship is based on a training agreement between the apprentice and employer. Employers must follow strict guidelines. Time taken is flexible, depending on the apprentice's educational qualifications and experience at the start, but Modern Apprenticeships usually take three years. Apprentices are normally paid a wage.

There are two levels of Modern Apprenticeships: Foundation and Advanced. Foundation Modern Apprenticeships are open to school and college leavers from 16 and focus on achieving a level 2 NVQ. Advanced Modern Apprenticeships (Modern Apprenticeships in Wales) are open to young people aged 16–24 and lead to at least one NVQ at level 3. Both levels aim to equip young people with the key skills such as working with others and problem solving.

The Government has announced that in England Foundation and Advanced Modern Apprenticeships are to be replaced by Apprenticeships and Advanced Apprenticeships. Apprenticeships for adults are also to be introduced.

In Scotland Modern Apprenticeships are part of the Scottish Enterprise's Skillseekers initiative.

Further information Contact the local Connexions Service or ring learndirect on 0800 100 900.
www.realworkrealpay.info
www.scottish-enterprise.com

HIGHER EDUCATION

Degrees

Courses and qualifications in higher education are constantly evolving. The traditional route to a degree is still through a 3- or 4-year full-time or 4-year sandwich course, but part-time and even distance-learning modes of study are becoming more widespread. Students may specialize in a single subject or in two major subjects in a joint degree or take various combinations of subjects in a 'combined' degree. The great majority of degrees are now structured on a modular basis, with modules carrying a number of credits depending on their length. Modules are available at levels (normally 1, 2 or 3) and whereas some courses require students to take a level 1 before they take a level 2, others allow students to pick up modules at different levels in a different order. This way there is maximum choice and flexibility.

There is a nationally recognized credit rating of courses (under what is generally called the CATS scheme – Credit Accumulation and Transfer). For example, for an honours degree students need to accumulate 360 credits, with 120 credits being awarded after each of three years of full-time study. Credits may also be given by institutions to students for in-company training, professional studies and experiential learning, so long as these relate to the proposed course of study. The European Credit Transfer Scheme (ECTS) also provides for Europe-wide credit transfer. This is operated by the Socrates/Erasmus Programme which also offers HE students the opportunity to study at universities in other European countries.

Higher National Diplomas

These are full-time or sandwich courses in vocational subjects such as science, engineering and business. They may be taken as a qualification in their own right or, in some cases, as a stepping stone to a degree. Higher National Diplomas (HNDs) may be linked to a degree in the same subject at one or more universities and allow successful diplomates entry to the final year of the degree course. Others allow students on to the second year of a degree. In some cases students who start degree courses and find them too challenging can transfer on to an HND programme. Higher National Certificates (HNCs) are available in similar subjects, mainly followed by people in work who wish to study part time. Some full-time HNCs are also available. Although of a similar standard to HNDs they do not generally cover such a full syllabus.

Discussions are currently under way to bring HND/Cs into the Foundation degree framework (see below).

Diploma of Higher Education – England and Wales only

Most Diplomas of Higher Education (Dip. HE) courses take 2 years full time or 3 years part time at higher education institutions. Nursing Dip. HEs take 3 years (except for graduates). Entry requirements for school-leavers vary – some, but not all, require a minimum number of UCAS points (i.e. A levels or equivalents).

Courses are comparable in standards and sometimes similar or identical in content to the first 2 years of an honours degree. As free-standing courses they are available only in a small number of subject areas. Most are vocationally related, for example in health care or management studies. They may form an integral part of vocational training. Many diplomates go on to degree courses towards which their Dip. HE may count; some universities award a Dip. HE after successful completion of 2 years of a degree course.

Foundation degrees

Foundation degrees are a new vocationally focused higher education qualification introduced in 2001, designed by universities in partnership with employers. Courses develop work-specific skills relevant to a particular employment sector, and are the equivalent of 2 years' academic learning. Students who are already in employment can combine study at a higher education institution with distance or Internet-supported learning and work-based learning in programmes to suit their circumstances. A foundation degree may be used as credit towards honours degree studies or towards professional qualifications.

At the time of writing it is the government's intention that foundation degrees will become the standard higher education vocational qualification at intermediate level, and that many pre-existing intermediate qualifications such as HNDs will be converted to foundation degrees.

Entry requirements – Widening access

Traditionally, to enter a degree course one normally needed 2 or 3 passes at A level (or 4 or 5 Scottish Highers). For an HND normally 1 pass at A level is required. In recent years, however, many universities have accepted applicants with alternative qualifications such as International or European Baccalaureate or Vocational A levels. Recent changes in post-16 examinations in England, Wales and Scotland mean that universities are making offers based on the new UCAS tariff, which sets out how much credit is attached to different types of examinations (see p. 8). Many universities have welcomed applications from 'mature' candidates without these kinds of school or college leaving qualifications. In 2002 over 75,000 of accepted student applications for full-time courses were from people aged 21 or over. Over 36,000 of these were over 30. The number of mature students on part-time courses is even higher. Mature applicants are required to show evidence of recent academic study to demonstrate that they will be able to cope with the course. Those with a suitable background (of education, work or training) may be admitted straight on to a course. For those without there are various ways to prepare.

Foundation years

These are also known as year 0 and are taught in universities (occasionally colleges) and lead straight on to the first year of the degree, making a 4-year course in total. These are mostly in disciplines such as science or engineering where students without a strong background in specific subjects can catch up.

Access to higher education courses

These courses have been around even longer and are run at adult and further education institutions. They may be directly linked to degree courses at a nearby university or may be free standing. They are in subjects ranging from teaching to social work, science to law or humanities. All include an element of numeracy, information technology and English.

Other preparatory programmes range from courses which help

students to improve A level grades to those which update special areas of knowledge, to those which deal with study skills. They may have titles such as 'Return to study', 'Wider opportunities', 'Make your experience count'. Some universities run summer schools as a 'taster' for potential students. Residential colleges are intended for those over 21. They run a variety of courses, some intended as preparation for higher education or professional training, others designed to stretch students' minds and open up their horizons.

Associate student schemes

Students are not formally enrolled on degree programmes, but sample some units of degree courses. Assessment is optional. Some students decide to progress to degree study.

The Open University

The Open University is the UK's largest institution of higher education. No academic qualifications are required for admission for undergraduate degrees, but places are limited and students are admitted on a first-come basis. Students study at home in their own time using specially prepared materials, such as books, videos, radio and TV programmes, and, increasingly, online. There are also weekend and residential summer schools. Students build up credits towards ordinary and honours degrees. It is possible to complete a degree in 3 years but most people take 4 to 6 years, combining study with work or family responsibilities. There is also an associate student programme and many shorter courses for professional people, scientific and technical updating, community and personal interest. There are various postgraduate programmes and a range of management courses taught through the OU Business School.

Further information The Open University, Walton Hall, Milton Keynes MK7 6AA.
Website: *www.open.ac.uk* (this includes addresses of regional centres)

University of London External Degrees

The External programme has a long history. It differs from the much newer Open University in offering in-depth study of single subjects rather than interdisciplinary courses. London University acts only as an examining body, with students studying either independently or, more commonly, at a college or by correspondence course. The basic entry requirement is 2 A levels and 3 GCSEs, or equivalent, but mature applicants are assessed on an individual basis. Successful students gain a London University degree (or a more recently introduced Diploma which, as in other universities, may allow progress to a degree).

Further information The External Programme, Senate House, University of London, Malet Street, London WC1E 7HU.
Email: *enquiries@external.lon.ac.uk*
Website: *www.lon.ac.uk*
UCAS publishes an annual *Mature Student's Guide*. For list of access courses see the website: *www.ucas.com/access*

Financing Your Studies

The system of funding students through further and higher education has changed radically in recent years and continues to change. At the time of writing the position is as follows.

NON-ADVANCED COURSES

These are courses run mainly in further, tertiary or adult education colleges.

Students aged 16–18 studying in their local colleges do not have to pay fees. Students aged 19 and over are normally expected to make a contribution, based on income. Education Maintenance Allowances which offer some young people staying on in full-time education after year 11 a weekly income dependent on their parents' means are available through Local Education Authorities. Students with financial difficulty may also apply for help from Learning Support and Access funds, administered and distributed by the colleges. Contact the college's Awards or Welfare Officer. Help may also be available for certain kinds of residential course (e.g. agriculture or horticulture) outside the area.

Students aged over 18 are eligible for Career Development Loans for vocational courses (see p. 20).

Further information Check with the local Jobcentre or phone the learndirect helpline: 0800 100 900, or look at the Department for Education and Skills website: *www.lifelonglearning.co.uk/moneyto learn*

A booklet *Money to Learn* is available from the DfES, telephone: 0845 602 2260.

ADVANCED COURSES

Free tuition and mandatory awards for degrees and other higher education awards have been replaced by a new method of funding.

There are two elements to the cost of studying: tuition fees and living costs.

Tuition fees

The government currently sets a maximum on what universities can charge as a contribution towards the cost of teaching students, for example, for 2003/4 it has been set at £1,125. Local education authorities (LEAs) will pay all or part of the fees for full-time students depending on income, either that of the parent or that of the student if he/she is classed as an independent student. Tuition fees are not payable by Scottish domiciled students attending Scottish universities.

Part-time students on low incomes can receive help with tuition fees; this is administered by the college/university, not the LEAs.

Living costs

Maintenance grants, which used to be paid by LEAs, have been replaced by a system of Student Loans. These loans are interest free and students start paying back the loans only after they have finished their studies and are earning a minimum annual salary, in 2003 set at £10,000.

Full time

Amounts change every year but for 2003/4 students could borrow up to £3,165 if living at home, £4,000 if studying away from home (£4,930 if in London). A portion of this is now means-tested.

Part time

Students can apply for a loan of £500 a year; this is means-tested. Other categories of students who are eligible for some financial help include those with child or adult dependants, those who have just left care and those with disabilities.

Other sources of help

Universities and colleges administer Access Bursary Funds, Hardship Funds, and Hardship Loans. Some universities offer other bursary schemes – ask individual institutions. Some charities also have funds available for students in particular categories.

Reference libraries will have directories of grant-making trusts.

CAREER DEVELOPMENT LOANS

These are deferred repayment bank loans administered on behalf of the government by 3 banks (Barclays, Co-operative, and Royal Bank of Scotland). Borrowers do not need to have an existing account with these banks to qualify. The loans are intended only to help with vocational courses and training which can be at any level, from NVQs to post-graduate awards. Study can be full time, part time or by distance learning. Students can borrow between £300 and £8,000 to cover up to 80% of training costs over 2 years or less plus 1 year of practical work experience if it is part of the course. The DfES pays the interest until a month after the course finishes, when the student starts to repay the loan.

Further information Details from the above banks or the CDL Information Line: 0800 585 505 or website:
www.lifelonglearning.co.uk/cdl

SOURCES OF INFORMATION

England and Wales: *Financial Support for Higher Education Students in 2003/4.*

For all information on student finance telephone DfES information line: 0800 731 9133 or look at website: *www.dfes.gov.uk/studentsupport*

Scotland: Student Awards Agency for Scotland, telephone: 0845 111 1711; Fax: 0131 244 5887. email: *saas.gov@scotland.gsi.gov.uk*

Website: *www.student-support-saas-gov.uk* (for Scottish students only).

Northern Ireland: Department for Employment and Learning, Student Support Branch, telephone: 028 90 257710; Fax: 028 90 257747. email: *studentsupport@delni.gov.uk*

Website: *www.student-support.org.uk*

The Student Loans Company Ltd, 100 Bothwell Street, Glasgow G2 7JD. Helpline: 0800 40 50 10.

Website: *www.slc.co.uk*

The Mature Student's Guide to Higher Education (UCAS).

Late Start and Return to Work

A VARIETY OF ROUTES FOR RETURNERS, CAREER CHANGERS AND LATE STARTERS

There have never been as many or as flexible opportunities for catching up on missed educational and training opportunities as there are now. Adults who need educational or vocational qualifications – or simply more knowledge – for courses or careers they want to start or return to after a gap of some years can choose from an ever-increasing variety of courses and methods of study. For details of what is available nationally and locally see guides listed under 'Especially for Job-Changers and Late Starters' on p. 37.

PREPARATORY COURSES

Most re-entry courses were started by women, for women wishing to return to work, but men are rarely excluded. These preparatory courses have various titles, such as 'Women into Work', 'Ready for Work' and 'New Opportunities for Women'.

Courses vary in content, organization, level and quantity of work expected. Some are mainly confidence-restoring and 'diagnostic': they help students to sort out their aims, motivation, level of confidence and circumstances, and then balance these with the available job opportunities and obstacles which may arise. Others include work experience or work-related skills training, introduction to new technology and job-hunting techniques.

OPEN LEARNING

(The terms *open learning* and *distance-learning* are often inter-changeable.)

What is *open learning*? Essentially it is a system which enables more people to make use of educational and training facilities. Flexibility and accessibility are the key-words. All colleges are trying to attract more adults to their courses, whatever their chosen method of study. Open learning aims to remove traditional barriers to education and training, such as rigid entry requirements, the need for full-time attendance, fixed-length courses, and the need to live or work within daily travelling distance of college or training centre.

Flexibility is provided in two ways: by making entry requirements less rigid and by giving students a choice of study methods to fit in with their work or domestic commitments. For example, *distance-learning* courses have been steadily increasing in recent years. These are a kind of 'souped up' correspondence course with study by post being supplemented by audio and videotapes and/or IT, plus personal, telephone or email contact with a tutor. One of the best-known providers is the National Extension College (NEC, Michael Young Centre, Purbeck Road, Cambridge CB2 2HN. *www.nec.ac.uk*).

Accessibility partly depends on where courses are held – some areas are much better provided for than others. Students can generally enrol on open-learning courses at any time and work at their own pace. Many courses require attendance on one or two days a week or even less, making it possible for many more people to participate than in the past. The growth of multi-media provision and the potential offered by the Internet have given a boost to open learning and are opening it up to many more people.

Open learning is increasingly used to train people who are in work (see learndirect p. 25). The definition of the term 'open learning' is complicated by the fact that it refers both to a concept and to specific institutions and initiatives.

OPEN COLLEGE NETWORKS

These should not be confused with the Open University. Open College Networks do not themselves run courses, but consist of groups of colleges which collaborate to provide accreditation for adult learning in their geographical area. This is carried out through a system of credits and levels (see CATS, p. 13). These can help individual learners plan their pathways through their local further and higher education system and, in many cases, enable them to have their achievements recognized by other Open College Networks. Although the 31 Networks differ in the way they work, they all adhere to a framework giving four levels of award, ranging from entry to A level/NVQ level 3.

Further information National Open College Network, Kedleston Road, Derby DE22 1GB.
www.nocn.org.uk

THE OPEN COLLEGE OF THE ARTS

This was set up in 1987 to provide training in the arts by open-learning methods to people wishing to develop their artistic and creative abilities at home. It is affiliated to the Open University (see p. 16). Courses currently available are in painting, drawing, sculpture, textiles, art and design, interior design, garden design, calligraphy, reading, photography, creative writing, music, singing, understanding art, understanding dance. The two main elements of a course are books, tapes and videos and tutorial support. Students can choose to study either by correspondence, with help and guidance from a personal tutor, or by face-to-face study at locations throughout England, Wales, Scotland and Ireland. Many tutors are based in colleges and art centres, while others are practitioners with an interest in teaching. Optional summer schools, life classes, visits, etc., are arranged by many tutors.

Some courses carry the option of assessment for academic credit points awarded by the University of Glamorgan, and OCA has a credit transfer agreement with the Open University. The OCA can be particularly useful for people who think they might want to work in the arts, but need to test their abilities and build up a portfolio, including those who have to study at home because of domestic circumstances.

Further information Open College of the Arts, Unit B, Redbrook Business Park, Wilthorpe Road, Barnsley S75 1JN.
www.oca-uk.com

LEARNDIRECT

learndirect is a government-supported online course provider. The aim is to enable people to acquire specific knowledge, mostly work related, without enrolling for a traditional course which may involve many months of study before they come to the particular area of learning they need. Courses may be as short as 15 minutes or take several hours. They can be assessed through a personal computer at home, at work, or at one of the learndirect centres set up in easily accessible locations including shopping malls, sports centres and railway stations. Courses do not lead to national qualifications but some are designed to help lead towards the achievement of a formal qualification including undergraduate and post-graduate qualifications through work-based learning.

Further information *www.learndirect.co.uk*

Employment Legislation

A brief outline of the main legislation and regulations affecting employment.

Sex Discrimination Act 1995
The Sex Discrimination Act 1995 makes it unlawful to discriminate on the grounds of sex, including in employment and education or in advertisements for jobs.

The Equal Pay Act 1995
The Equal Pay Act 1995 stipulates that women must be paid the same as men when they are doing equal work and vice versa.

Disability Discrimination Act 1995
The Disability Discrimination Act 1995 made it unlawful for employers with 15 or more employees to discriminate against a disabled employee or job applicant by treating them less favourably or by not making reasonable adjustments.

In 2003 this legislation was extended to cover small employers.

The Race Relations Act 1976
The Race Relations Act 1976 makes it unlawful to treat a person less favourably than others on racial grounds. It covers grounds of race, colour, nationality (including citizenship), and national or ethnic origin.

Equality and Diversity

Further anti-discrimination legislation was introduced in 2003 – the Employment Equality (Sexual Orientation) Regulations 2003 and the Employment Equality (Religion or Belief) Regulations 2003.

Anti-age Discrimination

New anti-age discrimination legislation is planned for 2006.

Maternity Leave

Women are entitled to 26 weeks' ordinary maternity leave, normally paid, regardless of how long they have worked for their employer. If they have been in continuous employment by the beginning of the fourteenth week before their expected date of childbirth, women are entitled to additional maternity leave. This starts immediately after ordinary maternity leave and adds a further 26 weeks. Additional maternity leave is usually unpaid.

Paternity Leave

To be eligible for paternity leave an employee must be the biological father of the child or expect to have responsibility for the upbringing of the child and must have worked continuously for their employer for 26 weeks, ending 15 weeks before the child is due. Most employees are entitled to Statutory Paternity Pay and can choose to take one or two weeks consecutive leave. The leave can start following the child's birth but should be completed within 56 days of the first day of the expected week of birth.

Adoption Leave

To quality for adoption leave an employee must be newly matched with a child (i.e. not a step-parent adopting a partner's children) by an adoption agency and have worked continuously for an employer for 26 weeks before the date of notification of matching. Adoption leave is available to an individual or to one of a couple adopting jointly and equates with maternity leave, starting from the date of placement or from a fixed date which can be up to 14 days before the expected date of placement. Partners of adopters are entitled to paternity leave.

Parental Leave

Parents who have completed one year's qualifying service are entitled to 13 weeks' unpaid parental leave for each child born after 15 December 1994 and 18 weeks' leave for a child entitled to a disability living allowance born after 15 December 1981. Parents' rights to return to the same or similar job are also protected. Parental leave can be taken at any time up until the child's fifth birthday or until 5 years after adoption or in the case of children with a disability, up until their eighteenth birthday.

Flexible Working

Parents of children under 6 can apply to work flexibly and employers have a statutory duty to consider their application seriously. Flexible working can include flexitime, job-sharing, term-time working, voluntary reduced working time (see the work life balance website www.dti.gov.uk/work-lifebalance for a full list of flexible working options).

Time Off for Dependants

Employees have a legal right to take time off for family emergencies such as unexpected illness or accident, or childcare breaking down. Employers are not obliged to pay for the time taken but are not able to penalize employees for their absence as long as the reason is genuine.

Part-time Working

The Part-time Workers (Prevention of Less Favourable Treatment) Regulation 2000 ensures that part-time workers are not treated less favourably than their full-time colleagues doing comparable work. This means they must receive comparable treatment regarding rates of pay (including overtime when they have worked more than the normal full-time hours), access to career break schemes, maternity and parental leave, holiday entitlement, training and development, company pension schemes, promotion and transfer and redundancy.

Protection is also provided for employees wishing to return to part-time work where formerly they were employed full time.

Working Time

The working time regulations stipulate that employees may not be asked to work more than 48 hours a week although they can agree to opt out. Other provisions include a limit of an average of 8 hours' work in 24 which nightworkers can be required to work, a right to a day off each week and a right to 4 weeks' paid leave per year (see *www.dti.gov.uk/er/work_time_regs* for greater detail). Working time includes travelling where it is part of the job, working lunches and training. It does not include day release, travel between home and work or lunch breaks.

Young workers (over the minimum school leaving age but under 18) should not work more than 8 hours a day. There is no opt out for young workers although there are some exemptions for those in the Armed Forces or on board ships.

www.dti.gov.uk
www.eoc.org.uk
www.disability.gov.uk
www.homeoffice.gov.uk
www.agepositive.gov.uk

Working in Europe

The Single European Act guarantees the freedom for every EU citizen to work, to seek work, to set up business or to provide services in any EU member state. Community citizens may not be discriminated against on grounds of nationality. This means that EU nationals are free to work and to practise their professions anywhere in Europe. In fact, the situation can be more complicated, as qualifications must be recognized in other member states.

Undoubtedly, with the spread of multinational companies, more people will spend part of their working lives with big companies abroad. Yet many professionals wishing to set themselves up in practice or to apply for comparable posts in other member states still face barriers, due to the differing nature of qualification systems in the member states. The European Commission has introduced a number of directives in an attempt to address these issues.

SECTORAL DIRECTIVES

Initially, the Commission aimed to harmonize qualifications profession by profession. Sectoral Directives were issued for the professions of doctor, dentist, midwife, general care nurse, pharmacist, veterinary surgeon and architect. This means that those qualified in these jobs in one EU member state can work in another member state, although they do need to register with the appropriate professional body.

GENERAL DIRECTIVES

The sectoral approach proved to be lengthy and difficult (it took 17 years for the architects to agree!) and so the Commission decided to tackle the remaining professions by means of General Directives based on the principle of mutual recognition of qualifications.

The first General Directive (89/48/EEC) covers professionally regulated qualifications at degree level and above, and the second General Directive (92/51/EEC) covers professionally regulated qualifications at below degree level.

Further information about the directives and who to contact to have qualifications recognized in other member states is available from: DfES Qualifications for Work Directorate, Room E4B, Moorfoot, Sheffield s1 4PQ.
www.dfes.gov.uk/europeopen

TRANSITIONAL MEASURES DIRECTIVES

Transitional Measures Directives assist crafts or trades people, such as construction workers, hairdressers, insurance agents and brokers, who want to work in an independent or self-employed capacity in another member state. These directives require the authorities in the host member state to accept proof of work experience (generally 5 or 6 years in self-employment) in the home member state as a substitute for the relevant national qualification in the host member state. Experience and training must be certified by authorities in the home member state and, providing they meet the requirements of the directive which covers the area of work, a Certificate of Experience is issued.

Further information Certificate of Experience Unit, Department of Trade and Industry, 2nd Floor, Kingsgate House, 66–74 Victoria Street, London sw1e 6sw.
www.dti.gov.uk

NATIONAL REFERENCE POINTS FOR VOCATIONAL QUALIFICATIONS

The National Reference Point (NRP) network is an organization of centres across Europe that can help and advise on the recognition of qualifications.

The UK National Reference Point for Vocational Qualifications (or UK NRP) is operated by NARIC and acts as a national agency in a European network of reference points for vocational qualifications in the member states. The UK NRP operates an assessment service, which can produce an evaluation report detailing the comparable UK level and closest award, modular equivalence, background information and grading system conversion.

The main focus of this service initially is to provide information to individuals, employers, professional associations and other interested organizations in the UK about European vocational qualifications. However the UK NRP will also act as a signpost to the other NRPs across Europe for those wanting information about the validity of their UK qualifications in Europe.

Further information is available from National Reference Point for Vocational Qualifications, UK NARIC, Oriel House, Oriel Road, Cheltenham, Gloucestershire GL50 1XP, Tel: 01242 260225, email: *vq@ecctis.co.uk*

Information on all aspects of careers and working in Europe and further afield is available from Careers Europe, Onward House, 2 Baptist Place, Bradford BD1 2PS.
www.careerseurope.co.uk

Sources of Help

CAREERS ADVISORY SERVICES

As a result of devolution the different countries of the UK now all have their own careers advisory services.

England

In England the main source of information and guidance for young people is the Connexions Service. Connexions is a new support service for young people aged between 13 and 19, offering help in a range of areas including careers. Local Connexions Partnerships are the best point of contact for information on initiatives such as Modern Apprenticeships as well as advice on further and higher education and career choice. The address of local Connexions Services can be found on *www.connexions.gov.uk*.

Some Connexions Partnerships also offer a service to adults but adult guidance is more normally provided through a network of Information Advice and Guidance Partnerships. Details on local services can be obtained from Connexions Partnerships or Jobcentres. Adults can also contact the free learndirect helpline – 0800 100 900 – to talk to an adviser or to be referred to a local IAG Partnership adviser or find online information on the website *www.learndirect-advice.co.uk*.

Scotland

Careers information, advice and guidance in Scotland is provided by Careers Scotland, an all-age service with centres throughout the country. It operates a helpline – 0845 8 502 502 – or information on careers and learning or details of local centres can be accessed through the Careers Scotland website: *www.careers-scotland.org.uk*.

Wales

In Wales careers information, advice and guidance can be obtained from Careers Wales, an all-age service bringing together the seven careers companies which cover all areas of Wales. Information on careers and learning can also be found on the Careers Wales website: *www.careerswales.com* which also gives details of the local careers companies. Adults can also ring the learndirect helpline – 0800 100 900.

Northern Ireland

The Northern Ireland Department for Employment and Learning provides an information, advice and guidance service for young people and adults. Careers officers are based in 35 JobCentres and Jobs and Benefits Offices throughout Northern Ireland. Contact can be made through a freephone number: 0800 353530 or careers and learning information can be accessed on *www.delni.gov.uk*.

Higher Education Careers Services

Universities and colleges/institutes of higher education have their own guidance services tailored to the needs of their students and graduates. As well as information on local courses and career opportunities they provide a vast amount of national information produced by AGCAS (Association of Graduate Careers Advisory Services). Students of all ages are advised to make early contact with their service.

The addresses of HE Careers Services can be found on *www.prospects. ac.uk*

GENERAL HELPLINES AND WEBSITES

learndirect national helpline: 0800 100 900 – help and information on finding courses.

www.learndirect-advice.co.uk

www.dfes.gov.uk – Department for Education and Skills website, with portals for young people, adult learners and parents linking to other useful sites.

www.worktrain.gov.uk – comprehensive site bringing together information for young people and adults on occupations and careers, education, training and learning, and job search, with links to other sites.

www.connexions-direct.com – site designed specifically for young people with information to help in making decisions about careers and education and addresses of local Connexions services. Also included jobs4u, a careers database.

www.ucas.com – the UCAS website provides information on applying to higher education, a course search facility leading to a developing database of entry profiles which give in-depth information on course content and requirements and direct links to university and college sites.

www.prospects.ac.uk – the UK's official graduate careers website offering careers advice and information for graduates. The website covers how to choose a career, information and advice on jobs and employers, the graduate job market, work experience and working abroad along with job vacancies and resources for further study.

www.careers-portal.co.uk – this online careers service from Trotman Publishing is part of the National Grid for Learning and provides careers and higher education information on the web, including links to many useful sites.

PUBLICATIONS

Many of the sources listed below are available in careers libraries and reference libraries. A few are too expensive for most individuals to buy, while others may be worth investing in and may be ordered through bookshops. There is a growing number of computer programs providing help with career decisions, occupational information and course choice, and many Connexions services, schools, colleges and universities will have these available for use by clients.

Higher and Further Education Information

University and College Entrance: The Official Guide (The Big Guide), published annually by the Universities and Colleges Admissions Service (UCAS).

UCAS/Universities Scotland: Entrance Guide to Higher Education in Scotland, published annually by UCAS.

Directory of University & College Entry (formerly known as the *Laser Compendium*), published annually by Trotman.

CRAC Degree Course Guides, published by Trotman. Compare individual courses within disciplines.

CRAC Which Degree Guides, 2 vols. covering a group of related study areas, published by Trotman.

The Potter Guide to Higher Education, published by Dalebank Books. Does not include course information, but gives profiles of universities and colleges.

The Student Book, published by Trotman. Contains facts as well as opinions on subjects of study and institutions.

The European Choice: A Guide to Opportunities for Higher Education in Europe, free from DfES Publications, PO Box 99, Sudbury, Suffolk CO10 2SN

Experience Erasmus: The UK Guide to Socrates–Erasmus Programmes. Lists more than 500 degrees and diploma subjects at UK institutions which include study in other EU institutions, from ISCO-Careerscope Publications, 12A Princess Way, Camberley, Surrey GU15 3SP.

The Sixthformer's Guide: The Annual Guide to Visiting Universities and Colleges. Lists open days and gives advice on what to ask and look out for on a visit. Also from ISCOCareerscope Publications (see above).

CRAC Directory of Further Education (DOFE), published annually by Trotman. Lists full- and part-time vocational courses at all levels outside universities.

The Disabled Students' Guide to University, published annually by Trotman.

Careers Information

'Working In' series of booklets on individual career areas, published by DfES and downloadable from *www.connexions.gov.uk*.

AGCAS (Association of Graduate Careers Advisory Services) publishes a series of regularly updated booklets covering most graduate career areas.

Working Abroad: The Complete Guide to Overseas Employment by Godfrey Golzen and Jonathan Reuvid, published by Kogan Page.

Especially for Job-Changers and Late Starters

Second Chances – A National Guide to Education and Training for Adults, published by Lifetime Careers Wiltshire. A comprehensive guide to education and training at all levels.

The Mature Students' Directory: Lifelong Learning Opportunities for the 21 Plus, published by Trotman.

The Which? Guide to Changing Careers, published by Which? Books.

Returning Women: Their Training and Employment Choices and Needs by Veronica McGivney, published by the National Institute of Adult Continuing Education (NIACE).

Major careers publishers include Hobsons, Kogan Page, Trotman, How to Books, Lifetime Careers Wiltshire. Check catalogues for current publications.

Part Two

Main Careers in Alphabetical Order

Accountancy

PROFESSIONAL ACCOUNTANT

Entry qualifications At least 2 A levels and 3 GCSEs (A–C) including maths and English language or equivalent. Over half the total entrants (around 90% of chartered accountants, 40% certified and 60% public finance) are *graduates* (any discipline). (See also 'Accounting Technician' route below, p. 49.)

In Scotland, for training with The Institute of Chartered Accountants of Scotland either a degree or membership of the Association of Accounting Technicians.

The work The image of accountants as deskbound figure-crunchers is quite wrong. An accountancy qualification leads to a vast variety of jobs, in virtually any environment: manufacturing industry or television; retail or merchant banking; professional consultancy; public service. There is scope for accountants interested in the intricacies of accounting procedures and their technological development, or in high finance, or as a way into general management, and also for people who intend to become entrepreneurs. (See WORKING FOR ONESELF, p. 648.)

There is a vast variety of jobs in all types and sizes of business and public enterprise. An accountancy qualification is also an excellent preparation for jobs in merchant and other banking, insurance and the City.

There are some opportunities for employment (but *not* in public practice) in the EU, and in most other countries.

Work falls broadly into three categories:

1. *Public* (illogically also called 'private') *practice.*
2. *Industrial and commercial accountancy.*
3. *Public sector accountancy.*

Public Practice Accountants

Public practice firms (ie accountancy firms) vary in size from 1 to several thousand, and in type from high-powered international practices which deal mainly with large companies and are at the very centre of the country's commercial activities, to small suburban practices which deal mainly with private clients and local businesses. Normally each accountant deals with particular clients' affairs so that there is personal (at least written or telephone) contact with individuals.

As the financial scene becomes ever more complex, accountants now often specialize in one particular accountancy aspect: for example, taxation, computer systems, mergers, corporate finance. However, the bulk of public practice work is taxation and accounting-service auditing. Auditing means analysing and verifying clients' books and ensuring that the annual balance sheet presents a 'true and fair' picture of the client's financial affairs. Auditing is done on clients' premises so it involves meeting people and possibly travelling. Audits take anything from a few hours to several months, depending on the client's size and type of business. Audits may be done in streamlined offices using the latest technologies, or it may mean having to create order out of chaos when, for example, a farmer's 'office' consists of a drawerful of bills. Auditing is largely desk-work (or desk-top computer work), but it also involves discussions with clients – anyone from clerk to managing director – if specific items in the books are not clear. Apart from auditing and making suggestions about how to improve their systems and procedures, accountants also advise their clients on personal and business financial matters, from how to invest a small legacy to setting up a business or liquidating one. Some accountancy firms provide *management consultancy* services (see MANAGEMENT CONSULTANCY, p. 364).

Industrial and Commercial Accountants

They can be divided into *financial* accountants, concerned largely with internal audits, taxation, wage and salary structure, financial record-keeping; and *management* accountants. This is a fast-growing accountancy specialization (and it overlaps with management consultancy). Management accountants assess the relative importance, value and cost of all aspects of a business (or public enterprise): labour, raw materials, transport, sites, administration, marketing, etc. Every person's, machine's, department's, vehicle's, etc., contribution to the effectiveness of an organization, and their interdependence, can, with the help of computer systems and mathematical models, be assessed separately and as part of the whole operation. Management accountants might, for example, compare the relative cost of using a cheap new raw material which would necessitate more expensive machine maintenance and require mounting a marketing campaign to launch the changed product, against the cost of going on using the more expensive traditional raw material – taking into account, among other factors, what the competition abroad might do, and how staff would feel about the change. Or they might assess the cost of moving a factory to a cheaper site, considering increased transport cost, recruiting and training new staff. Like management consultants, their work requires interviewing all the people whose work affects the efficiency of the organization concerned. Having compared the financial results of alternative courses of action, management accountants present the information to the decision-makers at the top of the organization and may be involved in future strategic planning and forecasting.

Because management accountants take part in decision-making and business control they need a broader understanding of business organization in general and of the type of business with which they are concerned than do financial accountants. They often move into consultancy sections of auditing firms, or into *management consultancy* (see p. 364).

Public Sector Accountants

Accountants and auditors working in local and central government, the health service, national audit and other public service bodies are, like industrial and commercial accountants, concerned with all aspects of financial management. The emphasis of their work is on the efficient and effective use of funds and the need for public accountability.

In the 1990s public service organizations became more commercially orientated. Involvement in the management of change, e.g. contracting out of services, and advising on alternative options for the use of limited funds are important aspects of the finance manager's job. Work in the national audit bodies involves auditing public income and expenditure, certifying accounts and carrying out value-for-money studies.

Companies providing services to the public sector increasingly seek to recruit public service accountants and auditors. Significant numbers of finance managers become top-level general managers.

Training There are 6 main professional qualifications, each awarded by a different body:
1. Institute of Chartered Accountants in England & Wales.
2. Institute of Chartered Accountants of Scotland.
3. Institute of Chartered Accountants in Ireland.
4. Association of Chartered Certified Accountants.
5. Chartered Institute of Management Accountants.
6. Chartered Institute of Public Finance and Accountancy.

There are differences between the syllabuses and the training programmes that each body offers. There is a core element of accountancy knowledge which all accountants must master – but emphasis varies.

Accountancy courses cover economics; statistics; computer applications and systems; corporate finance; financial management; taxation; trustee work; share organization; management accounting; relevant law; EU accountancy implications; auditing. The emphasis on different aspects of accountancy differs in the various professional bodies' examinations; some syllabuses overlap more than others.

It is generally believed that chartered accountants get all the best jobs, or indeed that all qualified accountants are 'chartered'. But that is not so at all. The various qualifications are equally marketable. Choice of one qualification rather than another only partly depends on the ultimate career aim: it also depends on what training is available locally; and on the type of training method preferred.

Main differences in various qualifications' usefulness in the job-market

Only appropriately qualified *chartered* and *certified* accountants may, by law, become registered auditors and audit limited companies' accounts. People who want to go into public practice must therefore choose one of these two qualifications. *Chartered* and *certified* accountants can also go into the public sector, and work as management accountants in industry and commerce, so these two qualifications leave the widest range of options open. (More than half of all qualified accountants work in industry and commerce.)

Chartered management accountants' training concentrates more on running a business and planning its future than do the others. So people who definitely want to go into industry/commerce might choose this qualification. They too can choose to work in the public sector.

The *Chartered Institute of Public Finance and Accountancy* qualification differs from the others in that it is specifically tailored to the very large amount of work in the public sector – public utilities; National Health Service; local and central government.

Training methods vary between the various bodies, and they are complicated. (Candidates should read carefully all the accountancy bodies' training literature.)

The essential differences between the various bodies' training methods are:

Institute of Chartered Accountants in England & Wales

To train as a Chartered Accountant (ACA), students must complete a training contract with an organization authorized to train. This ensures that they receive the correct work experience, which is a vital part of the qualification. Training contracts can last between 3 and 5 years, although a graduate will normally receive a 3-year contract. Authorized training organizations can vary from small accountancy firms to large international firms (more commonly known as the 'big 4') to commercial organizations and public sector organizations, such as the NHS or National Audit Office. The work experience will be varied and every client will be different.

As well as a minimum of 3 years' work experience, students must also pass the Institute's exams. There are 2 stages of exams: the Professional Stage comprising 6 papers, and the Advanced Stage, which involves a test of advanced technical competence and an advanced case study. Chartered accountancy training develops a blend of technical knowledge, communication skills and commercial awareness, and a broad understanding of the legal implications of the work.

Institute of Chartered Accountants of Scotland
The majority of students who train with ICAS enter through the graduate entry route. Depending on degree studied, ICAS awards exemptions from the first level of exams. They also provide a route into chartered accountancy training for those students who decide to go straight into employment, rather than going to university. This new route involves up to 3 years studying towards membership of the Association of Accounting Technicians (AAT). Students who qualify for AAT membership can continue their professional development and progress on to chartered accountancy training. To qualify as a chartered accountant students must secure a training contract with an approved employer authorized by ICAS. The 3-year training programme combines classroom-based study and exams with supervised work-based training in employer training offices. Students can train with ICAS anywhere in the UK.

Association of Chartered Certified Accountants
Training is the most flexible although it must total 3 years. Students do not have to enter into training contracts but can train while in part- or full-time salaried employment by various part-time methods. Alternatively, they can study for the exams full time and get practical experience afterwards. They may change employers, and type of

employer, during their training and thus can get varied experience. They need not make up their mind at the outset whether they wish to go into industry/commerce or into public practice. Three years' training in an Approved Training Practice is obligatory for those who ultimately want to become Registered Auditors in public practice. This experience can be gained before, during or after passing the professional exams. Exams leading to Associate Membership (ACCA) are at 3 levels. Those with a relevant HND/HNC or foundation course may be exempt from all or part of level 1. A relevant degree should gain some exemptions at level 2. Study can be full time, by day- or block-release, evening classes or correspondence courses. Certified accountancy students are not automatically entitled to study leave, but companies registered on the Employer Accreditation Scheme offer it. About 40% of all UK accountancy students now choose certified accountancy.

Chartered Institute of Management Accountants

To gain Associate membership, CIMA students need a minimum of 3 years' relevant practical experience and to pass 3 stages of examinations. They can gain the practical experience (which could include a sandwich year taken in industry) before or after passing the examinations and they can be working in a variety of business areas, including public and private sectors, industry and commerce. They may change employers during this period. Students qualified above the minimum entry level may be given exemptions from parts of the syllabus. The method of study chosen will depend on the employer and the student: options include full-time, part-time, evening, weekend and correspondence courses.

Chartered Institute of Public Finance and Accountancy

CIPFA's education and training scheme incorporates a Foundation stage. Students with an accountancy degree, an HND/C in Business and Finance or Accounting, the AAT qualification or an NVQ in Accounting at level 4 (see Accounting Technician training, p. 50) are exempt from this stage. CIPFA students must be employed in a public service finance post. They follow a structured practical experience

47

scheme integrated with theory studied through open learning packages which can be supplemented with taught college courses. The whole scheme takes between 3 and 4 years to complete. Both the syllabus and work experience reflect the increasingly commercial focus of public service and the need for financial management skills.

Personal attributes Academic ability; numeracy; ability to speak and write concisely; business sense; logical mind; ability to negotiate without self-consciousness with people at all levels within an organization; tact in dealing with employers and clients; a liking for desk-work. Training demands determination, motivation and staying-power.

Accountants in public practice: A confidence-inspiring manner; ability to put things clearly to lay people.

Industrial/commercial accountancy: Ability to communicate with and extract information from people at all levels of intelligence and responsibility; enjoyment of decision-making.

Public sector accountancy: Ability to advise and explain financial matters to councillors and other public sector representatives.

Late start Individual cases judged on merit. ACCA offers a mature student entry route which waives entry requirements. It may be difficult to find training vacancies, but there are opportunities, particularly for people willing to undertake preparatory study (see 'Training', p. 44).

Work life balance A career break should be no problem for ICA and ACCA members. There are lectures and journals which help to keep accountants up to date with developments. Some reduced professional membership subscriptions. It is possible to work in most parts of the country and also to run a small practice from home. More difficult with other 2 bodies but possible if well established first. CIPFA has a Career-Break membership category.

Part-time opportunities are increasing especially in public practice. Job-sharing should be possible. Part-time training may be possible.

Further information Institute of Chartered Accountants in England

& Wales, Education and Training, Gloucester House, 399 Silbury
Boulevard, Central Milton Keynes MK9 2HL.
www.icaew.co.uk/students

Institute of Chartered Accountants of Scotland, CA House, 21 Haymarket Yards, Edinburgh EH12 5BH.
www.icas.org.uk

Institute of Chartered Accountants in Ireland, 11 Donegal Square
South, Belfast BT1 5JE.

The Association of Chartered Certified Accountants, 64 Finnieston
Square, Glasgow G3 8DT.
www.accaglobal.com

The Chartered Institute of Management Accountants, 26 Chapter
Street, London SW1P 4NP.
www.cimaglobal.com

The Chartered Institute of Public Finance and Accountancy, 3 Robert
Street, London WC2N 6BH.
www.cipfa.org.uk

Related careers ACTUARY – BANKING – CHARTERED SECRETARY
– INFORMATION TECHNOLOGY – INSURANCE – MANAGEMENT –
PURCHASING AND SUPPLY – SCIENCE: *Statistics* – TAX INSPECTOR

Accounting Technician

Entry qualifications There are no prescribed entry requirements for
the Association of Accounting Technicians' Education and Training
scheme or ACCA's Certified Accounting Technician (CAT) scheme,
but students are advised that they need reasonable numeracy and
literacy skills in order to cope with the qualifications.

The work There is no legal requirement for accountants to be professionally qualified; 'accountant' is not a 'protected title' in the way
'solicitor' or 'architect' is. This 'second tier' technician qualification
was created because there is so much accountancy work which, while
requiring responsibility, expertise and training, does not require the
breadth of *professional* accountancy education (see above, p. 41).

Broadly, professional accountants conduct audits (which technicians are not empowered to do) and deal with high-powered financial management and advice, etc.; accounting technicians collect the information on which professional accountants base their decisions, and deal with straightforward accountancy. This involves more deskwork than does professional accountancy, but it also involves contact with clients.

The vast majority of accounting technicians work in professional accountants' offices or under the direction of professional accountants in industry, commerce or the public sector. However, some are 'sole' or 'company' accountants in firms too small to warrant employing a professional accountant, and some accounting technicians set up on their own, dealing with private clients' (individuals, shopkeepers, etc.) VAT, income tax and similar matters. Some keep small firms' books and visit such clients at regular intervals on a contract basis. Others put advertisements in local papers and do 'one-off' jobs for people who need some straightforward accountancy advice, or help with tax returns. So accounting technicians can choose whether to take on secure employment and do mainly desk-work, or to have contact with a variety of clients and be their own boss (see WORKING FOR ONESELF, p. 648).

AAT members who want to become professional accountants (see above) normally get exemption from at least the professional accountancy bodies' (see above) Foundation examinations.

Training The AAT has introduced a new 'competence-based' scheme in 3 stages: Foundation, Intermediate and Technician. Assessments are conducted through exams, skill tests and work-based projects, and at Technician stage students will specialize in either accounting practice, industry and commerce or the public sector. These are accredited as NVQs/SVQs in accounting at levels 2, 3 and 4 (see p. 10). The CAT scheme from ACCA is assessed solely by exams, in preparation for continuing on to professional examinations if wished. It offers internationally relevant syllabus options and can be studied for online.

Personal attributes A methodical approach; liking for figures, computer and desk-work. There is room in this work for those who prefer to work on their own but with limited responsibility as support staff to more highly qualified/experienced colleagues, and for those who, though unable to take the professional examinations, wish to do responsible work and have contact with colleagues and clients. For accounting technicians who want to set up on their own: confidence-inspiring manner; self-confidence; ability not to worry as work may be sporadic rather than regular (see WORKING FOR ONESELF, p. 648).

Late start Very good scope for various kinds of older entrants such as unqualified but experienced accountancy staff, returners to office occupations, mid-career changers. Older people with relevant experience or knowledge may be exempted from some examinations.

Work life balance Career-breaks are unlikely to present any problems as long as people keep up with changes in taxation and other accountancy matters. Evening classes and correspondence courses (including Open University) can act as *refresher* training. AAT offers reduced membership subscriptions for those on maternity break.

There is very good scope for part-time work, both in employment and working on one's own. Job-sharing should be possible.

Further information Association of Accounting Technicians, 154 Clerkenwell Road, London ECIR 5AD.
www.aat.co.uk
The Association of Chartered Certified Accountants, 64 Finnieston Square, Glasgow G3 8DT.
www.accaglobal.com

Related careers BANKING − INSURANCE − LOGISTICS − PURCHASING AND SUPPLY − STOCK EXCHANGE AND SECURITIES INDUSTRY

Actuary

Entry qualifications Over 95% *graduate* entry, most graduates have degrees in a mathematical subject.

For school-leavers: A minimum of 2 A levels, one of which must be at least grade B in a maths subject, the other at least grade C, and 5 GCSEs (A–C) or equivalent including English.

Scotland: 3 H-grade passes including maths (grade A) and English.

The work Actuaries use probability and finance theory together with statistical techniques to highlight and solve financial problems, to suggest appropriate courses of action and to model/assess the financial implications of such actions. In other words, they 'work out the odds'. Their work has a strong mathematical bias and is essentially desk-work performed in a variety of settings. Some 40% of actuaries work for insurance offices, concentrating on the technical side of life assurance and pension funds, investigating such matters as relative life expectancies of various groups in the population, and assessing the effects of lifestyles and characteristics on premiums and policies and investment. In other insurance branches – accident, fire, motor – actuaries assess risks and pin-point variables in the light of changing conditions and lifestyles, and advise on reserves necessary to cover long-term liabilities. In the Government's Actuary's Department actuaries advise on public service pensions and insurance schemes. Though they are concerned with various aspects of people's lives and welfare (cushioning the effects of old age, accident, sickness which are the reasons for insurance schemes), actuaries do not usually have much contact with people outside their own office.

About 50% of actuaries work in consultancy. Much of their work involves advising pension funds, or the companies which finance the funds. They also provide specialist advice to insurance companies.

There are also openings in merchant banks, the Stock Exchange and other financial institutions, as well as some opportunities (usually to do with pensions) in industry and commerce.

Actuaries can go into middle and higher business management, especially in life assurance companies and pension funds.

Training *For school-leavers*: (Increasingly unusual – most companies employ graduates.) On-the-job training (minimum 3 years) plus 6–7 years' part-time study (mainly by correspondence) and discussion classes for Institute of Actuaries' (England and Wales) or Faculty of Actuaries' (Scotland) examinations.

For graduates: On-the-job training and on average 3–5 years' (depending on degree subject) part-time study as above. A good degree in mathematics, statistics or economics qualifies a student for exemption from some early parts of the professional examinations. A first degree or post-graduate diploma (1 year full time, 2 years part time) in actuarial subjects can lead to further exemptions.

Personal attributes Liking for concentrated desk-work; an analytical brain; probing curiosity; pleasure in solving complicated problems; ability to interpret mathematical and statistical information and express results clearly; business sense.

Late start Only advisable for very able mathematicians because of the long training; also difficulty in finding training posts.

Work life balance A career break may be possible for experienced actuaries who have kept up with developments, especially relevant legislation.

Actuaries do not work the long hours that are common in the City. In theory the work could be done part time and by job-sharers or freelancers although most actuaries work full time for large financial companies. Opportunities exist in investing, banking or management consultancy worldwide.

Actuary

Further information Institute of Actuaries, Napier House, 4 Worcester Street, Gloucester Green, Oxford OX1 2AW.
www.actuaries.org.uk
The Faculty of Actuaries, Maclaurin House, 18 Dublin Street, Edinburgh EH1 3PP.
www.actuaries.org.uk

Related careers ACCOUNTANCY – BANKING – CIVIL SERVICE – INSURANCE – STOCK EXCHANGE AND SECURITIES INDUSTRY

Advertising

Entry qualifications No rigid requirements; in practice usually at least A level English. Most entrants are now *graduates*.

Graphic design, typography, etc., require art-school training (see ART AND DESIGN, p. 105).

The work Advertising specialists work in:
1. Agencies.
2. Company advertising departments.
3. The media and for suppliers of advertising services (e.g. studios, film production, market research).

AGENCIES

Agencies plan, create and place advertisements on behalf of advertisers who appoint them to handle their 'account'. This may be a detergent, a package holiday, government information or financial services. Only 40% of advertising expenditure is concerned with persuading people to *buy*; advertisements are also used to get money for charities, votes for political parties, support for legislation, to encourage energy saving or investment, to fill jobs.

Agencies vary in size, speciality and scope. A very few employ up to 500 people, most under 50. Some specialize: for example, in business-to-business or recruitment advertising. Some will be responsible for creating the communications (creative agencies) and others will be responsible for media planning and buying (media agencies). Some may be full service (i.e. they have creative and media under the same roof). The largest agencies are now usually part of a communications group which can offer clients a wide range of specialist services ranging from packaging design (see p. 108) to broadcast production (see TELEVISION, FILM AND RADIO p. 620), market research, marketing and/or brand consultancy, sponsorship, PUBLIC RELATIONS (see p. 496) and promotional marketing, etc. Some agencies, especially regional agencies, will offer these services 'in-house' and yet others will buy in services as and when needed from outside suppliers.

Account Executive/Account Planner

Agency staff work in groups on individual accounts. The *account executive's* main responsibility is liaison with the client; the *account planner's* with organizing and interpreting research into consumer attitudes and developing the strategy on which the advertising will be based. Account executives are usually in charge of several accounts, each dealing with a different product, and are the link between clients and agency. They acquaint themselves thoroughly with each client's product, investigate the competition's product and ensure the client's claims for the product can be substantiated. Account planners acquaint themselves with the potential consumers who form the 'target group' (the people at whom the advertisement is to be aimed) and commission the necessary research. Once the group have decided upon a campaign proposition or theme, the account executive discusses it with the client. When the brief and the budget are agreed, work on 'creating the advertisement' starts.

The account executives coordinate the work, control the budget and present progress reports to the client. Their work involves travelling if clients are scattered over the country or abroad.

The executive's job requires self-confidence and diplomacy, as clients often have to be persuaded that the type and tone of a campaign suggested by the agency will be more effective than the client's own idea. Planners' jobs tend to be more strategic and intellectual in approach.

Media Executive

Planning, research and buying are the three media functions; they may be carried out by different people within the department, or the whole media operation may be the responsibility of a group of individuals assigned to a particular campaign.

Media planners' jobs are crucial to the success of any campaign. In consultation with account handlers and creative staff they work out how best to spend the available budget in order to generate most sales/influence. They choose the channels of communication – newspapers, magazines, radio, television, websites, posters and so on – which are most appropriate for any particular campaign and reach the target group most economically. Media planning decisions are based on information and statistics provided by *media research* and an understanding of media consumers. Computers are widely used to compare effectiveness and costs, but creative requirements – for colour, movement or sound – require subjective judgement.

Media buyers are responsible for negotiating the purchase of advertisement space or air time and the selection of different options within a medium (i.e. different magazines).

Market Research
(see also p. 371)

Before an advertising campaign is planned, facts are compiled about the product's uses, its advantages and limitations, competitors' products, distribution and so on. Facts and opinions are also gathered about its potential users – the target group: not just in terms of who they are, how much money they have and where they live, but in terms of their attitudes and behaviour. Some facts come from desk research, collecting information from a variety of published sources and the client's own records. Others may need specially commissioned research, ranging from statistics compiled by part-time interviewers questioning members of the public, to sophisticated behavioural studies involving trained psychologists.

Creative Department

Once the account group has been briefed and a strategy agreed with the client, the creative team of *copywriter* and *art director* together develop the advertisement.

The advertising 'message' is translated into a 'communication' that makes an instant impact on the target group. Words and pictures must complement each other.

Copywriters must be literate and imaginative, but they must choose their words under considerable constraints – from the disciplines of the brief and the restrictions of the space or time available, to the obligations of the Code of Advertising Practice and legal requirements. An interest in commercial success and an understanding of people's ways of life and priorities are far more useful than literary leanings.

Copywriters and art directors work with television producers and directors to create television and cinema commercials. There is no hard and fast rule about who exactly does what, and whether the visual or verbal aspect is the more important.

The *art director* is responsible for the visual appearance of advertisements, deciding whether to use photography, illustration, computer graphics or typography, and commissioning and supervising their production. The typographer chooses type which is easily readable, fits the layout and reflects the character of the product. The artist (only the larger agencies employ their own) may produce anything from a 'rough' to a finished 'visual' (see 'Graphics . . .', p. 108).

The atmosphere in agencies is often relaxed and informal, but the pace and pressure are very demanding indeed. The decline in the number of people in agencies means fierce competition for any openings. Considerable talent, the right kind of personality and commitment are needed to survive and succeed.

Traffic and Production Manager

This role involves liaising between other departments within an agency and clients and keeping up to date with all projects, in order to ensure that they are completed in time and within budget. The production manager makes sure that creative departments have necessary approvals and scripts, organizes print buying and the purchase of services such as photography when needed and keeps track of overall expenditure.

ADVERTISERS

Many advertisers incorporate advertising into marketing (see p. 371). *Brand managers* are responsible for the marketing policy for a product, including its advertising. Relatively few have their own advertising departments, which vary in size. If a manufacturer creates and places all the advertising directly, the department may be much like a small agency. There is less scope for employees to work on different types of products simultaneously, but there may be a broader range of work covering different aspects of marketing.

Retailers' advertisement departments may deal with store and window displays, exhibitions, fashion shows, promotions, sponsorship, Internet activity, classified recruitment advertising and public relations, for example, using an advertising agency only for display advertisements.

Advertising departments are useful training grounds, giving experience in a range of work.

MEDIA

The advertising departments of media owners are responsible for selling space or air time to advertisers, directly or through agencies. The *research section* provides information about readers or viewers; it helps advertisers pin-point target groups. The *promotions section* may have its own creative department, which works in 3 areas: projecting the medium to advertisers, to distributors and to retailers on behalf of advertisers. *Sales representatives* are responsible for selling advertisement space or air time; this may include telephone selling, trying to get classified advertisements (which may involve having to put up with being rebuffed, and trying again). *Media managers* are responsible for ensuring that advertisements comply with the Code of Advertising Practice, which may involve checking copy claims and possibly asking for changes to be made before accepting copy.

Training Considerable patience – apart from talent – is needed to get a job. Nearly three-quarters of jobs are in London. Once in, training is a combination of practice and theory. Agency policy varies concerning how far vocational qualifications listed below are looked for or encouraged and possession is no guarantee of a job.

Pre-entry training is not essential. The larger agencies tend to run in-service training schemes, sometimes supplemented by external courses. The Institute of Practitioners in Advertising runs a phased programme of training courses designed to cater for the training needs of executives employed at IPA member agencies at each stage of their career development. Some agencies take several graduates (any discipline) each year; many advertisers have management training schemes which can lead to advertising jobs.

Secretaries/PAs occasionally progress to executive or copywriting positions; their chances are better with a small specialist agency (for example, a recruitment agency) or in an advertising department, but they are never great. Other ways into the industry are through production departments (see PUBLISHING, p. 500, and PRINTING, p. 470) and 'traffic control' (progress chasing – keeping the work flowing to schedule through all the different departments and processes).

Those wanting to take a pre-entry course can choose from:

(a) A growing number of university courses – degrees and higher national diplomas – with a substantial advertising component.

(b) Foundation degree in Business (Advertising & Marketing Communications) full time, 2 years *or* post-graduate Diploma in Advertising, full time, 30 weeks at West Herts College.

(c) Full-time, part-time or distance-learning courses leading to the CAM Foundation's Certificates (available at pre-entry stage or when in employment).

NVQs at levels 3 and 4 are available.

However, these vocational qualifications do not necessarily increase the chance of entry as the advertising industry recruits from a wide base of subjects in order to vary the range of knowledge and experience within a team.

Personal attributes Business acumen; interest in social and economic trends; flair for salesmanship; numeracy; communication skills; ability to work in a team; ability to stand criticism whether justified or not; ability to work under pressure; stamina; resilience; persistence; interest in popular culture.

For creative people: Discipline; originality; strong feeling for uncomplicated images and 'messages'; willingness to produce the kind of words/artwork that are best for the campaign, whether artistically first-rate or not.

For planning and research: Objectivity; a logical, analytical brain but ability to make lateral strategic leaps – often based on intuition – that then have to be backed by solid evidence and a creative appreciation.

Late start Little opportunity without previous relevant commercial experience although some agencies do look at more varied working backgrounds when recruiting for the account planning department.

Work life balance The advertising industry has produced a guide to best practice in work life balance for both agencies and individuals. There is increasing recognition of the need to accommodate more flexible working to retain talented individuals – both male and female – particularly given the development of technological support. There is also increasing incidence of flexible working to accommodate outside pressures such as further study, other creative endeavours, children and other dependants amongst staff who have demonstrated their worth.

Prospects for career breaks are reasonable for experienced planners or for successful executives who have 'kept their hand in' with freelance work.

Further information CAM Foundation, Moor Hall, Cookham, Berks SL6 9QH.
www. camfoundation.com

Advertising

Institute of Practitioners in Advertising, 44 Belgrave Square, London
SW1X 8QS.
www.ipa.co.uk

Related careers MANAGEMENT – MARKETING AND SELLING –
PUBLIC RELATIONS – RETAIL MANAGEMENT

Agriculture and Horticulture

Entry qualifications Entry at all levels, from no qualifications to degree.

The work Agriculture and horticulture cover a wide range of land-based industries, both traditional and, increasingly, non-traditional. Pig and poultry rearing, fish and deer farming, fruit, vegetable and flower growing, shooting, nature trails, vineyards – these and many other activities make up an industry that in the last few years has been going through one of its biggest ever changes, more particularly on the agricultural side. This is due to a number of factors: increased efficiency leading to over-production, which in turn has led to the imposition of quotas on what a farmer can produce. Farmers' incomes have dropped significantly, which means fewer staff can be employed and more farmers and their families work part rather than full time. Smaller units are disappearing, while larger ones survive by becoming even more efficient. Numbers employed in general farm work have dropped dramatically and anyone looking to a career in farming in future must be prepared to develop good management and/or specialist skills. Bad publicity about chemical pollution, intensive farming and recent food scares, plus pressures from a more health-conscious public, mean more farmers have been switching to less intensive, organic methods of production. The foot and mouth outbreak hit farming in some areas especially badly but all farmers are having to find other ways to use their resources, for example by diversifying into the tourism or recreation industries (e.g. bed and breakfast, golf driving ranges). This may not mean a big increase in income, and many farms are not suitable for such developments, but somehow farmers have to find ways of 'adding value' to their products or activities – perhaps making ice cream from surplus milk, or encouraging the public to 'pick your own' fruit. Government schemes to pay farmers to 'set aside' land from production and to subsidize the planting of woodlands are part of an escalating movement towards seeing farmers not just as producers of food, but as custodians of the countryside.

Management posts in agriculture and horticulture are often held by people who started out in practical work and then became supervisors. Increasingly, though, qualifications such as HNDs and degrees are essential for such jobs as farm manager, unit manager, manager of a country park. As farms and horticultural units grow in size, the range but not the number of management jobs is increasing. A manager of, for example, an animal unit needs scientific, technological, veterinary, accounting and IT knowledge. Marketing skills are increasingly in demand.

Research is usually concerned with a particular aspect of crop production or of animal husbandry. This could be concerned with pest control, plant disease, soil chemistry, genetics, nutrition, taste preservation (researchers work closely with technologists in the food industry – see 'Food Science and Technology', p. 547). Work may be wholly or largely theoretical, involving study of scientific journals and papers as well as collaboration with scientists from other disciplines. It often involves experimental work in the laboratory or in trial growing areas. Researchers work for research establishments, for botanical gardens, in industry, in the Civil Service (mainly the Department for Environment, Food and Rural Affairs (Defra)).

Advisory work is carried out by government (through Defra) and by commercial firms which supply agricultural and horticultural goods and equipment. Advice may be given on pest control, selection of the best variety of crop, choice of feed, marketing, finance, diversification.

AGRICULTURE

The main branches of 'traditional' practical farm work are:

Animal Husbandry

Beef cattle: work varies according to size and type of farm. Some farms only rear calves, others fatten cattle through to slaughter.

Dairy cattle: a 100-cow herd can be worth a large sum of money, so this is highly responsible work. Tasks involve feeding, milking and following strict hygiene maintenance routines.

Pigs: farms breed pigs for sale, or buy young pigs and fatten them for sale as bacon or pork, or they do both. Extent of automation varies.

Poultry: highly specialized holdings concentrate either entirely on egg production or on hatching chicks – often in fully automatic giant incubators – or on rearing table birds. Some poultry units resemble a cross between a laboratory and a modern factory, with indoor, clean work. Increased demand for free-range eggs means more scope for alternative forms of egg production, but there are still few farms where looking after poultry means feeding birds in the farmyard.

Sheep: hill farms usually concentrate on large flocks; on lowland farms sheep may form part of a unit and shepherds also do other work. Shepherds work with, and may train, dogs.

Working in Arable Crops

The wide variety of crops grown on British farms tends to be concentrated in the east of the country. Most arable work is highly mechanized, but requires considerable skill in operating and maintaining sophisticated machinery.

On the whole, the larger and/or more mechanized the farm, the greater the degree of specialization. Individuals need not stick to one specialization throughout their career, though some prefer to do so. Livestock workers are expected to drive tractors.

General Farm Work

People who do not want to specialize can carry out general duties, driving tractors, helping with livestock, repairing buildings, clearing ditches, etc. The range of jobs depends on the type and size of farm.

HORTICULTURE

There are two main divisions: commercial – growing plants for sale – and amenity – making and maintaining gardens as pleasant environments. Horticulturalists, therefore, may work in different settings – as sole employee or as one of a large team; in the depths of the country or in the middle of a town.

Commercial Horticulture

This includes the production of fruit, vegetables, flowers, plants of all kinds in market gardens, nurseries, garden centres, greenhouses and fruit farms. Some sell directly to the public, while others sell only to other horticultural concerns. Some specialize in, for example, bulb production, soft fruit, cut flowers or house plants. Others grow a wide variety of plants. Many tasks are now mechanized, but some are still done by hand – some pollination, disbudding, collecting seed, grafting, for example. Much effort now goes into producing strains that are disease-resistant and/or have a longer growing season (e.g. through genetic engineering). Computer systems are often used to control the environment in order to produce exactly the right conditions for different plants. Garden centres are a feature of most towns, offering pot-grown plants which customers can plant in their gardens at any time of year, plus a huge range of garden tools and accessories. Jobs in these offer the most contact with members of the public, who expect staff to be knowledgeable. Experienced horticultural workers can become plantation assistants on fruit stations or quality inspectors for commercial canning and quick-freezing stations, or manage 'pick your own' farms (weekend work).

Amenity Horticulture

Its purpose is to provide pleasant open-air environments in town and country. It includes town and country parks; picnic areas off motorways; National Trust and similar properties; nature trails; theme parks; bowling greens; golf courses. It frequently involves nursery work and arboriculture (see 'Forestry', below). Staff have to cope with the sometimes conflicting demands of the gardening programme and events held in the park (e.g. open-air concerts). A park manager may spend a large proportion of time on such non-horticultural activities as paperwork and rubbish disposal. Current reductions in staffing levels often affect types of planting, e.g. bedding plants may give way to grass and shrubs. The work involves contact with the public and often helping with recreational activities, such as sitting at cash-desks for open-air concerts, usher and patrol duty, although in some parks these duties are carried out by keepers with no horticultural training (see also LEISURE/RECREATION MANAGEMENT, 'Training', p. 338). There may be more of a career structure (and day-release) in this type of horticulture than in commercial concerns.

Landscape and Garden Contractors

The work overlaps with landscape architecture (see p. 313) and amenity horticulture. It includes design and construction of new gardens and regular maintenance of existing gardens. Increasingly, contractors are employed by local authorities (and even by the Royal Parks) to maintain public gardens and parks.

Training Although it may still be possible to get a job in farming and horticulture without going to college, there is much more chance of a proper career for those with formal training. Expertise and management skills are of increasing importance. The main training routes are:

Foundation and Advanced Modern Apprenticeships (see p. 11) Available in agriculture and commercial horticulture.

NVQs/SVQs

Available in agriculture and horticulture at levels 1–4. Work-based training with part-time courses can lead to these; some full-time courses also lead to credits towards NVQs.

National Certificate route

City & Guilds National Certificate courses normally last 1 year full time. No set academic requirements, but students are required to have had 1 year's previous practical work, sometimes 2, on a farm or holding. Also, as competition for places is keen, those with some good GCSE grades or with other certificates, e.g. City & Guilds, have more chance of acceptance. Most NCs are in general agriculture or horticulture, but a few are specialized, e.g. in dairy farming or greenkeeping.

Advanced National Certificate courses last 1 year and are specialized. Examples are agricultural mechanization, deer management, arable farm management, commercial fruit production. Some colleges offer a National Certificate in Farm Management – of a similar level to the ANC.

Edexcel BTEC/SQA route (see pp. 8, 10)

BTEC First Diploma and National Certificate and Diploma/SQA Scottish Group Award courses can be in general agriculture or horticulture or specialized. Examples are livestock, crop husbandry, land-based business and farm diversification. Higher National Diplomas (3-year sandwich) offer an alternative to a degree course for those looking for a career in practical farming or horticulture. A range of additional courses are available, mainly in new technologies, management and farm organization; these are especially suitable for people who have spent some time working in the industry.

Degrees

3 or 4 years. Entry requirements normally include 1 or 2 sciences at A level. There is a wide variety of courses: examples of titles, apart from general agriculture or horticulture, are crop science, crop technology and resource management, agriculture and land management, agri-

cultural botany, agricultural and food marketing, agroforestry, animal production science. Little actual farm work is included in degree courses, which are intended for future advisers, researchers, teachers or managers. Entrants to full-time courses are frequently required to have had 1 year's practical experience. This is a good idea even where it is not obligatory.

Full- and part-time Foundation degree courses, sometimes including a year's work experience, are also available.

Kew Diploma

3-year, degree-level course in amenity and botanical horticulture. Entry requirements are minimum 5 GCSEs, including English, maths and a science, plus 2 A levels, preferably in science subjects, in addition to formal horticultural training to at least NVQ level 2. A small number accepted straight from sixth form but will be expected to take 2 years' preliminary practical training before starting their course at Kew.

SPECIALIZATIONS

Forestry

This is a small specialization, although until recent tax changes made it less attractive, commercial conifer planting had been increasing. The Woodland Grant Scheme is encouraging farmers to plant trees instead of crops; and environmentalists would like to see the planting of more hardwoods (which take a long time to grow and attract a wide range of wildlife) and fewer conifers. In commercial forestry trees are grown as a renewable resource and harvested like any other crop. Other woodlands are maintained for sporting or recreational purposes. Urban forestry is growing in importance; known also as arboriculture, it covers the establishment, care and maintenance of trees for amenity purposes (see 'Amenity Horticulture', above).

Employers include the Forestry Commission, local authorities, commercial companies that own forests all over the country, co-operatives and individual landowners. There are opportunities to work abroad. Managers – senior forest officers – plan afforestation programmes and may be in overall charge of a single plantation, a group of forests or a whole district. Though an administrative job it involves driving and walking. It includes responsibility for fire protection, wildlife protection, disease identification and control, planning and control of recreational areas, possibly marketing. Forest workers carry out practical tasks under supervision usually of foresters or forest officers.

Training Forest workers do not need formal qualifications, but may be given in-service training and/or sent on block-release for courses leading to NVQs levels 1 and 2, BTEC First Diploma or City & Guilds/ SQA certificates.

Most foresters or forest officers train by taking *either* a BTEC National Diploma *or* SQA-based college diploma *or* a degree or Foundation degree in a forestry-related subject or a post-graduate course. Those seeking the highest level management posts may need to take the Professional Examination of the Institute of Chartered Foresters (forestry graduates take only part 2, ND holders take parts 1 and 2).

Traditionally, diploma holders have been taken on as supervisors, responsible for overseeing day-to-day operations, and graduates as assistant or area managers. Graduates have more scientific knowledge than diplomates, but the distinction has become blurred and promotion is possible for both types of entrant.

Fish Farming and Fisheries Management

This is the breeding and rearing of various types of fish for food or sport. Most fish farms are small owner-run businesses, but there are larger ones employing several staff. Other employers of fisheries managers are water authorities, angling clubs, estate owners, fish processors. Like all animal husbandry this is usually a 7-day-a-week job and involves unsocial working hours.

Training There is no prescribed entry and training route: the usual ways into this growing industry are through a BTEC/SQA National Award (see pp. 9, 10) in Fishery Studies; or a BTEC sandwich Higher National Diploma; or the Institute of Fisheries Management correspondence course for its certificate and diploma (no entry requirements). Work-based training may lead to NVQs/SVQs at levels 2 and 3.

For research posts: degree in biological or agricultural science, usually followed by a post-graduate course.

It is possible to progress to management from a technician post.

Engineering in the Land-based Sector

Engineers in the land-based sector apply engineering principles to all kinds of agriculture and horticulture as well as in amenity-related fields. As the world's non-renewable and slowly renewable resources are being rapidly used up, it is essential to make the most efficient use of natural resources. This involves recycling processes; exploring and using new sources of energy; and, above all, incorporating new and sustainable technologies in the design and manufacture of agricultural equipment. Engineers in this sector may be involved in the sales, marketing and servicing of equipment; in designing and constructing farm and horticultural installations; in product planning; mechanizing procedures; crop storage and processing, and the design and maintenance of outdoor sports surfaces. The work is related to food technology (see p. 547) and professional engineering (see p. 216) and professional environmentalist work. There is scope for work abroad, especially in developing countries.

Farm/Garden Mechanic

All farmworkers must be able to cope with running repairs; many arable units which use machinery worth thousands of pounds employ their own farm mechanics who are in charge of maintenance, repairs and adaptation of all types of mechanical gadgets. On large units there may be several mechanics; usually there is only one. However, the majority of mechanics are employed by agricultural and garden machinery dealers, carrying out servicing and repairs in a workshop or in the field where the machinery is being used.

Training For levels of engineering see p. 216.

Courses are available leading to City & Guilds National Certificate or BTEC/SQA awards, as well as degrees in agricultural engineering. NVQs are available. Holders of a Higher National Diploma or a degree in a related subject (geography, science, agriculture) can take a post-graduate course in agricultural engineering.

Farm or garden mechanics may follow a formal training scheme accredited by the British Agricultural and Garden Machinery Association.

Social and Therapeutic Horticulture

This covers the use of horticulture in a range of therapeutic activities. It may form part of a planned rehabilitation of a physically disabled patient or it may provide education, recreation or vocational training for people with learning difficulties. Most therapists (who may be called horticultural instructors/organizers or project workers) work in sheltered workshops, hospitals, residential homes, training centres or in special education.

Training There is as yet no career structure, although the majority of the work is carried out by professional care staff and horticulturalists. A few colleges are introducing diploma courses and Thrive (a registered charity) offers a Professional Development Diploma in Therapeutic Horticulture, a part-time 1-year flexible learning course studied through a combination of workshop blocks and home study for people with qualifications in either horticulture or occupational therapy. A certificate course has also been developed for individuals new to this field to provide them with a basic understanding of the principles and practice of horticultural therapy.

Personal attributes *For most jobs*: attention to detail; physical robustness and ability to cope with irregular hours; reliability; good powers of observation; ability to work without supervision.

For managers: ability to recruit and cope with permanent and seasonal staff; ability to take decisions, knowing that these may be subject to the vagaries of nature; enjoyment of responsibility.

Late start On the whole this is not advisable as trainee vacancies tend to go to young applicants (partly because the pay structure is age-related), although there are no age limits on training schemes or courses. Some farmers' children return to farming as a second career when their parents wish to retire.

Work life balance A career break should be no problem for those in management jobs before the break, except that competition for jobs is fierce. The Forestry Commission has a career break scheme for men and women who retire temporarily for domestic reasons.

Many more people than in the past are working part time, especially in agriculture.

Further information Lantra, Lantra House, Stoneleigh Park, Nr Coventry, Warwickshire CV8 2LG.
www.lantra.co.uk
Royal Botanic Gardens, Kew, Richmond, Surrey TW9 3AB.
www.rbgkew.org.uk
Institute of Chartered Foresters, 7a St Colme Street, Edinburgh EH3 6AA.
www.charteredforesters.org.uk
Institute of Horticulture, 14/15 Belgrave Square, London SW1X 8PS.
www.horticulture.org.uk
Institute of Fisheries Management, 22 Rushworth Avenue, West Bridgford, Nottingham NG2 7LF.
www.ifm.org.uk
The Institution of Agricultural Engineers, West End Road, Silsoe, Bedford MK45 4DU.
www.iagre.org

British Agricultural and Garden Machinery Association, 14–16 Church Street, Rickmansworth, Herts WD3 1RQ.
www.bagma.com

Thrive (Horticultural Therapy), The Geoffrey Udall Centre, Beech Hill, Reading RG7 2AT.
www.thrive.org.uk

Related careers ANIMALS: *Veterinary Nurse/Surgeon* – LANDSCAPE ARCHITECTURE – SCIENCE: *Scientist*; *Technician*

Animals

VETERINARY SURGEON

Entry qualifications Normally at least 2 science A levels plus one other. Some universities require chemistry and/or biology; some 3 science A levels. The science subject not offered at A level should be offered at a high grade at GCSE. This is the most competitive of degree courses; very high A level grades are required. Veterinary schools require applicants to have gained practical work experience, such as working in a veterinary surgery, on farms or in stables, kennels or catteries.

General Practice

The work Some veterinary practices deal mainly or exclusively (except in cases of emergency) with small or 'companion' animals; others deal with farm animals or horses; some are mixed practices, but even here veterinary surgeons are likely to develop particular areas of interest and expertise. Veterinary surgeons must provide a 24-hour service, but most practices are organized so as to provide reasonable time off and holidays.

Veterinary surgeons treat animals both in their surgeries and at their owners' premises. It is important for them to be able to communicate effectively with animals' owners. This means a different approach for pet-owners, who have an emotional attachment to their 'companion animals', and for farmers to whom their animals are an investment. While always committed to the welfare of an animal, the veterinary surgeon must allow a farmer to balance an expensive new treatment against an economic return. In farm animal practice, veterinary surgeons are concerned not just with treating individual animals but with advising on the well-being and productivity of the entire stock.

Veterinary surgeons in practice often take on additional part-time appointments. Farm practitioners may be Local Veterinary Inspectors for the Department for Environment, Food and Rural Affairs, testing cattle for tuberculosis or brucellosis or carrying on inspections at cattle markets. Some practices carry out supervision of meat hygiene in abattoirs or poultry slaughterhouses; others work at licensed greyhound tracks. District councils need veterinary surgeons to inspect the riding establishments, zoos, pet shops and dog-breeding and boarding kennels which they license.

Newly qualified veterinary surgeons normally start as assistants in established practices, moving on to a more senior assistantship and then to a partnership in an existing practice or setting up a new practice.

State Veterinary Service

The State Veterinary Service is concerned not with individual animals but with the 'common herd'. Its responsibilities include: the control and eradication of notifiable disease; diagnostic and consultancy work on notifiable and non-notifiable disease; epidemiological studies; disease monitoring and surveillance; special investigations and surveys; public health liaison and human diseases related to animals; red meat and poultry hygiene; the operation of animal health schemes; improved farm animal health.

Veterinary surgeons are employed as *Veterinary Field Officers* or *Veterinary Investigation Officers*. They work closely together, with the field officer generally carrying out a major part of the statutory work while the investigation officer provides diagnostic services based on laboratory tests. The Central Veterinary Laboratory contracts (as a Civil Service agency) to carry out research into conditions of economic importance to British farm livestock. Immediate practical farming problems as well as long-term applied and fundamental research projects are dealt with. It also provides services for the State Veterinary Service.

Other Opportunities

Veterinary surgeons are also employed in research institutes of the Agricultural Research Service and Medical Research Council; animal welfare societies; the Royal Army Veterinary Corps; industry, mainly pharmaceutical companies and those making animal feeds and fertilizers; universities; the Animal Health Trust, a voluntary organization for veterinary research and the promotion of post-graduate veterinary education. There are also opportunities in developing countries, and veterinary surgeons who qualify from one of the 6 UK veterinary schools may practise in EU member states. However, they have to satisfy that country's registration requirements.

Training Degree courses last 5 years (6 at Cambridge) and are divided into pre-clinical (animal husbandry, anatomy, physiology, biochemistry), para-clinical (pathology, pharmacology) and clinical (medicine and surgery, veterinary public health). During the vacations students must spend 6 months gaining experience in aspects of veterinary work under the supervision of veterinary surgeons in practice, in veterinary laboratories and in other areas of veterinary work.

In some veterinary schools training may be shortened by 1 year for science graduates.

Personal attributes Scientific interest in animals and their behaviour and development, rather than sentimental fondness for pets; powers of observation; a firm hand; the ability to inspire confidence in animals (i.e. total absence of nervousness) and in their owners; self-reliance and adaptability; indifference to occasional physically disagreeable conditions of work.

As veterinary surgeons deal with owners as well as animals, excellent communication skills are essential, as are time management, leadership and the ability to work well in a team.

Late start As there is such stiff competition for degree course places, it is unlikely that anyone over 30 would be accepted, though there is no official upper age limit.

Work life balance In general practice, a career break would have to be negotiated with partners. A retraining course has been organized every other year for those wishing to return to practice. Veterinary surgeons in the State Veterinary Service are civil servants (see p. 158).

There are opportunities to work part time or as a locum.

Further information Royal College of Veterinary Surgeons, Belgravia House, 62–64 Horseferry Road, London SW1P 2AF. *www.rcvs.org.uk*

Veterinary Nurse

Entry qualifications Five GCSEs (A–C), including English language and either 2 physical or biological sciences or 1 science and mathematics. Alternative qualifications of a comparable or higher standard may be accepted in lieu of the usual requirements at the discretion of the RCVS.

The work Veterinary nurses assist veterinary surgeons in their practice and occasionally on visits, undertaking a wide variety of veterinary care and supporting work. In the practice they assist with consultations and look after hospitalized animals, monitoring their condition and providing necessary care and treatment. Veterinary nurses prepare the operating theatre, ensuring that it is clean and that equipment is maintained. They also assist veterinary surgeons during operations and help to monitor anaesthesia. Veterinary nurses also undertake a range of veterinary investigations and treatments, under the direction of their employing veterinary surgeon. These can include the collection and examination of specimens, dental hygiene work, administration of vaccines, dressing changes, 'well pet' clinics and puppy parties, etc. In addition to providing nursing care for animals, veterinary nurses are also responsible for ensuring the hygiene of clinical areas of the veterinary practice. They work mainly in 'small animal' practices, i.e. those dealing with domestic animals kept as pets, and for the RSPCA and other animal welfare and research organizations. Opportunities also exist for training in equine veterinary nursing, in specialized veterinary practices dealing with horses.

The hours are usually long and irregular. Animals become sick and have to be cared for at weekends and during the night, which will mean going to work on Saturday and Sunday, and sometimes overnight.

Some veterinary surgeons' practices employ only one veterinary nurse who may then have little companionship. Most of the working day will be spent with the employer.

While predominantly a young person's job, there are a growing number of opportunities for career development and progression. These include senior nursing posts in specialized veterinary hospitals, veterinary nurse teaching posts, commercial work with pharmaceutical companies, practice management and specialization into areas such as pet behaviour or nutrition.

Training Minimum age for enrolment as trainee is 17; practical work may start earlier.

Training for the Veterinary Nursing Certificate is work-based, incorporating NVQs at levels 2 and 3, plus study by day- or block-release courses.

A potential trainee must first find a job with a veterinary practice or hospital approved by the Royal College of Veterinary Surgeons as a training centre and then enrol with the RCVS as a trainee. The syllabus covers anatomy and physiology, hygiene and feeding, first aid, side-room techniques (analysing specimens and preparing slides), and the theory and practice of breeding and nursing. Trainees are continuously assessed at work and external examinations are taken at the end of the first and second year of training.

Trainee vacancies are sometimes advertised in the *Veterinary Record*, and prospective trainees may themselves advertise for jobs. Letters to local veterinary surgeons and animal research and welfare societies may also bring results; and the RCVS will provide a list of those veterinary practices and centres that are approved as training centres.

Veterinary nurse training is also available alongside a degree or diploma course. There are currently eight universities and colleges that offer full-time higher education courses incorporating the Veterinary Nursing Certificate and NVQs.

Advanced qualifications in veterinary nursing are available.

Personal attributes A love of animals and a scientific interest in their development, behaviour and welfare; lack of squeamishness; a willingness to respond to instructions, and yet to act independently when necessary; readiness to work well both alone and with others; a sure, firm, but gentle grip; patience. Ability to type and drive is helpful.

Late start There is no upper age limit, but most trainees are under 25. This is to some extent dictated by the low wages received during training.

Work life balance There are many opportunities for part-time and locum work for qualified veterinary nurses. Most trainees work full time. Any career break would have to be negotiated with employer.

Further information Royal College of Veterinary Surgeons, Veterinary Nursing Department, Belgravia House, 62–64 Horseferry Road, London, SW1P 2AF
www.rcvs.org.uk

HORSES

Entry qualifications Four GCSEs, including an English subject, for riding instructors, but requirements waived for entrants over 18. None for grooms and stable managers. But see 'Training', below.

The work Looking after horses nearly always means hard physical work that has to be carried out daily in all weathers. Hours tend to be long, especially in summer, and most people work a 6-day week. Most new entrants have had unpaid experience. Staff may live in or out, but grooms and stable managers usually live on the premises because of the early-morning start. Meals may be provided.

Riding Instructors

They teach children and adults, both in private lessons and in classes, and accompany riders out on 'hacks'. Classes may be held early in the morning or late in the evening, to suit pupils coming before or after work. Some instructors work for one establishment full time, others work freelance or part time. Many combine teaching with general stable work. Setting up one's own riding school requires considerable capital, experience and business knowledge.

Groom/Stable Managers

They work in and may eventually manage a variety of establishments, e.g. hunt, racing, showjumping and eventing stables, livery yards (which look after other owners' horses), riding schools, studs. They clean stables, feed and water horses, watch out for and report any symptoms which indicate a horse may be sick, clean and maintain tack. They prepare horses for competition – eventing, showjumping, dressage, driving, polo, showing, etc. At a stud, grooms also look after the brood mares and care for their foals. They may also assist with breaking and training. This is highly skilled work. 'Plum' jobs like travelling with show horses are rare. However, British grooms are in great demand abroad.

Instructors

Training The 2 main examining bodies in the horse industry are the British Horse Society and the Association of British Riding Schools. The BHS exams consist of 2 parallel streams: riding, and horse knowledge and care. Intending instructors must take both, together with teaching tests. The route is:

Stage 1 (minimum age 16).

Stage 2. Candidates for Stage 2 must first have passed the separate BHS Riding and Road Safety Test. This together with the Preliminary

81

Animals

Teaching Test (minimum age 17½) leads to the Preliminary Teaching Certificate. (On completion of 500 hours of teaching experience, and completion of the Stage 3 (minimum age 17) the full *Assistant Instructor Certificate* (AI) is awarded.)

Stage 4 (minimum age 18 for riding, 19 for care). This, together with the Intermediate Teaching Examination and a full Health and Safety at Work first aid certificate, leads to the *Intermediate Instructor* (II) award.

Stable Manager's Certificate (minimum age 22). Those who pass this plus the Equitation/Teaching Examination gain the full *Instructor's Certificate*.

BHS instructional qualifications are currently recognized in 29 countries through the International Group for Qualifications in Training Horse and Rider.

Grooms

People who want to become grooms and stable managers, but have no particular riding ambitions, can take either the BHS horse knowledge and care tests, Groom's Certificate, Intermediate Stable Manager's Certificate and Stable Manager's Certificate (without the riding tests) or the ABRS exams. These consist of *Preliminary Horse Knowledge and Riding*, the *Groom's Certificate* (minimum age 17) and *Groom's Diploma* (minimum age 18). No educational qualifications are required for the ABRS exams.

The National Pony Society runs examinations for stud workers.

Training for horse exams is normally at an equestrian college or riding school/training yard. An apprenticeship scheme is available. Duration of training depends on a student's ability and standard when starting. It is also possible to work for these exams while working as a groom. There are also some fee-charging schools. It is important to check that any training establishment is approved by the BHS and/or is a member of the ABRS. Increasingly, equestrian studies courses are being offered at colleges of agriculture and further education colleges, leading to BTEC National and Higher National awards and incorporating BHS qualifications. Degree courses are now also available. It is anticipated that in future people with qualifications will have the most opportunities in managing equestrian establishments of all kinds.

Foundation Modern Apprenticeships are available for those looking for work-based training, as are NVQs at levels 1–3.

Personal attributes Physical stamina and ability to work outside in all weathers; indifference to getting dirty; willingness to work 'unsocial' hours and sometimes by oneself.

For instructors: authority; ability to express oneself clearly; patience; a liking for children.

Work life balance There may be some part-time work for riding instructors at local riding establishments. Part-time work is on the increase.

Further information British Horse Society, Stoneleigh Deer Park, Kenilworth, Warwickshire CV8 2XZ.
www.bhs.org.uk
Association of British Riding Schools, Office No. 2, Queens Chambers, 38–40 Queen Street, Penzance TR18 4BH.
www.abrs.org/abrs
National Pony Society, Willingdon House, 102 High Street, Alton, Hants GU34 1EN.
www.nationalponysociety.org.uk

OTHER WORK WITH ANIMALS

There is a wide range of other opportunities to work with animals. They range from guide dog trainer to gamekeeper, pet shop assistant to RSPCA inspector, zookeeper to dog beautician. Some of these fields offer a very limited number of openings. Often no specific academic qualifications are needed and training is on the job. Most are essentially practical, manual occupations with limited prospects. (None is a suitable alternative for anyone who narrowly misses becoming a veterinary surgeon.)

Animals

Further information Universities Federation for Animal Welfare, The Old School, Brewhouse Hill, Wheathampstead, Herts AL4 8AN. *www.ufaw.org.uk*

Archaeology

Entry qualifications Degree course requirements. Maths or a science and modern language at GCSE normally required. For *classical archaeology*, Latin or Greek at either level. For *conservation*, chemistry at A level. Archaeology GCSE and A level are available, but are not required.

The work Archaeology is the science of gaining knowledge from the past from the study of ancient objects. Excavations tend to be the most publicized aspects of the work, but the actual digging up and recording work is becoming less centre stage as emphasis on preservation and limiting of damage to sites increases. Though archaeologists need a broad knowledge of the whole field, they normally specialize in one geographical area or period, for example landscape, regional, prehistoric, Anglo-Saxon or theoretical archaeology. Some archaeologists also specialize in particular artefacts, for example coins, weapons or inscriptions.

Among the many broad archaeological specializations are archaeological science, conservation, heritage management, underwater archaeology, environmental archaeology, geophysical survey, archaeological computing and landscape archaeology. These can be studied through a wide variety of post-graduate courses.

Some archaeologists work in museums (see MUSEUMS AND ART GALLERIES, p. 392). Most work for local authorities, independent trusts, English Heritage, the Royal Commission on Ancient and Historical Monuments in Scotland and Wales, the National Trust, Forestry Commission, British Gas. There are many more archaeologists than related jobs.

Archaeology

Training BA or BSc in archaeology as a single subject or in combination with a wide variety of other disciplines. These can be followed by a 1-year Master's degree in various specializations. NVQs in archaeology may become available.

The Institute of Field Archaeologists is the professional institute for archaeologists with various membership levels.

Personal attributes Deep curiosity about the past; intellectual ability well above average; artistic sensibility; patience; manual dexterity (for handling delicate and valuable objects). For excavation, physical stamina.

Late start Advisable only for people who already have a relevant degree or scientific skills and/or hobby experience. Archaeological degrees tend to attract mature students.

Work life balance Prospects for returners depend on previous experience.

A report published by the Cultural Heritage NTO in 2003 found that under 15% of those working as field archaeologists or in a museum/visitor services worked part time although opportunities were better in educational and academic research.

Further information The Council for British Archaeology, Bowes Morrell House, 111 Walmgate, York YO1 2WA.
www.britarch.ac.uk
The Institute of Field Archaeologists, University of Reading, 2 Earley Gate, PO Box 239, Reading RG6 6AU.
www.archaeologists.net

Related careers ARCHIVIST – MUSEUMS AND ART GALLERIES

Architecture

ARCHITECT

Entry qualifications Some schools of architecture require specific GCSE and A level passes. The Royal Institute of British Architects (RIBA) recommends students should have minimum 2 academic subjects at A level (which will ordinarily be a mix of arts and science subjects) and 5 GCSEs (these to include English, maths and double award science).

The work Architecture is a multi-disciplinary profession requiring a combination of artistic, technological and sociological expertise. The challenge of architecture is to produce, within a given budget, an aesthetically pleasing design which will stand up to wear and tear and is the kind of building in which people will want to live or work. Architects must fully understand traditional and new building methods and materials and appreciate their potential and limitations. They must also understand and be interested in contemporary society and changing lifestyles, the community's expectations and needs, and social problems which may lead to loneliness or vandalism. They need to question householders, office workers, teachers, hospital staff, managers, social workers, etc. to come up with a design for a building that is 'user friendly' and which works. For example, the design and layout of a housing estate and its walkways can provide a haven for muggers; a redesign can mean a dramatic drop in antisocial behaviour. This, together with strict financial constraints, makes architecture today a more demanding discipline than it has ever been. Tasks range from converting houses into flats to designing hospitals, retirement homes and factory complexes or cultural institutions such as art galleries, museums and concert halls.

Architects receive instructions (the 'brief') from their clients or employers on the type, function, capacity and rough cost of the building required. Then they do their research – and at that stage they may question some assumptions on which the client based the brief.

When the type of the building has finally been decided upon, the design work begins. This starts with producing, perhaps jointly with colleagues, a sketch scheme of the floor plans and the elevations, and perspective drawings. Several designs may have to be produced before one is finally approved.

The next stage is to prepare contract documents, which will include detailed drawings and specifications; estimates of cost; and applications for necessary planning consents from the local authority. At this stage, especially if the scheme is a big one, consulting engineers (see p. 229) and quantity surveyors (see p. 593) may be appointed. When the contract for the work has been awarded to a building contractor, the architect will usually coordinate the project team, with responsibility for certifying payment to contractors, and for inspecting the work in progress. This involves regular visits to the building site, issuing instructions to the contractor's agent or foreman and discussing any problems that might arise. Site visits may involve walking through mud and climbing scaffolding.

The architect is normally also responsible for the choice or design of fittings and the interior design of the buildings. (See ART AND DESIGN, p. 105.)

An architect can work in different *settings*: in private practice; in the architects' and planning departments of a local authority; in a cooperative; with a public body; with a ministry; or in the architect's department of a commercial firm large enough to have a continuous programme of building or maintenance work.

In private practice the client may be an individual, a commercial firm, a local authority or other public body. It is usual for private practices to specialize, but not exclusively, in houses, schools or offices, etc. In private practice architects normally work only on design and not, as in other categories, on design and maintenance.

In local authorities architects may work on a wide variety of buildings, such as one-family houses, blocks of flats, schools, sports centres and clinics. They also collaborate with private architects employed by the authority for specific schemes.

For other public bodies such as government departments, the architect's work is less varied and is largely confined to the organization's particular building concern: e.g. hospitals for the Department of Health.

The same applies to architects working for a commercial concern. Their work is confined to that organization's particular type of building: e.g. hotels and restaurants for a large catering organization; shops for a retail chain.

The majority of architects are salaried employees, but they may become junior partners and later principals in a firm, or set up on their own. But to start a firm requires a good deal of experience, capital and contacts. More than half of practices employ 5 or fewer full-time architects.

Architects' prospects can be badly affected by recessions and at these times they have to be prepared to take on any work they can find. There are reasonable opportunities to work abroad and UK qualified architects are often in demand overseas. Architects qualified in the UK can register in other EU member states subject to local regulations.

Training The normal pattern of training is a 5-year full-time course, with 1 year of professional experience after the third year and a second year of professional experience at the end of the course, making a minimum of 7 years. Besides full-time courses, some schools of architecture offer part-time courses, but this method of training is not suitable for everyone, as students need to be working in an architectural practice to be accepted and it takes even longer than the normal training; however, it does provide a route to qualification for self-funding students. Subjects studied include architectural history, design and construction, town planning, environmental science, materials science, building control, some sociology, economics, law. The development of design skills through projects is central to an architect's education and increasingly involves CAD (computer-aided design).

For *interior designers*, architectural training need only be up to degree level. It must be followed by a specialized art-school course (part or full time) and practical experience.

NOTES: 1. Architecture, planning and landscape architecture are related disciplines. There are some courses which start with a combined studies year so that students can delay specialization until they know more about the whole field. But courses must be chosen with care: practising architects whether in private practice or public employment must be registered with the Architects Registration Board (ARB) and only qualifications prescribed by ARB lead to admission to the Register. For further information and a list of schools of architecture offering prescribed qualifications see *www.arb.org.uk*. Course titles can be misleading, e.g. 'Architectural Studies' may or may not be a recognized course.

2. For candidates who are not quite certain whether to commit themselves to a 7-year training it is useful to know that the first 3-year stage of training, on most courses, leads to an honours degree in its own right, and therefore to all the graduate jobs for which no particular discipline is specified.

Personal attributes A practical as well as creative mind; an interest in people and an ability to respond to changing lifestyles; self-confidence to put over and justify new ideas; mathematical ability; drawing skills; the ability to deal with legal and financial questions; a reasonably authoritative personality; an aptitude for giving clear instructions and explanations.

Late start The RIBA has a well-established system of external examinations offering a route to qualification for mature students who have at least 6 years' working experience in architectural practice to enter the Part 1 programme and 3 years' professional experience to enter the Part 2 programme. In Spring 2003 the RIBA's Examination for Office-based Candidates was relaunched under a new partnership between the RIBA and Oxford Brookes University, to provide a better-supported route and wider opportunities for mature students to complete their architectural studies while working. For more information see the 'Courses' on the Oxford School of Architecture website at *www.brookes.ac.uk*.

Work life balance Career-breaks are possible for those who keep up by reading journals and attending occasional lectures and seminars. Architects are strongly advised to 'keep their hand in' and do *some* work throughout the break, however sporadic – although current Professional Indemnity Insurance can now make this a somewhat expensive undertaking.

Updating courses are a feature of the profession under its CPD (Continuing Professional Development) requirement for all architects and some returners take one of the post-graduate courses available to develop a new specialization in, for example, urban design, planning or conservation of historic buildings.

A fair proportion of women architects work part time, but combining domestic and professional responsibilities will take its toll on career development. While there is little opportunity for part-time work in the public sector, up to middle-level jobs it should be possible to organize job-sharing and other flexible working. However, with increasing numbers of women choosing to study architecture, government legislation to support family-friendly working, and the Royal Institute of British Architects' stated commitment to supporting equality of opportunity in the profession, this may be set to change.

Further information Royal Institute of British Architects, 66 Portland Place, London W1B 1AB.
   www.architecture.com
Royal Incorporation of Architects in Scotland, 15 Rutland Square, Edinburgh EH1 2BE.
   www.rias.org.uk
The Royal Society of Architects in Wales, Bute Building, King Edward VII Avenue, Cathays Park, Cardiff CF10 3NB.
   www.architecture-wales.com

Royal Society of Ulster Architects, 2 Mount Charles, Belfast, N. Ireland BT7 1NZ.
www.rsua.org.uk

Architects Registration Board, 8 Weymouth Street, London W1W 5BU.
www.arb.org.uk

Related careers *Architectural Technologist/Technician* (*see below*) –
ART AND DESIGN – ENGINEERING – LANDSCAPE ARCHITECTURE
– SURVEYING – TOWN AND COUNTRY PLANNING

Architectural Technologist/Technician

Entry qualifications For associate membership of BIAT, British Institute of Architectural Technologists, an accredited degree in architectural technology or the built environment; a NVQ/SVQ level 4 in Architectural Technology. A BIAT approved HNC/HND in Building Studies with Architectural options is currently acceptable but this requires qualifying as a Technician member before qualifying as a Technologist member.

The work *Architectural technologists* work alongside and often in partnership with other professionals such as architects and planners, both in private practice and in public employment as well as with large firms of building contractors. The work may vary considerably according to the size and structure of the office. It may include any or all of the following: collecting, analysing and preparing technical information required for a design; preparing technical drawings for the builder and presentation drawings for the client; administration of contracts; liaison with clients and with specialists such as quantity surveyors; site supervision; collecting information on performance of finished buildings (which means contact with satisfied and possibly dissatisfied clients); office management. Technologists do responsible work but on the technical rather than the creative side. Those with a few years' experience in employment can set up on their own and, working for private clients or building contractors, design conversions; or help out in architectural firms which need occasional extra staff. Prospects vary according to economic climate. Technologists who want to become architects must take the full architectural training; their BTEC award is normally accepted in lieu of A levels. Few technologists, however, switch to architectural training.

Architectural technicians provide support to other architectural professionals by ensuring the necessary technical information is available and use CAD or traditional methods to produce the specifications and plans needed throughout a building project. They cannot practise on their own account.

Training Having gained the necessary academic qualifications (see 'Entry requirements'), to gain professional status it is necessary to complete BIAT's Professional and Occupational Performance Record (or POP record). For Architectural Technologists, this takes 2–3 years followed by a professional assessment interview; for Architectural Technicians 1–2 years.

Personal attributes Accuracy and attention to detail; ability to visualize and draw (although some of this can be done via a PC); technical ability; communication skills; interest in architecture, materials, structures and the environment (natural and within buildings); liking for teamwork; some design flair.

Late start Not advisable because of low salary while training, although part-time study could be combined with part-time or agency work. Young trainees tend to be preferred, but previous experience in construction is an asset. BIAT offers a non-standard route for those aged 30-plus who have a minimum of 10 years' experience.

Work life balance Theoretically there is no reason why qualified technologists should not return, although professional membership may require a reassessment of skills, expertise and knowledge.

There is not much opportunity for part-time employment, although flexible working hours and practices are available, especially for those who are self-employed.

Architecture

Further information The Education Officer, British Institute of Architectural Technologists, 397 City Road, London EC1V 1NH. *www. biat.org.uk*

Related careers SURVEYING: *Surveying Technicians* – ENGINEERING: *Engineering Technicians*

Archivist

Entry qualifications Good honours degree (subject not strictly relevant). Some knowledge of Latin is desirable.

The work Archivists' work involves the selection, preservation, arrangement, description and making available of documents, such as official records of central and local government and courts of law, or private documents such as title deeds, business records, family papers. Archivists help members of the public with their research, whether they are professors of history, solicitors in search of evidence, students working on projects or genealogists. They may also be involved in promotional activities including exhibitions, presentations or media work. At a more senior level, archivists will undertake traditional management tasks as they take control of budgets, staff and strategy. There is considerable scope for trained archivists who prefer to specialize in records management.

Most archivists work in central and local government record offices. Other posts are in professional institutions, universities, and a wide variety of other establishments, including ecclesiastical foundations, businesses, hospitals, charitable organizations, specialist museums, libraries and research bodies.

Training Nearly all posts now require formal training: 1-year postgraduate course for an MA or Diploma in Archives Administration. Subjects include palaeography, record office management, research methods, conservation methods, editing, information technology, some history and law. It is necessary to have up to 1 year's work experience to be successful in applying for a course.

Archivist

Personal attributes Communication and people skills; a logical mind; an understanding of new technologies and research techniques; a commitment to continuing professional development.

Late start In general the profession welcomes late starters, but there are practical difficulties involved in undertaking the necessary work experience and post-graduate course to qualify.

Work life balance The attitudes of different employers will obviously vary, but part-time posts are available and job-sharing may also be possible. It is usually necessary to go wherever there is a vacancy, both for the first job and later for promotion. Vacancies can be very scarce in some parts of the country.

Further information Society of Archivists, Prioryfield House, 20 Canon Street, Taunton, Somerset TA1 1SW. *www.archives.org.uk*

Related careers ARCHAEOLOGY – INFORMATION WORK – MUSEUMS AND ART GALLERIES

Armed Forces (Officer Entry Only)

In recent years the Armed Forces have been in action more than at any time in the last 40 years. But in addition to the recent conflicts in Iraq, the Balkans, East Timor and Afghanistan which have dominated the headlines, servicemen have taken part in peacekeeping/peace enforcing operations and provided humanitarian aid in many parts of the world. The Armed Forces work at many different levels and service personnel have to be flexible, ready to deal with many different situations and rapid deployment to anywhere in the world.

Entry qualifications Minimum 2 A levels and 3 acceptable GCSEs. See individual forces.

The work Frontline servicemen and women operate and maintain increasingly technically sophisticated equipment, but in a peace-keeping role their primary weapon is often their own communication skills and ability to respond coolly to a sensitive situation. All 3 services have to be self-sufficient, i.e. they have to house, feed, clothe, equip, transport, select, train and provide medical and welfare services to servicemen and servicewomen at home and overseas. Many jobs are unique to the services, but all now offer opportunities to gain qualifications relevant to civilian life. Recruiters look for a particular mix of abilities and personal qualities to try to select people who will fit in and enjoy the way of life. Although the majority will spend their time without experiencing combat, nevertheless they can never forget that at any time they might have to take part in action against an enemy.

Most officers have a dual responsibility: as a leader and manager of a group of men and women, and as a specialist. All three forces have been actively recruiting more women and most jobs are open to them with new ground being broken all the time.

As jobs are so diverse, and training for them is so specific, it is not possible to give more than an outline of the various entry routes in this book. A great deal of information and help is available to people considering joining any one of the services; they should contact their school or university liaison officer, or local recruiting office, or write to the addresses given below.

The Army

Regiments and corps are divided into Arms (those involved in battle) and Services (those providing many kinds of services to the Arms). Each has its own responsibilities, e.g. the Royal Signals handle communications (often using very advanced technology); the Royal Engineers handle engineering and construction, as well as running mapping services for all 3 forces. Would-be officers apply to a corps or regiment, though not all are open to all entrants. Age limits vary, as do entry requirements. (Nearly 80% of recently commissioned officers are graduates.)

Main entry routes and types of commission

Short-Service Commission (SSC) – minimum usually 3 years and can be extended up to 8 years.

Minimum age 17.9 and up to 28. 140 UCAS Points and 5 GCSEs at grade C or above including English language, mathematics and either a science or foreign language.

Intermediate Regular Commission (IRC)

The IRC offers a mid-length career and can be applied for after a minimum of 2 years' SSC, subject to being recommended. The IRC entitles officers to serve for a maximum of 16 years but they may apply to convert to a full-career Regular Commission (Reg C) after 2 years' 'service', subject to being recommended. The IRC is the normal first commission for Welbexians (see below).

Regular Commission (Reg C)

The Reg C offers a full career potentially to the age of 60, although officers may leave at any time subject to meeting minimum notice periods and specified return of service following career courses. It is awarded to recommended and selected IRC officers who have served a minimum of 2 years' IRC.

The Gap Year Commission (GYC)

The GYC is open to young men and women who wish to take time out between leaving school and taking up a firm place at university. Those who pass the selection procedures at the Regular Commissions Board (RCB) are commissioned into their chosen regiment or corps as 2nd Lieutenants on probation and attend a 4-week course at Sandhurst. They serve for a minimum of 4 months (maximum of 18 months) with a front line unit (although not where active service operations are in progress), ending their service shortly before entering university. Thereafter there is no reserve liability and no subsequent obligation to serve in the Army.

The Undergraduate Army Placement

This is very similar to the GYC but is specially tailored for students at university who wish to do a placement year as an Army officer.

There are various schemes to give financial support to sixth-formers and undergraduates; the Army Scholarship scheme is designed to attract candidates of the highest ability into a career as an Army officer by giving financial assistance, first to parents or guardians towards the cost of the candidate's school education and second to the candidate for his/her degree training. The scheme culminates with a lump sum payment at Sandhurst.

Welbeck College is a sixth-form residential college which offers a 2-year A2 level course to motivated young people who would like, in the future, to commission in one of the more technical areas of the Army. Most Welbexians will be commissioned into one of the following Corps: Royal Engineers, Royal Signals, Royal Logistic Corps,

Royal Electrical and Mechanical Engineers. The Welbeck Course is designed both to qualify students to take degrees in engineering and science and to develop their personalities and leadership qualities prior to their officer training at Sandhurst.

The Army Undergraduate Bursary scheme is for undergraduates who wish to commit themselves to the minimum of a 3-year SSC after graduation and the 44-week officer training course at Sandhurst. The Army provides financial support and opportunities for paid training that supplement the normal education grant. Bursaries can be awarded for any degree course including veterinary science, nursing and pharmacy. Financial sponsorship is not available for the Army Legal Services Branch of the Adjutant General's Corps or for applicants for the Royal Army Chaplains' Department.

A special Cadetship scheme applies to applicants for the Royal Army Medical Corps and Royal Army Dental Corps.

Women in the Army

Some 9% of Army officers are women and the number of female Colonels and Brigadiers is increasing due to improved maternity packages encouraging longer service. The Infantry and Royal Armoured Corps remain closed to women.

Royal Navy

Over half the Navy's officers are graduates, who can be from almost any discipline. There are several branches, each providing a specialist service:

Warfare officers are responsible for the safe and efficient handling of a ship while on watch and they may also train to operate weapons systems. They can go on to specialize, for example training as a principal warfare officer, with the tactical expertise to direct fighting operations, or as a submarine service officer or in mine warfare and clearance diving (women at present do not serve in the Submarine Service or as divers). Other officers in the Warfare branch train as hydrographic surveyors or as meteorology or oceanographic officers, advising the command team on the environmental conditions and how they will affect aircraft or weapon performance.

Officer Aircrew develop the exacting skills necessary to fly the Navy's high-performance aircraft not only in defence situations but also in humanitarian roles such as search and rescue sorties. Pilots and observers work together as a team, carrying out equally demanding tasks. Air traffic control officers use some of the most sophisticated radar and communications equipment available to ensure the safety of both naval and civilian aircraft.

Engineer officers work with highly advanced technology and its complexity means that they specialize as one of the following: weapon engineer officers (surface ships), weapon engineers (submarines), marine engineer officers (surface ships), marine engineers (submarines) and air engineers (mechanical and electrical).

Training Management officers are responsible for education and much of the training, from general academic studies to advanced technical training.

Information Systems officers are responsible for the management of complex IS systems ashore and afloat.

Supply officers work in ships and also at shore establishments. They are concerned with both the technical and the personnel aspects of a ship's organization. Their main duties are: administration; correspondence; welfare and personnel matters; naval stores; catering; pay and cash. While at sea, supply officers also have quite separate operational duties.

Medical and Dental officers, Nursing officers in Queen Alexandra's Royal Naval Nursing Service, take care of the health and well-being of naval personnel.

The Royal Marines are the Navy's amphibious infantry and they have their own entry and training requirements. The training is the physically hardest of all in the forces and includes a very demanding commando course.

Armed Forces (Officer Entry Only)

Main entry routes

There are 2 main entry routes for warfare, supply, engineer and aircrew officers:

1. Non-graduate entry for those with 140 UCAS points. On completion of their initial professional training, all non-graduate Warfare and Supply officer entrants receive a Foundation degree in Naval Studies and subsequent accreditation towards an Open University honours degree, at no financial cost to the individual.

2. Direct Graduate Entry.

Financial support through scholarships or sponsorship is available at both levels of entry. University sponsorship is offered either as a bursary, a university cadetship or through the Defence Technical Undergraduate Scheme.

Training Management officers enter by Direct Graduate Entry and must be under 34 and hold a degree or equivalent in a mathematical, computing, engineering or scientific discipline.

Medical and Dental officers may apply for cadet entry (and be sponsored through university) or for Direct Graduate Entry on completion of their degree.

All entrants join on an initial commission of 12 years for RN officers and 8 years for RM officers. They are eligible for competitive selection to a career commission (16 years) or for selection to a full-term commission (to age 55).

Women in the Royal Navy

Entry and conditions of service are now mainly the same as for men. However, they do not serve as divers, in submarines or in the Royal Marines.

Royal Air Force

As in the other forces, officers in the Royal Air Force are leaders, managers and specialists. Pilots and navigators fly fast jet, multi-engine and rotary wing aircraft. Air traffic controllers are responsible for directing the movements of aircraft in the air and of aircraft and vehicles on the airfield. Fighter controllers report on radar pictures and control what goes on in the air by planning air operations and guiding aircraft to their targets. Intelligence officers gather and interpret data largely obtained from sensors in reconnaissance aircraft to help with planning operations. Engineers specialize in work either on aircraft and weapons or on communications and radar systems. Supply officers are responsible for provision of all kinds of equipment and the movement of cargo and personnel by all means of transport. In the administrative branch, officers work in accountancy, estates management, personnel and welfare services. Others work as education and training officers, station catering managers and physical education officers.

For most branches in the RAF there are two types of commission: *permanent* (up to age 38 or for 16 years, whichever is the longer, with possible extension to age 55) and *short service* (3–6 years, varying from branch to branch; 12 years for pilots and navigators, with the option to leave after 6 years' 'productive service'). For most branches both types of commission are available.

Main entry routes

For all commissions the minimum academic standard is 2 A levels and 5 GCSEs (A–C) or equivalent, including English language and maths. There is a large graduate intake to 20 officer branches.

Aircrew: aged 17½ to 24 (pilots) or 26 (navigators). *Air traffic control, fighter control, flight operations* and *intelligence officers*: aged 17½ to 29. *Provost/Security*: aged 21 to 29. *RAF Regiment*: males aged 17½ to 25. *Engineer Officer*: aged 17½ to 38 with an acceptable engineering degree. *Supply Officer*: aged 17½ to 29. *Catering Officer*: aged 17½ to 38 with Higher National award, degree or professional qualification in catering. *Training Officer*: aged 21 to 38 with a degree (occasionally Higher National award) in science, engineering or similar subject. *Administrative Officer*: aged 17½ to 34. *Physical Education Officer*: aged 22 to 26 (exceptionally 38) and must have relevant degree in physical education or sports science. Relevant professional qualifications are required to join the *Chaplain, Dental, Legal, Medical* and *Nursing* branches.

Various types of sponsorship are available, including sixth-form scholarships and university bursaries.

Armed Forces (Officer Entry Only)

Women in the RAF
Women now serve in all branches except the RAF Regiment.

Personal attributes Depend very much on the branch or job, but all officers need certain qualities of leadership, initiative, ability to get on with people from all kinds of background, liking for teamwork, adaptability, physical fitness. Must enjoy and be willing to contribute to community life.

Further information Your local Army, Royal Navy or RAF Careers Office or Jobcentre or Careers/Connexions Service.

Army: *www.army.mod.uk*
www.armyofficer.co.uk

Officer Entry, Freepost (LON 15445) Bristol BS38 7UE.

Royal Navy: *www.royal-navy.mod.uk*

Director of Naval Recruiting, Victory Building, HM Naval Base, Portsmouth PO1 3LS.

Air Force: *www.raf.mod.uk*

Art and Design

Entry qualifications See 'Training', below.

New technologies and changing concepts of what is meant by art and design make this a very rapidly changing career field. Computer-aided design and the increasing requirement for multi-skilling have blurred the boundaries between areas of work. The distinction between artist and designers is also less clear. One definition is that artists work to express their own creativity while designers work to a brief of some sort but many artists work to commissions as well. Art and design is usually referred to as 2-dimensional, taking in areas from magazine and webpage design to photography and textiles, and 3-dimensional, covering a huge range of creative activity from sculpture and fashion to theatrical set design and industrial design. Artists and designers may specialize in one material, such as oils or metalwork, but increasingly they choose or are required to bring a range of skills to their work.

FINE ART

Post Turner prize this can mean performance art, installations and artistic video as much as painting and sculpture. Although commissions for murals and sculpture are more common since the 'percentage for art' scheme encouraged art commissions for public buildings, it is still very hard to make a living through fine art although some do manage it. Artists in residence posts and Community Art work projects provide opportunities for some fine artists.

The majority of fine artists also teach and for that they need Qualified Teacher Status (see p. 611). Part-time teaching is now *very* difficult to find. Others combine fine art with applied art, such as pottery, jewellery-making or illustration but success can depend on a certain amount of business acumen.

A fine art degree can lead to a career in related areas such as arts administration in galleries, museums or funding bodies.

DESIGN
(see also ENGINEERING, 'Design', p. 225)

The function of the designer, who is, broadly, a specialist combining artistic talent and training with sufficient technical and business knowledge to appreciate the requirements of an industry, is still evolving. Design careers tend not to be structured, although the last 20 years have shown that there are certain employment patterns that new entrants can aspire to. Most designers start as assistants and work first in the area of specialization in which they trained. Later, with experience and evolving interests, they can switch specializations, or at least sub-specializations. For example, a 3-dimensional designer might switch from light engineering to furniture or interior design; a graphic designer from typography to photography; a fashion/textile designer from fashion (see p. 113) to floor-covering or wallpaper, etc. Sometimes 3-dimensional-trained designers switch to visual communication – but the switch the other way round is less likely. A few later combine several design categories.

Titles in industry are arbitrary and mean little; an assistant designer may have more scope for creativity and decision-making than a designer or even design director. Not all industrial employers are used to working with designers; the contribution the designer is expected or indeed allowed to make varies from one job to another. For example, sometimes the bias is towards technical expertise: the designer is expected to state, through design, exactly how a product is to be manufactured or printed. Sometimes the bias is towards creativity, and the designer is expected to put forward ideas for totally new products. Usually, the visual appearance of the product is the most important aspect of the designer's brief.

Designers usually work with a team of experts from different disciplines, both technical (engineers, printing technologists, etc.) and business (buyers, marketing people, etc.). This teamwork is one of the important differences between artists and designers. Designers cannot just please themselves: their ideas on what is good design and what is not have to be adapted to fit in with commercial and technical requirements.

Though the designer's work varies from one field of design to another, the end-product always has to fulfil at least 3 demands: it must look up-to-date, perform its function adequately, and be economically produced so that it is profitable. For example, a poster must attract attention and be easily readable; a tin-opener or a fridge must work well, look good and last; a biscuit pack must attract attention, fit into shelf-displays, keep its contents fresh, and open easily; a machine tool must serve the engineer's stated purpose, be easy and safe to handle and clean; and all these products must be manufacturable within given cost-limits. Designers must fully understand the purpose of the product they are designing and its marketing and manufacturing problems. They must know the limitations and potential of materials and machines available for production. Sometimes a change in technology allows the designer to develop a revolutionary design: e.g. the removal of buffers from high-speed locomotives allowed the design of a totally different engine shape.

Starting as design assistant, the trained designer gains useful experience when carrying out simple 'design-technician' rather than design tasks. For example, the beginner may translate a designer's idea for a product into detailed working drawings: this requires technical know-how rather than creativity. In furniture design, for example, the task might be specifying how to fix A satisfactorily to B in manufacturing terms without spoiling the appearance.

One designer is usually responsible for several design assistants (now sometimes called design technicians); the size of design teams varies greatly. Designers and design assistants work in various settings:

in advertising agencies; manufacturing concerns' design departments; architects' offices; interior design studios; design consultancies, and many others. Organizing freelance work either on one's own or with colleagues on a design consultancy basis is complex and requires experience: newly trained designers should try to gain experience as staff designers first. They need to know a lot not only about production problems and organization, but also about how to deal with clients and finance.

The ratio of opportunities to qualified applicants is more favourable in the less glamorous and more technical field of *product design* than in *interior, set* or *textiles* and *fashion design*.

There will never be as many creative top-level jobs as there are aspiring designers, but there is scope for design assistants or 'technicians' whose work varies in creativity and responsibility; for example, making working drawings from designers' scribbled outlines; model-making; or, in communication design, trying to get as near the designer's intended effect as possible with a restricted number of colours and within printing constraints. There is a vast range of jobs in product design which require technical competence, an appreciation of what constitutes good design and *some* creativity rather than creative genius.

Prospects are reasonable for people who *want* to design for industry and appreciate that it is teamwork, but *not* for failed artists. Many of the best product and fashion designers go abroad where British training is greatly appreciated.

Graphics or Graphic Design or Visual Communication

This is concerned with lettering; page design; illustration, including photography; the design of symbols or 'logos'. It ranges from the design of books, magazines, websites, all kinds of advertisements (posters, packaging, etc.), to the visual corporate identity symbol of organizations, i.e. presenting the image of that organization in visual, instant-impact-making terms. Nearly all graphic design work is carried out on computers and experience with relevant software is usually essential.

Visual communication includes 'visual aids' for industrial and educational application. This is an expanding area: instructions and/or information are put over in non-verbal language, with symbols taking the place of words. Symbols are used as teaching aids in industrial training; as user-instructions in drug and textile labelling; as warning or information signs on machinery; on road signs. Symbols may be in wall-chart or film-strip form, or on tiny labels as on medicine and detergent packages, or on textile labels, or on huge posters. Symbol design, whether single or in series, requires great imagination, social awareness, logical thinking.

Visual communication also includes TV graphics: captions, programme titles, all non-verbal TV presentation of information, such as election results, trade-figure trends, etc.; packaging, publicity and advertising; stamp and letter-head design. Graphic designers work in advertising agencies, in design units, or in manufacturing firms and other organizations' design departments. Television absorbs only a tiny proportion. Web design is a growing specialization, employing freelancers as well as in-house designers (see p. 286).

There are few openings in general book and magazine illustration and design, but there is considerable scope in technical and medical graphics, which require meticulous accuracy rather than creative imagination. There is also some scope in the greeting-card trade and in catalogue illustration. Much of this is considered hackwork by creative artists.

3-Dimensional Design

This can be divided conveniently into *product design* and *interior design*. Almost all 3D design is produced on computers.

Product design
This covers the design of all kinds of consumer goods (e.g. domestic appliances, or suitcases) and of machine tools, mechanical equipment, cars, as well as pottery, furniture, etc.

There is pressure on manufacturing industry to pay more attention to design than it has in the past. But there is no general agreement on how this is to be brought about. Many engineers and manufacturers still believe that with a bit more design training, engineers can cope with the aesthetics and ergonomics (ease of handling and cleaning, convenience in use, legibility of instructions). But most progressive manufacturers now agree that engineers must work *with* design specialists who, for their part, must have a thorough understanding of engineering principles and production constraints.

The proportion of 'design input' and 'engineering input' varies from product to product. Designers talk about a 'spectrum' – for example, in the manufacture of a plastic cup the 'engineering input' is very small, the 'design input' large; at the other end of the spectrum is a gas turbine, where the design input may be confined to the lettering of the instructions and the colour (which is, however, important, as it affects the 'work environment', which affects industrial efficiency). In between the two extremes are appliances such as food processors and CD players. The engineer designs the components and says how they must be arranged to do the job; the industrial designer is primarily concerned with the appearance and ergonomics of the product.

Between the first sketch and the final product there may be many joint discussions, drawings, modifications, working models and prototypes. The designer negotiates with the engineer; design technicians develop the product through the various stages. Designers and engineers work in teams – whether the team leader is an engineer or a designer varies according to the type of product, the firm's policy and, last but by no means least, the engineer's and designer's personalities.

Product designers need such extensive knowledge of relevant engineering and manufacturing processes that they tend to stay within a particular manufacturing area. The greatest scope is in plastics, which cover a wide range of products, from toys to complex appliances and equipment.

Interior design

Interior designers work in specialized or general design consultants' studios; large stores; for a group of hotels or supermarkets; in private practice or local authority architects' offices. A considerable knowledge of architecture is required in order to know how to divert drains, move walls safely, or enlarge a shop window satisfactorily. The job of the interior designer, besides being responsible for such things as the management of contracts, is to specify the nature of an interior – how it is made, built and finished – as well as selecting the finishes and fixtures and fittings.

Planning interiors for a hotel, shop, aircraft, etc., needs research before the design starts. Beginners often spend all their time on fact-finding: the different items of goods to be displayed; the number of assistants required in a new shop; the kind of materials suitable and safe for furnishing a plane. They also search for suitable light fittings, heating equipment, furnishing materials, and they may design fixtures and fittings.

The term 'interior design' is often interpreted rather loosely, and some jobs require less training and creativity. This applies particularly to work done by assistants in the design studios of stores or architects' offices; in showrooms of manufacturers of paint, furniture, furnishings, light fittings, wallpaper, etc.; in the furnishing departments of retail stores, and in specialist shops. In these settings, interior designers may advise customers or clients on the choice and assembly of the items needed. This may mean suggesting colour schemes, matching wallpaper and curtains, sketching plans for room decoration, or advising on the most suitable synthetic fabric for a particular furnishing purpose. As stores' estimators and home advisers, they may go to customers' houses to give advice or even only to measure up for loose covers and curtains. Some stores and specialist shops employ interior designers as buyers in furniture and furnishing departments, and paint, wallpaper and furnishing fabric manufacturers may employ them as sales representatives. In these jobs 'interior designer' is a courtesy title rather than a job description.

Set design
The work requires a knowledge of period styles, structures and lighting techniques, an understanding of drama and an ability to analyse a play, to help visualize the right kind of set for a theatre production or TV programme. Limited scope.

Exhibition and display design

Combines some of the work of interior and set design with model-making and graphic design. Exhibition design is usually done by specialist firms. Exhibitions are often rush jobs, and designers may help put up stands and work through the night before opening. Exhibition designers also work in museums (see p. 392). Limited scope. See also TELEVISION, FILM AND RADIO, p. 620.

Display design

Closely allied to exhibition design, but can be a specialization on its own. The essence of window and 'point-of-sale' design is communication: the display designer must present the store's or shop's image, attract attention and persuade the passer-by to buy. Window display can consist of merely putting a few goods in the window or a show case, or it can be a highly sophisticated exercise in marketing, using specially designed models (see 'Model-making', below) and specially chosen merchandise to convey a 'theme' and marketing policy. In stores there may be a *display manager*, a *display designer* and several *display assistants* or *technicians* who make/arrange the props and merchandise. Reasonable scope.

Studio-based design (glass, jewellery, silverware, stained glass, etc.)

Design and production by designer-craftspeople who run their own small-scale studios or workshops where each article is made individually. This is a fairly precarious way of making a living. However, some studios survive, especially in tourist areas, selling to local shops and individual customers. They have 'studied the market', and perhaps compromised, producing designs which sell rather than those which they would ideally like to produce.

Model-making

This includes the design and/or making up of models for window and exhibition display, and the making of scale models for architects, planners, and interior-design and product-design studios. Many designers, architects, etc., find that their clients are better able to judge a design if they see it in 3-dimensional model form rather than as drawings.

Model-makers use the traditional materials – wood, plaster, fabric, etc. – and also the new synthetics. They usually work in specialist studios and firms, but some work in other types of design studio. There is more scope here for manual work requiring some creative ability than for pure artistic design. It is an expanding field.

Textiles/Fashion
(see also FASHION AND CLOTHING, p. 248)

Textile design includes printed and woven textiles, carpets and other floor coverings, wallpapers, and plastic surface coverings and decoration. There are few openings in manufacturing firms. One of the difficulties is that thorough knowledge of manufacturing methods is essential, but it is difficult to get a job with suitable firms.

Textile designers work on their own more frequently than do other designers. They usually work through agents who show their designs to manufacturers. Fashion collections are held two or more times a year, furnishing collections usually twice.

Training
BTEC National awards, SQA Scottish Group Award or Vocational A levels

Nearly all of these are 2-year full-time courses for people aged 16 or more. For those with no particular educational qualifications there is a BTEC Intermediate GNVQ in Art and Design; the National Diplomas/Certificates in Design are for those who already know in which area they want to become involved. In some cases students with A level art (or mature entrants) may enrol for the second year of these courses.

The National Diploma has been replaced in many colleges by the Vocational A level. This is a broad-based course equivalent to A level standard and acceptable for degree entry. In Scotland there is a named Scottish Group Award in Art and Design.

Art and Design

Foundation course
1-year full-time (2-year part-time) Art Foundation (in Scotland incorporated into a 4-year art and design degree course) for students aged 17 or more, most of whom have several GCSEs and have studied in the sixth form. This course should be 'diagnostic' to help students decide on their eventual specialization. There are many aspects of design which school-leavers cannot know about, and by taking a Foundation course students may be drawn to one of the less well-known design fields. However, Foundation courses are not all the same, so students need to look carefully at what is on offer.

Access courses (see p. 15)
These are designed for adults returning to education after a break. They usually last 1 year and may be full or part time.

Higher education courses
The number and variety of art and design courses can be confusing. Course titles are not always indicative of course content and prospectuses should be studied carefully before a choice is made. (A detailed listing of all higher education Art and Design courses can be found in *The Art & Design Directory*, published by ISCOCareerscope.) Entry requirements vary considerably and a student's portfolio of work may be a deciding factor.

HND/HNCs
They vary considerably and some may be almost indistinguishable from degree courses while others are much more employment focused. Some incorporate a work placement. Many lead on to the final year of an honours degree.

Foundation degrees
In many higher education institutions Foundation degrees are replacing art and design HNDs. These are work-related courses, and usually take 2 years full time and part time 3 to 4 years.

Degrees

Entry qualifications vary – as a guide 1 A level and 3 GCSEs (A–C) plus – normally but not invariably – a 1-year Foundation course; or BTEC National Certificate or Diploma or Scottish equivalent. Individual colleges vary in their precise requirements; some demand, for example, GCSE (A–C) maths or craft design and technology and English. Acceptance also very much depends on applicant's portfolio, i.e. on proof of creative ability.

Again, course content varies considerably. Art and Design subjects can be studied individually or in combination, either with a related subject or with another subject such as a language. Most courses are modular and offer a range of selectives in addition to the compulsory modules. Some are academically focused while others put more emphasis on developing skills. Institutions are not uniformly equipped and it is worthwhile checking that they are up to date with technology where appropriate. Prospective students who expect to work freelance should look out for modules on marketing and business start-up.

Art and Design teachers in schools need to achieve Qualified Teacher Status (see Teaching p. 611). Art and Design lecturers in further education and higher education usually need professional experience as well as a relevant degree and increasingly a teaching qualification.

Post-graduate training

Although a degree or HND is the basic requirement for anyone wanting to get on in the design world, it is usually necessary these days for artists and designers to update their skills or acquire new ones at some stage, often between 3 and 10 years after gaining their first degree or HND. There are post-graduate courses in most design specializations, for example in film, in TV graphics, computer-assisted art and animation, conservation, theatre design.

The Open College of the Arts

Set up in 1987 as a charitable trust, the Open College of the Arts provides home-based education in the arts using similar methods to those of the Open University (see p. 16), to which it is affiliated. Courses that can be taken by distance learning, with or without tutorial support provided by one of a network of tutorial centres, include basic art and design, drawing, painting, graphic design, textiles and photography. OCA courses do not lead to nationally recognized qualifications, but they are very useful to mature entrants needing to gain basic knowledge and a portfolio before applying to mainstream courses.

Art Therapy

The work This is a growing field. Its purpose is twofold: painting and other art forms help withdrawn patients to express themselves and relieve tension, and seeing patients' work helps psychiatrists pinpoint patients' thoughts and problems. The majority of art therapists work – usually on a sessional basis – in hospitals and institutions for those with psychiatric problems and learning difficulties, with children and with adults, individually and in groups; some work with children with special needs. Art therapy is not so much a career in itself as a field in which practising artists with the necessary human qualities can do useful work.

Training Post-graduate 1-year full-time or 2-year part-time courses are essential.

Personal attributes All careers in art and design require resilience, self-confidence and exceptional talent.

Especially for design: Ability to work as one of a team; creative sensibility and imagination coupled with a logical analytical mind; an interest in science and technology; curiosity and a desire to solve technical problems; perseverance; an interest in the social environment and in the community's needs, tastes and customs; the ability to take responsibility and criticism; willingness at times to lower one's artistic standards in the interests of economic necessity or technical efficiency.

For freelances and senior staff jobs: Business sense; the ability to communicate with employers and clients who commission the work but are possibly not themselves interested in art.

For 'technician' jobs: Considerable manual dexterity, technical ability and some creativity.

Late start It is not unusual for people to do a fine art degree in later life – on one course several were in their seventies. On vocationally-orientated courses qualifications may be waived for applicants with experience.

Work life balance If experienced and established, designers can set up on their own; some return to outside employment after a career break, but competition from recent art-school leavers is likely to be stiff.

Freelancers can work their own hours but these may be longer than if in employment.

Further information National Society for Education in Art and Design (NSEAD), The Gatehouse, Corsham Court, Corsham, Wilts. SN13 OES.
www.nsead.org
Design Council, 34 Bow Street, London WC2E 7DL.
www.designcouncil.org.uk
Chartered Society of Designers, 32–38 Saffron Hill, London EC1N 8FH.
www.csd.org.uk
British Association of Art Therapists, Mary Ward House, 5 Tavistock Place, London WC1 9SN.
(for information please send s.a.e.)
British Display Society, 146 Welling Way, Welling, Kent DA16 2RS.
BTEC and SQA (see pp. 8, 10).
Open College of the Arts, Houndhill, Worsborough, Barnsley, South Yorks. S70 6TU.
www.oca-uk.com

Art and Design

Related careers ADVERTISING – ARCHITECTURE – CARTOGRAPHY
– ENGINEERING – FASHION AND CLOTHING – LANDSCAPE ARCHI-
TECTURE – MUSEUMS AND ART GALLERIES – PHOTOGRAPHY –
TEACHING – TELEVISION, FILM AND RADIO

Banking and Building Society Work

Take-overs and mergers, along with the introduction of Internet and telebanking, continue to bring about branch closures and a reduction in traditional face-to-face customer services. Institutions offering high street financial services have gone through a period of rapid and dramatic change. Competition has intensified, spurred on by new technology and legislation. Distinctions between different institutions have blurred with activities and services formerly offered by one particular kind of institution now being offered by others. Banks offer mortgages and insurance, while building societies offer cheque accounts. The clearing banks have investment banking divisions or subsidiaries, while the investment banks (as well as the clearers) have bought stockbroking firms. More and more one hears the term 'financial services group' to convey the range of financial activity.

Banking can be broken down into services to individuals and services to companies, though there may be overlap (especially in the clearing banks) in terms of both activity and career opportunity. For example, a high street branch manager may be involved with individuals and with corporate clients; a trainee might have a spell in a department marketing corporate services and then move into a role as a personal accounts executive.

Retail/Personal Banking

Entry qualifications Many but not all banks ask for a minimum of 4 GCSEs (A–C), or Scottish equivalent. Those with A levels, Advanced GNVQ/VCE, a BTEC National award, or Scottish equivalent, or a degree will normally be recruited to an accelerated training programme.

The work Banks and building societies provide a wide range of financial services to personal customers, largely through their branch networks. They take deposits and make loans, transmit money from one account to another, exchange foreign currency and travellers' cheques, offer mortgages, insurance policies, pensions and investment schemes. They also offer financial advice on a range of matters.

The rapid take-up of telephone and Internet banking means that many financial services staff now work in call centres. UK-based call and contact centres still represent major employment opportunities within the sector despite an ongoing trend to relocate many such operations to developing countries.

Staff at all levels in a branch deal with people as well as money and figures. From an early stage in training considerable emphasis is placed on the ability to relate to customers, identify their needs and promote the bank's services.

Trainees normally start in the general office, where they learn basic procedures such as sorting and listing cheques so that they can be 'read' electronically and operating the terminal linked to the central computer on which customers' accounts are updated. Trainees usually commence duties as a cashier. Cashiers are in the front line of the intensifying battle for customers so they must make a good impression. Courtesy, efficiency and helpfulness are important.

After a spell at the counter, trainees undertake other customer service duties, for example setting up standing orders/direct debits and opening accounts. Promotion to senior clerical duties involves the development of supervisory skills and the more specialized technical knowledge needed to deal with, for example, customers' investments; the sanction of small personal loans and analysis, with the management team, of more detailed lending propositions; or executor and trust work, dealing with trusts and wills in which the bank may look after customers' or their dependants' interests, advise people who have been left money on investment, or explain complex money matters to bewildered heirs. As clerical officers are promoted to junior management grades they take on increased responsibility for customer service and the smooth running of the branch.

Managers may be responsible for one branch or several. Within policy laid down by the bank, they have considerable responsibility for approving loans, dealing with business customers from the small to, sometimes, the very large, overseeing the smooth running of their branches and marketing the bank's growing range of services and 'products'.

Those on accelerated management training programmes might spend only very short periods in the clerical functions. They are not necessarily expected to master the tasks but need to appreciate their importance in the overall service the bank offers its customers. There are also opportunities in regional and head offices where, for example, specialist advice is available and new 'products' are developed. A career with a bank can also develop into non-banking functions, e.g. personnel.

New technology has led to large cuts in staff among the banks. The impact is more marked in lower-level jobs; in an intensely competitive climate, the banks continue to recruit and train those who have the potential to become senior managers. The banks all have well-developed graduate recruitment and training programmes, but in theory it is still possible to reach senior levels from a modest start. (Many graduates also opt to develop their careers on the corporate side of the business.)

Training Largely on the job, with residential courses at more senior levels. Day-release may be available for those preparing for the exams of the Institute of Financial Services, but it is often restricted to Associateship Examination candidates and those on accelerated pro-grammes. There are evening and distance/flexible learning courses for other candidates.

Call/contact centre staff can take a range of qualifications which are either offered by external providers or internally through their employer. Qualifications are available for various levels of staff, from customer advisers to supervisory and management levels. The

Foundation level qualifications are equivalent to A level or NVQ level 2/3 and are very practically orientated.

Personal attributes Meticulous accuracy; the interpersonal skills to deal with customers; a clear, logical mind; tact; courtesy; a feeling for figures and interest in work with data-processing equipment.

Late start No precise figures are available for the profession overall. In the past the proportion of full-time late entrants has been small, but banks are now looking very seriously at mature applicants with experience and the right personal qualities.

Work life balance Most of the major banks operate a career-break/return-to-work scheme. They vary in detail but, broadly speaking, are open to male and female staff, for a period of 2–5 years. Some guarantee a return to the organization at one's previous grade. Normally the member of staff is expected to undertake refresher training for 2–4 weeks a year and to keep abreast of developments.

Developments such as telebanking have increased opportunities for flexible working.

Wholesale/Corporate Banking

Entry qualifications There are some opportunities for school-leavers with GCSE or A level or equivalent, but their prospects may be limited. Most banks recruit mainly graduate trainees.

The work Companies and governments require financial services broadly equivalent to those offered to individuals, but the scale and complexity are much greater. Among the services offered by the banks to their corporate customers are: banking, which is basically taking deposits, transferring funds and lending money; corporate finance, which includes advising on mergers and acquisitions, raising capital, business strategy, competitors and outside factors; and treasury, which involves buying and selling foreign currency to protect against disadvantageous currency movements. The banks are also involved in investment management on behalf of institutional investors of large sums of money, such as pension funds and investment trusts, and the securities business (see p. 585) – making issues and buying and selling shares.

Corporate banking can start with the local branch manager, but the more complex work will be done in the corporate divisions of the clearing banks, their investment banking subsidiaries, and the investment banks. Not all banks offer the same range of services. Staff are required for a range of tasks from analysis to sales. In most jobs staff should be capable of analysing, researching and selling the results, but team work is a common feature of this area of banking.

An important related activity is dealing – in currencies and various financial 'products' designed to help firms finance their businesses. Banks may deal speculatively on their own account to make a profit, or on behalf of clients to help them manage financial risks.

After the rapid expansion of the mid-1980s, numbers have been steadily declining, affected by both fierce competition and recession. However, though the level varies, the larger banks will maintain some regular recruitment as a long-term investment. For those who are successful, the financial rewards are high, but, as recent years have shown, high rewards are often balanced by high risks, especially on the dealing side. It is not a business that carries 'passengers'.

Most 'bankers' and corporate financiers will be graduates, but dealers are often non-graduates who start in a support function. Specialist staff, e.g. experts in a particular industry, have good opportunities to move between banks.

Training Largely on the job with the opportunity and encouragement to obtain relevant qualifications.

Personal attributes High intelligence; ability to work as a member of a team and to relate to clients at a high level; flexibility; competitive drive; ability to think analytically and practically. *For dealers*: confidence, quick wits, entrepreneurial flair, independence.

Late start Some entrants over 30, with relevant industrial/professional experience. A 'fresh' start for job changers without such experience is unlikely.

Work life balance High street banking groups are introducing flexible working practices.

In corporate banking job-sharing and part-time work are not widespread and mainly confined to clerical/secretarial areas and possibly support functions like personnel. Employers claim resistance from clients who want continuity of service from their bankers.

Further information Institute of Financial Services, 4–9 Burgate Lane, Canterbury, Kent CT1 2XJ.
www.ifslearning.com
Chartered Institute of Bankers in Scotland, Drumsheugh House, 38B Drumsheugh Gardens, Edinburgh EH3 7SW.
www.ciobs.org.uk
London Investment Banking Association, 6 Frederick's Place, London EC2R 8BT.
www.liba.org.uk
Building Societies Association, 3 Savile Row, London W1X 1AF.
www.bsa.org.uk

Related careers ACCOUNTANCY – ACTUARY – INSURANCE

Beauty Specialist

Entry qualifications For school-leavers, 2 or more GCSEs depending on course, but some schools ask for biology or chemistry; see 'Training', below.

The work Practitioners may use one of several job-titles, but the two most common terms are *beauty therapist* and *beauty consultant*.

Beauty Therapist

Most *beauty therapists* use the full range of available treatments on the face and body. These extend from make-up, facials and wax or electric depilation (removal of superfluous hair) to massage, saunas, diet and exercise. They know when to deal with a skin complaint themselves or when to advise the client to see a doctor. It is possible to learn one or two techniques only, e.g. a *beautician* works on the face and neck only; a *manicurist/pedicurist* on the hands/feet; the *electrologist* (or *epilationist*) uses various means to remove unwanted hair; a *masseur/masseuse* performs face/body massage. (*Aromatherapists* massage with aromatic oils.)

Beauty therapists work in private high street salons (sometimes combined with hairdressers), in their own or clients' homes, in health farms or cosmetic firms' salons. Clients may be of all ages, male or female.

It is not always easy for students to find jobs, but beauty and fitness treatments are becoming more popular. Some beauty specialists set up on their own: the initial financial outlay on equipment depends on the treatments offered. The town hall will advise on necessary licences (see WORKING FOR ONESELF, p. 648). For those trained in hairdressing there are some opportunities in television (see p. 625) and with psychiatric and other patients for whom beauty care can be part of their rehabilitation.

Beauty Consultants (Sales Consultants, Sales Representatives)

Usually work in the perfumery department of large stores, occasionally in luxury hotels (at home or abroad), on liners, or at airports. They are usually under contract to a cosmetics firm and travel round the country, working for a week or two each in a succession of stores or shops.

They sell and promote the firm's products and try to win regular customers. They answer questions on skin-care and make-up problems, and may give talks and demonstrations.

Top jobs are as cosmetic buyers for stores, at the head offices of cosmetic firms, and as training consultants.

Professional training

Training For jobs in a reputable salon or health farm, it is important to take a course leading to one of the mainstream qualifications. NVQs (see p. 10) are available at levels 1 to 4 and students should make sure that courses lead to these qualifications, as they are likely to become very important in the future (e.g. for getting insurance cover). Courses are available in both local education authority colleges and private schools. The advantage of maintained college courses is that they are free for younger students, although they generally last longer than private ones. Most good private courses last from 5 to 12 months (some are longer). Fees for private colleges range from a few hundred pounds to several thousand, depending on range of skills taught. Syllabus includes theory – anatomy, physiology, diets, salesmanship, salon organization – and practical work: giving facials, different types of massage, make-up, sometimes electrical treatments, etc.

Main courses are:

1. In-house training or Advanced Modern Apprenticeship leading

to NVQ/SVQs levels 2 and 3. A level 4 NVQ is available for those progressing to management positions.

2. A number of universities and colleges offer 2-year BTEC HND courses in Beauty Therapy or related subjects. 2-year Foundation degrees and related 3 or 4 years honours degree courses are also available.

3. Courses leading to awards of one of the national or international beauty therapy examining bodies, for example, the Confederation of International Beauty Therapy and Cosmetology and ITEC (International Therapy Examination Council). Minimum age usually 18.

NOTE: It is important to check the usefulness of courses not included above with one of the organizations mentioned under 'Further information'.

Courses given by cosmetics houses for sales consultants
Minimum age depends on age range at which product is aimed, e.g. teenagers or mature people. Majority need to be 24+ and must have several years' selling experience and must be good salespeople. Training is mainly in-store and lasts a few weeks. Subjects dealt with are facials, simple massage, eyebrow shaping and make-up, for both day and evening. These courses qualify students as sales consultants, but not as beauty therapists.

It is useful to take a hairdressing training as well as beauty training. It widens the choice of jobs later.

Personal attributes A liking for people of all ages; a friendly, confident manner; tact; courtesy; an attractive, well-groomed appearance; good health; business sense; ability to express oneself easily; foreign language sometimes an asset.

Late start Beauty specialists' work is very suitable for late entrants. Many salons prefer women who are nearer in age to the majority of clients than young school-leavers are. Nurses and physiotherapists sometimes choose this work as a second career.

Beauty Specialist

Work life balance Career-breaks present no special problem, except for need to find new clients.

Part-time work is fairly easy for experienced people.

Further information BTEC and SQA (see pp. 8, 10)

ITEC, 10/11 Heathfield Terrace, Chiswick, London w4 4JE.
www.itecworld.co.uk

Confederation of International Beauty Therapy and Cosmetology (CIBTAC), 70 Eastgate Street, Gloucester GL1 1QN.
www.cibtac.com

Hairdressing and Beauty Industry Authority, Fraser House, Netherhall Road, Doncaster DN1 2PH.
www.habia.org.uk

Related careers TELEVISION, FILM AND RADIO: *Make-up artists/ Designers*

Bookselling

Entry qualifications None laid down, but good general education essential.

The work All bookselling is a branch of retailing, but there is a difference between a specialist bookshop, where customers expect to find knowledgeable staff, and non-specialist bookshops with a limited range of titles and various non-book products on sale. The latter are more suitable for people interested more in a retailing career than in books. Specialist bookshop staff must be well read in order to be able to advise customers and answer queries. Reading should cover a wide field rather than only one's own interests, but in large bookshops staff usually specialize in one or two subjects. Customers are often left to browse undisturbed amongst the stock and are offered help and advice only when they want it.

Assistants' duties include daily dusting and filling and tidying shelves and display-tables. This also helps them to learn the stock and remember where titles are shelved. Assistants also write out orders, keep records and may do some bookkeeping. In many bookshops, ordering, stock control, etc. is now computerized. Assistants may pack and unpack parcels and carry them to the post; bookshop work is physically quite hard.

One of the most interesting and most skilled parts of the job is helping customers who have only a vague idea of what they want or cannot explain what they have in mind. It may involve tracing titles in bibliographies and catalogues.

Book-buying – selecting a small proportion of the vast number of new titles published each month – is a highly skilled and often tricky task. Several members of staff may be responsible for buying within one or more subject areas. They have to be able to judge what will interest their particular customers, whether to buy a new title at all and how many copies to order. New titles are ordered before reviews have appeared so staff must trust their own judgement. They must also judge how much reliance to place on the recommendation of publishers' representatives.

Managers may take part in or do all the buying – it depends on how experienced their staff and how large the shop. Above all, the manager tries to give the shop an 'image' to attract a nucleus of regular customers. This is done partly by the choice of books in stock and partly by the method and type of display and arrangement of the shop as a whole. The manager is also responsible for the stock-control system (as would be the case in any other kind of shop).

Far more people want to work in bookshops than there are vacancies. Bookselling is not a high margin business; nevertheless some owner-managers of small bookshops do reasonably well if they have researched the market thoroughly before setting up shop (see WORKING FOR ONESELF, p. 648). The Booksellers' Association publish *Starting & Running a Bookshop*.

Training Staff learn mainly on the job, although some large shops and chains have formal training schemes.

Personal attributes An excellent memory; commercial sense; wide interests and extensive general knowledge; pleasure in reading and handling books; a liking for meeting people with various interests; a helpful friendly manner and the knack of making diffident customers who are not well read feel they are welcome; the ability to work well in a large team or in a very small shop or department; a calm temperament.

Late start No greater problem than young entrants.

Work life balance A career break should not present any problems.

There is good scope for part-time work especially in bookshops with extended working hours.

Further information The Booksellers' Association of United Kingdom and Ireland Ltd, 272 Vauxhall Bridge Road, London SW1V 1BA. *www.booksellers.org.uk*

Related careers INFORMATION WORK – RETAIL MANAGEMENT

Careers Work

Entry qualifications Usually a degree and for the Connexions Service a background of work with young people.

Careers Work with Young People

In England most careers guidance for young people is now offered through the Connexions Service, a universal service for young people aged 13–19 which brings together a range of social, health and educational agencies to offer an integrated service. Within this service all advisers are employed with the generic title Personal Adviser but some may specialize in providing careers guidance. In some areas the Connexions Service subcontracts careers advisory work to companies specializing in providing careers services.

Scotland and Wales Careers advisers working with young people are based in all-age guidance services – Careers Scotland and Careers Wales – which also carry out careers work in schools and colleges.

Careers work with young people involves helping them to make sound and realistic career choices and to implement those choices. This covers a wide range of activities from encouraging an unemployed school-leaver back into education or training to helping a school to plan an ongoing careers education programme to suit various age and ability groups. Personal/careers advisers need to keep up to date with developments, trends and impending changes in education, training and the jobs market. Some may specialize in information work, publishing local careers information in print or on websites and overseeing careers/Connexions libraries in centres and schools. Others may work solely with young people with special needs.

Personal advisers work in Connexions centres, in youth and community centres, in outreach work – anywhere where young people may be found – and may work with students in groups or as individuals. Since the introduction of the Connexions Service individual work with young people has tended to focus on young people at risk of dropping out of education and training.

Careers Work in Higher Education

In higher education, careers advisers carry out a range of activities similar to those in Connexions/careers services but at a level appropriate to the age, maturity, sophistication and educational level of their clients. A degree and employment experience are essential; beyond that, backgrounds vary enormously. There is no pre-entry training; in-service training may be arranged by the employer or by the Association of Graduate Careers Advisory Services.

Careers Work with Adults

Educational guidance for adults in England is provided through local Information Advice and Guidance (IAG) networks. Advisers working in these aim to help adults understand and take advantage of the full range of educational and training opportunities available. The work includes information, assessment, advice and counselling, so, again, a wide variety of backgrounds may be appropriate.

Other Careers Work

There are opportunities for careers work in a number of other organizations, but they are limited in number and the entry qualifications of practitioners are very varied. Employers of careers advisory staff include *professional bodies*, *charities* and *vocational guidance organizations*. Again, backgrounds differ widely. Some people have experience in careers work, in teaching, in personnel or in the relevant profession. Vocational guidance organizations often look for psychology graduates.

An increasing number of experienced careers advisers are setting up on a self-employed basis.

Training 1. 1-year full-time (2-year part-time) course leading to the Qualification in Careers Guidance. Courses are offered by a number of universities. After completion, careers advisers wishing to work in the Connexions Service must also undertake an NVQ/SVQ in Advice and Guidance level 4.

2. A combination of work-based and off-the-job training leading to NVQ/SVQ in Advice and Guidance level 4. This qualification is a requirement for all career guidance specialists working within the Connexions Service.

Personal Advisers are also required to undertake in-house Connexions Service training programmes. Connexions Service training is currently under review.

A guidance qualification is not mandatory for work in higher education or with adults but 60% of higher education careers advisers now have a qualification as do an increasing number of adult guidance workers. The Association of Graduate Careers Advisory Services offer post experience qualifications at 3 levels – Certificate, Diploma and an MA.

Psychometric testing is increasingly being used in careers work, and careers advisers using such tests are usually required to have a certificate of competence from the British Psychological Society.

Personal attributes Ability to get on with and understand people of all levels of intelligence and temperament; interest in industrial and other employment trends and problems; sympathy with rather than critical attitude towards other people's points of view; organizing ability; willingness to work in a team; ability to put facts across clearly and helpfully; ability to gain people's confidence and to put them at ease however shy and worried; insight and imagination to see how young people might develop and to understand adults' particular difficulties; ability to communicate with individuals, with groups and in writing.

Late start Applicants are normally over 21 and maturity and variety of experience are assets in this work. Relevant jobs are those which involve dealing with a variety of people, preferably in a work situation.

Work life balance There are opportunities for part-time work and job-sharing and other flexible work patterns are now common.

Further information Institute of Career Guidance, Third Floor, Copthall House, 1 New Road, Stourbridge, West Midlands DY8 1PH. *www.icg.uk.org*
Association of Graduate Careers Advisory Services, Administration Office, c/o Careers Service, The University of Sheffield, 8–10 Favell Road, Sheffield S3 7QX.
www.agcas.org.uk
www.connexions.gov.uk

Related careers PERSONNEL/HUMAN RESOURCES MANAGEMENT – PSYCHOLOGY – TEACHING – YOUTH AND COMMUNITY WORK

Cartography

Entry qualifications For *cartographer*: degree or Higher National award: A levels in geography, maths or science often required. For *cartographic draughtsman/woman*: 4 GCSEs (A–C) including maths and English or equivalent.

The work Cartographers are concerned with map-making. A map in this context covers any type of chart, plan, 3-dimensional model or computer image representing the whole or sections of the earth, or of other parts of the universe. While their work in producing 'traditional' maps and wall charts with which everyone is familiar, such as those used in schools and universities, by walkers and motorists and for land and air surveying, is as important as ever, there is steady demand for more specialist maps and charts. Planning professionals may need maps showing traffic flow or the distribution of housing, employment or industry; forest officers need to see areas of planting, thinning and felling; highly accurate details of the sea bed are needed by scientists looking for oil or minerals. There are increasing calls for charts showing the spread, or contraction, of animal and plant populations and human habitation. The penetration of space and of the earth's crust has extended cartographers' horizons and set new challenges in finding new ways of representing the results of such exploration.

Cartographers are concerned with every stage of preparation and interpretation. They have to determine what data are needed for any particular map, discuss how to collect it, evaluate the information that comes in and apply it to map production. This is the *editorial* function. The actual collection of data is done by other specialists such as surveyors (see p. 590), specialist photographers (see p. 454), computing people (see p. 281) or by historical or archaeological researchers. Infra-red photography, often taken from satellites, remote sensing and seismic measurements are techniques widely used in data collection. Information technology is having enormous impact on the way cartographers work, as is shown by the increasing use of GIS – Geographical Information Systems. These enable the storage, processing and display of information on a computer screen. GIS consist of a database, a statistical/mathematical analysing capacity and a means of graphic display. One of the many benefits of GIS is that they enable data to be scanned from existing 'hard copy', manipulated and processed before being displayed in new and graphic ways on a screen or printed out. Cartographers are developing electronic map forms which are replacing at least some products previously printed on paper.

This is a fairly small profession and entry and training opportunities have changed very much in the last few years. While editing is done by cartographers, production is usually the responsibility of the cartographic draughtsman/woman, although there is often overlap. The cartographic draughtsman/woman's traditional skill with hand and pen is now supplemented or replaced by the manipulation of computer images. Traditionally, the Ordnance Survey was the largest employer of cartographic staff; owing to reorganization and the introduction of GIS, staff numbers have been reduced. Other government departments, such as the Ministry of Defence, that used to use large numbers of staff are in a similar situation. The main civilian employers are BT, the Civil Aviation Authority, utility companies and, of course, map publishers. There are some openings in universities and with local authorities.

Training Trainee posts with part-time study are very rare; pre-entry training is normally required, often to be followed by further study.

There are a few single honours degree courses in cartography. It can be studied as part of a degree in Topographic Science (the collection, analysis and presentation of geographical information), or in combination with subjects such as geography, maths, computer science or surveying. There are a growing number of degrees and

Higher National Diplomas in Geographical Information Systems (GIS).

Cartographic draughtsmen/women can take one of the handful of BTEC/SQA National Diploma courses in cartography, surveying and topographical studies.

Personal attributes Patience; diligence; great accuracy; good colour vision; powers of observation; willingness to experiment; sense of design useful.

Late start Very few opportunities.

Work life balance In principle, a career break should be no problem for qualified cartographers who have kept up to date, but likely to prove difficult when jobs are decreasing.

Part-time work is possible, but again affected by job situation.

Further information Mr R. W. Anson, British Cartographic Society, Department of Planning, Oxford Brookes University, Headington, Oxford OX3 0BP.
www.cartography.org.uk

Related careers ARCHITECTURE: *Architectural Technologist* – ART AND DESIGN – SURVEYING

Chartered Secretary and Administrator

Entry qualifications None laid down for entry to Foundation Programme of Institute of Chartered Secretaries and Administrators, but must be 17 or over. Exemptions for graduates and BTEC Higher award holders (see 'Training', below).

The work This has nothing to do with personal secretarial work (see SECRETARIAL AND CLERICAL WORK, p. 550). Instead, it is general administration and management in public, private and voluntary sectors.

The main element in professional administration, wherever it is carried out, is coordinating (and possibly also controlling) various individuals and/or departments within an organization. Administrators are generalists who coordinate the activities of specialists. They form a link between people and their separate activities; they make sure that different sections or departments dovetail, and fit into the whole. Increased use of information technology in all organizations means they need a good grasp of information systems – how they work and what they can do. At senior level, administrators have an 'overview' over whatever their organization does; at junior level, they may, for example, coordinate the work of the accounts department; at middle level they ensure that, for example, production, distribution and personnel departments are informed of each other's needs. Professional administrators often work for a time in the various departments, to find out how each works and where it fits into the whole. Like other professional qualifications, professional administration can lead to the top in whatever the type of organization. The work is immensely varied, and so are the top jobs. Senior administrators may be involved in the choice and design of complicated computer systems aimed at improved decision-taking by top managers.

Qualified chartered secretaries can become company secretaries: public companies are by law required to have company secretaries, i.e. people who have either a legal, an accountancy or the ICSA qualification. According to type and size of company, company secretaries can be chief executives – possibly called director, or secretary-general – responsible only to the Board or whoever are the policy-makers; or they can be the chief administrative officer responsible to the director or chief executive.

As it is an adaptable qualification, chartered secretaries have a wide choice of jobs. They can also set up in public practice, offering clients a range of services.

Training The Institute's examinations consist of 3 programmes; Foundation, Pre-professional and Professional, all made up of modules. The first two programmes give a broad business education, covering law, accounting, information systems, organizations and personnel. The Professional Programme is a post-graduate level qualification and focuses on managing the affairs and protecting the integrity of the organizations.

Study can be full time or part time, by flexistudy (distance learning with tutorials) or distance learning. Typically, students take 4 modules a year. Graduates in any discipline are exempt from the first 2 programmes, and are expected to qualify in 18 months. All students are expected to complete the examinations within 5 years. Holders of BTEC/SQA Higher National awards start with the Pre-professional Programme.

People with other professional qualifications may also be given exemptions.

Personal attributes A flair for administration; common sense and good judgement; numeracy; interest in current affairs; tact; discretion.

Late start Good opportunities, especially now that access to ICSA examinations is 'open'.

Work life balance A career break should be no problem for people who had responsible jobs before the break. Because of the flexible examination structure it is possible for people to study while on a break.

There are fair possibilities for part-time work, particularly in small firms.

Further information The Institute of Chartered Secretaries and Administrators, 16 Park Crescent, London W1B 1AH. *www.icsa.org.uk*

Related careers ACCOUNTANCY – HEALTH SERVICES MANAGE-MENT – LAW

Chiropody
(Podology, Podiatry, Podiatric Medicine)

The profession is in the process of changing its title from chiropodist to podiatrist, and the professional body is now known as the Society of Chiropodists and Podiatrists.

Entry qualifications A BSc (Hons) in Podiatry.

The work Podiatrists diagnose and treat foot diseases and functional and constitutional foot disorders; they inspect children's and adults' feet to prevent minor ailments from growing into major ones. When patients need their shoes adapted, podiatrists give the necessary instructions to surgical shoemakers or shoe-repairers; they also construct special appliances themselves. They are unusual among the professions supplementary to medicine in that they diagnose and treat conditions without medical referral. Most can undertake invasive skin/nail surgery under local anaesthetic, and a growing number are qualified to perform minor bone surgery. Podiatrists can choose the environment in which to work:

1. *Private practice*: This is the most remunerative work and scope is growing. Podiatrists may practise in surgeries in their own homes and, occasionally, visit patients in their homes. Private practice can be lonely work (even though patients are seen all day) but many work in group practices, partners renting premises jointly or using rooms in one of the partners' homes as a surgery.

2. *Hospitals and community health clinics*: Podiatrists employed by the NHS work in a variety of settings from orthotics laboratories to patients' own homes.

3. *Industry*: Firms where staff are on their feet all day often employ full-time or part-time podiatrists.

In both (2) and (3) podiatrists enjoy the companionship and social facilities of a large organization. Some combine part-time work with private practice.

Some retail chains such as Boots the Chemist now employ State Registered podiatrists in high street branches. There are also increasing opportunities in sports clubs and leisure centres.

Training Only graduates with a degree in podiatry from one of 13 schools of podiatry are eligible for State Registration, which is essential for all public jobs, and for membership of the Society of Chiropodists and Podiatrists. The courses are modular and much of the content is practical and includes treatment of patients under supervision. Theory includes the basic medical sciences, anatomy, physiology, medicine and surgery, and local anaesthesia.

Courses which do not lead to degrees do not lead to State Registration and Membership of the Society of Chiropodists and Podiatrists. All recognized courses last at least 3 years, full time.

Personal attributes A high degree of manual dexterity; ability to get on with people greatly enhances chances of promotion and of having a flourishing private practice. However, unlike many other careers with patients, shy, retiring people may get on well, providing they are even-tempered.

Late start Good opportunities, with some relaxations in entry requirements.

Work life balance A career break should not be a problem if up to date with developments. *Ad hoc* arrangements for *refresher* courses can usually be made.

There is ample scope for part-time work (although not for promotion), but no part-time training. Job-sharing possible.

Chiropody (Podology, Podiatry, Podiatric Medicine)

Further information The Society of Chiropodists and Podiatrists, 1 Fellmongers Path, Tower Bridge Road, London SE1 3LY. *www.feetforlife.org*

Related careers NURSING – PHYSIOTHERAPY

Chiropractic

Entry qualifications Usually 3 good A levels including biology and chemistry, or equivalent. Mature students with suitable alternative qualifications are considered. Foundation years are available for those without the standard qualifications.

The work Chiropractors diagnose, treat and prevent mechanical disorders of the musculoskeletal system and the effects of these disorders on the function of the nervous system and general health. In practice this usually involves using their hands to 'adjust' or 'manipulate' the spine and joints where signs of restriction in movement are found and can also involve working on muscles. Patients consult them for a wide range of disorders, arising from accidents, stress, lack of exercise, poor posture or illness. Chiropractors may use X-rays for diagnosis but largely rely on their own diagnostic skills. They do not use drugs or surgery and they support their treatment with advice about their patients' work, diet and exercise.

Chiropractors trained in the McTimoney method of chiropractic may choose to specialize in treating animals, which must be referred to them by a vet.

Chiropractic is one of only two complementary medicines to have statutory recognition and regulation. It is illegal to practise unless registered with the General Chiropractic Council.

Chiropractors work in private practice, either on their own or within a group practice. Many NHS GPs endorse chiropractic and will refer patients for treatment which may be funded through the NHS. However, most patients consult chiropractors privately.

Training 3 institutions currently offer courses leading to qualifications recognized by the General Chiropractic Council: the Anglo-European College of Chiropractic, the University of Glamorgan and the McTimoney College of Chiropractic.

The Anglo-European College offers a 4-year honours Master of Chiropractic (MChiro) degree with an additional foundation year for those who do not meet the standard entry requirements. In the final year of the course, students treat patients at the college clinic under supervision.

The Welsh Institute of Chiropractic at the University of Glamorgan offers a 4-year BSc (Hons) Chiropractic. Again a foundation year is offered for those without the standard entry requirements.

The McTimoney College offers a 5-year full-time mixed-mode course, which combines home study with college contact time at weekends. Students can follow the course while employed but this is a demanding option. An access course is available for those who do not meet the normal entry requirements.

Following graduation most chiropractors spend a year in employed but supervised practice under the Post-registration Training Scheme and it is expected that this will soon become a requirement for registration to practise in the UK.

Chiropractors are also encouraged to participate in continuing professional development (CPD) throughout their careers. The regulating body, the General Chiropractic Council, will shortly implement mandatory CPD as a requirement for annual reregistration.

Personal attributes Dexterity; interest in the working of the body; empathy; interest in wellness and health promotion; communication skills; ability to work alone; business acumen.

Late start About 40% of entrants to the Anglo-European College and 93% of entrants to the McTimoney College are mature students. An access course or Open University science foundation course may be suggested as good preparation for those without the necessary academic background.

Work life balance Chiropractors are self-employed so once established can choose their own hours. It is currently possible to be restored to the register after a career break without further qualification. However, the GCC is in the process of consulting with the profession on continuing professional development which may be a mandatory requirement for reregistration in the future.

Further information General Chiropractic Council, 44 Wicklow Street, London WC1X 9HL.
www.gcc-uk.org
British Chiropractic Association, Blagrave House, 17 Blagrave Street, Reading RG1 1QB.
www.chiropractic-uk.co.uk
McTimoney Chiropractic Association, 3 Oxford Court, St James Road, Brackley, Northamptonshire NN13 7XY.
www.mctimoney-chiropractic.org

Related careers MEDICINE – OCCUPATIONAL THERAPY – OSTEO-PATHY – PHYSIOTHERAPY

Civil Aviation

Air Traffic Control Officer

Entry qualifications 2 subjects at A level and 5 GCSEs (A–C). Must include English language and maths at either level. Graduates or people with other qualifications welcomed. High standard of physical fitness, eyesight and hearing required.

The work Teams of ATCOs control and monitor the movements of aircraft taking off, landing and when *en route* in designated controlled airspace. An aircraft leaving a controller's area of responsibility is coordinated with the next ATC unit, which may be an airfield or an air traffic control centre in the UK or in Europe. Pilots of aircraft are, in fact, in 2-way radio communication with controllers from the time they request permission to start engines until the engines stop at their destination.

The work is responsible and highly skilled: it may involve the safe 'stacking' of aircraft in an airfield's 'holding area' while awaiting approach; the 'sequencing' of aircraft using radar to maintain a safe distance between them, and ensuring that aircraft flying the same routes at varying speeds, heights and directions are always safely separated horizontally and vertically. ATCOs use computers in their calculations. After gaining operational experience, a small proportion of ATCOs specialize in ATC computer work.

ATCOs spend most of their time – normally wearing headphones – monitoring data about relevant aircraft, either looking at a radar display unit or out over an airfield. The international language of ATC is English, so UK ATCOs talk and are talked to in their own language. Foreign pilots sometimes have problems expressing themselves clearly, especially when under pressure. Although ATCOs must make quick decisions, they can ask pilots to repeat anything which is not quite clear.

The great majority of operational ATCOs work shift duties, and all ATCOs must be prepared to do so; as far as possible shifts are planned well in advance, but last-minute changes are sometimes necessary.

Training Trainee ATCOs follow an initial 74-week course at the College of Air Traffic Control near Bournemouth, followed by practical training at operational units. Training is given in all aspects of ATC, and in basic meteorology, navigation, telecommunications and principles of radar and associated techniques; an 'introduction to flying' course is also given in which trainees normally reach 'solo' standard.

Personal attributes Good eyesight (including normal colour vision); medically fit; a calm cool temperament; ability to conceal and control excitement in emergencies; ability to concentrate both in busy and in quiet periods; a good quick brain, with quick reactions and the ability to be decisive; the ability to work as part of a team.

Late start Normal maximum age 29 unless with substantial relevant experience. Suitable applicants may be offered deferred entry so that they can complete a professional training or a degree course before joining the service.

Work life balance Career-breaks are available.

There is no initial part-time work but some flexible working can be considered during career to suit personal needs.

Further information National Air Traffic Services Ltd (NATS), 1 Kemble Street, London WC2B 4AP.
www.nats.co.uk

NOTE: Air Traffic Control Assistants (ATCAs) assist ATCOs in their tasks by undertaking certain routine functions, particularly with data preparation and display, at both airfields and airways control centres.

Cabin Crew (Stewardess and Steward)

Entry qualifications Minimum and upper age limits for trainees and minimum height requirements vary between airlines. No set educational qualifications, but good GCSE standard, preferably including English and maths, and conversational ability in a foreign language. Some catering or nursing experience, or minimum 1 year in a responsible job which involved dealing with people, e.g. in a travel agency.

The work The cabin crew welcome passengers, supervise seating and safety-belt arrangements, and look after air-sick travellers, babies, and children travelling alone. Stewards and stewardesses serve meals, and sell drinks, cigarettes, etc. in a variety of currencies.

They 'dress the plane' to see that blankets, head-rests, magazines, cosmetics, etc., are available and in good order, and make necessary announcements over the public-address system. They deal with any emergencies and write reports after each flight, with comments, for instance, on the behaviour of unaccompanied children.

Most of the time cabin crews are airborne waiters and waitresses. From the moment the plane is airborne they are continuously busy, working at great speed in a confined space.

Duty hours vary from one airline to another and are likely to be changed at the last minute because of weather and other 'exigencies of the service'. Normally on European routes cabin crews are 'on' for 4–6 days with a good deal of night duty; they are then off-duty for 2–4 days. On long-distance trips they may be away from home for 3 weeks, but that would include several days' rest at a foreign airport.

The farther the destination, the more chance of sightseeing. On short routes cabin crews may fly backwards and forwards for a month without seeing more than the airport at their destination. On long-distance trips crews often change planes at 'slip-points' and stay for a few days' rest, living in luxury hotels at their airline's expense.

British-trained crews are in demand by American and other foreign airlines if they speak the appropriate language.

Training About 4–6 weeks at airline training school. Subjects include meal-service, first aid, documentation, airborne procedure, foreign currency exchange, security procedures, emergency drill with swimming-pool lesson in the use of the inflatable dinghy and life-jacket, practical fire drills, customer service, grooming and deportment.

Personal attributes A likeable personality; calmness in crises; common sense; efficiency; sensitivity to anxious passengers' needs; well-groomed appearance.

Further information Individual airlines.

GROUND STAFF
(some examples)

Passenger Service Assistant/Agent
(titles vary)

Entry qualifications Usually good GCSE-standard English, maths, and previous customer service experience. Minimum age usually 18.

The work Passenger service assistants see that passengers and luggage get on to the right plane, with the minimum of fuss. They check-in luggage, which involves checking travel documents, and check-out passengers at boarding gates. They answer passengers' questions on travel connections and similar matters.

Other duties carried out by experienced PSAs include: load-control – preparing information for aircraft loaders on luggage weight; cargo documentation for customs clearance; checking that planes leave with the right meals, cargo, baggage.

PSAs work in uniform, and do shift work. They move about the airport all day, rarely sit down.

Training Several weeks' induction and on-the-job training.

Sales Staff
(titles vary)

Entry qualifications Usually good GCSE-standard English, maths, geography, a foreign language.

The work Sales staff sit in airport and city offices and answer questions on international flight connections; make fare calculations (in various currencies); sell tickets over the counter and over the phone. Bookings are made to and from all over the world; each reservation must be related to reservations made elsewhere and reservation vacancies available for any particular flight at any given moment. This is called 'space control'. Reservations staff use computerized information systems: they can see on their computer terminal exactly what the present reservation situation is on any flight of their airline.

Senior sales staff may call on travel agents, business houses and other important customers to explain ancillary services such as car hire, hotel accommodation, package holidays, and 'sell' their own particular airline, both passenger and cargo services.

Sales staff may do shift work, though less so in senior positions.

Training Short on-the-job training with some lectures.

Personal attributes For all 'public contact' jobs: an orderly mind; communication skills; a liking for meeting many people very briefly; a calm, helpful manner; good speech and appearance.

Commercial Management, Flight Operations and Flight Planning

Entry qualifications Vary with different airlines and according to supply and demand. Some promotion from sales staff; most entrants have A levels; many have degrees or BTEC/SQA/HND in Business Studies (see pp. 8, 10).

The work The administration of flight programmes, which cover many thousands of flight-miles, millions of tons of freight and ever-growing 'passenger throughput', is a highly complex undertaking. Staff organize the airline's fleet of planes over its network, making the most efficient use of each aircraft, e.g. ensuring that as far as possible outgoing freight is replaced with return-flight freight, and that the 'turn-round' time in airports is as short as possible, while allowing time for maintenance, loading, etc. 'Aircrew management' involves arranging individual crew members' schedules, taking into consideration maximum flying hours allowed; rest-days ('stop overs') abroad, etc.

Apart from this planning work, staff are also responsible for ensuring that at all times aircrew have all the information they need before each take-off, throughout the planned itinerary. This involves discussions with a variety of departments and individuals; keeping detailed records; being prepared for emergencies.

Training Through airlines' own training schemes, lasting 2 to 3 years, or BTEC/SQA Higher awards or degree, followed by shorter airline training. Schemes vary between companies and according to expansion or contraction of airline industry.

Personal attributes Drive; organizing ability; liking for working under pressure.

Late start May be possible for cabin crew, passenger service assistants and sales staff (see 'Entry qualifications', above).

Work life balance A career break may be possible, but depends on vacancy situation. Also, returners have to start again with basic training.

Part time opportunities in some jobs, for example cabin crew, passenger services, but this affects promotion. Also some short-term contracts with 'package tour' companies for cabin crews.

Further information Individual airlines.

Related careers HOTEL AND CATERING — LANGUAGES — TRAVEL AGENT/TOUR OPERATOR

Civil Pilot

Entry qualifications None are laid down by the Civil Aviation Authority for the Commercial Pilot's Licence, but 5 GCSEs (A–C), including English, maths and a science, are assumed. Airlines sponsoring pilot training courses require applicants to have at least 5 GCSE passes at grade C or higher (including English language and mathematics) and 2 A level passes, preferably in maths and physics.

The work The pilot has to fly the aircraft safely at all times, in accordance with the company's operating procedures, complying with instructions from Air Traffic Control. The pilot is required to have a very good knowledge of the aircraft and to be able to deal with any emergency situation arising while in flight or on the ground. In a multi-crew aeroplane, one of the pilots is Captain of the crew of the aircraft.

In an airline, the first job is as First Officer. Promotion to Captain, which is not automatic, may come 3–15 years later. (Earlier in small airlines and later in the largest airlines.) The Captain has total responsibility for the aircraft, crew and passengers. He/she usually has a co-pilot and there may be up to 4 pilots on long haul flights.

The Captain begins to plan the flight at least an hour before start-up time. After meeting the other flightcrew members in the Operations Department, and checking on the serviceability of the aircraft and its systems for the flight, the pilot studies the procedures to be used for the take-off and climb, *en route*, and descent and landing, together with the availability of diversion aerodromes along the route and any Notices To Airman (NOTAMs) affecting the route. After study of the meteorological forecast, the pilot works out the amount of fuel to be carried, taking account of the weights of the passengers and cargo. The pilot then calculates the take-off and landing weights (vital data in case of emergency action) and the optimum cruising heights for the route. Finally, at the aircraft, having carried out external and internal checks, the pilot signs a Technical Log accepting the aircraft as being fit for the flight. In modern aircraft, a great deal of this planning work is computerized and the pilot can load the route data into a Flight Management System computer within the aircraft.

On most aircraft, apart from on take-off and landing, the flight is flown using the autopilot, and one of the pilot's tasks is to set its controls and then monitor it to see that it flies the required route. On 'short hauls' (within Europe) the pilot and crew are busy all the time. On long hauls there can be long hours flying at cruising height over the ocean, with only routine monitoring checks to go through. This can be difficult in an unexpected way: pilots get bored, especially at night, yet the need for alertness is as great as ever.

UK pilots are increasingly working for companies within Europe. There is some small demand for pilots (aeroplane or helicopter): on air taxis; crop spraying; aerial photography; oil rig support operations; weather and traffic observation; flying privately or flying company aircraft, and especially for instructors in flying clubs.

Fixed Wing – i.e. Aeroplanes

Training The majority of UK students at approved Flying Training organizations are sponsored by airlines. While the major sponsor of UK pilots is British Airways, larger airlines such as Britannia Airways and EasyJet also occasionally offer sponsorship.

Basic training lasts about 15 months on full-time courses. The syllabus includes Air law, Aircraft general knowledge, Flight performance and planning, Human performance and limitations, Meteorology, Navigation, Operational procedures, Principles of flight,

Communication and multi-crew cooperation training. Flight training is carried out both in aircraft and in simulators.

The first qualification is the Commercial Pilot's Licence (CPL), but to fly in an airliner as co-pilot the basic requirement is the CPL plus Instrument Rating (IR), and the pilot must also have passed the Airline Transport Pilot's Licence Aeroplanes (ATPL) ground examinations. Ratings are qualifications in particular aspects of flying and in flying particular types of aircraft. The type of aircraft a pilot may fly depends on the aircraft ratings included in the licence. To become qualified as Captain of a large airliner a pilot must have the ATPL, and several thousands of flying hours.

Trainee pilots can qualify by attending a full-time, integrated course in flying and ground training. This course costs from £55,000 and this route is usually only followed by sponsored students. An alternative route is to first gain a Private Pilot's Licence (PPL) and then 150 hours flying experience before undertaking modular courses for the ground examinations, for the CPL and then the IR. This route still costs about £55,000 but the courses may be taken when funds permit.

Rotary Wing (i.e. Helicopters)

Demand for commercial helicopter pilots fluctuates but due to a decrease in the number of military-trained pilots leaving the forces, prospects for commercially qualified helicopter pilots are improving. A full-time integrated course leading to a commercial pilot's licence lasts around 9 months and costs about £45,000. A flexible modular course is also available which can be completed on a part-time basis. Commercial operators run occasional sponsorship schemes.

Personal attributes At least average intelligence; commitment; dedication; enthusiasm for aviation; mental agility; high standard of fitness; justifiable self-confidence; leadership qualities; ability to take decisions; well-balanced personality; ability to get on with others.

Late start 30% of newly qualified pilots are late entrants (see 'Training' above), but there are upper age limits to airline sponsorship schemes, typically 27 on entry.

Work life balance A career break should be possible as all pilots need retraining throughout their career. Work is often irregular.

Position of women Only about 3% of professional pilots are women. Once trained they have no greater difficulty getting work than men. The airline sponsorship schemes are open to women as well as men. British Airways and other major UK airlines employ women pilots and some are now Captains.

There are only about 20 women professional helicopter pilots. As the armed services have not been training them until relatively recently, their only avenue has been through sponsorship or by paying for the training themselves.

The British Women Pilots Association has over 300 members and helps with advice and (small) scholarships.

Further information British Helicopter Advisory Board, Graham Suite, West Entrance, Fairoaks Airport, Chobham, Woking, Surrey GU24 8HX.
www.bhab.demon.co.uk
British Women Pilots Association, Brooklands Museum, Brooklands Road, Weybridge, Surrey KT13 0QN.
www.bwpa.demon.co.uk
British Airline Pilots Association, 81 New Road, Harlington, Hayes, Middlesex UB3 5BG.
www.balpa.org.uk

Related careers *Air Traffic Control Officer* (*see above*) – ENGINEERING – SURVEYING

Civil Service

The Civil Service exists to administer the business of the government. This covers a vast range of activity from defence procurement to the issue of driving licences, and the Civil Service is one of the largest employers in the country with more than half a million staff.

Opportunities exist at all educational levels. There is a strong tradition of and commitment to training to enable staff to function effectively and progress up a well-defined career structure. Training may be work-based, or on courses as appropriate, and may cover anything from time management to human resources development to understanding EU Enlargement.

Over the last few years the Civil Service has been undergoing major changes with far-reaching developments still taking place. The aim is to make the Civil Service more efficient, businesslike and responsive.

Although by definition the Civil Service is an administrative organization and its careers in administration are well recognized, within its vast and varied structure it offers opportunities in virtually every career area. Approaching half of its staff are specialists, some of whom were recruited after their specialist training, while others were given the opportunity to acquire specialist qualifications after joining the Civil Service. There are also increasing opportunities for mature entrants and job changers, at all levels.

The work of government departments – and their staff at all levels – is immensely varied. It affects virtually every aspect of modern life – health, education, the environment, transport, agriculture, defence, foreign affairs, social security, energy policy, taxation and so on. These broad headings cover a vast and complex range of activities and concerns of which it is possible here to give only a few examples.

The Department for Environment, Food and Rural Affairs offers opportunities for senior staff to participate in meetings in Brussels on the development, negotiation and implementation of EU agricultural policy, but it is also responsible for the management of sea fisheries and consumer protection. The Ministry of Defence is one of the largest consumers of the products of British industry with vast annual expenditure to manage. In the Home Office staff might be concerned with the administration of prison management and reform or with how the Data Protection Act is working. The Scottish Executive and the National Assembly for Wales, with their regional responsibilities, embrace a range of activities handled by different departments elsewhere, e.g. education, agriculture and fisheries, transport, health.

Across all departments and levels there is a broad spectrum of functions, both strategic and operational. Some civil servants advise ministers; others deal direct with members of the public; some research the implications of policy options; others provide support services in, for example, computer operations, personnel, finance or general support work.

Civil servants face similar pressures to those in industry, and the work is no less stimulating. Efforts continue to make the Civil Service more 'businesslike' with all the demands and satisfactions for its staff which that implies. Management is increasingly decentralized, allowing more flexibility in decision-making and managing budgets and staff.

Many civil servants now work in 'executive agencies' which operate like businesses under a Chief Executive who is set financial and quality of service targets and given the financial and management freedom to pursue them. The idea is to make managers more accountable and visible and for the new ethos to filter down through the staff, with financial rewards for outstanding performance.

Recruitment to most Civil Service jobs at all levels is by individual government departments through national or local newspaper ads, or departmental websites. A large number of mature applicants are recruited in this way from private industry and commerce as well as junior staff. Recruitment is at 3 main levels: senior manager, junior manager and administrative assistants.

Senior managers are largely recruited through Fast Stream, the Civil Service's accelerated training and development programme for entrants with the potential to reach the top grades. This is a highly competitive centralized recruitment competition held twice annually (for some options only once) and although the basic qualification asked for is a 2.2, candidates need to be in the top 10% of students in terms of intellect, interpersonal skills and personal qualities. Candidates can apply for the General Fast Stream which has five options: Central Departments covering all the major departments except the Diplomatic Service; Science and Engineering; the European Fast Stream; the Diplomatic Service; and Clerkships in Parliament. There are also Fast Streams for statisticians, economists, for the Government Communications HQ (GCHQ) and the Secret Intelligence Service (SIS).

People already working in the Civil Service can also apply to the Fast Stream, though there is usually a two-year service requirement.

Fast Stream

Entry qualifications A 2.2 degree in any subject but this minimum requirement does not reflect the intensive competition for places. Generally applicants need to be British nationals. Candidates for the European Fast Stream are required to have an A level or equivalent in one of the 19 other official languages of the EU or to have independent evidence of competence.

Method of entry and training The initial application process for the Fast Stream is now online. Fast Stream candidates are required to take an online self-assessment test before applying and feedback is given to help candidates decide whether the Fast Stream is for them. Practice Qualifying Tests are also available online.

The Stage 1 Qualifying Test is an online questionnaire, lasting about an hour, taken through any Internet access. Successful candidates are then invited to a regional centre to take a computer administered Stage 2 Qualifying Test made up of 3 aptitude tests, taking in all about 3½ hours. (Further changes are planned by 2005 and for the latest information about applying see *www.faststream.gov.uk*).

Candidates reaching Stage 3 attend the Civil Service Selection Board in London and undertake a series of written and group exercises and interviews. There is a further stage for applicants to the Diplomatic Service, Diplomatic Service Economists and Clerkships in Parliament.

Candidates who narrowly miss selection may be recommended for other Civil Service posts.

Fast Stream entrants begin with a series of intensive placements or 'postings' which last from 1 year to 18 months. They are given real responsibility from the start and may be seconded to business or industry, or to work abroad, and can expect to be senior managers within 5 years. European Fast Streamers are guaranteed a placement in Europe and language tuition and while they can remain based in the UK Civil Service, encouragement is given to those wishing to enter recruitment competitions for permanent posts in the EU Civil Service.

The work Senior civil servants are responsible, under ministers, for formulating and implementing the policy of the government of the day. As indicated above, the subject matter of the work varies considerably, but the work of civil servants at this level falls into several broad categories. It includes researching and analysing policy options; developing the organization and procedures necessary to translate policy objectives into practice; dealing with parliamentary business, including briefing ministers and drafting replies to parliamentary questions; drafting legislation; dealing with operational matters affecting the day-to-day responsibilities of a department; working in a minister's Private Office. There is scope for liaison and negotiation at a senior level within and between departments, with outside organizations, and with foreign governments. The balance of tasks varies between different postings.

As mentioned above, the Civil Service is moving towards greater accountability and responsibility for individual managers. Ultimately, however, ministers make final decisions. These decisions (including the nuts and bolts of legislation) are made on the advice and recommendations of their civil servants, so there is a real opportunity to contribute to matters of national and international importance from an early stage of a Fast Stream career. There is also considerable intellectual challenge in mastering complex issues and giving impartial advice, whatever one's own politics or those of the government of the day.

Personal attributes High intelligence; capacity to grasp all issues involved in a problem, to weigh up facts, conflicting opinions and advice and to make a decision; ability to extract the main points from a mass of detail and to write balanced and concise reports; ability to hold and delegate authority; enjoyment of responsibility; the ability to manage both people and resources; the ability to communicate and work well with other people at all levels – junior staff, colleagues, outside organizations and ministers.

Junior Managers

Entry qualifications Requirements vary according to department and role but as a guide at least 2 A levels or equivalent. Many applicants have degrees. There may be a nationality requirement.

Method of training and entry Entry is by competitive tests and interview. Recruitment is organized individually by departments or agencies.

Training is largely in house, with regular opportunities to review progress. All junior staff are encouraged to develop a personal training programme to meet their own career plans. There are opportunities for more specialized training leading to external qualifications as appropriate and many departments organize their own management development programmes.

The work Junior managers, also called executive officers, are the first line of management in the Civil Service. Their role is more operational than strategic and is generally concerned with applying policy. The subject matter obviously varies a great deal from one department or agency to another, but they may be involved in several broad types of work. Junior managers *manage staff and resources*, allocating, monitoring and controlling the team's work, motivating them and helping them to develop their potential. Many *handle casework*, making decisions on the basis of often complex law, regulations and precedent. A major part of the work of many junior managers involves *dealing with the public*, as customs officers, or within Jobcentres, for example. *General administrative duties* are an essential part of the work and essential to the smooth running of a department or agency; they may include finance, personnel, estate management, purchasing and support for senior colleagues, including arranging meetings and writing reports.

Some junior managers have more specialized responsibilities and are recruited and trained accordingly. Examples are the Immigration Service, Inland Revenue, Customs and Excise and the Diplomatic Service (see p. 164). There are also opportunities to train in accountancy (see p. 169) or information technology (see p. 169).

Promotion is linked to regular formal appraisals and junior managers can move to senior posts. They may also apply to join the Fast Stream.

Personal attributes Practical intelligence; organizing ability; enjoyment of a measure of responsibility; a liking for paper work and for dealing with people; ability to manage staff.

Administrative Assistant

Entry qualifications Requirements vary but in practice 4–5 GCSEs or equivalent.

The work Administrative assistants are employed by all government departments to do routine clerical work: filing, sorting, keeping records. They may also deal with inquiries from the public, and may operate computer systems or electronic mail equipment. They are encouraged to take appropriate day-release classes and examinations. There are good prospects for promotion. Modern Apprenticeships may be available for young entrants.

THE DIPLOMATIC SERVICE

Entry qualifications 1. For Diplomatic Fast Stream, see Fast Stream p. 160. Candidates have to pass a medical (special provision is made for people with disabilities) and security vetting. No particular language skills required but a definite advantage.

2. See Junior Manager p. 162.

3. See Administrative Assistant p. 163.

4. There are also occasional openings for research officers, economists, legal advisers, architects, surveyors, engineers and other specialist staff.

The work Staff spend about a third to a half of their career working at the Foreign and Commonwealth Office in London. For the remainder of their time they are serving overseas in any of the more than 160 countries with which the UK maintains diplomatic relations or with UN or NATO postings. During a working lifetime anything from 6 to 10 'tours' of 2–4 years each are spent working at British embassies, high commissions and other missions in a variety of countries. The willingness to serve anywhere in the world is, therefore, vital.

Work is very varied. In the course of their careers staff may work on trade promotion, political reporting and analysis (especially in the Fast Stream), consular services to British nationals living or travelling overseas, immigration work, aid administration, personnel and financial management or combating international crime or terrorism.

Promotion is generally on the basis of performance on the job and there is a continuous process of appraisal.

Training The Diplomatic Service attaches great importance to proper training. New entrants at all levels usually undertake a short induction course which acquaints them with the organization and working of the service and its place in the machinery of government. Specialized job-related courses are arranged for staff who are going to take up jobs in, for example, commercial or consular work, and there are also courses designed to develop individual skills and potential, for example in management, effective speaking or international economics. The Diplomatic Service, not surprisingly, attaches great importance to language training. For some jobs full-time language training for up to 2 years is provided; all staff, even when it is not essential for their jobs, are encouraged to learn something of the local language and are entitled to at least 100 hours of free tuition. Language allowances are paid to staff who reach a certain level of proficiency. Diplomats can master several languages during their careers.

Personal attributes Members of the Diplomatic Service must combine the skills of salespeople, political analysts and public relations officers. They must have a calm and reliable personality; a persuasive, confidence-inspiring manner; the ability to make friends easily and put down roots instantly; and the adaptability and resourcefulness to cope with the constant upheaval of moving from one place to another. The Diplomatic Service is not so much a job as a way of life. It demands balance, staying power, curiosity about the way other nations live and the confidence to put forward the British point of view.

SPECIALISTS AND PROFESSIONALS IN THE CIVIL SERVICE

The Civil Service employs a wide range and substantial number of specialists and professionals. There are opportunities for those with considerable previous experience outside the Civil Service; the newly qualified; and those seeking opportunities to obtain professional qualifications.

The basic entry and training structures of these careers and their different functions and applications are discussed in detail in other sections of this book. This section looks at their roles within the Civil Service. Most departments and agencies do their own recruitment and although there is specialist central graduate recruitment, scientists, engineers and statisticians are also recruited through the Fast Stream.

Non Fast Stream entrants usually require a good degree in the appropriate subject. Information on specialist recruitment can be found on *www.careers.civil-service.gov.uk*.

Scientists
(see SCIENCE, p. 520)

Scientists in the Civil Service may be involved in research and development; providing scientific services; statutory advisory and inspection duties; scientific contributions to the formulation of government policies. Within these broad areas of work is a vast range of activity and interest covering aspects of life as diverse as the food we eat, the air we breathe and the weapons that defend us.

For example, scientists in the Department for Environment, Food and Rural Affairs study problems caused by animals, from the causes of BSE to bird collisions with aircraft. Others are concerned with food additives and the evaluation of new food products and processes, including high profile issues such as the trialling of GM crops. Dstl (the Defence Science and Technology Laboratory) is one of the largest employers of scientists and engineers and recruits graduates from a range of disciplines. The Home Office maintains the Forensic Science Service, which provides the scientific backing to the search for criminal evidence, using sophisticated techniques to analyse a wide range of materials such as blood, fibres, glass, paint and soil.

There are opportunities in most scientific disciplines, both major areas like chemistry, physics and computer science, and smaller, more specialized fields like animal nutrition, meteorology and plant pathology.

Engineers
(see ENGINEERING, p. 216)

There are opportunities for every type of engineer in the Civil Service. The Ministry of Defence has the greatest requirement, and for example needs engineers to design test software for combat simulators and develop improved helicopter rotor blades. At the Department of

Transport, Local Government and the Regions, while civil engineers might design new roads and bridges and manage huge projects, electrical engineers develop computer-based traffic control systems. DTLGR engineers work in multi-disciplinary teams seeking an integrated approach to pollution control over a range of industries.

Surveyors
(see SURVEYING, p. 590)

There are a variety of opportunities for surveyors in the Civil Service. The Valuation Office Agency provides valuation services to the Inland Revenue and other government departments throughout the UK. Surveyors in the Defence Estates Agency are responsible for all the property owned by the Ministry of Defence, one of the largest landowners in the UK; there are also overseas projects to be managed. Defra offers advice, often as a chargeable service, to farmers, growers and landowners on all aspects of land and estate management. Smaller numbers of openings are available in other departments including the Department of Health, the Department for Education and Skills, Ordnance Survey and national museums. All types of surveyor are needed, but different departments have different requirements.

Economists
(see ECONOMICS, p. 213)

Economists work in about 30 government departments, analysing the economic implications of virtually every aspect of government policy. A key part of this work is the interpretation of economic and other statistics. In some departments, for example the Treasury, economists specialize; in others they apply economic principles to a variety of different situations.

Statisticians
(see SCIENCE, p. 520)

Across the range of government activity statisticians collect, analyse and interpret data on a variety of subjects and for a variety of purposes. Statistics on subjects as diverse as transport, health, education, trade and household expenditure are used both to shape and reflect policy and to inform industry, the academic world and the general public on aspects of modern life.

Press and Publicity
(see PUBLIC RELATIONS, p. 496)

The Civil Service is one of the largest employers of press and public relations specialists. Overall their job is to explain government policies and measures to the public. This might involve advising a minister on dealing with the news media; planning a publicity and information campaign on, for example, drink-driving; organizing an exhibition to promote British trade overseas; working on a range of publications dealing with subjects as diverse as recruitment, overseas aid or detailed statistics on social trends. The Central Office of Information offers the greatest number of opportunities, but there are openings in most departments both for new graduates and for experienced professionals.

Lawyers
(see LAW, p. 323)

Lawyers in government service have a great number of roles, many of which mirror work done in private practice and industry, some of which are unique to government. Lawyers have a key role in drafting legislation and assisting ministers in steering it through Parliament. They are also advisers on the formulation and implementation of policy. Many are involved in prosecution and litigation over, for example, serious VAT fraud. Lawyers working on the administration of justice might be advising on the discipline, conduct and welfare of the judiciary or settling cases before the European Court. There are also opportunities to advise on a range of matters concerning the Civil Service as a large organization – employment legislation, employee accidents at work, conveyancing and pay agreements. There are opportunities for both qualified lawyers and for graduates who wish to qualify through government service.

Accountants
(see ACCOUNTANCY, p. 41)

Accountants in the Civil Service are at the forefront of many developments designed to promote accountability and introduce financial management disciplines. They are also involved with government's dealings with industry and commerce and with tax matters. There are openings for those with a professional accountancy qualification and opportunities for some administration trainees and junior managers to train and qualify as accountants.

Research Officers

Research officers study the impact of government policies and provide information on which policy is based. Most opportunities are with the Ministry of Defence, DTLGR and Department of Social Security.

Information Systems and Technology
(see INFORMATION TECHNOLOGY (IT)/INFORMATION SYSTEMS, p. 281)

Computers are in widespread use throughout the Civil Service. Applications range from sophisticated weather forecasting and research into climatic change, through a Home Office electronic photofit system to help catch offenders, to the Department for Education and Skills' administration of the country's largest and most complex pension scheme (for teachers). All levels and types of IT personnel are needed.

Civil Service

Late start (Civil Service generally) There is no upper age limit (except for a few schemes which involve long-term training). There may be increasing opportunities for mature candidates, especially those with managerial, professional, technical or scientific qualifications and/or experience. In 2002, the average age of new entrants to the Civil Service at senior level was 45.

Work life balance The Civil Service has been at the forefront of introducing flexible working practices, having introduced career breaks and job-sharing in the 1980s and more recently term-time working and work-sharing. The government White Paper *Changing Patterns in a Changing World* published in 2000 required Civil Service departments to offer work life balance options to their staff. Under the Modernizing Government and Civil Service reform programmes all departments have been looking imaginatively at opportunities for flexible working and introducing initiatives such as a cross-department database and register through which to introduce potential job-sharers to each other. Current action on work life balance includes addressing the issue of individuals having to choose between a good work life balance and progression in their career, and encouraging support for work life balance practices at senior levels.

Further information Phone 0117 982 1171 for careers brochure.
www.cabinet-office.gov.uk
www.civil-service.gov.uk

Related careers LOCAL GOVERNMENT

Construction

Entry qualifications *For degree*: 2–3 A levels, to include maths/science for some courses. *For technician training*: see BTEC/SQA National and Higher National, pp. 8, 10. *For craft training*: none specified.

The work The construction industry is one of Britain's largest, employing one in 14 people. It is made up of companies ('contractors') of all sizes, from international giants employing thousands of skilled craft workers and professional staff, including architects, chartered builders, surveyors and chartered engineers, to small 'jobbing builders' employing one or two craftsmen/women and taking on additional people as required. Many small builders work partly on their own and partly as sub-contractors to larger firms, sometimes providing a specialist skill which the main contractor may not be able to offer. Large companies have their own design departments and execute large-scale projects such as housing estates, large office blocks, hospitals, etc. Smaller firms – and often large ones too – work to plans drawn up by the client's architect and may sub-contract work to specialist firms of plumbers, tilers, smaller general builders, etc. On large projects the client, or the client's representative, appoints a *clerk of works* (see p. 173).

The construction trade (particularly, but not only, firms concerned with large projects) is very dependent on the economic climate. Currently the industry is buoyant and needs to recruit 380,000 people into all levels over the next 5 years. There are still too few registering on construction degrees, so experienced managers are usually in demand.

Levels and organization of work are very much less well-defined than, for example, in the engineering industry. In the construction industry it is possible to start at any level and work your way up the career ladder or to owning your own business. There is currently a drive to ensure that the construction workforce is qualified, whether at operative or management level. There is, therefore, increasing scope for people with specialist and management qualifications, but there will always be scope for craftsmen and craftswomen who are qualified, good at their job and also have organizing ability to build up their own business. Knowledge of basic crafts like bricklaying, carpentry and plumbing is useful even for managers; knowledge of new materials and technologies is essential in all parts of the industry.

Graduate route – Design, Engineering, Finance, Management and Planning

Creative people, financial experts and legal professionals all play a part in getting the project off the ground. Once the construction work begins, construction managers, engineers and surveyors organize all the people working on site to ensure that what is built matches the original designs.

Some job titles in this area include: architect (see p. 87), architectural technologist (see p. 92), landscape architect (see p. 313), building services engineer (see p. 217), civil engineer (see p. 216), structural engineer (see p. 217), building surveyor (see p. 595), quantity surveyor (see p. 593), town planner (see p. 635) and construction manager.

Construction Managers

Unlike a lot of the other occupations construction managers tend to manage people and work processes rather than having specialist knowledge of engineering or design. They must see that work is carried out in the right sequence with the right materials – which must be available at the right time – and at the right cost. They organize the labour force, so must understand the work of bricklayers, carpenters, etc. Depending on the size of the firm, work may include organizing the financial side (paying wages, paying for materials, etc.).

Some construction management jobs are site-based (there may be a site office), some are office-based; nearly all jobs involve some site visits; and many jobs, at least for large firms, involve working away from home at times, occasionally overseas.

As well as the construction manager there are other jobs and specializations which may be needed on a construction site (which vary very much between firms):

1. *Planner*: At pre-tender stage is involved in the decision about how the tender can be adjusted. When tender is accepted, produces charts showing sequence of operations. Works closely with contract manager. In large companies will use a computer for this. Planners need experience of estimating, buying or contracts management.

2. *Site engineer*: In charge of technical side of an individual project. Sets out the positions and levels of the building to ensure it is placed in the correct position in accordance with the designs. Oversees all the work on site, including quality control (see 'Civil Engineering' and 'Structural Engineering', pp. 216–17).

3. *Site manager/site agent* (used to be called 'general foreman'): In charge of the contract. Ensures the designs and specifications are understood by the foremen/women; plans and coordinates materials and labour. Sees that building keeps to the plan and time schedule (see 'Technicians', below, and 'Surveying Technicians', p. 600). May control work of young engineers.

4. *Production controller*: Works on incentive schemes; measures work done by operatives as part of productivity control; takes part in construction planning at site level. Some specialize in work study and/ or industrial relations.

5. *Contract manager*: Oversees several projects. Moves from site to site ensuring that work is progressing according to plan. Plans movement of machines and labour to minimize delays and time-wasting. Has overall responsibility for completion of projects to correct standard at the right time.

6. *Clerk of works*: Other construction management specialists work for the contractor; the clerk of works is employed by the client (or client's representative). May be employed full time on a contract basis or on a self-employed private practice/consultant basis. Works from

an office on site and is responsible for seeing that the work is carried out according to the specification. As the only person on site not working for the contractor the clerk of works can be rather isolated, so needs to be confident and self-sufficient. On large schemes duties may include supervising several other clerks of works specializing in, for example, heating and ventilating or electrical installation.

7. *Building control officers*: They are responsible for checking sites to see that work complies with building regulations. In certain circumstances they may advise contractors on alternative methods of construction. Up until recently they worked only for local and other public authorities, but they can now work in the private sector.

Technicians route

Technicians are valuable members of the team who support the work of engineers, architects, quantity surveyors, etc. The role of technicians overlaps with that of managers and, in fact, many managers start as technicians (see 'Training'). Technicians do many of the detailed costings, work out quantities and prepare drawings. On site they may be involved in surveying, measuring and detailed planning of the work. They are the people who make things happen. Some jobs that mainly exist at technician level are:

Buyer: Selects from the design drawings the materials and services needed; contacts suppliers and sub-contractors to obtain the most competitive prices; ensures materials are available on time and within budget.

Estimator: Calculates the likely cost of materials (from door handles to concrete), labour and plant equipment, and the time needed for the project when the firm is tendering for a contract. Also analyses costs of existing projects to provide a guide for future estimates.

Craft route

There is a huge range of occupations that craftspeople work in, for example bricklaying, painting and decorating and roofing. Other more unusual or specialist trades are shopfitting, plant operating, demolition and steeplejacking (for a full range of information visit *www.bconstructive.co.uk*).

Training

Manager

Either on the job by training first as a technician (see below) and then taking BTEC/SQA Higher National awards. Successful completion plus appropriate experience leads to exemptions from various examinations of the Chartered Institute of Building.

Or 3-year full-time or 4-year sandwich degree in construction management, building studies, built environment. Most give full exemption from Chartered Institute of Building's Final examination.

Clerk of works: As above followed by evening or correspondence course for Institute of Clerk of Works' Intermediate and Final examinations. (BTEC National and Higher awards give some exemptions. Experience may also be taken into account.) Membership of the Institute is compulsory before sitting the examinations. Some local authorities give day-release.

Building control officers qualify in building, surveying or relevant engineering subjects at BTEC/SQA or degree level.

Technician

Either via the Construction Industry Training Board's youth training programme (see below) *or* as a trainee with a company and day- or block-release (both may lead to BTEC/SQA National awards) *or* by studying full time for BTEC National Diploma (or SQA equivalent) (see pp. 8, 10). Courses can be in construction or building services engineering (see ENGINEERING, p. 216).

Craft

There are 2 main routes:

1. Work-based training – Foundation and Advanced Modern Apprenticeships (see p. 11). The CITB administers the Construction Apprenticeship Scheme (in Scotland, the Scottish Construction Apprenticeship Scheme). This provides young people over 16 with a

4-year work-based programme leading to an NVQ/SVQ in their chosen occupation.

2. College-based route – full-time courses, usually 2 years, leading to a Vocational A level in Construction and the Built Environment, Edexcel BTEC Construction National Diploma (see p. 10 for SQA equivalents) or City & Guilds qualifications.

Personal attributes *Construction crafts*: Some manual dexterity; an inquiring and logical mind; willingness to work both in a team or alone with the minimum of or no supervision; good attention to detail; a reasonably careful nature or at least awareness of dangers unless basic rules are observed.

Construction technicians and management: Ability to work with all kinds of people and help them work as a team; technical and practical aptitudes; good at organization; willing to work outdoors in all weathers; commercial sense.

Late start Most apprenticeships have an age limit of 23. There may be training and retraining schemes for adults (see p. 22) with or without related experience and/or qualifications, e.g. as surveying technician, see p. 600.

Work life balance Depending on the length of absence, a career break may be difficult without retraining. So far nothing is known about returners (see WORKING FOR ONESELF, p. 648).

Part-time work may be possible if working for small contractor or for oneself.

Position of women There are over 188,000 women employed across all occupations in the construction industry, making up 9% of the workforce. Almost 50,000 of these women are in professional, technician or management roles. Women in the craft trades accounted for 1% of the workforce in 2002. Women currently make up 2% of sole traders in the construction industry and 7% of entrepreneurs running small businesses employing between 1 and 10 people.

Further information Construction Industry Training Board (CITB), Bircham Newton, King's Lynn, Norfolk PE31 6RH (for England and Wales); or 4 Edison Street, Hillington, Glasgow G52 4XN (for Scotland).
www.citb.org.uk

Chartered Institute of Building, Englemere, King's Ride, Ascot, Berks SL5 8BJ.
www.ciob.org.uk

Institute of Clerks of Works, 41 The Mall, London W5 3TJ.
www.icwgb.com

Institute of Building Control, 21 High Street, Ewell, Epsom, Surrey KT17 1SB.
www.building-control.org

JTL, Stafford House, 120–122 High Street, Orpington, Kent BR6 0JS.
www.jtlimited.co.uk

Scottish Electrical Charitable Training Trust, Bush House, Bush Estate, Penicuik, Midlothian, Edinburgh EH26 0SB.
www.sectt.org.uk

Women and Manual Trades, 52–54 Featherstone Street, London EC1Y 8RT.
www.wamt.org

Related careers AGRICULTURE AND HORTICULTURE – ARCHITECTURE – ENGINEERING: *Civil Engineering* – SURVEYING

Consumer Scientist/Home Economics

Entry qualifications None laid down; depends on 'Training' (see below).

The work Consumer scientists, sometimes still known as home economists, act as a link between producers of household goods and services and their consumers. This covers a wide range of jobs. Within industry they also act as a link between technologists who design and develop new products but often know little about consumer preferences and requirements, and marketing and general management staffs. So consumer science, at least at senior level, requires communication skills as well as an understanding of technological and of social trends.

Consumer scientists work in various settings: industry, social services, public relations, public utilities, consumer advice and protection, retailing, hotels and catering. Increasingly they are working in community care and in health and welfare fields. As food technology teachers they are involved in health and design and technology education. There is nothing clear-cut about the professional consumer scientist's work: people with related kinds of training may do the same, or similar, jobs; and once qualified may branch off into related fields such as catering, marketing, consumer and trade magazines, and books.

The majority work in manufacturing industry on development, quality control, promotion and marketing of products, appliances and equipment used, or services provided in the home. Before new or improved food and washing products, dishwashers, cookers, central heating systems, etc. are put into production, consumer scientists discuss details of design and performance with engineers, scientists, designers, marketing people. They put the customer's point of view; they test prototypes in the laboratory under 'ideal conditions', and they also use them in the same way as the customer might – being interrupted in their work and not always following the instructions as they should. For instance, they test whether a new type of butter-substitute creams easily, even if kept in the fridge too long and if clumsily handled; how a washing machine behaves if switches are turned on in the wrong order, or how easily a new cooker cleans when it is really dirty. As a result of laboratory and 'user' tests, alterations are often made before a product is put into production. In the retail industry, consumer scientists work in, or manage, food- and textile-testing laboratories, some become management trainees and then go into retail management (see RETAIL MANAGEMENT, p. 512).

Some consumer scientists are involved with educating the public, for example in the need for, and methods of, energy conservation (e.g., home insulation and other fuel-saving devices). The work combines dealing with lay people who have much less technical knowledge, and with experts who have very much more.

Under the heading *customer relations* or *marketing*, work involves writing clear, concise user-instructions for explanatory labels and leaflets which accompany fish-fingers, freezers, synthetic fibre carpets, baby foods, etc., as well as dealing with inquiries and complaints correspondence.

Consumer scientists also identify demand for new products or changes in existing ones. This may involve field work – interviewing potential customers in their homes (see 'Market Research', p. 57 and MARKETING AND SELLING, p. 371) and thinking up innovations which could be marketed profitably.

In the *media* consumer scientists prepare features and programmes: they cook and cost elaborate as well as very cheap dishes, or arrange and cost domestic interiors which are then photographed and described, or demonstrated on TV. They also use their skills in assessing and reporting on equipment and on issues relevant to the consumer at home and at work.

In local authority *social services departments* consumer scientists advise low-income families on budgeting and general household management; and they may run the home-help service and advise on the efficient running of the authority's residential homes. Those who have studied a housing option may work in local authority or private *housing management*. There are also openings in health education.

In *hospitals* they become domestic administrators at top management level.

They may also work in the *Trading Standards Department* (see p. 639) in consumer services.

Experienced consumer scientists can work as freelance consultants: firms may wish to research and/or promote a new product and need a consumer scientist for a particular project rather than permanently. For example, they work as freelances, writing explanatory leaflets, developing and checking recipes and equipment, etc. Some prepare food for magazine photography or TV commercials; some write books and articles for consumer magazines.

Job prospects are good, especially for graduates, although competition for top jobs (most are in cities) is keen. However, the combination of technical knowledge and understanding of family and consumer needs can be useful in a variety of jobs; consumer scientists willing to be adaptable can find work in a wide range of organizations. Greatest scope is in food and domestic appliance manufacturing, in retail, fuel and energy industries.

Training No particular qualification leads to any particular type of job. It is possible for anyone with basic approved training or related training (see 'Accommodation and Catering Management', under HOTEL AND CATERING, p. 272) and the right experience and personality ultimately to do as well as a graduate. But the more thorough the training, the wider the scope of job.

1. *Degree*: Entry requirements: 2 A levels and 3 GCSEs (A–C) (no specific A levels, although home economics preferred, but maths, English language and a science at least at GCSE level). Degree courses in Home Economics or related subjects such as Food and Consumer Studies (*see also* TEACHING, p. 610).

2. *BTEC/SQA Higher National awards* in Home Economics or

related subjects, e.g. Food and Consumer Studies: Entry requirements: 1 A level (preferably home economics) and 3 GCSEs to include English language, maths or a science. Diploma and degree courses include varying amounts of nutrition, food preparation and science; design and performance of equipment and materials, including textiles; business and marketing studies; consumer and social studies; communications and the media; information technology. Students can choose from a range of options, e.g. the carer in the community, ergonomics, housing and community health, product development, press and public relations.

3. *BTEC/National awards* in Home Economics or related subject or in Scotland SQA National Units: broadly the same subjects as HND but not in such depth; some courses concentrate more on practical skills such as cooking; home management; care of textiles, etc.

4. Foundation degree: no set requirements. There are a few 2 year full-time or part-time Foundation degrees in related subjects.

5. Modern Apprenticeships: there are Foundation and Advanced Modern Apprenticeships in Food and Drink Manufacturing leading to a level 2 or 3 NVQ. There are also a range of NVQ/SVQs in related occupations.

Personal attributes Practicality and organizing ability; interest in consumer affairs, ability to understand both consumers' and manufacturers' points of view; ability to communicate easily both with more highly qualified professionals and with often poorly educated, possibly illiterate consumers; liking for people; humour.

Late start Mature entrants are welcome on all courses and may be given exemptions if they have relevant experience.

Work life balance A career break should be no problem for people who keep up with developments.

Good opportunities for part-time working; no reason why job-sharing should not be tried. Some part-time courses are being developed.

Further information Institute of Consumer Sciences, Lonsdale House, 52 Blucher Street, Birmingham B1 1QU.
www.instituteconsumersciences.co.uk

Design and Technology Association, 16 Wellesbourne House, Walton Road, Wellesbourne, Warwickshire CV35 9JB.
www.data.org.uk

Institute of Food Science and Technology, 5 Cambridge Court, 210 Shepherd's Bush Road, London W6 7NJ.
www.ifst.org

Related careers DIETETICS — HOTEL CATERING — PUBLIC RELATIONS — TEACHING — TRADING STANDARDS OFFICER

Dance

Teaching and performing are two separate careers. There are three kinds of performer in Western dance:

1. classical ballet;
2. contemporary;
3. musical theatre.

PERFORMING

Entry qualifications No specific educational requirements, but a good general education is essential for ballet dancers. Many dance schools offer A levels and GCSEs, and A levels are essential for students interested in the growing number of degree courses in dance performance or teaching.

Ballet Dancer

The work Ballet dancers lead dedicated lives. Their days are spent practising, rehearsing and performing. They have little spare time and may not indulge in such activities as cycling, riding, etc., lest they develop the wrong muscles. They meet few people who are not in some way involved with ballet.

They are usually attached to one particular company and may be on tour for much of the year.

Ballet companies have only a few vacancies each year so opportunities are limited. Once a member of the *corps de ballet*, a talented dancer has a chance of rising to solo parts and understudying bigger roles, but it is rare indeed to rise to principal dancer status. Even a successful dancer's professional life is short; only the very exceptional still get engagements in their middle thirties. There are some opportunities abroad – dance is a very international activity.

Training Serious training must have started by the age of 11 and certainly no later than 16 with a professional teacher who prepares pupils systematically for one of the officially recognized major dancing examinations: e.g. those of the Royal Academy of Dancing, the Imperial Society of Teachers of Dancing or the British Ballet Organization (RAD, ISTD, BBO).

The best training is given at professional schools which give general education for GCSEs and a thorough drama and dance training. It is advisable to apply only for courses accredited by the Council for Dance Education and Training.

There are part-time ballet schools all over the country but pupils from the few full-time vocational schools (some of which are attached to companies) probably stand a better chance of getting into a company when they finish.

Ballet training includes national and character dancing, mime, history, art and literature, and usually French (most technical terms are in that language).

Before accepting a pupil, good schools insist on a thorough orthopaedic examination, which is repeated at regular intervals throughout training.

NOTE: Since the ending of local authority discretionary grants, government-backed Dance and Drama awards have been introduced for vocational courses leading to recognized qualifications at leading private schools. These provide funding towards tuition fees and means-tested help with other expenses. For further information phone 0114 259 3612 for a copy of the DfES booklet *Dance and Drama Awards*. With the creation of the new Conservatoire for Dance and Drama, dance and drama students at affiliated institutions will be eligible for the same financial support as other HE students.

Personal attributes Suitable physique, including strong back and feet; intelligence; intuition; emotional depth; musical talent; the ability to take criticism without resentment; a strong constitution; complete dedication; a distinct personality.

Contemporary Dancer

The work The work and lifestyle of the contemporary dancer is very like that of the ballet dancer, requiring the same degree of dedication. As contemporary dance groups are structured differently from classical ballet companies and are often much smaller, there is not the same hierarchy and route to principal dancer.

Training This is quite different from that of classical ballet, although contemporary dancers may have started with classical training as children and may continue to take classical dance classes occasionally (as classical dancers may take contemporary classes). Their kind of dance makes different aesthetic and physical demands and requires specialized training. Students frequently take a foundation course before starting their vocational training, which should begin by age 18. Most contemporary dance courses are degrees (for example the degree in Contemporary Dance run by the London Contemporary Dance School and validated by Kent University).

Personal attributes Similar to those of a ballet dancer; however, physical requirements are more flexible as contemporary dance aims to be inclusive of all body shapes and sizes.

Musical Theatre Dancer

The work Modern stage dancers perform in musicals, pantomime, cabaret, on TV, and in light entertainment generally. They are not usually attached to a company, but appear in individual shows. As well as learning dances, they often have to learn scripts and songs. They are more likely to be on short-term contracts and to have longer periods out of work than other dancers. Even when not working, they have to keep up their practice, which means paying for private classes at a dance centre.

For the fully trained first-rate dancer prospects are fair. But like other entertainers, a dancer must be prepared for months of 'resting', meanwhile earning a living in some other way yet being available to attend auditions. If lucky, they may get a long run in the West End, a tour, or a television series.

Training 3 years full time, preferably. Most start vocational training at 16. Over 80% of dancers currently employed in the West End have been through accredited vocational dance courses. At auditions, dancers must show potential; and do not rely on examination passes (they may be expected to have reached Elementary). The modern stage dancer should also have some training in voice production, drama and singing.

Personal attributes A strong stage appearance and presence; resilience; versatility; enterprise in tracking down jobs; sense of rhythm.

Teaching

Entry qualifications To teach dance in state primary and secondary schools (i.e. not dance schools) Qualified Teacher Status is required: *either* a degree leading to QTS *or* a degree in dance *or* in performing arts (titles and content vary) followed by a Post-graduate Certificate in Education (see TEACHING, p. 610). Entry requirements may be waived for mature entrants.

The work A dancing teacher may teach both children and adults, or may specialize in teaching one or the other. Adults are taught in private schools/classes or in local authority adult education centres.

Children are taught in ordinary schools; dancing schools; specialized professional schools.

Ordinary schools
Full-time or visiting part-time teachers teach dance to GCSE, mainly to improve children's poise and deportment.

Dancing schools
These are intended for children who do not have dancing lessons at school. They may be run by a teacher who hires a hall for the purpose, or they may be in a dancing school which caters for both children and adults.

Children are usually prepared for recognized dancing examinations (see 'Ballet Dancer, Training'). This ensures that children are being properly taught even though they do not intend to become professionals.

Professional schools
Dancing is an essential part of the curriculum in what is generally an arts-orientated private school; the teacher deals with especially talented children who hope to become professional dancers

Job prospects are good for teaching adults and children. Royal Academy of Dancing and Imperial Society of Teachers of Dancing examiners often go abroad to organize, teach and examine.

Leading to Qualified Teacher Status
Training Applicants to degrees in dance should check prospectuses very carefully before choosing a course, as the 'dance component' varies from a few hours to a substantial proportion.

The dance teaching societies (e.g. ISTD and RAD) have their own entrance requirements for student teachers and need to be contacted individually. Students can teach only the syllabus they have been trained in, and usually work in private schools and classes. Degree courses are available for the ISTD and RAD syllabuses. A fast-growing area, in which there are some specialized teaching courses, is that of community dance. The emphasis is frequently on contemporary or ethnic dance.

Other courses A number of vocational schools now offer 3-year degree courses. Universities and colleges around the country also offer BA Honours courses which include dance but there is considerable variation in the balance between academic study and practical work.

Personal attributes The ability to explain and demonstrate steps and movements; a fine sense of rhythm and some proficiency at the piano; a liking for people of all ages; imagination; endless tact and patience; good appearance; graceful movements. (See also TEACHING, p. 610.)

Teaching Keep Fit and Exercise

This area has expanded rapidly in the last few years. Movement classes have mushroomed, changing their style frequently in order to follow the latest (often imported) fashion. Many people have cashed in on the dance/exercise craze without a proper knowledge of how the body works and what kind of movement is suitable for each type of student. The most suitable basic training for teachers in this area is either a proper dance course; or physical education teacher training; or a 2-year part-time course organized by the Keep Fit Association and run in conjunction with local education authorities; or courses leading to the RSA Certificate in Exercise to Music.

Choreography

The work The dancer who has exceptional imaginative powers and the ability to interpret music in terms of dancing may ultimately do choreography. This is dance composition: the grouping of dancers and sequence of dances which make up the entire ballet. In musical theatre, a choreographer may direct within a wide range from the production numbers on TV which involve scores of dancers, to the unexacting dances of a seaside concert party.

Choreography is not a career for which a novice can be trained unless there is a noticeable talent. Years of experience of classical or contemporary dance and a musical training are needed (see MUSIC,

p. 398). However, some dance courses now include choreography or offer it as an option.

Work life balance Many dancers take up teaching after a break from performing.

There are good opportunities to teach part time.

Further information Council for Dance Education and Training, Toynbee Hall, 28 Commercial Street, London E1 6LS (for addresses of accredited dance schools).

Imperial Society of Teachers of Dancing, 22–26 Paul Street, London EC2A 4QE.
www.istd.org

The Keep Fit Association, Astra House, Suite 105, Arklow Road, London SE14 6EB.
www.keepfit.org.uk

Royal Academy of Dance, 36 Battersea Square, London SW11 3RA.
www.rad.org.uk

Related careers DRAMA – MUSIC – TEACHING

Dentistry

DENTAL SURGEON

Entry qualifications 3 good A levels (or equivalent) usually including at least 2 sciences (biology and chemistry are preferred). Chemistry, biology, physics and maths must usually be included at GCSE. (See 'Training' for arts A level candidates.)

The work Dentists (or dental surgeons) look after oral health by offering both preventive and restorative treatment. In addition to fillings and repairing teeth, dentists also extract teeth and design and fit artificial dentures. Some also carry out surgical operations on the jaw, while others specialize in orthodontics, which is the improvement of irregular teeth, mainly in children. The preventive aspects of dentistry are very important, especially encouraging good oral health care at home. Prospects are good and qualifications are accepted in the EU.

General Practice

The majority of dentists work in general practice. Most general practitioners are self-employed, often offering a combination of NHS and private treatment.

Dentists in general practice have the best financial prospects and the greatest independence, but they are also likely to work the hardest. They may be in a partnership, or in practice on their own, working in their own premises with their own equipment and employing their own dental nurses (see p. 195).

It is usual to begin as an assistant or associate in a practice, perhaps with a view to becoming a partner later. An associate takes on his or her own 'list' of patients and basically rents practice space from the practice owner.

Community Dental Surgeon

The Community Dental Service (CDS), as the name suggests, works within the community, largely providing care to those who may find it difficult to get treatment in general practice, such as those with disabilities. Those working within the CDS are also responsible for things like school dental checks. Unlike general practitioners, they are employed by the local health trust.

Hospital and University Dental Surgeon

Hospital dentists are usually specialists in a particular field and will require further training following their dental undergraduate degree. For those who go on to practise surgery, their work will include reconstructive surgery, for example for those involved in car accidents. A large part of their work involves extractions under general anaesthetic, as this can no longer be done in general practice.

Another option for dental graduates is dental teaching or research. Teaching posts are generally based in dental schools and hospitals. Those going into dental research can look forward to working on the development of new treatments as well as looking at the causes of dental disease.

Training 5-year course at dental schools attached to universities. Some dental courses may be preceded by a 1-year preliminary science course for students without the appropriate A levels (students with A level physics, chemistry, biology, zoology or maths are exempt from it), although not all dental schools offer this option.

Dental training lasts for 5 years. The syllabus covers anatomy and physiology, the uses of dental materials, design and fitting of dental appliances, pathology, some medicine, general as well as dental surgery, anaesthesia, orthodontics, children's and general preventive dentistry, radiology, dental ethics and relevant law.

Practical work on 'phantom heads' normally begins in the second year, and work on actual patients during the second or third year of the dental course.

A year's vocational training in a practice under the supervision of an experienced dentist is required for new graduates who want to work in NHS general dental practice. There is also the option of undertaking General Professional Training (GPT). GPT lasts for 2 years, with 1 year spent in general practice and the other spent working in a hospital.

Personal attributes Manual dexterity; a methodical and scientific approach; good personal skills; good health. Left-handedness is not a disadvantage.

Dentist in general practice especially: The ability to establish easy relationships quickly with people, and give confidence to the nervous (the growth of the practice depends almost entirely on the patients' personal recommendations); organizing ability.

Community dental surgeon especially: The ability to get on with children.

Hospital dentist especially: The ability to work well as a member of a team.

Further information General Dental Council, 37 Wimpole Street, London W1G 8DQ.
www.gdc-uk.org
The British Dental Association, 64 Wimpole Street, London W1G 8YS.
www.bda.org

Related careers MEDICINE

PROFESSIONS COMPLEMENTARY TO DENTISTRY

For people interested in dentistry but without the necessary qualifications for dental training, there are four careers: *dental therapist, dental hygienist, dental nurse* and *dental technician.*

Dental Therapist

Entry qualifications Minimum age for training 18.

5 GCSEs (A–C), including English language, and either a recognized dental nursing qualification or 2 A levels.

The work Dental therapists do 'operative work'; they work in hospitals and community dental services. They work under the direction of a dentist who prescribes the treatment to be given; this includes simple fillings, extraction of deciduous teeth, cleaning, scaling and polishing teeth and giving guidance on general dental care. Dental therapists always work under the direction and prescription of a registered dentist. Their responsibility is therefore limited. Many of the patients are very young – in welfare clinics under 5, in school clinics mostly under 11. In the past dental therapists worked in hospitals and community dental services but since July 2002 they have been able to work in all areas of dentistry including general practice. They must be enrolled with the General Dental Council in order to practise in the UK.

There is now intense competition for the very few training places per year.

Training 2 year full-time course. Students learn how to scale, polish, fill and extract teeth. They also work on patients, under supervision. Theoretical training includes anatomy, physiology of the teeth and jaw, some radiography, some dietetics – enough to understand the effect of different foods on the development of children's teeth.

Personal attributes Considerable manual dexterity; conscientious-ness; some interest in science; a way with children.

Further information The British Dental Association, 64 Wimpole Street, London WIM 8AL.
www.bda-dentistry.org.uk
British Association of Dental Therapists, Dental Auxiliary School, Heath Park, Cardiff CF4 4XY.
www.badt.org.uk

Dental Hygienist

Entry qualifications Minimum age for training 18. 5 GCSEs (A–C), preferably including English language and a science subject, and either a recognized dental nursing qualification or 2 A levels. Candidates are given a manual dexterity test.

The work Dental hygienists also do 'operative work'. They do scaling and polishing under the direction of dentists, but do not do any fillings etc. An important aspect of the work is preventive dentistry.

They work with adults as well as with children, in general practice as well as in community health clinics and hospitals.

More dentists in general practice, especially in partnership, now employ hygienists, but there are no promotion prospects.

Training 2 years full time at dental teaching hospitals. Training is similar to that of therapists, but the extraction and filling of teeth are not included. Some time is spent in learning how to talk about oral hygiene to children and adults.

Personal attributes As for therapists, plus the ability to express oneself lucidly.

Further information The British Dental Hygienists Association, 13 The Ridge, Yatton, Bristol BS49 4DQ.
www.bdha.org.uk

Dental Nurse

Entry qualifications None laid down, but most hospital training schools demand some GCSE passes, which should include English language and a science. None required for admission to the examination for the National Certificate of the Examining Board for Dental Nurses.

Minimum age for training usually 17.

The work Dental nurses do no 'operative work'. They act as the dentist's 'third hand', handing them the right instruments at the right time. They also look after the instruments, do sterilizing, get out patients' treatment cards, help with filling in forms and filing, do secretarial and reception work.

Dental nurses work wherever dentists work, i.e. in general practice, in community dental clinics and in hospitals.

Training Most dentists train their own nurses, but some prefer those who were trained at a dental hospital, for a period varying from 12 to 24 months. The type of training differs slightly from one hospital to another, but it is mainly practical, with some lectures and demonstrations.

Most dental nurses now qualify through the NVQ/SVQ level 2 in Oral Health Care Support and the level 3 in Dental Nursing. It is expected that these qualifications will eventually replace the long-established National Certificate in Dental Nursing.

Personal attributes Good communication skills; some manual dexterity; a smart appearance.

Further information British Association of Dental Nurses, 11 Pharos Street, Fleetwood, Lancashire FY7 6BG.
www.badn.org.uk

Dental Technician

Entry qualifications For BTEC National Certificate or Diploma in Science (Dental Technology): 4 GCSEs (A–C), including maths and a science.

The work Dental technicians construct and repair dentures, crowns and other orthodontic appliances. They work either in commercial dental laboratories where work for individual dentists is carried out, or in hospital dental laboratories. It is highly skilled work.

Training *Either* (in commercial laboratories or dental practices) a 4-year apprenticeship with day-release for BTEC National award; *or* (in dental hospitals and health authorities) a 3-year training scheme with block-release for the BTEC National award.

Successful students may take a 2-year part-time course for the BTEC Higher National Certificate or Diploma.

Dental technicians at present do not need to be registered with the General Dental Council but negotiations are under way for statutory registration.

Personal attributes Great manual dexterity; patience; accuracy.

Further information General Dental Council, 37 Wimpole Street, London w1g 8dq.
www.gdc-uk.org
Dental Technicians Education and Training Advisory Board, 5 Oxford Court, St James Road, Brackley, Northants nn13 7xy.
www.dentalguide.co.uk

Late start 1. *Dentists*: Unusual. Dental schools vary in their attitude to mature students and judge each case on its merits – acceptance depends largely on the number of years students would have after qualifying. There is, usually, no relaxation in entry requirements. Over-35s are unlikely to be offered a place. No employment problem once qualified.

2. *Professions complementary to dentistry*: Young students are given preference for training usually, but mature entrants are also considered.

Work life balance There are good opportunities for part-time employment. Those working in the NHS have access to the flexible working practices – part time, job-sharing, term-time working, etc. – being introduced under the Improving Working Lives standard. There are refresher courses for dentists, dental therapists and dental hygienists who have taken a career break. As continuing professional development is mandatory for dentists, a Keeping in Touch Scheme (KITS) has been developed to keep them up to date with clinical and professional developments while they are away from practice, whether NHS or general practical.

Related careers MEDICINE – NURSING – SCIENCE

Dietetics

Entry qualifications 2 to 3 A level passes, preferably chemistry and another science subject. Also mathematics and English to GCSE standard.

BTEC National Diploma in science with an appropriate merit pass or an Access course in science may be acceptable.

The work The dietitian's special skill is to translate the science of nutrition into understandable and practical information about food and health. Career opportunities have greatly diversified as healthy eating habits become increasingly recognized as a vital part of preventing disease and promoting good health.

Dietitians are concerned with food and health in its widest sense and their work is preventive and therapeutic. They have to know about food production and processing; social, economic and psychological factors that influence food choice; the digestion, absorption and metabolism of food, its effect on nutritional well-being; how to treat disease and prevent nutrition-related problems.

Dietitians work in many different settings. Currently, about half of the profession are employed in the National Health Service, where they work in hospitals or in the community as 'hands-on' dietitians or as managers.

Hospital dietitians advise people who need special diets as part of their medical treatment, e.g. a carefully controlled diet for kidney disease or an appropriately formulated liquid feed which is passed through a tube. With other health professionals they work as part of a clinical team. They also help in developing food policies and liaise with the catering services to ensure that healthy food is available for both patients and staff, and special dietary needs are met. Many hospital dietitians eventually specialize, e.g. in the treatment of children, diabetes or eating disorders. Whatever the reason for referral, the dietitian works with the patient (or carer) to plan changes to their eating patterns. As well as treating the medical condition, diets must take into account usual food habits, cultural customs and social and financial position in a non-discriminatory way. The dietitian must provide support and encouragement through sometimes difficult times of adjustment.

Community dietitians' work is more about health education, although many run clinics in doctors' surgeries and health centres for people needing specialist dietary advice. As there are so few dietitians, an important part of their job is to work closely with primary healthcare teams. This includes keeping nurses, doctors, health visitors and other health professionals up to date on the latest food issues so that they in turn can communicate important health messages as widely as possible. Dietitians also work with the media and speak to groups and societies to ensure that accurate nutrition information is available to their local communities.

Another important aspect of community work is working in partnership with local people to tackle food issues that they are concerned about, e.g. cooking skills, access to affordable, healthy food. Community dietitians may also work with schools, social services, agencies involved with the under-5s, workplaces, services for elderly people and local authorities to help promote positive, enjoyable changes in food choice. This work may involve: helping to develop and implement food policies; developing educational resources; nutrition education for staff or carers; liaison with catering services and individual advice for people with special dietary needs, e.g. people with chewing or swallowing difficulties.

Outside the NHS dietitians work in rapidly expanding areas such as:

education, for example as educators in centres of higher and further education, for other health-care workers such as doctors and community nurses and for the media.

research, for example into evaluating and improving dietetic treatment and developing the science of nutrition and dietetics.

industry, for example with trade associations, food retailers, food manufacturers, catering organizations, public relations and marketing companies – in a consultancy role, giving advice on nutrition to businesses and their customers.

freelance dietetics, for example in private practice, sports nutrition and the media.

Experienced dietitians are in demand, but getting that first job may mean moving to another part of the country. There are some openings in the developing countries and in the EU (for dietitians who speak the relevant languages). British qualifications are not automatically recognized in the USA, Canada and Australia, but reciprocity of recognition may be obtained in the future.

Training State registration with the Council for Professions Supplementary to Medicine is essential for a dietitian wishing to work in the National Health Service and a definite advantage when working outside the NHS. There are alternative routes:

1. A recognized 4-year degree course. The syllabus includes: physiology; biochemistry; microbiology; nutrition and food science; diet therapy; health education; catering; psychology and sociology.

2. Graduates with degrees which include human nutrition, physiology or biochemistry may take a recognized 2-year post-graduate diploma. All courses include a period of approved practical clinical training in hospital and community settings.

Personal attributes An interest in science, people and food; enjoyment of communicating with people from all walks of life; an ability to explain complex things in a simple manner; a positive and motivating attitude and an understanding, non-discriminatory approach; confident spoken and written communication skills; patience and a sense of humour.

Late start No age-bar in jobs, mature students welcome on degree courses. (See Access to higher education courses, p. 15.)

Work life balance A career break should present no problem. The British Dietetic Association offers courses for returners to the profession. Other refresher courses may be organized by hospitals and colleges.

Opportunities for part time and job-sharing at all levels of seniority. At present there are no part-time training opportunities, but some colleges and universities are developing more flexible study routes, including part-time courses.

Further information The British Dietetic Association, 5th Floor, Charles House, Queensway, Birmingham B3 3HT. (please send an s.a.e.)
www.bda.uk.com

Related careers CATERING – CONSUMER SCIENTIST/HOME ECONOMICS – MEDICINE – SCIENCE: *Biochemist*; *Chemist*; *Food Science and Technology*.

Drama

ACTING

Entry qualifications No rigid requirements. See 'Training', below.

The work A career only to be contemplated by those who feel they could not possibly be happy doing anything else. Complimentary notices for school or college plays are rarely pointers to professional success, because being the best of a group of local performers is irrelevant when competing with the best from all over the country. In addition, luck plays a large part: being in the right place at the right time is as important as being good at the job.

Entry to this overcrowded profession is extremely difficult. There are 'casting agreements' between theatrical, TV, film and commercials producers which control the employment of actors and virtually restrict employment to Equity members. Equity (the actors' trade union) in turn strictly controls the entry of new members.

Television

Provides well over half the total of acting jobs, but is not easy to get into: producers can pick and choose and tend to choose players who have had repertory experience or who have done exceptionally well at drama schools or in fringe theatre work. TV drama is recorded on video tape or film in short scenes or 'takes'. Each take rarely lasts for more than a couple of minutes. The actor may be asked to film scenes out of story order, which requires a high level of discipline. Rehearsal time is scarce; the technique now widely used is the rehearse/record method. The actors rehearse each scene on set, then record it immediately. Making TV drama can be very boring. At least two-thirds of an actor's time on set is spent sitting around waiting for technical problems to be sorted out. Added to this, actors have very little control over the finished product; the director, camera operator and editor have more control than they do. However, generally TV work pays better than theatre work and exposes the actor to a wider audience.

Theatre

Performers may give 8 performances a week. In repertory, there are often rehearsals during the day as well, which leaves little free time. Reasonably priced digs near the theatre are rarely luxurious; theatre dressing-rooms tend to be cramped and uncomfortable.

No actor ever has a 'secure job' – contracts may be as short as 2 weeks; rarely longer than a year.

Apart from the conventional theatre, there has in recent years been a considerable growth in 'fringe theatre'. Companies are often set up by players working as cooperatives (for a very small wage), taking plays into small halls, pubs, schools, etc. This type of acting – without a proper stage – requires adaptability, devotion and special technique; it is not much easier to get into than conventional stage work.

Commercials

Work comes through casting agencies. Work is never regular; TV commercials' producers always look for fresh faces, and an actor or actress who is currently advertising, for instance, a baby food, is unlikely to be used for some time, either for a competitor's food or for, say, a sophisticated drinks or fashion advertisement. Once established, actors and actresses sometimes appear in commercials which are written to suit their particular style, or they do 'voice overs' – the speaking but not the visual part of the commercial. Commercials are not a way into acting, but useful bread-and-butter jobs.

Films

The film industry is very small. There is very little work; nobody can hope to be *only* a film actress or actor today. The decision whether to accept a tiny part in a TV soap opera or wait for a hoped-for break in a film is always a difficult one. A performer who has accepted a part must stick to it and not let the producer down if something better turns up – this is essential to retain all-important agents' or casting directors' goodwill.

Acting is never easy, however good a player is. It gives great satisfaction, however, to people with stamina, real talent and lots of luck. At any one time over two-thirds of professional actors and actresses are out of work. An inquiry also showed that the chances of success are best for students who have attended one of the established schools (see 'Training', below) whose acting courses are accredited by the National Council for Drama Training. Another advantage of accredited courses is that their graduates, who are legally entitled to work in the UK, are automatically awarded membership of Equity. Most of the schools with accredited courses belong to the Conference of Drama Schools. Those who have been to one of the lesser-known schools which are totally out of touch with the changing needs and techniques of the theatre and broadcasting, or those few who somehow slipped in without any systematic training at all, are much less likely to find work. Entry to good schools, however, is very competitive (RADA, for example, auditioned over 500 people in 2002 for 34 places). 'Graduates' from established drama schools do not normally have great difficulty in getting their first job often due to the high level of exposure they receive from their end of course showcase. They are usually fixed up within a few months of leaving drama school. It is the second step, into bigger and better repertory, or into TV, West End, etc., which is the problematical one – and which vast numbers never manage to take at all. It means going to London, finding a good agent who will take a newcomer, and earning a living, yet being available if the hoped-for audition comes.

Entry requirements and training Drama schools are not too rigid on academic requirements for entry; acceptance at good drama schools depends on audition where talent is the primary criterion, but candidates considered most suitable will have 5 GCSEs and 2 A levels, especially in English language and/or literature.

A BTEC in Performing Arts would normally be considered in place of 2 A levels. It is important to contact individual schools as entry requirements vary and some may ask for specific subjects at A level.

Most players who earn their living at acting have been to NCDT accredited schools.

NOTE: The majority of accredited courses are now in the maintained sector, with courses leading to a degree qualification. Students who are studying for their first degree and are applying for these courses should be eligible for a grant and student loan from their Local Education Authority (LEA).

The government's Dance and Drama Awards (DaDA) were introduced in 1999 to provide help with fees and maintenance for students wishing to attend vocational courses in dance, drama and stage management at independent dance and drama schools. Contact the Department for Education and Skills on 0845 602 2260 for booklet or *www.dfes.gov.uk/dancedrama* for details on how to apply.

Vocational drama courses normally last 3 years. Schools' curricula and ethos vary considerably, but all accredited courses are seen to prepare the student for professional acting work, of all types, upon graduation. Students unlikely to succeed are asked to leave, or leave of their own accord, well before the end of the course. Students who have already got a first degree, or have substantial experience (normally 3 or 4 years) in acting, may take a 1 or 2-year post-graduate course.

Academic drama courses at university normally focus on literary criticism, history and literature of the theatre, not vocational acting training.

Personal attributes Good health; well-cut features, but not necessarily beauty; the ability to learn lines quickly; a good memory; great self-confidence; imagination and sensitivity to interpret any part; resilience, to ignore or benefit from the constant and public criticism from teachers, producers, directors, colleagues and the critics; an iron constitution; a sense of rhythm, at least (preferably an aptitude for dancing and singing); outstanding acting talent and a 'stage personality'; grim determination.

Late start Not impossible, but difficult owing to stiff competition for drama school places, although increasingly drama schools are favouring more mature applicants, asking students of 18 to reapply after a year or two.

Work life balance A career break is possible, providing contacts are kept up. The work is part time by its very nature and performers are strongly advised to have a second string to their bow.

Drama Therapy

Drama therapy aims to use various dramatic techniques (including mime and improvisation) to provide therapeutic experiences for people with physical and mental disabilities and psychiatric patients. It is practised by both specialist drama therapists and other professional staff involved in the care and treatment of such patients.

Training Either via part-time course while working in the health or community services (for details write to the British Association of Drama Therapists, 41 Broomhouse Lane, Hurlingham Park, London SW6 3DP) or via the 1-year full-time course, Drama and Movement in Therapy, operated by Sesame (a charity) at the Central School of Speech and Drama. Students should have had previous relevant experience, e.g. psychiatric nursing, teaching, social work or drama. For details write to the Central School of Speech and Drama, Embassy Theatre, 64 Eton Avenue, London NW3 3HY.

Stage Management

The work Stage managers and their teams are responsible to the director, during rehearsals, for the implementation of her/his instructions. This usually includes such things as the recording of actors' moves and other stage directions in the prompt book; collecting props, sound effects, etc., for the director's approval; relaying the director's requirements to the scenic, costume and lighting departments; ensuring that the actors are in the right place at the right time for rehearsals, costume fittings, etc. During the run of the play stage managers are in charge of everything on stage and backstage, and are responsible for seeing that each performance keeps to the director's original intention. Stage managers may also conduct understudy rehearsals. They often work all day and are in the theatre until the lights go out. Stage managers are engaged by theatrical managements for one particular production, or for a repertory season, or occasionally on a more permanent basis.

There is a shortage of trained and experienced stage managers. Many directors start as stage managers. First jobs are the most difficult to find.

Training Full-time stage management courses at drama schools for 2–3 years. Admission to the courses is by interview and only those who are interested in stage management for its own sake or as preparation for work as a producer or director, but not as a stepping-stone to acting, are accepted. As with acting, those who have attended courses accredited by the National Council for Drama Training have the best prospects.

The subjects studied include history of drama and theatrical presentation; literature; the elements of period styles; stage management organization and routine; play study; carpentry; stage lighting; voice; movement; make-up.

NOTE 1: Stage management training does not lead immediately to work in television and films, but, if supplemented with experience, it may do so.

NOTE 2: There are also a very few full-time courses for theatre *electricians* and *sound engineers*.

Personal attributes Organizing ability; natural authority and tact for dealing with temperamental and anxious actors; a practical approach; ability to deal with emergencies from prop-making to mending electrical equipment; calmness during crises; interest in the literary and technical aspects of theatrical production; the ability to speak well – both lucidly and concisely; visual imagination; a genuine desire to do stage management in preference to acting: frustrated actors do not make good, or happy, stage managers.

Late start Should be fair opportunities for people with amateur dramatic experience; maturity helps in a job which involves organizing others.

Work life balance Need to be willing to work all evening and often during the day. A career break should be no problem if good experience before the break.

Work may be sporadic rather than part time.

Further information National Council for Drama Training, 1–7 Woburn Walk, London WC1H 0JJ.
www.ncdt.co.uk
Conference of Drama Schools, PO Box 34252, London NW5 1XJ (for free publication *The Conference of Drama Schools Official UK Guide to Drama Training*, write to address above including 44p s.a.e.).
Local theatre; drama schools

Related careers LAW: *Barrister* – LEISURE/RECREATION MANAGEMENT – SPEECH AND LANGUAGE THERAPISTS – TELEVISION, FILM AND RADIO

Driving Instructor and Examiner

Driving Instructor

Entry qualifications Minimum age 21. 4 years' full (not provisional) car driving licence without disqualification. Registration as an Approved Driving Instructor (ADI).

The work The majority of instructors work on their own. This is more lucrative, but also more precarious, than working for one of the big driving schools. Hours are irregular and long: far more pupils want lessons at lunch time, after work or at weekends than during normal working hours. Most instructors teach between 6 and 12 pupils a day.

Being a good driver is not the most important aspect of instructing: instructors must like teaching and have the natural ability to do so; they must be able to put themselves into the position of a nervous, possibly not very talented, learner. They usually drive all day and every day through the same streets, which can be dull. The attractions of the work are, largely, being one's own boss; developing learners' road sense and driving technique; talking, during lessons, to a variety of people.

Business depends on area: it is essential, before investing in a dual-control car, to find out whether or not the area is already saturated with instructors.

Personal attributes Organizing ability; business acumen; ability to get on with all types of people and to put them at their ease; complete unflappability and fearlessness; some mechanical aptitude; teaching talent; endless patience; ability to criticize tactfully and explain lucidly.

Training Instructors must pass the Driving Standards Agency's 3-part examination: an IT-based theory test (Part 1), a practical driving test (Part 2) and a test of instructing ability (Part 3). Parts 2 and 3 must be completed within 2 years of passing Part 1. Only 3 attempts at each of these two parts are permitted. The syllabus for Part 1 includes road procedure, traffic signs and signals, car control, pedestrians, mechanical knowledge, driving test, disabilities, law, publications and instructional techniques. Part 2 is a stringent test at advanced level. In Part 3 the examiner plays the part first of a new learner and then of a pupil at about test standard. After passing Part 2, trainees are allowed to hold a 6-month training licence and charge for instruction, but they must pass Part 3 before being registered as an Approved Driving Instructor.

Examiners

Driving Examiner

Entry qualifications and training A full, clean and unrestricted licence and at least 5 years' driving experience. Selection includes a theory and hazard perception test, a special driving test and a formal interview. The interview focuses on 4 key competencies: working in a team, providing a quality service, communication, analysis and problem-solving and handling change. Training begins with a 4-week intensive residential course which covers some driving but focuses on learning the assessment and interpersonal skills required. On passing the course, examiners are allocated to a training centre to begin a 9-month probation period.

Traffic Examiner

Entry qualifications and training 5 GCSEs (A–C) or equivalent plus 5 years' relevant experience. Initial training takes place over a 9-month period and is classroom and practical based.

Vehicle Examiner

Entry qualifications and training City & Guilds Motor Vehicle Technicians Part 2 or BTEC/SQA equivalent and at least 4 years' experience in repair, maintenance or inspections of motor vehicles. Initial training follows a similar pattern to traffic examiner (see above).

The work *Driving examiners* are Civil Servants. They work as members of a team under a senior examiner, attached to one of over 400 test centres throughout the country. They test learner drivers of cars and other vehicles to ensure that candidates are competent to drive without endangering other road-users and that they drive with due consideration for other drivers and pedestrians. To do this the examiner takes drivers over an approved route and asks them to carry out various exercises. While doing this the examiner must take notes without distracting the driver's concentration and must make a fair assessment. The work is highly concentrated and, for work as responsible as this, can be fairly repetitive.

Traffic examiners, also Civil Servants, investigate, by observation on the road, by inquiry of operators and by examination of drivers' records, whether laws concerning operation of vehicles (such as the hours a driver may be in charge of a vehicle without rest period) are being observed. Examiners do not have to examine vehicles' mechanical conditions.

Vehicle examiners are employed by the Vehicle and Operator Services Agency to carry out a variety of mechanical testing and inspection tasks, including checking of HGVs; supervising the tachograph scheme; checking operators' maintenance arrangements; inspecting vehicles and preparing reports following road accidents. They may appear in court as expert witnesses.

Personal attributes Air of authority; friendliness; tact; ability to concentrate constantly; unflappability.

Late start Most instructors and examiners have had some other job before; maturity is an asset.

Driving Instructor and Examiner

Work life balance *Instructor* It is possible to have a small number of pupils, but it is never possible to work during school-hours only. Summer months are the busiest time. A career break might mean having to start up again and continued driving would be essential.

Examiners The Civil Service is encouraging the introduction of flexible working in all departments.

Driving tests take place on Saturdays and in the evening during the summer months. As demand for driving tests is variable, the DSA particularly welcomes examiners who are willing to work to a flexible pattern. Driving examiners can opt to work less than full time, in which case their area office will contact them with an offer of work when available.

Further information *Driving instructors and driving examiners*: Driving Standards Agency, Stanley House, 56 Talbot Street, Nottingham NG1 5GU.
www.dsa.gov.uk
Traffic and vehicle examiners: Vehicle and Operator Services Agency, Berkeley House, Croydon Street, Bristol BS5 0DA.
www.vosa.gov.uk

Related careers TEACHING

Economics

Entry qualifications Degree in economics; A level maths or statistics preferred, but not essential, for all courses.

The work Economics is concerned with the organization, utilization and distribution of productive and financial resources, nationally and internationally. This includes the study of political, industrial and social relationships and interactions.

Economics comes under the Social Sciences umbrella (but is not a 'science' in the same sense as physics or chemistry). Economic theories are 'applicable' or 'inapplicable' rather than 'correct' or 'incorrect'. Even if worked out on mathematical models and tested on the computer, premises are based on sweeping simplifications rather than on unassailable facts and figures. Hence the variety of 'schools' of economists (e.g. Keynesian, monetarist), each with different answers to the same economic problems. Economics therefore involves making judgements, choosing to adhere to one set of principles rather than another.

Economists work in a wide variety of settings – in urban and regional planning, in industry, commerce, the City, the Civil Service (the largest employer), in financial and industrial journalism, as organizers or researchers in trade unions and in management consultancies and overseas in development programmes. They try to identify the causes of problems like inflation or traffic congestion and suggest courses of action which might solve or ease the problem. Some economists specialize in, for example, the economics of energy resources, the car industry, agriculture, transport.

Extent of specialization varies enormously. Some economists

become very knowledgeable about a particular aspect or part of an industry; others in an area of economics. One assignment required an economist with a background in the catering industry to suggest sites for and types of new hotels which a major company wanted to build. Work involved research: what makes hotels successful at home and abroad? In what proportion do food, accommodation, hotel location, service, pricing, affect a hotel's profitability? What constitutes 'good' food, accommodation, etc.? The economist spent a year asking questions in hotels – of guests and staff and management – analysing relevant companies' accounts, and then presented the report. Another economist who specialized in 'agricultural economics' prepared a report on measures to improve the productivity of an underdeveloped Third World country. New specializations emerge as society's needs, priorities and problems change. For example, economists in the Civil Service are concerned with all aspects of our lives, from energy conservation to services for the disabled, from monitoring the performance of the higher education system to cost/benefit analysis of a new motorway scheme.

Economists who take jobs as *economists* act as advisers, whatever type of employer they work for. They do not normally take or implement decisions, and they have to be prepared for their advice to be ignored. Economists who want to be involved more directly with the work of the organization that employs them would be wise to go into management in industry or commerce (see MANAGEMENT, p. 351; BANKING AND BUILDING SOCIETY WORK, p. 119; ACCOUNTANCY, p. 41).

An economics degree can be a general graduate qualification; and it can be a 'specialist' qualification – for work in systems analysis, statistics, market research, investment analysis, cybernetics, operational research (see under relevant headings).

Training Most degree courses include, as 'core' studies, micro- and macro-economics. Specializations to choose from include agricultural economics, monetary theory and policy, economics of less-developed countries, public sector management, econometrics, economic forecasting, economic geography, transport studies. Economics can be combined with almost any other discipline including accountancy, geography, computing, law, sociology, languages, maths, philosophy and a physical science. The content of individual courses and the emphasis given to the many aspects of the subject vary greatly from one to another, but quantitative methods are of increasing importance.

Personal attributes Numeracy; interest in political and social affairs; analytical powers; resilience, to be able to persevere when events prove research and theories wrong, and when suggestions are being ignored; ability to explain complex research findings to lay people.

Late start Should be no problem for people who have commercial, financial or similar experience.

Work life balance It is essential to stay in touch during a career break through reading journals, going to meetings and reading reports, etc.
    Freelance working is possible for established consultants.

Further information No central organization.

Related careers ACCOUNTANCY – INFORMATION TECHNOLOGY (IT)/INFORMATION SYSTEMS – INFORMATION WORK – JOURNAL-ISM – MANAGEMENT – MANAGEMENT SERVICES: *Operational Research* – TOWN AND COUNTRY PLANNING

Engineering

ENGINEERING DISCIPLINES

The main *branches* or *disciplines* are:

Mechanical Engineering

Mechanical engineers work in all branches and all functions; they are concerned with the application of the principles of mechanics, hydraulics, thermodynamics, to engineering processes. They have a vast choice of end-product to work with and environment to work in: literally no industry is closed to them; they work in hospitals; in computer manufacture; robotics; all types of research establishments. Engineers who want to help humanity as directly as possible, who want to see the application of their efforts to the alleviation of suffering and discomfort, can work in *medical engineering* (see below); engineers who want to go into technical sales or into marketing, or general management can take their mechanical engineering training into anything from mobile phones to agricultural machinery, oil extraction to food processing.

Civil Engineering

Civil engineering covers the design, planning, construction and main-tenance of, first, the 'infrastructure': transport systems, water supplies and sewage plants; and, secondly, large-scale structures, ranging from oil platforms to power stations. Transport systems include roads, bridges, tunnels, ports and airports. Transport planning and management is another, growing, activity. Providing water supplies may involve building reservoirs; controlling the flow of rivers; ensuring safe drinking water and effective irrigation systems in developing countries; and the disposal and treatment of waste to prevent pollution.

Civil engineers work for local and central government, in industry and for international organizations. Many work as *consulting engineers*, called in by large organizations to design and carry out a project. Others work for civil engineering contractors supervising construction projects and dealing with building contractors; they may also do design work. Many British firms work on overseas contracts.

Structural Engineering

This is a specialized branch of civil engineering. Structural engineers are particularly skilled in non-traditional construction materials and techniques. Those working for civil engineering firms might design large-scale constructions such as grandstands and bridges. Those called in as consultants by architects might design the foundations and skeletal framework of large buildings such as skyscrapers and hospitals.

Environmental Engineering (Heating and Ventilating Engineering/Building Services Engineering)

Environmental engineers are concerned with heating, lighting, acoustics, ventilation, air conditioning, noise and air pollution and its control. They are called in as consultants by civil engineers and architects on building projects from hospital to airport, office block to housing estate, chain store to underground station. This branch straddles mechanical, electrical and structural engineering.

Electrical and Electronic Engineering

The two overlap. Broadly, *electrical engineering* is concerned with the use and generation of electricity to produce heat, light and mechanical power: electrical engineers work in generating stations, distribution systems and on the manufacture of all kinds of electrical machinery from tiny motors for powered invalid chairs to heavy motors for industrial plant. They are also concerned with research into the more efficient use of, and new sources of energy for, electrical power.

Electronics is mainly concerned with *computers, telecommunications, automation, instrumentation and control.*

1. *Computers*: The electronic engineering industry is concerned with producing the machinery – the 'hardware' – which gives house-room to the software, i.e. the programs, and with producing the components and products which 'computer systems' need to perform their tasks. This includes microprocessors, visual display units, printers, etc. (For details of software/programming jobs see INFORMATION TECHNOLOGY (IT)/INFORMATION SYSTEMS, p. 281).

The proportion of design, research and development engineers is greater in electronics than in other branches. (Mechanical, electrical and chemical engineers, physicists, and computer scientists also work in computer manufacture.)

2. *Telecommunications*: Includes, for example, the extension of old-fashioned telephony into 'multi-facility' services such as 'conference calls': facilities for telephone conversations between several participants in different locations; and for 'confravision': centres in various towns equipped with closed-circuit television as well as with 'conference call' services are rented by the hour to business people who then 'hold meetings' with colleagues or customers without having to travel. Other telecommunications developments include optical fibre systems; the extension of radio networks; satellite and cable television.

Telecommunication technologies used in offices and, increasingly, at home, include electronic mail, fax machines and facilities like Ceefax, etc. The Internet generates ever more demand for faster connections and greater security.

3. *Automation, instrumentation and control*: This is concerned with automatic control devices, from the operation of automatic flight control systems in aircraft to nearer-home gadgets such as automatic ovens and central-heating time-clocks, and robotics.

Then there is the vast area of computer-controlled equipment which has become possible as a result of the development of *microelectronics*: the design, development and production of scaled-down, minuscule electronic circuitry – the 'chip'. The chip affects virtually every industrial, commercial, scientific and professional activity but it can do nothing by itself: electronics specialists develop its potential and 'program' (instruct) it to perform the precisely defined task for which it is intended.

Examples are hotel, aircraft and theatre seat reservations; supermarkets (bleeping checkouts that keep the warehouse management informed of the precise level of stock of every item in every store at any time); document storage and retrieval systems (see INFORMATION WORK, p. 295). In manufacturing, 'robotics' – assembly-line work done by programmed robots – is developing fast. Scientific applications include weather-forecasting; computer-aided design in civil and structural engineering; dating archaeological discoveries.

Medical or Biomedical Engineering

Medical engineering is a combination of electronic, electrical and mechanical engineering and physics. The health care industry is one of the world's largest industrial sectors and is expanding, creating a demand for new technology from improved hip replacements to an artificial retina chip which can partly restore lost vision. Medical engineers also design aids for people with severe disabilities, for example artificial replacement limbs or custom-built transport. They work in industry on the design and development of medical devices; in hospitals with medical staff providing non-clinical services; in research; and in government agencies.

Previously medical engineers took a degree in either mechanical, electronic or electrical engineering combined with a post-graduate qualification or work experience, but there are now an increasing number of medical engineering degree courses. Medical engineering is a multi-disciplinary subject which integrates a professional engineering course with a basic knowledge of anatomy, physiology and cell biology. Students may choose to study rehabilitation engineering, tissue engineering – the creation of biological substitutes for the replacement or restoration of tissue function lost through failure or disease – or medical imaging. Some courses have a foundation in mechanical or electronic engineering but others may be more focused on materials engineering or physics.

Medical engineering is often overlooked as an alternative to medicine for people who want to be closely involved with alleviating disabilities.

Chemical Engineering

Chemical (or process) engineers are concerned with the design and development of laboratory processes, and with their translation into large-scale plant, for the production of chemicals, dyes, medicines, fertilizers, plastics, etc. Their expertise in designing and managing plant in which chemical processes take place is also used in food processing, brewing, paper, textile and other industries. Biochemical engineers specialize in the design and development of industrial plant in which biochemical processes can take place (see 'Biotechnology', p. 532), e.g. developing alternative sources of energy and converting noxious waste into useful by-products or at least into harmless substances. Chemical engineering has far wider application than is often believed: many chemical engineers do work in oil refineries and other heavy industry, but there is wide scope elsewhere, for example in textiles and electronics. 'Green' issues are of increasing importance.

Manufacturing Engineering
(see p. 227)

This branch covers all aspects of manufacture. It embraces knowledge of many aspects of engineering and ensures that labour, equipment and materials are used efficiently.

Manufacturing engineers need both technical and 'people management' skills, so that goods of the right quality are produced at the required time at the right price. They plan the production methods and systems (which nowadays often involve computer-controlled tools) and may modify machinery to suit a particular task. They liaise with other departments such as design, R & D, purchasing and sales.

Naval Architecture

Despite the title, the work is engineering rather than architecture. It is concerned with the design, repair, construction and economic operation of craft which float on or under or hover just above the water. Craft can be of any size from sailing dinghy to supertanker, hydrofoil to oil rig. Naval architects work for the armed services as well as for ship- and boat-building firms. A small branch.

Aeronautical/Aerospace Engineering

Concerned with aircraft design and construction and space and satellite research, as well as with planning, operation and maintenance of airlines' fleets of aircraft and aircraft components. They work for aircraft manufacturers, airlines and the Ministry of Defence. This is a small branch of engineering; a greater proportion work in R & D, fewer on production. People who want to work in this area can take electronics or physics degrees and leave more options open.

Agricultural Engineering
(see AGRICULTURE AND HORTICULTURE, p. 71)

Other Branches

Some engineering specializations described elsewhere (or advertised) have different titles from all those mentioned here. They may be small branches, or offshoots of, or options within, established engineering branches. Titles may describe jobs which can be done by people from various disciplines (e.g. in robotics). Or they may describe emerging new branches which are also still under the umbrella of an established branch.

Engineering can no longer be neatly categorized into the traditional disciplines. It is a fast-changing profession, developing as a result of scientific discovery (scientists discover; engineers exploit discoveries and make them work productively as well as in response to need). For example, new sources of energy will be needed in the future: engineers are working on the development of wind, wave and solar energy – and become *energy engineers*. Technological tasks are so complex now that people from various disciplines have to pool their expertise: at the same time, some disciplines are becoming so unwieldy that they sub-divide. That applies specially in *electronics* and *mechanical engineering*. New titles do not have as precise meanings as have traditional engineering disciplines.

Here is a very brief (and superficial) guide to some of the current engineering job-titles and the – probable – umbrella discipline, or function, which should be the first port of call for information on what knowledge is required and what work involved:

Computer systems, control engineering: umbrella discipline – *Electronics*.

Offshore, oil, fuel, energy engineering: umbrella disciplines – *Mechanical*, *Electrical*, *Electronic* or *Chemical Engineering*. (Energy engineering can also describe the energy-saving function in large organizations.)

Nuclear engineering: umbrella disciplines – *Physics* and *Electronics*.

Industrial engineering: umbrella discipline – *Manufacturing Engineering*, but can also be combination of *Management* and *Engineering*.

Process engineering: umbrella discipline – *Chemical Engineering*.

Plant, installation, test and commissioning engineering: umbrella disciplines – could be *Mechanical*, *Production* or *Chemical Engineering*, but also used for functions carried out by *Mechanical* or almost any other specialist engineer.

Qualified engineers are divided into three sections on the Engineering Council's Register: *Chartered Engineer*, *Incorporated Engineer* and *Engineering Technician*.

CHARTERED ENGINEERS

(see p. 231 for Incorporated Engineers and Engineering Technicians)

Entry qualifications For registration see 'Training'. Entry require-ments for accredited degrees are usually 3 A levels or equivalent, generally including maths and a physical science (for Chemical Engin-eering usually maths and chemistry with another science). The grades required differ between universities. Introductory courses for appli-cants with alternative subjects are available at some institutions.

The work Engineering is not so much one career, more an expertise which opens doors into a vast range of jobs. Engineers probably have a wider choice of environment in which to work, and of type of job, than any other professionals.

The purpose of engineering is the design and manufacture of the 'hardware' of life. Engineers have a hand in the creation of anything in use anywhere – from chips (both kinds) to chairs; cable TV to toys; motorways to kidney-machines; robots to milk bottles. They are the wealth creators without whom the country's economy cannot improve, and they are also a type of aid worker: by designing irrigation and similar schemes for the Third World they reduce famine and poverty. So engineering can be the right choice as much for the person who wants to improve the quality of life all round as for the person who wants a prestigious top managerial or professional job.

There is a range of engineering functions (see below), each appeal-ing to different temperaments and talents. Engineers can concentrate on, for example, creative design; on developing ideas, seeing them translated into the end-product and sold at a profit; on managing people and/or resources and/or processes; on research into, say, laser beam applications or into robotics.

Apart from the many aspects of practical 'active' engineering, there is the vital commercial exploitation of ideas and products. Technical sales and marketing (see below) are now often considered the sharp end of the profession, and engineers do well in both these areas.

It is estimated that most engineers spend about one-third of their time discussing work with colleagues, customers or clients, staff, bosses; but there are backroom jobs for loners.

An engineering qualification is much underrated as a way into more glamorous-sounding and more difficult-to-get-into careers – e.g. marketing (see p. 371), industrial management (see p. 351), public relations (see p. 496), television (see p. 620) and other graduate employment. Engineering is, in fact, very much a 'transferable skill' – and that is immensely useful at a time when everybody is likely to change jobs several times in a working life.

Even non-engineering employers who recruit graduates often now prefer science and engineering to arts graduates. Their specific knowledge can be useful in an age when technology has a bearing on virtually any type of business; their analytical approach to problem-solving is invariably useful, even when the problem is not a technical one. So even young people who are not planning to spend their lives as engineers, but want to go into anything from merchant banking to journalism, might well consider taking an engineering degree as a stepping-stone. Engineering need be no more a vocational course than an arts degree.

There are post-graduate courses in business management, systems analysis, transport, etc., which can be taken either immediately after qualifying or a few years later (after the *career break*, p. 237). Courses in 'information engineering' (combining computing and electronic engineering) and 'mechatronics' (combining mechanical and electronic engineering) aim to train engineers to manage computer-based engineering systems.

Job prospects are good on the whole, because engineering is such an adaptable skill; the broader the areas of application of the discipline, the better the prospects; for example, mechanical and electronic engineers are needed in very many more areas of employment than are naval architects. Within electrical, electronic, mechanical and manufacturing engineering it is possible to switch from one branch to another. This usually requires taking a post-graduate course (possibly part time, while working). Many engineers, from any discipline, go into industrial and commercial management (see MANAGEMENT,

p. 351) and into management consultancy (see p. 364). Others, especially electronics engineers, go into information technology (see p. 281). Chartered engineers can become maths, physics and engineering science teachers. There are opportunities in the EU and elsewhere abroad. The title 'European Engineer' (EUR ING) enables greater mobility and recognition for engineers working in Europe. To gain this title, professional engineers must show they have completed a package of degree, training and experience lasting not less than 7 years. Competence in a second European language could improve employment prospects.

Engineers normally specialize in two dimensions: in one *branch* or *discipline*, and then, after training, in one *function*, or type of activity. The main functions within each branch are outlined below.

Design

This is the most creative of the engineering functions and is the core of the engineering process. Design engineers create or improve products which can be manufactured and maintained economically, perform satisfactorily, look good and satisfy proven demand. Looks matter more in consumer goods – microwave ovens, telephones – than, for example, in machine tools. Design engineers may also design a new, or improve an established, engineering process. Most designers work to a brief. For example, a car manufacturer's marketing department may request that next year's model within a given price range should incorporate fuel-saving and/or safety devices (which may have been perfected in Research or which Research may be asked to work on); and that the model should incorporate certain visual features which seemed to 'sell' a competitor's model; design engineers may add their own, totally new ideas.

Their job is to find efficient and economic solutions to a set of problems. They must investigate materials and processes to be used in the manufacture of the product, which means they have to consult experts from other disciplines; but it is the design engineer who specifies what goes into the manufacture of the product and what processes are to be used.

Because the work of design engineers varies so enormously, the job is impossible to define precisely. Designing an aircraft which is a team effort has little in common with adding a feature or two to an established type of machine tool or TV component. Most work is done in 'design offices', where several graduates assisted by technicians work under a *chief design engineer*. Some designing, in electronics for example, is done in the laboratory. CAD – computer-aided design – is now used extensively. An experienced design engineer can choose whether to be part of a team that designs, say, a whole new airport, or whether to work alone on simple, straightforward design.

Personal attributes High academic ability; an urge to put new technologies to practical use; creativity; imagination and interest in problem-solving; ability to coordinate the work of others; interest in marketability of product; ability to work as one of a team or to lead it.

Research and Development (R & D)

In some organizations research and development are two separate departments; in some the two, plus design, go together. But most typically, research and development form one department, with design a separate, but very closely linked one.

R & D engineers investigate, improve and adapt established processes and products, and they may create new ones. The work is essentially experimental, laboratory-based, but the 'laboratory' could be a skid-pan on which new tyre-surfaces are tried out, or a wind-tunnel in which to experiment with aircraft models.

While there is some extending-the-frontiers-of-knowledge kind of research, most engineering research is 'applied', i.e. aimed at maximizing sales and profits; or at saving precious resources; or exploiting newly discovered materials or processes.

Work comes from several sources: *design engineers* may want to use a new material, but they need to know more about its 'behaviour' before using it; *manufacturing engineers* may ask R & D to investigate why there is a recurrent fault in a particular production process or product; the *marketing department* may complain that a particular aspect of a competitor's fridge or mobile phone makes the competitor's product sell better: R & D would investigate the better-selling product, and come up with suggestions. Research and development is very much team work.

Personal attributes Practical bent; high academic ability; imagination; perseverance in the face of disappointing research results; interest in following up ideas which have profitable application; ability to work well with colleagues from other departments; willingness to switch from one project to another if Marketing or Manufacturing have urgent problems.

Manufacturing (previously known as Production)

The manufacturing function broadly covers changing raw materials into all types of articles. This involves the selection of the most suitable material and the application of the manufacturing process and system in order to manufacture the products.

Products can range from pizzas to cars, CDs to beer cans. The engineer must see that labour, equipment and materials are used efficiently and that the product is completed at the correct quality and cost, in the right quantity, at the right time. The work environment could be a huge (and noisy) heavy engineering plant; it can be a large, but very quiet, highly automated workshop.

In the past, manufacturing engineering was usually done by practical people with some knowledge of engineering processes. As manufacturing processes become ever more sophisticated, and as industry has begun to recognize the need for greater efficiency and streamlining, this activity has grown in importance (and status). It is now an important equal of other engineering branches and functions.

Production managers' work has much in common with personnel management: smoothing out problems on the shop-floor before they flare up into disputes; dealing with unions and with staff problems which might affect the department's productivity.

Personal attributes Organizing ability; practicality; ability to get on well with people of all types at all levels in the hierarchy – from operatives to heads of research and managing director; ability to keep calm under pressure and in inevitable crises; liking for being very much at the centre of action and solving problems.

Technical Sales and Marketing

Sales engineers use engineering expertise in a commercial context. They spend most of their time away from the office, meeting people. Selling engineering products ('specialist selling'), which may be selling anything from machine tools to oil rigs, domestic freezers to road maintenance equipment and service, combines sales techniques with technical knowledge. Customers may be lay people to whom the virtues of a product have to be explained, or highly professionally qualified people (more so than the sales engineer, possibly) who ask searching questions about the product's performance and properties. Sales engineers also act as links between prospective customers and manufacturers, passing on criticism of and requests for products and changes. They must find out, for example, what features – design, after-sales service, cost – make a competitor's product sell better in other countries or at home. (See also MARKETING AND SELLING, p. 371.)

Searching out new customers is an important part of selling. Some sales may take months of meetings and negotiating. Sales engineers may travel abroad a good deal, or they may have their own 'territory' near home – it largely depends on the type of product.

Personal attributes Outgoing personality; adaptability to use the right approach with different types of customers; perseverance, and indifference to the occasional rebuff; commercial acumen; interest in economic affairs; communication skills.

Consultancy

This function absorbs significant numbers only in civil and structural engineering, but numbers in other branches – notably mechanical, electronic and production engineering – are increasing. Consulting engineers work in partnerships in private practice, rather like accountants or solicitors. A few set up on their own. Firms vary in organization and extent of specialization. Basically, consultants provide specialist services for clients in charge of large projects who may be public authorities, architects, other engineers or quantity surveyors. Consultants advise, provide feasibility studies, design to a brief, and, sometimes, organize projects. They are not in the construction/manufacturing business but may be in charge of putting work out to contractors and, as their client's agent, may then be responsible for supervising contractors' work, including authorizing payment.

Consultants may specialize: for example, civil engineers may specialize in motorway or in oil rig design, or in traffic management; electronic engineers may specialize in telecommunications or in medical electronics or in instrumentation and systems. Consultants are usually *design engineers* (see above), but as they move up the ladder they spend more time dealing with clients and getting business – i.e. on the commercial side of the job. Some go into or specialize in *management consultancy* (see p. 364). Civil and structural consulting engineers work abroad a lot, especially in the Middle East, usually on contract for a fixed number of years.

Personal attributes As for design engineers, plus a confidence-inspiring manner, persuasive powers for dealing with clients and contractors; for senior jobs: commercial sense.

Other Functions

Apart from these specializations, there are many jobs which are, usually, carried out within one of the main functions. Titles and the work they describe vary. They include *maintenance* (work on employer's premises) and *service* (work carried out on customer's premises), *test, installation, quality assurance, systems, control* engineers. These functions may be carried out by graduates early in their career, they may be top jobs or they may be carried out by technicians (see p. 231).

Considering the need for precision in engineering, job and function titles are often surprisingly vague and can, therefore, be misleading.

Training Although not a requirement to practise in the UK, only engineers registered with the Engineering Council are entitled to call themselves Chartered Engineers. The route to registration has recently changed. In the past this involved meeting set academic requirements. In future Chartered Engineers will have to meet the UK standards for professional engineering competence, known as UK-SPEC, which has been introduced to place more emphasis on the skills and competences engineers have gained through their academic education and experience, rather than the entry qualifications specified for accredited degree courses. Skills and competences may be demonstrated through academic qualifications, experience and training, a professional review and membership of a licensed member organization. Two academic routes are accepted as exemplifying the required knowledge and understanding: 1. an accredited BEng (Hons) degree, plus either an accredited post-graduate Masters or appropriate further learning to Masters level; 2. an accredited integrated MEng degree.

Candidates for registration also have to demonstrate professional competence, either through an industrial placement as part of their degree course, through an employers' accredited graduate training scheme or through developing their own profile of competence. There is no set time requirement.

Applicants who do not have an exemplifying qualification can quality for registration through submitting a technical report based on their experience and demonstrating their knowledge and understanding or by taking Engineering Council exams. With any necessary additional learning and development, an Incorporated Engineer can also register as a Chartered Engineer through submitting a technical report.

There is a Graduate Apprenticeship Scheme for students wishing to integrate work-based learning and higher education study. It is open to school-leavers, Advanced Modern Apprentices, undergraduates, graduates, post-graduates and experienced engineers who need to update their skills.

Applicants without maths and physics A levels can apply for courses which offer a foundation year after which they go on to study for a 3- or 4-year degree.

Sandwich courses are particularly suitable for students wanting to enter industry, as they are able to sample the industrial scene. Some large companies sponsor students for all or part of their course (i.e. pay them while they are studying), who thus gain work experience in that organization. College-based students work for a range of employers during their course. 'Thin' sandwich courses last 4–5 years, alternating 6 months' study with 6 months' work experience. 'Thick' sandwich courses last 5 years, with a year at the beginning and end spent with an employer and 3 years' full-time study in between.

INCORPORATED ENGINEERS AND ENGINEERING TECHNICIANS

Entry qualifications Incorporated Engineer: (For registration see 'Training' below.) 120 new tariff UCAS points for Accredited IEng degree or BTEC/SQA HND; Engineering Technician: in practice normally 4 GCSEs (A–C) including maths and science, and BTEC/SQA (pp. 8, 10). Technicians can also start by training as craftsmen/women through Modern Apprenticeships (see p. 11).

The work The technician scene is very confusing indeed to anyone outside the industry. There are, officially – that is according to the Board for Engineers Registration – 2 levels: *Incorporated Engineers* are those whose work overlaps with graduates and whose breadth of knowledge enables them to take responsibility for a wide range of tasks; *Engineering Technicians* are those who take responsibility for jobs in a more narrowly defined area. In practice, however, the distinction is blurred. The term 'technician' is loosely used to cover a whole range of job levels. Very many 'technicians' jobs are in fact done by graduates. Technicians become 'senior technicians' rather than 'Incorporated Engineers' in some organizations. Some go on to qualify as Chartered Engineers.

Chartered and Incorporated Engineers' work overlaps in all branches, but more in electrical, electronic, mechanical and production engineering than in the others. It also overlaps in all functions (see above) but much less in design and research where graduates' depth and breadth of training, and their creativity, are usually essential. After a few years' work, though, applicants' experience and ability rather than their qualifications count. At that stage, experienced technicians are on a par with *average* graduates (not with high-fliers). Degrees for Chartered Engineers became the normal qualifications about 25 years ago, when new technologies increased the complexities of engineering tasks (and as higher education became more accessible). Degrees or an HND became a requirement for registration with the Engineering Council as an Incorporated Engineer in 1997. But for every engineer who has the chance to make full use of degree-level knowledge – who is, say, responsible for the safe design of an oil rig or for a research project into the application of laser beams in surgery – there are hundreds of engineers whose jobs require sound professional expertise, but not the depth and breadth of knowledge needed for top jobs. Hence the increasing scope for technicians.

Incorporated Engineers have never managed to put themselves across as a professional entity, although in most branches they have their own professional institutions, and, within the engineering profession, they are fully recognized as vital experts in their field and essential colleagues. According to experience and training, they are either left to get on with tasks on their own, or are support staff with limited responsibility (both apply to average graduate engineers as well). Job-titles such as, for example, *plant, project, production, commissioning, development* or *sales* engineer can describe *either* a Chartered *or* an Incorporated Engineer. There is nothing precise about titles and demarcation by qualification in the engineering profession which depends so much on expertise and/or experience.

Work is as varied as that of Chartered Engineers.

Tasks include, for example:

In all branches: *Draughtsmanship* (usually computerized) which may be routine work, but may involve using initiative and special knowledge, and producing working drawings from designers' rough notes and/or instructions; or assisting professional engineers in research, design, development, perhaps building prototypes; *production* (see 'Manufacturing', p. 227): being responsible, for example, for one or several production lines or for continuity of supplies, or dispatch; *estimating*: costing projects or parts of projects; supervision of installation of equipment on customer's premises or in firm's own factory; *repair and maintenance* in anything from garage to hotel, hospital to factory; *after-sales service*: investigating complaints, for example. (Greatest scope in electrical and electronic engineering.)

Settings include:

Broadcasting (see p. 627).

Telephone companies.

Newspaper production.

Hi-fi, television and video servicing.

Commercial recording studios – for example, *balancing engineers* (who must be able to read music and have a good ear) are responsible for producing the required levels of sounds from various sources.

Civil and structural engineering sites – technicians help cost projects; supervise construction work; work out what equipment is required on bridge or road works; liaise with clients and, in municipal work, with local residents. In traffic management they may be in charge of compiling a 'street inventory' prior to the installation of traffic signals (finding out where gas and electricity mains are; what shops/schools and other 'traffic generators' there are) or organize traffic counts. They may also become *building control officers* for local authorities.

In *manufacturing* technicians work at all levels, from monitoring or servicing machinery to, jointly with personnel (see p. 444), working on job evaluation schemes. In *marketing and sales* where (see above) engineering knowledge is only one of the necessary skills, experienced technicians do very well indeed and can rise to the top. Finally, experienced technicians can set up their own workshop/business (see WORKING FOR ONESELF, p. 648).

Engineering

Prospects are good, especially for electronics, electrical and mechanical technicians. Even during recessions the demand for technicians often exceeds supply. Experienced technicians are also often able to get work abroad. Technician training is broadly based and, once trained, technicians can switch type of work.

Personal attributes A practical and methodical approach and an interest in technology are needed in all technician jobs. There is room for backroom types who like to get on with their work on their own, for those who like to work in a team, those who like to work in a drawing office or laboratory, and for those who enjoy visiting clients and customers. For some jobs (the minority) manual dexterity; for others, the ability to explain technical points in plain language and a liking for meeting people.

Incorporated Engineer

Training For registration as incorporated engineer with the Engineering Council (see 'Training' chartered engineer) the exemplifying qualifications are: 1. An accredited BEng in engineering or technology; 2. A BTEC/SOA HND or Foundation degree in engineering or technology plus appropriate further learning to degree level.

Trainee technician route

Advanced Modern Apprenticeships developed by SEMTA, the Sector Skills Council for Engineering and Science, are the recommended work-based route for trainee technicians and craftspeople. Entry can be with appropriate GCSEs (see 'Entry qualifications', p. 231), A levels, Vocational A levels/GNVQs or BTEC certificates or diplomas or SQA equivalents (see pp. 8, 10). Length of training depends on initial qualifications and eventual aim, but leads to an NVQ level 3 in a selected area. It will take a minimum of 3 years of combined theory and practical skills development, but each apprentice follows an individual programme agreed at the start. Engineering Advanced Modern Apprenticeships take 3–4 years to complete while working for an employer and studying part time at college. They involve 3 stages – an introductory stage during which the apprentice develops their training plan, stage 2 which provides a wide range of training in basic engineering skills and a final stage during which the apprentice will complete their on-the-job training for an NVQ/SVQ at level 3.

Many employers offer training programmes for technicians in manufacturing industry which combine theory with practical experience. Length of training varies according to the entrant's qualifications and ambitions. They will normally work towards NVQs/SVQs or BTEC National Certificate or Diploma or SQA equivalent.

Registration with the Engineering Council as Engineering Technician requires an NVQ/SVQ at level 3 or an Advanced GNVQ/GSVQ at level 3, or SQA Group Award or a BTEC National Certificate or Diploma plus at least 3 years' responsible employment with further training.

Full-time college route

Either a 2-year full-time or a 3-year sandwich BTEC National Diploma (or SQA equivalent). With training and responsible experience this can lead to registration as Engineering Technician (as above).

Students can then take a 2-year full-time or 3-year sandwich course for a BTEC/SQA Higher National Diploma.

Entrants with at least 1 relevant A level (usually maths or physics) and appropriate GCSEs (A–C) or GNVQ can go straight into a BTEC Higher award course.

CRAFT LEVEL ENTRY

Average ability in maths, science, technical/practical subjects. Employers normally test applicants' aptitudes. Many ask for a GCSE pass in maths.

Engineering craftsmen/women do skilled work and need sufficient theoretical knowledge to understand the principles behind the operations they carry out and to solve basic problems. They work in all branches and may be in charge of lower skilled workers. Their work, and their scope, is changing as a result of new technologies. First of all, the distinction between craftspeople and technicians is narrowing, with craft-trained people becoming technicians more frequently than in the past; and second, as a result of automation in all engineering spheres, the distinction between the specialist trades is blurring. Traditional crafts or 'trades' continue to be practised, including:

Machine-shop Crafts

Toolmaking: The use of precision machinery and tools to make jigs, fixtures, gauges and other tools used in production work. Apprentices may start in the toolroom, or they are upgraded from other trades.

Toolsetting: Setting of automatic (such as computer/tape numerically controlled) or semi-automatic machines for use by machine operators in mass production.

Turning: Operating lathes which use fixed cutting tool(s) to remove metal/material from a rotating workpiece.

Milling: Operating milling machines where metal/material is removed from a fixed workpiece by rotating cutter(s).

Jig-boring: Highly skilled work in which very heavy articles are machined to a high degree of precision.

Grinding: Obtaining a very accurate finish by removing small amounts of metal with rapidly revolving abrasive wheels. It is also used to sharpen tools.

Fitting

Fitters, whether working in mechanical, electrical or electronic engineering, combine the basic skills of the machine-shop craftsperson with the ability to use hand tools. In production work they may assemble cars, generators, TV sets, etc. They carry out maintenance and repair work on domestic appliances and office machinery either on customers' premises – private houses, factories, offices, etc. – or in workshops. Gas fitters install, service and repair gas-powered domestic appliances or industrial plant; marine engine fitters put together and repair ships' engines, etc.

Craftspeople may switch trades more easily than in the past, as well as learn new ones, but overall prospects are not as good as those for technicians.

Training See Modern Apprenticeships, p. 11.

Craftsmen/women increasingly train under the Advanced Modern Apprenticeship programme, leading to NVQs/SVQs at levels 3–4. There may be opportunity to specialize in one particular craft throughout or to train as a multiskilled craftsperson, spending time in a number of different departments before specializing.

Late start *Chartered Engineers*: Possible for technicians and people with related degrees or at least good, and recently acquired, science A levels.

Technicians: Good opportunities for people who have taken appropriate courses, especially in electronics and related fields or such specialized areas as TV and other electronic equipment servicing.

Craft level: Not advisable.

Work life balance Because of the pace of technological change, a complete gap of even a few years would be difficult to bridge. But there are various schemes for enabling people on a domestic break (mainly women) to keep in touch (see *www.wisecampaign.org.uk*). These include encouraging women to visit their former employers regularly during the break and, on their return, for them to have a 'mentor' or 'industrial tutor' who, in an informal way, helps them to catch up.

There are few part-time jobs at present, but some opportunities for engineers who have specialized or can specialize in computing and related work. Others work on 'one-off' contracts. Job-sharing schemes do not seem to have been tried on any scale, but there is no reason why they should not work.

Position of Women The proportion of women in engineering still remains very low. In 2003 women made up only 2.8% of Chartered Engineers, 1.0% of Incorporated Engineers, 1.1% of Engineering Technicians and 3% of Engineering Manufacturing Modern Apprentices.

There are several initiatives in place to encourage young women to consider engineering careers. SEMTA runs the Insight programme for young women in sixth forms or studying for Scottish Highers which offers successful applicants the chance to spend a week at university, staying in student accommodation and meeting others with similar interests. The programme provides opportunities to find out about different fields of engineering, spend a day with an engineering company and meet other women who have studied and are making successful careers in engineering.

WISE, Women into Science and Engineering, produces a number of publications, provides speakers and runs campaigns to increase awareness of engineering careers amongst young women. (The WISE *Directory of Initiatives* is produced yearly and lists awards, courses, visits and other initiatives on offer to women – available on *www.wise campaign.org.uk*.)

Further information The Engineering Council (for list of individual institutions as well as general information), 10 Maltravers Street, London WC2R 3ER.

www.engc.org.uk

SEMTA, Sector Skills Council for Engineering and Science, Engineering Careers Information Service (ECIS), 14 Upton Road, Watford, Herts WD18 0JT.

www.enginuity.org.uk

Institution of Civil Engineers, 1 Great George Street, London SW1P 3AA.

www.ice.org.uk

For a list of special courses (conversion and technician) for women: Engineering Council, Women's Engineering Society, 22 Old Queen Street, London SW1H 9HP.

www.wes.org.uk

Related careers AGRICULTURE AND HORTICULTURE – ART AND DESIGN – CONSTRUCTION: *Construction Managers* – INFORMATION TECHNOLOGY (IT)/INFORMATION SYSTEMS – SCIENCE – SURVEYING

Environmental Health Officer

Entry qualifications 5 GCSEs (A–C) and 2 A levels. Passes must include maths, English language and 2 sciences; one of the sciences must be at A level. BTEC alternatives (plus English language) may be acceptable.

The work Environmental health officers ensure that people are protected from a wide range of hazards in the environment in its widest sense – houses, shops, workplaces, leisure facilities, the air we breathe, our water supplies. Increasing public concern about the environment is reflected daily in the news: a leak of toxic chemicals; salmonella in eggs; contaminated water supplies; the effects of lead on children living near busy motorway junctions; an outbreak of legionnaire's disease; deaths from contaminated yoghurt; housing unfit through damp for human habitation. Environmental health officers deal with all these problems.

The majority of environmental health officers work in local authorities. Their role is both to advise on safety and hygiene and to enforce legislation. This involves visiting a great variety of sites; a high proportion of EHOs' time is spent out of the office.

EHOs ensure that safe and hygienic standards are met in the preparation, manufacture, transport and sale of *food*. This can mean visiting high-technology plants or market stalls, restaurants or slaughterhouses, to check on the cleanliness of equipment and staff, storage facilities and handling procedures. EHOs have powers to enter and inspect *housing* if they 'have reason to believe that the premises are not fit for human habitation' or they may be called in by the residents. They advise on repairs, improvements and sometimes demolition.

Responsibility for *places of work* overlaps with that of factory inspectors (see p. 253). EHOs check on working conditions, for example sanitary arrangements, overcrowding, temperature, ventilation, lighting and hours of work for juveniles.

Noise, pest control, water and waste, air pollution and *communicable diseases* are also the responsibilities of EHOs. They may also deal with caravan and camping sites, houseboats and leisure boats, swimming pools and leisure centres, and some aspects of animal welfare.

Some EHOs have a general role covering a wide range of responsibilities; others specialize in, for example, food hygiene, housing or atmospheric pollution.

Some work in industry, e.g. food manufacturing.

Training 1. 4-year sandwich degree course. Syllabus includes the basic sciences as applied to environmental health (control of infectious diseases and of vermin, for example); physical aspects of housing (dilapidations, unfitness); public cleansing; water supply; drainage, sewerage and sewage disposal; procedures under Housing Acts; hygiene of buildings (standards of heating, ventilation and lighting); food (hygiene and inspection), etc.

2. 2-year sandwich post-graduate course for graduates with appropriate degree.

The above courses include a period of integrated professional training with a local authority.

3. *In Scotland*. 4-year degree in environmental health at Strathclyde University, in conjunction with 48 weeks' practical training in a local authority, followed by a professional interview for the Diploma in Environmental Health.

Personal attributes Interest in people's living and working environment; ability to take decisions; sufficient self-confidence to go where one is not necessarily welcome, to be firm when necessary and to discuss complicated problems intelligently.

Late start There is scope for late entry, though the older one is, the more difficult it could be to get the necessary practical training.

Degree courses may relax the academic entry requirements for mature entrants.

Work life balance A career break should be no problem for those who keep in touch.

EHOs' major employers, local authorities, are among the most forward-looking on flexible working.

Further information The Chartered Institute of Environmental Health, Chadwick Court, 15 Hatfields, London SE1 8DJ.
www.cieh.org.uk
The Royal Environmental Health Institute of Scotland, 3 Manor Place, Edinburgh EH3 7DH.
www.rehis.org

Related careers HEALTH AND SAFETY INSPECTORS – HOUSING MANAGEMENT – TRADING STANDARDS OFFICER – SCIENCE: *Food Science and Technology*

Environmental Work

Entry qualifications Various but usually at least a first degree.

The work The popular image of environmental work is nature conservation or landscape preservation. But the sector encompasses the sustainable use of all natural resources, including the atmosphere and water. Most employment in environmental work involves supporting both the public and private sector in understanding and meeting increasingly stringent legislation and 'polluter pays' policies being introduced by government and the EU to protect the environment. It is indeed concerned with conservation but this heading covers a huge range of jobs, including the management of water resources, control of air and water pollution, waste management, decontamination of groundwater and soil, environmental risk management, modelling, impact assessment and auditing, energy supply, regeneration and the promotion of sustainable development. In addition there are those who formulate the policies on which much of this activity is based, and provide the research which underpins them.

Some environmental work is now becoming embedded in already established occupations, from farming and forestry to town and country planning. It is also increasingly a specialism within other professions. Major companies may employ specialist lawyers to advise them on environmental legislation or lawyers can specialize in prosecuting offenders against environmental regulations. Education for Sustainable Development is a statutory part of the National Curriculum but qualified teachers can also find employment outside school, for example setting up educational projects with companies or working with local communities to help them improve their environment.

Journalists, too, can specialize in writing about environmental issues, although regularity of work is dependent on the whims of the reading public.

Environmental work in practice is often a balance between enforcing regulations and promoting good practice, whether to a large corporation or to primary school children. The resource to be protected may be a local amenity such as a park or footpath or the very air we breathe and the water we drink. The ability to communicate well with people from all backgrounds is often as important to the job as scientific knowledge as much of the work involves increasing public awareness, explaining the issues involved to groups and individuals, weighing up conflicting interests and making judgements.

The main single employer in the sector is the Environment Agency, responsible for overseeing air and land quality, the regulation of waste management, conservation and ecology especially alongside rivers and coastal areas, and the prevention of flooding. The Agency employs more than 10,000 people across a huge range of specialist areas ranging from soil conservation to public relations. Local government, too, is a major employer, as is the voluntary sector. As the penalties for not complying with regulations can be severe, some large companies are starting to employ specialists to advise on their procedures and ensure that they are meeting legal requirements, though most depend on consultancies. Environmental work is an exciting new field, currently very much driven by legislation, which is changing and developing as new areas of expertise are needed. Much of it is overlapping, for example the management of water resources also involves the prevention of pollution and the protection of the natural environment. Below are some of the main areas of work.

Nature Conservation

It is estimated that the number of jobs in environmental conservation is increasing by 4% a year. The work is mainly concerned with retaining, restoring and improving habitats for wildlife. This includes ongoing work to preserve wildlife species throughout the world, many of which first have to be identified and recorded.

Closer to home, central and local government employs *ecologists* and *conservationists* at all levels, although, even with the expansion in demand, competition for jobs can be intense and many are academically over-qualified for their posts. Some will work on a variety of projects while others, employed as *rangers* or *reserve officers*, will be responsible for a single conservation area.

Competing pressures on the use of land mean that the work can often involve evaluating options and assessing the best use of the funds available. Many new developments require an Environmental Impact Assessment before planning permission is granted and this, along with the growing public interest in conservation and the increasing availability of funding from the National Lottery and the EU, has led to a steady expansion of jobs in this field. Few conservationists are employed in the private sector, although there are an increasing number of large consultancies offering a wide range of expertise who usually recruit experienced staff. The voluntary sector has openings for professional ecologists, often on short-term contracts, which may involve managing volunteers.

Waste Management

Waste management has become increasingly complex over the last few years. In the UK the traditional method of disposal has been to use landfill sites but the volume now involved and new directives from the EU are ensuring an urgent need to develop new approaches, for example creating demand for recycled products, recovering materials and harnessing the by-products of waste such as methane.

The waste management sector is increasingly employing people with scientific and technical expertise and managers with business qualifications. It is divided into three main sectors, those who regulate it – in England and Wales the Environment Agency and in Scotland the Scottish Environment Protection Agency (SEPA) – those who procure waste disposal services, usually county or in Scotland local councils, and those who provide the services. Industry is responsible for disposing of its own waste and often this may mean treatment on site. Finding suitable sites for waste disposal is a function of town and country planning (see p. 635).

Water Resource Management

Despite a drop in industrial use, there is still increasing demand for water and recognition of the requirement to protect the natural environment and this is leading to the need for new approaches to managing supplies. *Water resource planners* may work for the Environment Agency or for water companies, investigating future demand and looking for ways to meet it. *Hydrologists* and *hydrogeologists* provide the technical support on which decisions can be made. *Abstraction licensing officers* process applications to abstract groundwater or water from rivers.

Drinking water treatment and wastewater management employ a range of people: engineers, analytical chemists, biologists and microbiologists as well as regulators and consultants.

Environment Protection

The main employers in this category are the Environment Agency who regulate emissions to air and water in England and Wales and SEPA in Scotland. These agencies are responsible for monitoring the waste of some 7,000 industrial plants and ensuring that water and air quality is maintained. Farmers also have a duty to ensure that silage, for example, does not pollute local rivers or waterways and have to be supported and monitored. Environment Agency officers may work in multi-functional teams, with staff from related fields, and interpersonal skills and the need to be able to influence and negotiate are important.

Sub-surface – that is groundwater and soil – contamination is an area in which there has been enormous growth in demand for suitably qualified professionals. Until 5 years ago protection of this environment was largely voluntary but science-based regulations are now being introduced, resulting in a rapid expansion of consultancies in this field.

Training In a sector which overlaps with so many others and which is still developing it is still possible to enter environmental work from a variety of backgrounds. However, a degree in environmental science or geography or biology, usually including elements of ecology and biodiversity, is a good starting-point. Many entrants have post-graduate qualifications.

Some of the large consultancies may offer graduate training but ecologists taken on by organizations new to the field can find themselves defining their own jobs and responsible for gaining the knowledge and skills required.

There are a large number of Foundation degrees, reflecting the rapidly increasing need of employers for staff qualified in different aspects of environmental work. Course titles range from Wildlife and Countryside Conservation to Renewable Energy Technologies.

NVQs are also available in Environmental Conservation at level 2 and 3. These can be completed as part of a Modern Apprenticeship in Environmental Conservation or achieved through work-based training. NVQs are also available in Conservation Control at level 4 and in Conservation Consultancy at level 5.

The Chartered Institution of Water and Environmental Management (CIWEM) offers Certificate and Diploma courses, which can be taken through distance- or block-learning. Part 1, leading to the Certificate, provides a broad-based course with modules on environmental systems, environmental quality, environmental policy and regulation, and environmental management at post-graduate level. Part 2, leading to the Diploma, offers options in specialist areas. CIWEM also offers courses in practical environmental management, in partnership with Groundwork.

The Institute of Environmental Management and Assessment offers a number of short professional courses in environmental management systems and also a foundation course in environmental management.

Recently 10 professional institutions with a focus on the well-being of the environment came together to set up the Society for the Environment (SocEnv). The society is seeking chartership status and aims to introduce the title Chartered Environmentalist for professionals with suitable experience and qualifications. Further information can be found on *www.socenv.org.uk*.

Voluntary work is a recommended way to gain experience of dealing with people and to learn skills, for example the identification of species.

Personal attributes A committed interest in the care and conservation of the natural environment; an ability to work on own initiative; good communication and influencing skills; a willingness to seek and develop new approaches and solutions.

Late start This is a field in which experience can be more important than qualifications so may be possible for those from the right backgrounds.

Work life balance Career-breaks and flexible working should not be a problem for those employed by central or local government. Part-time work should be possible in conservation but may be more difficult in environmental management. Short-term contract work may be possible and, for those with experience, consultancy is an option.

Further information Chartered Institution of Water and Environmental Management, 15 John Street, London WC1N 2EB (publishes *Environmental Careers – The Inside Guide* – see *www.environmental-careers.info*).
www.ciwem.com

Institute of Environmental Management and Assessment, St Nicholas House, 70 Newport, Lincoln LN1 3DP.
www.iema.net

Lantra, Lantra House, NAC, Kenilworth, Warwickshire CV8 2LG.
www.lantra.co.uk

Related careers AGRICULTURE – ENVIRONMENTAL HEALTH OFFICER – LANDSCAPE ARCHITECTURE – LEISURE/RECREATION MANAGEMENT – TOWN AND COUNTRY PLANNING

Fashion and Clothing

The fashion and clothing industry is one of the largest in the country. Even at its highest fashion end it is concerned with business, not art. The vast majority of the industry is concerned with producing garments that large numbers of people want to wear, at a price they can afford. In the UK about three-quarters of production is for high street chain stores, with the retailers closely involved at all stages to ensure the right look and the right quality for their markets. Increasingly fashion and clothing is an international industry. Designs may be produced, patterns and lay plans developed, fabrics 'sourced' and garments made with each stage taking place in a different country; the finished garments may then be sold through shops in many parts of the world.

Entry qualifications Vary according to level and type of training.

Main Sectors of the Industry

In *haute couture*, garments to an exclusive design are cut and made up for individual customers almost entirely by hand. *Up-market ready to wear* follows couture trends but makes more garments in more sizes for sale through exclusive shops. These are the glamour end of the market, but are extremely small. They are fairly insignificant in employment terms, though not in influence.

Most employment opportunities are in the mass-production sector. It covers a huge variety of garments for different markets and for a multitude of purposes: clothing is about far more than fashion.

Womenswear is the largest sector of the market, but *menswear* has become very much more fashion-conscious, as has *childrenswear*, a growing area with its own special demands from babywear to teenage fashion (and still including a significant amount of school uniform). *Leisurewear*, including dancewear, sportswear and ski-wear, is a very lively market that has been enormously influenced by the development of special fabrics and finishes.

Workwear is a varied sector of the market, ranging from simple overalls for canteen staff to heavy-duty specialist protective clothing, e.g. for the chemical industry and oil rig workers. The technical and design problems for specialist applications may be very complex and must usually take health and safety legislation into account. *Uniforms* (for the police, armed services and so on) are a specialized sector of workwear and range from dress uniforms to gas-tight suits. *Corporate wear* (e.g. for bank, airline and hotel staff) is a growing market.

The work Very few *designers* become 'names' in *haute couture* or up-market ready to wear (or in 'diffusion ranges', which are good-quality wholesale production of designer name garments and have successfully brought good design down market in the last few years). Some young designers set up on their own, designing and making clothes for boutiques (sometimes their own), perhaps occasionally getting orders from store buyers. Most work in wholesale manufacturing, where high fashion is adapted for the high street.

Designers do not work in isolation but as members of a team with fabric designers or buyers, marketing specialists, production specialists, buyers from retail outlets. Very rarely is design an artistic 'gut feeling'. It is marketing-led, based on research. The designer almost always works within a trend (e.g. an ethnic influence) and within a firm's particular 'hand-writing', incorporating both into garments which will sell to a given type of market (e.g. trendy, classic, young, elegant, country). The designer's skill is in adapting something for a new market, making it look fresh while retaining the features that made it popular.

Different kinds of garments present different kinds of design challenges. For example, the designer of uniforms for paramedics is not concerned with high street trends but with considerations like how the garment will stand up to the weather, how to make sure it will not get in the way of the wearer's work, how to make it as hygienic as possible.

Some designers do their own pattern cutting, or it may be the job of a specialist *pattern cutter* or *technologist*. Pattern cutters cut an accurate pattern from which the 2-dimensional designer's sketch can be formed into a 3-dimensional sample garment.

Garment technologists are the bridge between design and manufacture. They take the sample and plan the way in which the garment will be made. They decide on, for example, what thread will be used, what seam and stitch types, what machinery will be needed, the costs at every stage. Sometimes a design proves too complicated or expensive, so the garment technologist will work with the designer to reach a compromise, perhaps changing some details in a way which will reduce the number and complexity of the manufacturing operations but still retain the designer's concept. Some garment technologists work for the large retailers, ensuring that the designs, quality and costs meet the retailer's specifications.

When the design is finalized, it returns to pattern cutters, who will return it to a 2-dimensional pattern suitable for mass production. A *pattern grader* then takes a standard size pattern and makes patterns to fit a range of different sizes. *Lay planners* work out how to place the pieces on the fabric in the most economical way. All these processes now make extensive use of computers.

The *production manager* is in charge of working out and managing production flow systems, ensuring that the manufacturing process, once it is broken down into a number of operations, will run smoothly, without bottlenecks, and keeping all the operators and equipment evenly busy.

The clothing industry invests very heavily in sophisticated machinery, so *engineers* are very important, ensuring that the machines are working effectively and advising on crucial investment decisions.

This industry is extremely varied. Job titles and functions are not clear-cut. People with different titles can be doing the same job and vice versa. People with different levels of qualifications can also be doing the same job. In smaller companies an individual may carry out several elements of the design/production process; in a larger company he or she may specialize in one particular function. There are also a number of liaison roles between retailers, designers and manufacturers.

Training There is a wide range of courses available at a number of levels. Titles include: textiles/fashion; fashion; clothing technology; fashion design with technology; design (fashion); fashion technology; knitwear design. Course title is little indication of course emphasis and content; for example, one BTEC HND in fashion/fashion marketing focuses on the design and development of leisure and sportswear garments with career options ranging from creative design to fashion forecasting. Another, in clothing technology, offers work experience in local manufacturing companies *and* TV and theatre wardrobe departments. Basically, most courses will include elements of design, pattern technology, garment technology, production management, business studies and raw materials. The balance and emphasis will differ, but most lead to a range of overlapping jobs. Some graduates start work at a lower level than their qualifications would seem to warrant, but they should be able to find a way up with experience. People who start with modest qualifications can also work their way up; prospects are better on the production than on the creative side.

Courses available:

1. Post-graduate degrees and diplomas: 1–2 years, full time or sandwich; entry requirements – degree or equivalent.

2. Degrees: 3–4 years, full time or sandwich; entry requirements – 2 or 3 A levels plus supporting GCSEs *or* BTEC National Diploma *or* Foundation course or Scottish equivalent.

Foundation degrees: 2 years. No entry requirements set and can lead on to an honours degree.

3. BTEC/SQA Higher awards: 3 years full time for the Diploma, 2 years part time for the Certificate; entry requirements – 1 A level and 4 GCSEs (A–C) *or* Vocational A level/Advanced GNVQ *or* level 3 NVQ or National Diploma or Scottish equivalent.

4. BTEC/SQA national awards: 2 years full time; entry requirements – 4 GCSEs (A–C) *or* Intermediate GNVQ or level 2 NVQ (see p. 10 for SQA equivalent).

5. Engineering: a few specialist degrees but other engineering qualifications suitable (see p. 216).

6. NVQs/SVQs are available at levels 1 to 3. No formal entry requirements.

Foundation and Advanced Modern Apprenticeships are available. Local colleges may offer City and Guilds courses at craft and operative level.

Personal attributes Depends on particular job. *For top-level designers*, visual imagination, creative genius *and* exceptional business flair. *For others*, visual imagination and colour sense; adaptability; willingness to discipline creative flair to the technical and economic necessities of design for a popular market; self-confidence; some manual dexterity; ability to work as part of a team. *For production specialists*, interest in the technology of fashion; organizing ability; creative approach to problem-solving; eye for detail; ability to delegate and deal with people.

Late start Depends on talent and drive. Competition from young college leavers is very stiff.

Work life balance Career-break may be possible. *Designers*: Depends on how established before break. *Production*: Probably no problem for those who have had good experience before the break. Changing technologies can easily be coped with by well-trained production managers.

Part-time work not usual, except as freelance designer or, very occasionally, as relief (holiday) cutter, etc.

Further information Skillfast-UK, 80 Richardshaw Lane, Pudsey, Leeds, LS28 6BN.
www.skillfast.uk.org

Related careers ART AND DESIGN – JOURNALISM – PHOTOGRAPHY – PUBLIC RELATIONS – TELEVISION, FILM AND RADIO

Health and Safety Inspectors

For *factory* and *agricultural inspectors*, normally an honours degree in any subject; for agricultural work, a relevant subject may be preferred. GCSE (A–C) in maths and a driving licence essential. For *specialist inspectors*: normally a good degree, several years' industrial experience and a professional qualification where relevant (e.g. Chartered Engineer).

The work The Health and Safety Executive is concerned with minimizing death, injury and disease stemming from work activities. Inspectors, who are civil servants, are concerned with the health, safety and welfare not only of workers, but of any of the public who may be affected by their work. They have a role in investigating major disasters where the public was placed at risk, but most of their work deals with prevention. They act as advisers, investigators, enforcement officers and sometimes prosecutors, collecting evidence and preparing and presenting cases. They deal with everything from a small workshop where disabled people may make toys to safety on offshore oil rigs.

The majority of inspectors are *factory inspectors*. They cover a large range of industries and workplaces, not only factories but, for example, hospitals, construction sites, shipyards, offices and shops. Depending on where they work, factory inspectors may deal with a limited number of industries or with a broad range. *Agricultural inspectors* are concerned with agricultural, horticultural and forestry establishments. There are also specialist inspectorates for railways, offshore safety, nuclear installations, mines and explosives.

Generally the work may be divided into 3 types or levels. Inspectors are the 'GPs' who carry out the day-to-day work, visiting sites across the whole range of industry to ensure that conditions, machinery and equipment, procedures and safeguards meet the requirements of legislation. For particular problems inspectors may call on the advice of specialists (analogous to consultants in medicine) who may be experts in very narrow areas. When required, Health and Safety Laboratories provide sophisticated research, investigation and analysis.

Inspectors are out of the office for as many as 3 days a week. They have considerable freedom to plan their work.

Training 2-year post-entry programme combining work experience and formal training leading to a post-graduate diploma in occupational health and safety.

Personal attributes Self-reliance; interest in technical matters and in people; diplomacy; ability to get on well with all kinds of people at all levels in the work hierarchy; fitness; initiative; ability to take responsibility; ability to communicate easily; curiosity.

Late start Very good opportunities. People with experience are needed, especially as the work is expanding. Track record may make up for lack of academic qualifications; each case is treated on its merit. Specialist inspectors always have previous experience.

Work life balance Inspectors are civil servants, see p. 158.
Flexible working arrangements available, such as part time and job-sharing, once training completed. Employees with domestic caring responsibilities who need to take time out from work, can apply for unpaid career breaks of 6 months to 5 years. To deal with emergencies, special leave, paid and unpaid, is available depending on certain conditions.

Further information Health and Safety Executive, St Hugh's House, Trinity Road, Bootle, Merseyside L20 3QY.
Helpline: 0151 951 3366
www.hse.gov.uk

The Private Sector

Many firms have their own safety officers whose job, broadly, is to ensure that all legal requirements are being met, and to advise management generally on all aspects of health and safety in the organization. There are no specific requirements for this work. Some practitioners are former health and safety inspectors or environmental health officers (see p. 239). The National Examination Board in Occupational Safety and Health offers certificates and diplomas leading to membership of the Institution of Occupational Safety and Health. Study is by part-time, block-release or distance-learning.

Further information Institution of Occupational Safety and Health, The Grange, Highfield Drive, Wigston, Leicestershire LE18 1NN. *www.iosh.co.uk*

Related careers ENGINEERING — ENVIRONMENTAL HEALTH OFFICER — SCIENCE

Health Services Management

Entry qualifications Entry is at all educational levels. There are formal training schemes for those with A levels or degrees. There is also direct entry with relevant professional qualifications and experience, and some managers move over from the clinical side.

The work Health services managers provide the framework within which patients are treated by doctors and other clinical and paramedical staff. Their wide range of responsibilities includes strategic planning; financial and human resource planning; the maintenance of buildings; the purchase and control of supplies and equipment; personnel management; contracting support services such as laundry, catering, and other patient services.

Most jobs are with hospitals or community units, e.g. for the elderly or mentally ill. Work varies according to the size and structure of the unit as well as the individual manager's specific job. Thus one manager might be working on improving services to the ethnic community, arranging for translators and seeking advice on cultural expectations, while another works on the funding of a new consultant's position – what paramedical and other support staff will he or she need, when and where can an out-patient's clinic be fitted in, what about extra equipment? Increasingly managers work in interdisciplinary teams (including doctors and other professional staff) to plan and develop new services, implement change (which is caused not just by legislation and reorganization but by medical and technological advances, changing population and so on), and manage staff, budgets and facilities. Negotiating skills are essential since resources are finite and various interests often conflict; for example, the cost of advances in one clinical speciality might mean a reduced budget in another.

Regional officers of the NHS Executive have a strategic role. They are responsible for long-term financial and manpower planning and helping to develop the role of the other tiers of the structure. Traditionally, able, ambitious managers moved from unit to district to regional management, but the NHS changes have upset that pattern. For example, to head a Foundation Trust, with the new management freedom and demands, might offer a more attractive challenge. At local level responsibility for health provision is now devolved to Primary Care Trusts on which Health Authority representatives work with local healthcare and social care professionals.

New careers for managers are emerging in primary care. GPs employ practice managers to run their practices. This may involve managing financial systems and monitoring contracts.

Careers in health service management are not confined to the NHS. It is increasingly common for people to move between the private and voluntary health service sectors and the NHS, and there is also increasing exchange between the social services and the health services. The large pharmaceutical and health supplies companies also look to recruit managers who have a good understanding of the health service.

Training Training opportunities are both considerable in number and different in kind. They are multi-level and multi-mode. Schemes may be run nationally, regionally, by commissions and by larger trusts. Entry qualifications include degrees, A levels and, for lower-level administrative work which can nevertheless lead to management, GCSEs. Trainees can work towards post-graduate qualifications (including MBA and diplomas in management); relevant business/professional qualifications (e.g. in finance, personnel, purchasing); Institute of Healthcare Management award. There is an increasing number of undergraduate degrees in health studies. Modes of study include full-time pre-entry courses, work-based training, day-release, distance-learning and open learning. There is now a level 4 Diploma in Practice Management. An individual's choice may be influenced not only by personal preferences and circumstances, but by what provision is available locally and the needs of a particular employer.

The NHS General Management Training Scheme (*NHS GMTS*) is intended to groom candidates for rapid promotion to senior management. Entrants must have a degree or acceptable professional qualification; in-service candidates may also apply. The scheme, which normally takes 24 months (though there is flexibility), combines work placements with formal management training. The training leads to a post-graduate Diploma in Care Management and an NVQ level 4 in management. A financial management and human resource management training scheme is also available (see *www.future leaders.nhs.uk*).

In-house and external schemes are available for employees of the NHS who wish to develop management skills and the launch of NHSU, the NHS corporate university, will increase the range of learning opportunities (see *www.nhsu.nhs.uk*).

In Scotland: Scotland has its own training schemes for health services managers. Major schemes for graduates and suitably qualified internal candidates are in general management, financial management, supplies management.

Because so many qualifications are appropriate and training opportunities exist at many levels, anyone interested should contact the regional health authority.

The Institute of Healthcare Management also provides continuing professional development to help managers adapt to the rapid changes and new developments going on in the health service.

Personal attributes Numeracy; flexibility; ability to discuss complex issues with specialists at all levels; organizing ability; ability to work as member of team; communication and negotiating skills; commitment to patient care.

Late start Good opportunities for those with appropriate qualifications and experience – the NHS does recruit managers from outside, usually from other parts of the public sector. The flexible training opportunities, for example the MESOL (Management Education

Scheme by Open Learning) programme (for those already in the health service) which offers three modes of study leading either to Open University or to IHSM qualifications, make the transition to or progress in health services management easier.

Work life balance The NHS is strongly advertising its commitment to flexible working, including part-time, job-sharing and term-time working. Staff are encouraged back after career breaks.

Further information Institute of Healthcare Management, 46–48 Grosvenor Gardens, London SW1W 0EB. *www.ihm.org.uk*

Related careers ACCOMMODATION AND CATERING MANAGEMENT – CHARTERED SECRETARY AND ADMINISTRATOR – HOTEL AND CATERING – MANAGEMENT

Hotel and Catering

Entry qualifications All educational levels. Considerable *graduate* entry. See 'Training', below.

The work The industry can be divided into two areas, *commercial services* and *catering services*. Under *commercial* come hotels – vast number of small ones, small number of large and/or luxury ones, motels, clubs, pubs and restaurants. *Catering services* include what is traditionally called institutional management: the provision of meals in schools and colleges, hospitals, etc., as well as industry, local and central government, passenger transport. Contract caterers may work in either area. There is not necessarily any greater difference between jobs in commercial and in non-profit-making catering than there is between individual jobs *within* each area.

Catering skills are highly transferable and there is considerable overlap between the different sectors. But for senior hotel management, experience in food and drink services as well as in accommodation services is necessary; for non-residential catering, experience of accommodation services is *not* necessary.

Job titles often tell one very little: 2 jobs with the same title may involve totally different tasks and levels of responsibility. Much depends on the size of establishment and the level of service it provides. It is an industry in which it is still possible to start at the bottom and, with aptitude, hard work and willingness to gain qualifications, reach the top and/or start one's own business.

In senior management, work often overlaps with other managerial jobs and involves less contact with the public (the reason which brings most entrants into this industry). Senior managers in a fast food chain may, for example, work entirely at head office with visits to units where they meet customers; in industrial catering they may be responsible for a group of catering units, visiting individual managers and liaising with head office; or they may investigate the latest 'catering systems' (see below).

The majority of catering jobs involve working when customers are at leisure, as do so many jobs in service industries. This can make a 'normal' social life difficult at times, but there are compensations to be had in being able to shop, play sport, etc. at less crowded times.

Success in most management jobs depends largely on motivating others to do their jobs well, and on efficient utilization of equipment and deployment of staff.

As in other industries, technology is 'de-skilling' some jobs and introducing new skills in others. Large industrial and institutional catering concerns and some chain restaurants increasingly use *systems catering* or *catering systems* instead of letting the chef decide what is for dinner and then getting the staff to prepare the meal. There are variations on the catering systems theme, but broadly this is how it works. Market research (see pp. 57, 371) identifies the most popular dishes within given price-ranges for given consumer-groups. Dishes are part- or fully prepared, and sometimes even 'trayed up' in vast production kitchens. Then they are transported, frozen or chilled, to the 'point of consumption', which may be many miles away. Finally, at the point of consumption, food is 'reconstituted', perhaps in a microwave oven. An example of this new technology is in a large hospital: here patients' food is put into covered trays similar to those on an aircraft; different materials are used in different sections of the tray so that when they have been transported from the kitchens the hot dishes can be heated up in large ovens in ward kitchens while the cold food, such as salad, stays chilled.

Managers must understand the technologies involved and their effects on ingredients, and they must be good organizers.

Hotel Manager

The work The manager's work varies enormously according to size and type of hotel. In large hotels, the general manager is coordinator and administrator, responsible for staff management, marketing and selling, financial control, provision of services, quality control and customer care. Departmental managers are in charge of specialist services: reception, sales, food and bar service, housekeeping, banqueting, etc. The manager deals with correspondence, has daily meetings with departmental managers and may be in touch daily or weekly with head office. Although managers try to be around to talk to guests (not only when they have complaints), most of their time is spent dealing with running the business side, making decisions based on information obtained from the accountant, personnel manager, sales manager, food and beverage manager, etc.

Managers do not normally have to live in, though they may have a bedroom or flat on the premises. Working hours are long, and often busiest at weekends and during holidays. They must be able to switch from one task to another instantly, and change their daily routine when necessary – which it often is.

Among managers' most important tasks: creating and maintaining good staff relations, as success depends entirely on the work done by others under their overall direction; giving the hotel the personality and the character which either the manager, or more often the owner, intends it to have; and being able to make a constantly changing clientele feel as though each of them mattered individually. However, the extent of emphasis on personal service varies according to the type of hotel.

In small hotels the manager may have a staff of about 15 to 30, and instead of several departmental managers, possibly 1 general assistant. Living in may be necessary, and off-duty time may be less generous than in large hotels. There are *far* more small (and unpretentious) hotels than large or small luxury ones. Many small and medium-sized country hotels are owned by companies and run by couples.

General Assistant – Assistant Manager

The work This varies according to the size and type of hotel. In small hotels, assistant managers help wherever help is needed most – in the kitchen, in the bar, in housekeeping. Although the work is extremely hard, it is the best possible experience – an essential complement to college training.

In large hotels, assistant managers may be the same as departmental managers (see above). They may take turns at being 'duty manager' available to deal with any problem that occurs on a particular shift. Trainee managers may spend some time as assistants in different departments before deciding to specialize.

Personal attributes *For top jobs*: Exceptional organizing ability and business acumen; outgoing personality; the wish to please people, however unreasonable customers' demands may seem; an interest in all the practical skills – cooking, bar-management, housekeeping, etc.; willingness to work while others play; ability to shoulder responsibility and handle staff; tact.

For assistants/managers of small hotels: Partly as for managers, but exceptional organizing ability is not necessary; instead, a liking for practical work is essential, and willingness to work hard and get things done without taking the credit.

Receptionist/'Front Office'

The work The reception desk is always near or at the entrance to the hotel. Receptionists are always at the centre of activities. Since they are usually the first contact guests have with the hotel on arrival it is essential that they make a good impression.

Head receptionists are assisted in large and medium-sized hotels by junior receptionists. They check bookings and deal with inquiries over the telephone or by post. To steer a course between unnecessary refusal of bookings and over-booking is skilled work. Receptionists deal with correspondence; they must be able to do straightforward book-keeping, type and compose their own letters: they notify other hotel departments of arrivals and departures, and keep the customers' accounts up to date. Almost all hotels have computerized reservations and accounts systems, which give instant information on a whole hotel group's vacancies, on guests' accounts, and possibly on the supply position regarding clean linen, beverages, etc. Reception also acts as general information office: staff answer guests' queries about, for example, train times, local tourist attractions or the address of a good hairdresser.

Receptionists work shifts, for example from early in the morning to mid-afternoon or from mid-afternoon to late at night. Especially in country hotels, they may live in; meals on duty are supplied free.

Head receptionists are usually responsible directly to the manager; theirs is considered one of the most important posts in the hotel business and can be a stepping stone to general management.

Personal attributes A friendly, helpful personality; an uncritical liking for people of all types; a good memory for faces – visitors appreciate recognition; ability to take responsibility and to work well with others; considerable self-confidence; a methodical approach; a liking for figures; meticulous accuracy; especially in tourist areas, modern language skills. *For top jobs*: Business acumen; good judgement of people; leadership.

Housekeeper

The work Except in small hotels, housekeepers do not do housework, but supervise domestic staff (mainly room-service attendants, formerly called chambermaids). Other duties include: checking rooms, seeing that they are clean, comfortable and that all the amenities are working (e.g. tea-makers and fridges); supervising laundry and ordering linen; pass-key control; room-service organization and supervision; liaison with other departments such as reception and maintenance; training and engaging staff and arranging work schedules. In a large hotel a head housekeeper may be in charge of a staff of 200.

In small and medium-sized hotels the housekeeper may be responsible for choosing and maintaining the furnishings, decoration and general appearance of bedrooms and lounges. In large hotels there may be one assistant or floor housekeeper to every floor, or every two floors; the executive housekeeper, who is immediately responsible to the manager, therefore has considerable overall responsibility.

Personal attributes Organizing ability; practical approach; an eye for detail; ability to handle and train staff.

Hotel Sales Management

A fringe hotel management career. Hotel sales managers work for large hotels and hotel groups. They sell 'hotel facilities' – efficiency, service, atmosphere, as well as conference and banqueting facilities. A hotel sales manager working for a group may approach large business concerns and try to fix contracts for business executives to stay regularly at the group's hotels. Jointly with tour operators (see TRAVEL AGENT/TOUR OPERATOR, p. 642) and airlines, etc., they build package tours.

Hotel sales managers come either via hotel management, or marketing (p. 371) or any other type of business experience.

Personal attributes Business acumen; numeracy; extrovert, friendly personality.

Restaurant Management

Eating places range from wine bars to large 'popular' and to exclusive *haute cuisine* restaurants. Restaurant managers must know how to attract and keep customers.

Catering for fluctuating numbers of customers with the minimum of waste is a highly skilled job, as is arranging staffing rosters to cope with busy periods without being over-staffed in slack ones.

Managers' responsibilities vary greatly according to type and size of restaurant. For example, if the restaurant is one of a chain, overall planning and ordering may be done at head office; in other places the manager may be given a very free hand to 'give the restaurant that personal touch', as long as menus keep within a given price-range and reach the profit target. The responsibility for menu-planning is usually the chef's (except in chain restaurants), but the manager must have considerable understanding of food and also of wine.

According to type of restaurant, managers spend varying amounts of time on 'customer contact'. Chef-proprietors have to spend some time away from their kitchens talking to customers. Except in lunch-only restaurants, working hours, though not necessarily longer, are more spread out, with some evening and weekend work.

Professional Cooks

Cooking always involves some physically hard work – the busier the kitchens, the tougher the job often is. Even with modern design and equipment, kitchens still tend to be hot, noisy and damp, and at times very hectic.

There are a variety of openings at various levels of skill and responsibility. For example, in large-scale *haute cuisine*, a chef heads a hierarchy of section chefs or *chefs de partie*, each responsible for one area of activity – larder, vegetables, pastry, etc. The chef may be responsible for budgeting, buying, planning – or this may all be done by a food and beverage manager, or at head office; responsibilities depend on type and size of organization worked for. In small restaurants, 2 or 3 cooks may do all the work. In simpler restaurants, convenience foods are used extensively and the cook's ability to produce palatable, inexpensive yet reasonably varied menus is the most important aspect of the work. It is no easier than, but very different from, *haute cuisine*. Production kitchens (see p. 261) leave little scope for creative cooking; every dish is prepared to recipes specifying such details as the size, weight, colour and often even the position on the plate of meat or cucumber slices, of sprouts or strawberries. But in experimental kitchens where new dishes and technologies are tried out, the work combines creative cooking skills, an understanding of the effects on the ingredients of being prepared in these unorthodox ways and, above all, managerial skills. There is also scope for creativity in small proprietor-run restaurants.

In large kitchens there are many cooking jobs without managerial responsibilities, but anyone who wants to progress beyond the kitchen-hand stage must take systematic training; home-cooking experience is not enough.

It is important to distinguish between courses for professional cooks, largely run by colleges of further education and some universities, and for *haute cuisine* for home cooking, mainly found in private schools. Cookery classes and schools do not always make this difference clear.

Freelance Cooks

Many people, both those professionally trained and gifted amateurs, make a living by freelance cooking. Clients range from company directors hosting lunches for a dozen clients to individuals wanting someone to cook for dinner or cocktail parties at their home. Some cooks specialize in party food for large or small gatherings. They need their own car or van to transport equipment and shopping. They must be able to budget and cook within various price-ranges.

Sometimes they cook for families on holidays abroad, or for travel agents' chalet-party package tours, working in ski resorts all winter, at the seaside all summer. This type of work usually includes general housekeeping.

Food and Drink Service – 'Waiting'

Food service can range from working behind a self-service food counter to highly skilled 'silver service' in a directors' dining-room or luxury hotel. *Beverage service* includes working behind a bar in a hotel or public house and, as *wine waiter*, helping a customer choose a suitable wine. Like cooking, waiting is at times physically hard and hectic, although the working environment is usually much pleasanter. In a restaurant the quality of the meal service is often as important to the customer as the quality of the food and can help to make or break its reputation.

Fast Foods

The products of this expanding part of the industry range from fish and chips to curry, pizzas to hamburgers. Outlets may be independent businesses, part of a large chain or franchises (the parent company, or franchisor, supplies materials and services and the right to use a trade name, in return for which the franchisee invests capital and pays a levy). Some sell takeaway food only, others also provide table service; all resemble small food-factories with a retail counter. All operations can be learnt quickly and staff often take turns cooking and serving; most chains train 'on the job' and in their own training centres. In what is very much a young person's environment, promotion from school-leaver entrant to supervisor level can be rapid. Management posts are filled either by very successful supervisors or by people with degrees or diplomas in catering, business studies or even arts subjects. The latter have to learn all the basic operations at first hand before undergoing management training. The fast food industry is highly competitive and requires considerable business expertise in order to maintain cash flow and to control stock. Success depends on high turnover, which in turn involves very long hours, but there are real opportunities for people to run their own business.

Pub ('Licensed House') Management

There are over 60,000 pubs in Britain, of which nearly a third are independent, half are owned by pub companies and the rest by breweries. Although the British pub has a traditional image, most now offer food, some with a separate restaurant, a few even have a theatre. Children are now allowed in parts of many pubs, while the loosening of licensing hours restrictions means that pubs can choose to open all day, including Sundays. Those who run pubs are proprietors, managers employed by the owner, or tenants or lessees, who rent or lease the pub for a given period. Many companies in the licensed trade now have graduate recruitment schemes and are keen to attract young people into the sector. It is a way of life rather than a job, as it means being tied to the bar during licensing hours, 7 days a week. Work involves purchasing, stock-keeping and record-keeping as well as bar service. Thorough knowledge of licensing laws is essential. Interest in entertainment trends and more than just a 'liking for people' of all kinds are essential. Specialist training and experience in bar and cellar work is required by anyone hoping eventually to become a licensee.

An important area of employment for people working in the licensed trade is leisure and recreation: sports clubs, leisure centres, private clubs, race courses and holiday centres nearly all have bars. Bar staff are the licensees and have their own 'franchise' – instead of working for a salary they 'rent' the bar on the premises and run it.

Industrial and Contract Catering

This covers the provision of meals at places of work. Service is provided either by staff employed by the organization itself, or, increasingly, by *catering contractors*. These run 'catering units' on clients' premises in factories, offices, old people's homes, hospitals, schools, colleges, and, with mobile units, at special/outdoor events. They may also operate vending machines. Contractors' staff can change the setting in which they work without having to change employers. Area and district managers are in charge of a number of units; unit managers and chef/managers work on the same premises regularly for a period.

Unit managers themselves usually only cook if fewer than about 50 meals are being served. Their main task normally is trying to achieve as even a flow of work as possible. Other tasks include: *menu-planning* – the complexity of this varies according to the range of meals to be provided, from a narrow range of standard dishes to a wide selection including directors' dining-room 'specials', and according to the importance attached to nutritional values and tight budget control. Expertise includes being able to provide at least 2 weeks' changing menus within several given price-ranges and at different grades of sophistication; *costing* – ingredients, labour costs, etc.; *purchasing*, which includes negotiating with suppliers and specifying, for example, the uniform size and weight of each lamb chop in an order of several hundreds.

Managers normally attend meetings with directors and/or personnel managers and also discuss improvements or complaints with staff representatives. They must keep up with technological develop ments and are usually responsible for, or for advising on, types of service, and purchase and maintenance of equipment. (That work may also be done by specialists.)

There is a wide choice of jobs: from preparing sophisticated snacks for a West End showroom, or a dozen *haute cuisine* lunches in a managing director's office with 1 or 2 assistants, to feeding 2,000 a day with a staff of 50 including 2 or 3 assistant managers.

In much contract catering, hours are more regular than in other parts of the industry, and staff often work weekdays only.

School Catering Service

This has undergone big changes in the last few years. Compulsory competitive tendering by local education authorities has meant that in many areas contract caterers, not the local authority itself, provide the service and, therefore, employ the school meals staff. Schools catering is basically the same as industrial catering, with special emphasis on catering for children's tastes, nutritional values and strict budget control. In some areas, only snacks are provided, in others much effort has gone into improving the standard and image of the service.

After training, caterers supervise the preparation of dinners, either at school kitchens or at centres from which up to 1,000 meals are distributed to a number of schools.

Promotion depends on the employing organization. Senior staff (who may be called school meals organizers) advise on buying, planning, staffing, kitchen management, nutrition, etc. They are also concerned with contract compliance, specifications and marketing. Cost control is very important. Organizers are responsible for geographical areas and do a good deal of travelling. Hours tend to be regular.

Hospital Catering

Hospital catering officers (now often called hotel services managers) organize provision of meals for patients, staff and visitors, which means meals for between 200 and 3,000 people, many of whom need meals round the clock. Some hospitals have opened up their conference/meetings facilities to outsiders. They usually prepare diets under the overall direction but not day-to-day supervision of *dietitians*. It is possible to enter as a school-leaver and train on the job. New entrants with vocational qualifications in hospitality and/or catering follow the NHS Hotel Services Development Programme.

Experience in hospital catering is very useful training for other specializations.

Hospital catering is also contracted out to specialist firms.

Transport Catering

This is often done by contractors using *catering systems* (see p. 261). Menu-planning in airlines involves taking into account climatic conditions at point of consumption; commercial facts such as air commuters' 'menu-fatigue' (business people travel the same routes regularly; frequent menu changes must be made or customers are lost to the competition); research into which dishes and wines 'travel well'.

Airline catering is very tightly cost-controlled; but in *marine catering* priorities are different: for passengers and crews at sea, meals are the highlight of the day. Proportionately more money is spent on food at sea than in the air, so sea-cooks and chefs have greater opportunities for creative cooking, and therefore for getting good shore-based jobs later.

Victualling ships – ordering supplies for trips sometimes several months long – is another catering specialization. Work is done in shipping companies' offices. Previous large-scale catering experience is essential.

Accommodation and Catering Management (previously called Institutional Management)

The work This is management in non-profit-making, mainly residential establishments: halls of residence, hostels; the domestic side of hospitals; as well as, increasingly, in commercial conference and training centres. It also includes non-residential work: private school catering; meals-on-wheels; social service departments' day centres.

Managers may be called bursar, warden, domestic superintendent, catering manager. The range of titles makes it difficult to compare level of responsibility, status or duties.

There are almost as many different types of establishments as there are of hotels, and there is considerable overlap between catering and accommodation management. The difference is one of emphasis and setting in which the work is done. Some jobs have more in common with running a hotel – for example, running a large conference or management training centre – than with other institutional management jobs, in which residents' general well-being and emotional needs as well as their creature comforts have to be considered (such as old people's homes, where the job is part catering, part social work).

A *manager* may be wholly or partly responsible for all or some of the following aspects of community life: meals service; budgeting; purchase and maintenance of kitchen equipment; planning additional building; furnishings and decoration; the use of the buildings for conferences or vacation courses; dealing with residents' and staff's suggestions and complaints; helping to establish a friendly atmosphere both among staff and among residents; in small establishments, first aid and home-nursing (but *not* responsibility for sick residents); acting as host and as general information bureau; dealing with committees.

Most jobs are entirely administrative, but in small institutions the manager occasionally has to help out with housework or cooking. Many (by no means all) jobs are residential; accommodation varies from bedsitter to self-contained flat for couples (with partner not necessarily working in the organization concerned).

Training The main choice is between a full-time college or university course and getting experience and training on-the-job, preferably as part of a formal training scheme, for example Modern Apprenticeship.

Main full-time routes

With 2/3 A levels or equivalent: 3-year full-time or 4-year degree (titles include hotel and catering management, hospitality management). These vary in emphasis on different catering aspects, but generally include supervision of food and beverage preparation (and some practical work); catering management principles and practice; catering technologies; specialist work such as airline catering; sales management and marketing; accounting; computer application; aspects of tourism, recreation and leisure industries; international catering and languages (some courses include opportunities to study in Europe or further afield).

There are a few post-graduate qualifications for people with a relevant degree or experience or any degree plus experience/interest in hotels and catering (including 'exceptional entry' courses for the Hotel and Catering International Management Association – HCIMA – Professional Diploma, see below).

With 1 A level or equivalent: BTEC/SQA Higher National Diploma (titles similar to those for degree). Core subjects include operational techniques and procedures; work organizations; physical resource management; human resource management. Options may include accommodation management; applied nutrition; conference and banqueting management; licensed trade management; languages; sales and marketing; small business enterprise.

With 4 GCSEs or equivalent: 2-year courses for Vocational A levels or SQA award (see p. 10) in Hospitality and Catering.

With some GCSEs or equivalent, or in some cases no qualifications, 1-year course for GNVQ/GSVQ Intermediate or NVQs/SVQs.

Main work-based routes

NVQs at levels 1–4 depending on the subject.

Modern Apprenticeships at Foundation and Advanced level. A Graduate Apprenticeship is currently being piloted, which will be open to graduates from any discipline.

In-house training schemes. Management schemes may require a degree or HND/HNC.

A Foundation degree has been introduced for employees in the hospitality industry which can be studied on a flexible basis.

Junior managers or supervisors with level 2 qualifications can enrol for the HCIMA Advanced Certificate in Hospitality Studies. This is usually studied in college one evening or afternoon a week.

With no set entry qualifications: NVQs/SVQs in a variety of catering subjects at levels 1–4 (see p. 10). In order to gain these it is necessary to have training and support from the employer. A formal training scheme, such as those provided by the Hospitality Training Foundation (HTF), or Modern Apprenticeships (see p. 11) are the best options. (Accommodation services, chef, fast food, pub and restaurant apprenticeships are available.)

Training and qualifications for the licensed trade are also offered by the British Beer and Pub Association, the British Institute of Innkeeping (for staff in pubs) and the Wine and Spirit Education Trust (for those in the wine and spirit trade).

Personal attributes *For all catering* (in varying degrees): organizing and administrative ability; outgoing personality; ability to motivate staff and to communicate with all types of people – from kitchen porters to managing directors, from salespeople to a coachload of pensioners; interest in people and in their creature comforts; some practical skills; ability to work under pressure; stamina; flexibility; tact when dealing with 'difficult' customers; sense of humour. *For self-employed cooks*: as above, plus business acumen.

Late start No problem. Admission to courses depends on experience and motivation rather than age and GCSEs.

Work life balance HCIMA has launched a Continuing Professional Development project which could be used by members to keep up to date with developments during a career break. Catering offers opportunities to set up small-scale businesses (see WORKING FOR ONESELF p. 648).

Half the workforce is part time, but there are still very limited opportunities at management level. Opportunities exist in cooking, housekeeping, junior reception, food service and barwork, and freelance catering offers possibilities.

Further information The Hotel and Catering International Management Association, 191 Trinity Road, London SW17 7HN.
www.hcima.org.uk
Hospitality Training Foundation, International House, High Street, Ealing, London W5 5DB.
www.htf.org.uk
British Beer and Pub Association, Market Towers, 1 Nine Elm Lane, London SW8 5NQ.
www.beerandpub.com
The British Institute of Innkeeping, Wessex House, 80 Park Street, Camberley, Surrey GU15 3PT.
www.bii.org
The Wine and Spirit Education Trust, Five Kings House, 1 Queen Street Place, London EC4R 1QS.
www.wset.co.uk

Related careers DIETETICS – CONSUMER SCIENTIST/HOME ECONOMICS – SCIENCE: *Food Science and Technology* – TEACHING – TRAVEL AGENT/TOUR OPERATOR

Housing Management

Entry qualifications Various levels. Considerable graduate entry.

The work Traditionally, housing managers are responsible for a wide range of functions relating to the administration, maintenance and allocation of accommodation let for rent. They may also be involved in the running of Housing Aid Centres; giving advice on rent and benefit schemes; housing research and the formulation of housing policy. Housing managers and housing assistants work mainly for housing associations and local authorities. However, as local authority housing stock has diminished, due to council houses being sold and not as many new houses being built, authorities have transferred their houses to housing associations and housing companies to manage. This means the number and scope of housing associations has increased, along with the number of people working for them. A small number work for building societies, property companies and voluntary bodies.

Day-to-day housing management adds up to an unusual combination of dealing with people, using technical knowledge and getting out and about. Duties may include interviewing applicants for homes; visiting prospective tenants in their homes to assess their housing needs; finding and monitoring bed and breakfast accommodation and trying as quickly as possible to move tenants into something more satisfactory; inspecting property at regular intervals and arranging, if necessary, for repairs to be carried out; dealing with tenants' complaints about anything from noisy neighbours and lack of play facilities for children to lack of maintenance. Rent collecting, which used to be the most important and time-consuming task, has all but died out: most tenants now take or send rent to the housing office.

Housing staff try to establish or maintain good tenant–landlord relationships and try to forge a conglomeration of dwellings into a community. To this end they may try to involve tenants in managing their block of flats or estate, or they may set up tenants' management committees. In Housing Aid Centres, housing staff advise on any problem related to housing, from how to cope with an eviction order or how to get a rent allowance, to where to apply for a mortgage.

At a senior level, the work involves top-level general and financial management using modern management techniques; the purchase of properties; the allocation of accommodation (which is the most onerous task); research into housing needs and into such questions as 'How can we retain neighbourliness in new developments?', 'What is a good environment?', etc.; advising architects and planners on social aspects of siting, design and lay-out of new developments.

The fact that there has been a considerable increase in owner-occupiers and a decrease in accommodation let for rent by local authorities has not diminished the importance of housing management, but it has changed its role. As stock for rent is reduced more, and more tenants are poor and on benefits, so the welfare element has become more important. New problems emerge such as the shortage of affordable housing for key workers in Central London and other areas. The emphasis now is more on efficient management, and on exploring innovative ways of coping with housing need. New approaches to the problem include shared ownership; rent-into-mortgage schemes; leasing short-life property from private landlords; more cooperation between local authorities, housing associations, and building societies and private property companies. There is also now more movement between housing associations and local authorities than there used to be. It is still easier, though, to move from local authority to housing association than the other way around.

Many housing managers prefer to stick to day-to-day management throughout their careers, because they enjoy dealing with people. At a senior level the jobs can be controversial. Directors of housing may have to implement policies with which they do not agree, e.g. sale of council houses.

In local authority departments which manage thousands of dwellings, staff usually specialize in one aspect of the work at a time. In housing associations, which manage a smaller number, one housing assistant or housing manager may deal with everything concerning a number of tenancies. Housing associations increasingly provide facilities for special groups, e.g. for the elderly, single-parent families, the disabled. Some run hostels for such 'special needs' groups as ex-prisoners or people who have been psychiatric patients and still need support while adjusting to living in the community.

The number of graduates moving into the profession is increasing. However, most housing associations will employ people with other transferable skills. These could be in general management, or accountancy, or with a degree in social science/administration or in surveying. As the stock of property increases, maintenance and conversion need more people with relevant knowledge. A recent specialism is housing consultancy. Consultants are people with housing experience who set up as freelances and advise on or help with state-of-the-art financial or general management, setting up rent-into-mortgage or other innovative schemes in which private and public sector organizations cooperate. They also help with in-house training.

Training There are several routes to the professional qualification, the Chartered Institute of Housing's Professional Diploma:

1. The recommended route: Entry with at least 1 A level and 4 GCSEs (A–C), for on-the-job training with day-release for the BTEC Higher National Certificate in Housing Studies. The HNC is followed by a further 2 years' part-time training for the Institute's Professional Diploma. Both the HNC and Professional Diploma are available by distance learning.

2. Candidates with 4 GCSEs (A–C) can first take the BTEC National Certificate in Housing Studies.

Training for full professional status takes 4 years for A level entrants and 6 for GCSE entrants. Candidates who do not aim at senior management jobs can stop after taking a National Certificate. At that level there are several specialized courses in, for example: Housing Management and Maintenance; Tenant Participation, and Supported Housing.

3. Graduates, any discipline, either take the 2-year part-time course for the Professional Diploma, or they can take one of several full-time university post-graduate courses in housing.

4. A number of degrees in housing (titles vary) have been recognized by the Chartered Institute of Housing.

The Institute's Professional Diploma covers various areas of study including social policy; building construction and maintenance; law relating to housing; management studies; housing finance. Before finally qualifying for the award candidates must pass the Institute's APEX, which tests a candidate's practical housing experience.

While housing associations often take graduates and do not expect them to train for the Professional Diploma, for career moves the Professional Diploma is increasingly required.

NOTE: There are no BTEC Diploma (i.e. full-time) courses in Housing Studies.

NVQs/SVQs levels 2, 3 and 4 in Housing are now available.

Personal attributes Ability to get on well with all types of people; an interest in social, practical and economic problems, and in planning; tolerance; ability to be firm; indifference to being out in bad weather; organizing ability and diplomacy for senior people.

Late start Late entrants welcome. Aptitude and relevant work, as well as 'life experience', are often more important than qualifications.

Work life balance Returners are very welcome indeed. Short courses and workshops are arranged through HERA (see below) and by individual housing organizations. The CIH has reduced membership fees for the temporarily retired.

There are excellent opportunities for part-time work and job-sharing.

Further information The Chartered Institute of Housing, Octavia House, Westwood Business Park, Westwood Way, Coventry, Warwickshire CV4 8JP.
www.cih.org
HERA, 232 Great Guildford Business Square, 30 Great Guildford Street, London SE1 OHS.
www.hera-group.co.uk

Related careers ENVIRONMENTAL HEALTH OFFICER – LOCAL GOVERNMENT – TOWN AND COUNTRY PLANNING

Information Technology (IT)/ Information Systems

Entry qualifications Nothing rigid: depends on job type (see below). Ability to think logically and communicate effectively is more important than specific GCSEs and A levels. For trainee programming jobs, in practice, at least 2 A levels or degree (any subject); for software programming/engineer, usually computing science degree – computing science A level not required for most of these courses.

The work Nearly all businesses in the UK now use IT in some form. The rapid expansion of the use of email for communication and e-business on the Internet have increased dependency on computers. The result is a continuing demand for the IT specialist who designs, develops, manages, maintains and supports systems for others to use.

In 2003 1.3 million people were employed in IT-related occupations. Of these 45% were employed in supplier organizations, that is those developing and supplying IT systems. The rest were employed by other organizations to manage and maintain the systems on which their business depends.

After its very rapid initial growth, the IT supply industry suffered badly in the recent economic downturn but seems to be stabilizing as the number of failing companies had dropped considerably by the end of 2003. Despite the downturn in employment in this sector there are still shortages of people with the right IT skills as skills needs are constantly changing. In 2001 measures were announced to train up to 10,000 people a year in ICT skills and 18 New Technology Institutes are currently being established nationwide to meet this target.

Computing and IT professionals are highly skilled practitioners and although qualifying routes are becoming more established, experience and potential can still be more marketable than qualifications. Demarcation between the various computer specialisms is constantly changing, and the emphasis is on team work, because devices are becoming ever more sophisticated, demanding new skills or newly combined skills. Teams of computer staff are headed by project leaders, who now have a well-defined planning and monitoring management role.

Software engineers/designers/developers, computer programmers, systems software programmers (titles are interchangeable)

Software engineers produce the technology which drives the IT industry. There are two kinds of software: that which controls the operating system of a computer or other hardware and the software that runs the applications or programs used on computers. Some of them work at the cutting edge, 'pushing out new frontiers of science', but most now work on updating, refining or adding to systems already in use, or increasing the compatibility of different products. The ongoing proliferation of increasingly sophisticated e-shopping and multimedia websites and other developments on the Internet is also increasing employment opportunities. Software engineers may be employed by software firms, or by consultancies who design and produce software for different clients, or by large companies to support in-house systems.

The work requires a high level of creativity and expertise and software engineers need to be familiar with different coding languages and applications. They are the only IT workers who must have a technological/scientific background, usually a relevant degree, and who work largely with other similarly qualified colleagues. They usually work as a team but some do work alone. Nevertheless the work may involve consultation with clients or colleagues and where software is being written for a specific purpose, liaising with the end-users to acquire an understanding of the processes to be covered. They also implement and follow up new programs, testing them and correcting defects. They write the technical specifications and test plans for their programs and may liaise with technical authors in the publication of user manuals.

Depending on the type of organization in which they work, software engineers may become team leaders or project managers, responsible for managing staff, budgets and keeping to timescales. Software design is now a very competitive business and most software houses work to tight deadlines. These may mean long hours and a strong commitment to the work.

Network Specialists

This group of specialists designs and supports the Local/Wide Area Networks (LAN/WANs) which allow computerized workstations to 'talk' to each other. Networking has become a means of integrating both computer applications and business functions. Jobs in this area cover network design, implementation, support and management. This is one of the most rapidly growing areas of IT and suitable staff are in short supply.

Systems Analysts and/or Designers

They identify the problem and design the solution to it. There are three stages to the job. First, they investigate and analyse the existing system – or lack of it – in the organization which is intending to install or update a computer system. In many organizations patterns of work have evolved haphazardly and, in the process, have become inefficient. The *systems analyst* spends several months getting to know the intricacies of the business, observing and talking to staff in all departments and at all levels – from junior clerk or packer to buyer or marketing and managing directors – to assess routines, bottlenecks, objectives. The work requires business acumen, knowledge of commercial practice and an ability to get people to talk freely about their work and to accept changes in old-established routines. When the old system has been translated into a logical sequence of procedures, the systems analyst writes a report on how the new system would affect the organization's staff, and how it would improve efficiency and profitability, and at what cost. If the report is accepted by the management, the systems analyst completes the analysis and design, using structured procedures, hands over the program specification to the programmers, and probably supervises the subsequent implementation, troubleshooting if necessary.

The systems analyst's role will often overlap with that of a business analyst, someone without a computing background, probably with a business degree, who analyses the problem from a business and financial perspective. They frequently work together.

Analyst/Programmers

In commercial computing – the vast majority of jobs are in this field, rather than in science or engineering – the jobs of *analyst/designers* and of *programmers* are normally merged into *analyst/programmers*. They see the whole project through, in teams under a project manager, until it is completed and validated. The vast majority of analysts and designers work for computer users; 'in-house' analysis and design used to be more usual than having the work done by software houses, i.e. consultancies which provide professional services for a number of clients. However, computing and IT skill shortages, downsizing and outsourcing have reversed this trend and many firms now employ consultants. Some analyst/designers (with ample experience) work as freelances.

Analyst/designers' work also covers advising employers, or clients, on what systems to buy; so they must be knowledgeable about and critical of the various systems available. They must be very good at explaining complicated matters to lay people – the computer users.

The attraction and challenge of this computing job is the mixture of tasks and of talents required: applying highly specialized technical knowledge; improving an organization's efficiency; assessing competing computer manufacturers' claims for new products. On top of applying technical know-how, systems analyst/designers must be very good at dealing with people: communication skills are vital. They must make the computer acceptable to staff and design the interface to be acceptable to the clients; traditional working methods and hierarchies may have to change; retraining has to be arranged and accepted, and staff reductions may have to be faced.

Applications Programmers/Developers

There is a spectrum of *applications programmers/developers*; some work to a 'loose specification', using great expertise and ingenuity; others work to a 'tight specification', need less expertise and have less scope for ingenuity. Most now become *analyst/programmers* (see above). The relationship between *systems analyst/design* and *applications programming/developing* has been likened to that of architecture and construction. Applications programmers/developers work to 'program specifications' – a description of what the program is to achieve – provided by the *systems analyst/designer*.

Applications programming/developing covers various stages. Applications programmers/developers roughly assess the time needed to complete the program, break it down into separate components, and then break down each component into individual step-by-step sequences of instructions upon which the computer can act. All this needs logical, analytical reasoning, but not mathematical skills. Then comes the translation into an appropriate language, which is usually typed directly into a computer terminal. Applications programmers/developers may produce programs to instruct particular machines to perform particular tasks: for example, to enable a chain of hotels to keep a constantly updated record of vacancies, or a hospital group to keep a constantly updated record of the lengths of waiting lists within the various specialities and the various hospitals within the hospital group. In large organizations teams of applications programmers/developers would deal with a variety of programs – writing for new applications; updating existing programs. Applications programmers/developers with considerable experience, working for software/systems houses, manufacturers, consultancies, users and, increasingly, as freelances, can also specialize in 'applications packages'. These are programs, or 'program systems' produced 'for stock', to be bought off-the-shelf by users with run-of-the-mill requirements: programs for stock control; payrolls; video games; office applications such as spreadsheets and databases for personnel systems. Writing applications package programs requires special skills: the programs must be 'user-friendly' (easy for laypersons to understand), well documented and flexible enough to be adaptable to particular users' differing needs.

There is usually a hierarchy of programmers, from trainee right up to *project team leader*, and then on to various management jobs. Most work in mixed-project teams with systems designers and other specialists as required.

As virtually everybody in computing, however high up, has to have had some programming experience, programmers have a choice of ladders. Most large installations have two branches: one dealing with developing systems and with those in the planning stage, employing the above staff plus specialists, e.g. *database administrators*; and another one dealing with the actual functioning of the system in use.

Webmaster

Web design is still a developing area. In large organizations web-masters may be employed as part of a team of IT specialists but often have a multidisciplinary if not arts background. The development of software which is reducing the need for technical know-how has led to an increase in the number of self-employed web designers who concentrate more on the visual design and content of the website. Good communication skills are essential as a major feature of the work is the ability to work with the customer and interpret their requirements. Web design courses are largely available at all levels but many designers still develop their own skills on the job and a willingness to keep up with technological change in this fast developing field is crucial.

Multimedia Specialists

Multimedia specialists draw on different types of media – text, graphics, audio, video and animation – to produce a single product, usually on DVD, CD-ROM or a website. Multimedia involves the coordination of the input of a number of specialists, so team working skills are impor-tant. Again this is a fast developing field and practitioners must be constantly updating their technical knowledge. Most multimedia specialists will use commercial authoring packages but some products involve software engineers in developing new programs.

Database Administration/Information

Data is now viewed by most organizations as a valuable corporate resource. These organizations usually see data as a separate area for control and management. Database administration personnel (often called information officers) design, manage and maintain the company's data and control access to it. This is a highly specialized and technical area. Considerable experience of database systems and business needs is required.

Hardware Engineers

They design and develop computers and related products ('peripherals') for computer manufacturers (see ENGINEERING, p. 216). Various specialists are involved, mainly but not only *electronic engineers, physicists, mathematicians*. At the moment titles of relevant degree courses vary (for example, IT or Computers and Communications); computing hardware professionals of the future must carefully study degree course syllabuses. Terminology of job-titles and specific functions varies, too. Hardware manufacture is a declining industry in Britain; major companies that once concentrated on this are now moving into selling software instead.

Some 'Spin-off' Jobs

With 'orthodox' (i.e. *applications* or *software programming, systems/ software design/analysis*) qualifications and experience, there are a growing number of opportunities in rapidly changing and expanding computer careers, suiting individuals with various bents, abilities, expertise. *Information technology*, including as it does telecommunications (and office automation), is developing faster than any industry ever has done: new jobs are constantly emerging – but beware: the unskilled or semi-skilled ones may be short-lived.

User Support Staff

Support staff provide a 'hand-holding' service to users who have bought a new system or updated and extended an existing one. Job content varies greatly. Support staff may be asked to provide training for everyone who will use or be affected by the new systems, from clerk to managing director; they may suggest additional or more efficient application of the system; or, if they work for manufacturers or software houses, they may visit at regular intervals to see all goes well – and possibly keep the customer informed of new equipment or software. The job combines ability to communicate and establish good relations with people at all levels in an organization, with technical expertise to keep up with technological developments.

Service Engineers

They work either for large users 'in-house' or for manufacturers, and visit customers – often irate and impatient – whose equipment has broken down (or apparently broken down: often it is simply wrongly used). Service engineers must thoroughly understand the complexities of hardware and software to be able to diagnose and rectify the trouble. This usually means plugging in a replacement part rather than actual repair. Unlike engineers at the hardware/software production end, service engineers get out and about and meet the users (see 'Incorporated Engineers and Engineering Technicians', p. 231).

Sales and Marketing

For details of general *sales and marketing*, see p. 371. However, in the computer hardware and software area specialist knowledge is vital. Computing is not only technologically the most sophisticated industry, it is also a highly competitive, cut-throat industry. Sales people usually specialize in systems for specific markets – i.e. commercial, scientific or educational.

Technical Writing

Writing manuals for – especially – workstations and PCs is a growing job area. It requires the ability to put over complex information clearly, succinctly and unequivocally, and it requires thorough understanding of what the device described can and cannot do, and how it functions. Manual-writers have to know very much more about their subject than the people for whom they are writing. Existing manuals are often criticized; manufacturers say they have difficulty finding people who combine the necessary technological expertise with the necessary communication skills. Technical writers may be employed by manufacturers or by consultancies or work as freelance or 'in-house'. 'End-user documentation' production is becoming a sophisticated area. Writers have to produce material – both in print and 'screen dialogue' – which is 'user-friendly', i.e. easily understood by amateurs, as well as documentation for experts.

Consultants

Systems analysts and *designers* can ultimately become independent consultants – advising prospective users on whether a system would be of use to them and, if so, which one. Considerable experience of the computer scene, plus specialist knowledge in a commercial (banking, retailing, etc.), or industrial or educational area, is essential.

Training This is still evolving. Experience is, on the whole, more important than paper qualifications, but experience is often difficult to get without qualifications. It is still just possible to start with a few good GCSEs as an operator or network manager and, with in-house training and preferably day-release, become an *applications programmer/developer* and then a *systems analyst* – if the conditions and the personality and ability are right. Because of the quick expansion and rapid developments in the whole computer area, training is still disorganized and haphazard, with several overlapping types of qualifications. Many people at the top of the profession now have no formal computing qualifications, because when they started their careers there were no relevant qualifications. Others have got on without qualifications because of the shortage of computer staff, but new entrants must aim at a qualification (though the only work for which a degree is invariably demanded is *software/systems programming/software engineering*). Training is also continuous, with the need for continuous updating (known as continuing professional development or CPD). Yet still far too few IT employers are prepared to train staff. Anyone joining the industry is advised to look for companies which participate in the British Computer Society's Career Development Accreditation or Framework schemes. Small companies may not have the resources to do this, but instead may have an arrangement whereby the BCS will 'authenticate' the CPD undertaken by their staff (who keep a record of their training).

Courses are at all levels from post-graduate to those for people with few educational qualifications. Non-degree qualifications are awarded by a number of different organizations, some specializing in a particular branch of the industry. The following are the main entry and training routes, but individuals should look very carefully at syllabuses to ensure that they choose a course to suit their particular interest and academic level. They need also to decide whether to take a full-time, part-time or distance-learning course (many can be taken by any of these methods).

1. Degree (full time or sandwich) in a computing subject (titles include computing science, software engineering, business computing, computer systems). Science A levels (physics and/or maths) are required for some, but not all, courses.

NOTE: see ENGINEERING, p. 216, for introductory/foundation courses for people with arts A levels who want to take a degree normally requiring science A levels.

2. Degree in a non-computing subject. The majority of IT entrants in the past have been from non-IT disciplines but as the sector develops this may change.

3. Full- and part-time Foundation degrees.

4. Post-graduate or post-HND computing course following a humanities degree, particularly languages.

5. BTEC/SQA (see pp. 8, 10) Higher National awards in computer studies, business information technology, software engineering, maths studies (with computing options).

6. British Computer Society (the main professional body) awards its own qualifications. The BCS Professional Examination has a modular structure set in three stages:

(a) Certificate – equivalent to the first year of a Higher National Diploma (HND);

(b) Diploma – equivalent to HND level; and

(c) Professional Graduate Diploma – equivalent to honours degree level. In addition, candidates undertake a Professional Project at either Diploma or Professional Graduate Diploma level, which aims to demonstrate professional competence in the development of a computer-based system. There are no formal entry requirements for the examination and both members and non-members of the BCS can enter for any part.

NOTE: The British Computer Society also manages in the UK the European Computer Driving Licence. This qualification involves 7 modules covering basic concepts of IT, management of files, word processing, spreadsheets, database filing, presentation and drawing, and information network services. It is awarded following a period of training recorded in a Log Book and successful completion of a number of tests. The BSC also runs the UK EUCIP (European Certification of Informatics Professionals). Introduced in 2003 and aimed at people with professional IT experience but no qualifications, individuals who have completed a non-IT education (at all levels), as well as younger students interested in entering the IT industry, it is a modular course and students can choose units corresponding to their own areas of interest.

7. Institute for the Management of Information Systems (emphasis is on business applications): offers through part-time or distance-learning courses in information systems management at Foundation, Diploma, Higher Diploma and Graduate Diploma level.

8. Edexcel BTEC National awards in computer studies or SQA Scottish Group Award.

9. City & Guilds (see p. 10) offers a range of vocational courses at different levels in applications programming/developing.

10. The Open University has introduced a range of flexible programmes aimed at the continuing professional development of individuals working in IT.

11. The e-skills Sector Skills Council oversees Foundation and Advanced Modern Apprenticeships in IT and Electronic Services, as well as NVQs at levels 1–5.

NOTE: Commercially provided training in IT is available in many forms, from full-time courses to computer-based training or through interactive learning systems. Major software providers such as Microsoft provide their own product-specific courses. If in doubt about the value of a qualification for a particular career aim check with the British Computer Society (see p. 294) before enrolling.

IT is the fastest expanding career area. For IT professionals who are flexible and prepared to continue learning new skills and for constant change and challenge, the scope is immense. IT is expanding in two dimensions:

1. It is penetrating ever more areas of activity, with more and more workplaces within each area installing or expanding systems; and

2. devices and systems are getting ever more sophisticated and versatile; as one generation of computers comes on to the market, the next one is in production, and the one after that on the drawing-board (or rather the researcher/designer's VDU). So computing professionals of all kinds have a promising future.

The prospects for people with an engineering/science background plus computing experience/training are excellent. There is increasing scope for specializing within a work area: people with experience in, say, *retail*, *banking*, the *law* or *agriculture* may become computing professionals by grafting computing skills on to their particular expertise. At present, IT remains a field where being able to demonstrate your prospective capability, rather than holding specific qualifications, is what may count most with recruiters.

Personal attributes *All professionals*: Communication skills, written and spoken; flexibility, willingness to adapt to new methodologies and to continue learning.

Systems analyst/designers: Well-above-average intelligence and powers of logical reasoning; numeracy; imagination to put themselves into the shoes of the people whose jobs they may be 'analysing away' or at least changing; tact and diplomacy; ability to get on well with people at all levels in an organization's hierarchy; a confidence-inspiring manner; curiosity; creativity to visualize how old-established methods might be changed; ability to explain complicated procedures in simple language; ability to listen; ability to take an overall view of a situation and yet see it in detail; business acumen, at least for many jobs.

Applications programmers/developers/programmers/analysts: Powers of logical thinking; numeracy; powers of sustained concentration; great patience and willingness to pursue an elusive problem till solved; liking for concentrated desk-work; ability to communicate easily with people in computing as well as with lay people. Programmers who hope to progress to systems analysis should note the different personal qualities required.

Systems programmers/software engineers: Very high intellectual ability; originality; research-inclined mind; imagination; interest in high technology and its implications and rapid developments.

Network managers: Practicality; liking for routine work; organizing/administrative ability for those wanting to get promotion.

Late start Good opportunities, especially for people with business or related experience and for mature students, who may take full- or part-time degree or other relevant courses.

Work life balance Depending on the type of work, as such a range of employers employ IT practitioners, including the Civil Service and the NHS, it should be possible to find flexible working. Self-employment through contracting is possible. Employers are willing to recruit career changers and returners with the right attributes. However, IT is a very competitive field and on the supply side the need to meet deadlines can mean a long hours culture.

Further information British Computer Society, 1 Sanford Street, Swindon, Wilts. SN1 1HJ.
www.bcs.org.uk

Institute for the Management of Information Systems, 5 Kingfisher House, New Mill Road, Orpington, Kent BR5 3QG.
www.imis.org.uk

e-skills NTO, 1 Castle Lane, London SW1E 6DR.
www.e-skillsnto.org.uk

Related careers ENGINEERING – MANAGEMENT SERVICES: *Operational Research* – SCIENCE

Information Work (Librarianship/ Information Science)

It has been said that we live in an information society. The sheer weight of information available increases all the time and impinges on every facet of modern life. We need information on which to base decisions on a whole range of issues. The fifth-former wants to find out where various A level combinations could lead him or her. A doctor needs to know the possible side-effects of a new treatment. An investor might look into the performance of various shares. A marketing manager wants to keep abreast of what the competition is up to. Information is vital to our education, our work, our leisure, our health.

Developments in technology have had an enormous impact on the 'information industry'. Not only has technology led to new ways of collecting, organizing and retrieving information, but it has also led to more information! The information specialist has to deal with a range of sources far beyond books and other printed material.

Entry qualifications For professional work, a degree; for assistant posts, nothing rigid, but 4 GCSE passes, including English, may be asked for.

The work Distinctions between the librarian and the information scientist have blurred. Differences are often a matter of the emphasis of their work, rather than a fundamental difference of role or purpose. Job-titles are not necessarily an indication of job content or emphasis. Information scientists may be chartered librarians; a librarian in a specialist library may work with highly technical information; some specialists have dual membership of the Chartered Institute of Library and Information Professionals and the Institute of Information Scientists. Information officer and research officer are other titles that may crop up in job adverts.

The common basic purpose of the librarian/information specialist is to see that relevant information is available and used effectively. For whatever purpose, the job of the information specialist is to *acquire*, *organize* and *exploit* information. This covers a vast range of activity. *Acquiring* might range from maintaining as broad and balanced a collection as possible to cater for a wide range of general interests, within a given budget, to trawling the international market to build up a highly specialist collection of academic or technical interest. *Exploiting* might mean inviting a children's author to read his or her stories to pre-schoolers or preparing a newsletter to keep specialists aware of developments in their field.

The *public library* service is vast and provides a wide range of services to the public. Librarians are responsible for the selection, purchase, cataloguing and arrangement of a wide variety of materials – books and periodicals, videos, cassettes, records, slides, compact discs and information packs, for example. Many libraries run special services, such as 'books-on-wheels', children's activities, services to business or the ethnic community. All provide information, sometimes in specially produced packs, and answer inquiries. Many libraries have computerized information systems.

In a smaller library, and early stages of their careers, librarians' work may cover several functions, but many jobs involve some degree of specialization. More senior positions involve managing staff and resources. As in most jobs, routine work is inevitable, but many of the routine tasks associated with libraries – issuing books, filling and tidying shelves – are not done by professional librarians but by library assistants. Most public librarians will be chartered librarians (see below).

Academic libraries in universities and colleges offer a service to both staff and students, and sometimes to outsiders. In consultation with academic staff, librarians carefully select materials to support the teaching and learning going on in the institution. Many academic librarians are specialists in a particular subject area and often have a degree in that subject. Others may manage special collections, e.g. early printed books, manuscripts, music or computer software. Important aspects of the work in academic libraries are helping students to understand and use effectively the facilities available (including the latest technology) and helping academic staff to keep up to date with developments in their subjects. Many posts in academic libraries are open only to those who have a post-graduate qualification (see below).

Industry and commerce need good information to make good decisions. As in other areas, the information specialist is responsible for selecting material; this could demand considerable specialist knowledge of the organization's area of operations in, for example, science or engineering, as well as information skills. Computer technology has had an enormous impact on the storage and retrieval of information, as well as on the range available, and information specialists will be expected to exploit this to fulfil their company's needs, whether it involves designing and implementing a system to catalogue all the company's information resources, or buying in the latest database. The provision of information for specific purposes is an important task and might involve compiling a list (perhaps from a computerized system) of key references on a particular topic; exploiting a network of outside contacts, e.g. trade associations, learned societies, other company libraries; preparing summaries or abstracts of new information. A reading knowledge of a foreign language can be very useful.

Information specialists are also employed in government departments, museums, research and professional bodies, and the media. There are some opportunities to work as a freelance consultant.

In public and academic libraries, where services are affected by public-spending policies, openings are not increasing in numbers. In information departments and special libraries the number of jobs is increasing. Graduates in physics, chemistry, computer studies and related science/technology fields are keenly sought; there is also a need for specialists in accountancy, economics, finance, law and management. (However, any degree subject can lead to work in this field.)

Training For chartered librarians: a CILIP-accredited 3- or 4-year information degree or 1-year full-time or 3- or 4-year part-time post-graduate diploma/masters. To gain chartered status, an additional 1-year professional in-post training.

For library and information assistants: part-time courses leading to City & Guilds, BTEC and SQA National and Higher National Certificates in librarianship and information studies.

NVQs at levels 2 and 3 or SVQs at levels 2, 3 and 4 in Information and Library Services.

Employers' requirements and preferences can vary. For some jobs a relevant first degree can be more important than further qualifications. Some people take relevant post-graduate courses, but do not go on to professional membership.

Personal attributes Good communication skills; curiosity; an interest in a variety of related topics without the desire to delve too deeply into any one; a methodical approach; a high degree of accuracy; organizing ability; a retentive memory; staying power for long, possibly fruitless searches; resourcefulness; interest in electronic information systems; capacity to switch instantly from one topic to another; ability to cope with frequent interruptions when doing jobs requiring concentration; ability to anticipate users' needs. Because library and information work has so many different aspects, practitioners' relative strengths in these areas may vary.

Late start No upper age limit. Educational institutions may relax normal requirements for mature students.

Work life balance A career break should be no problem if well qualified and up to date. Short courses can be used as refresher courses, though not intended as such. Formal schemes are increasing, particularly in the private sector.

Reasonable opportunities for part-time work at junior and up to middle-management level, but more difficult at senior levels. However, flexible working is becoming more common, including home working, job-sharing, term-time working and compressed hours, i.e. working more hours per day in return for a shorter working week.

Further information Aslib (The Association of Information Management), 3–7 Temple Avenue, London EC4Y 0HP.
www.aslib.com
Chartered Institute of Library and Information Professionals, 7 Ridgmount Street, London WC1E 7AE.
www.cilip.org.uk

Related careers ARCHIVIST – BOOKSELLING – MUSEUMS AND ART GALLERIES – PUBLISHING

Insurance

Entry qualifications For the qualifying exam of the Chartered Insurance Institute, 3 A levels or equivalent. Graduate entry gives exemption from part of the CII exams. GCSE entrants willing to study part time (often with employer's help) can move up the ladder, but the best prospects are for people with A levels, BTEC National, HND or degree.

Foreign languages are useful as insurance is an international activity and some jobs involve considerable travel.

The work Insurance is a method of compensating for losses arising from all kinds of misfortunes, from the theft of a video to an airliner crash, from a holiday cancelled through illness to the abandonment of a major sporting event. It is based on the principle that many more people pay regularly into a common fund than ultimately draw from it, and thus the losses of the unlucky few may be made good. The organizers of the system are the *insurers*, i.e. the *insurance companies* or *Lloyd's*. Lloyd's itself is not an insurance company, but a society whose individual members are grouped together into syndicates to accept and underwrite 'risks'. Each syndicate is administered by an agency which employs a *professional underwriter* (see below) to carry out the business. Banks and building societies (see p. 119) are also now moving into insurance. It is usual to specialize in one of the main branches of insurance: *marine and aviation, life and pensions, property, accident, motor and liability* and *reinsurance* (where very large risks are 'farmed out'), although transfers are possible.

Underwriters are responsible for assessing risks, deciding whether they are insurable, and on what terms and conditions they can be accepted. Some underwriting decisions are routine and based on guidelines laid down by the company for dealing with standard cases (for example, ordinary motor insurance). Others are highly complex and/or unusual and demand specialized skill or judgement (for example, the Channel Tunnel or an art treasure on special exhibit).

In the case of buildings, industrial plant and other commercial operations, underwriters may call on the advice of *surveyors*. The surveyor prepares a factual report on any aspects that might affect the underwriter's assessment of the risks (e.g. fire protection or security arrangements). Some surveyors go into risk management, which is concerned with identifying, assessing and minimizing the risks a company may face in its day-to-day activities. Insurance surveyors are often selected from existing staff and trained internally; they are not necessarily chartered surveyors. When risks are very complex, science or technology graduates might be recruited for this work.

When a claim is received *claims staff* assess the loss and determine the amount to be paid. As with underwriting, some cases are straightforward (though you might be dealing with people whose loss demands your tact and sympathy), while others are complex and require technical, legal and medical knowledge. For large or disputed claims insurance companies may call in independent *loss adjusters* to examine the claim and help to reach a settlement. Some loss adjusters come from the claims department of an insurance company, but others have relevant qualifications, e.g. in law, surveying, accountancy, engineering.

Insurance brokers act as intermediaries, bringing together the insurers and those who wish to be insured. Jobs include finding new business, looking after and advising existing clients, and placing the risks in the market (i.e. finding insurers to underwrite the policy). Brokers may be small high street firms or international giants employing thousands of staff. Only accredited brokers ('Lloyd's brokers') are allowed to do business with Lloyd's underwriters.

Training On the job over 3 years with day-release or evening study, distance or online learning for Associateship of The Chartered

Insurance Institute, followed by 3 years for Fellowship of CII. Other relevant qualifications may be taken into account. For some specializations, e.g. investment and pensions management, the CII exam is followed by Fellowship exams of a relevant institute.

Loss adjusters may take the Chartered Institute of Loss Adjusters exams after insurance company experience if they already hold a previous professional qualification such as ACII.

Personal attributes Some mathematical ability; a liking for paper-work; ability to grasp the essentials of a problem; sound judgement; determination and a certain amount of push; tact; a persuasive, confidence-inspiring manner; ability to communicate with people, often in difficult circumstances. For brokers, extrovert manner and entrepreneurial flair.

Late start Many employers are adopting a more relaxed attitude towards the age of recruits, but training vacancies can be more difficult to obtain after the age of 30. Mature entrants would be expected to follow the same training routes as young recruits, but the minimum academic requirements might be relaxed. In sales, maturity is an advantage.

Work life balance Employers are introducing career break schemes; details vary. Part time, job-sharing and working from home are becoming more popular within the industry.

Further information The Careers Information Officer, The Chartered Insurance Institute, 20 Aldermanbury, London EC2V 7HY.
www.cii.co.uk
The British Insurance Brokers' Association, BIBA House, 14 Bevis Marks, London EC3A 7NT.
www.biba.org.uk
The Chartered Institute of Loss Adjusters, Peninsula House, 36 Monument Street, London EC3R 8LJ.
www.cila.co.uk

Related careers ACCOUNTANCY – ACTUARY – BANKING AND
BUILDING SOCIETY WORK – INFORMATION TECHNOLOGY (IT)/
INFORMATION SYSTEMS – STOCK EXCHANGE AND SECURITIES
INDUSTRY

Journalism

Entry qualifications *Newspapers*: 5 GCSEs (A–C) including English language for traineeship, but nearly all school-leaver entrants have at least 2 A levels. 60% of entrants are graduates. For pre-entry course: 2 A levels in practice.

Magazines: Depends on editor; for pre-entry course: 1 A level, 4 GCSEs (A–C). About three-quarters of new entrants come from some kind of higher education course.

Pre-entry experience is essential.

The work Journalism covers a variety of jobs in a variety of settings (or 'media', which really should be 'media of communications'). Broadly, the main job groups are *reporter; correspondent or specialist reporter; feature writer; news editor; editor; freelance*. Division of duties depends on paper's size and organization.

NEWSPAPERS

Most newspapers now have computerized editorial systems, i.e. journalists input their copy through a keyboard directly into a computer. Virtually every journalist starts as trainee reporter. Reporters cover any kind of event: from council or Women's Institute meeting to political demo, fire, or press conference for visiting film star or foreign statesman. Reporters 'get a story' by asking questions and listening to other journalists' questions and interviewees' answers at press conferences, or in one-to-one interviews with individuals. For such interviews, reporters have to do some preliminary 'homework' – to interview a trade union secretary or famous novelist, for example, requires some background knowledge.

Reporters must compose stories quickly and meet tight deadlines. Accuracy, brevity and speed are more important than writing perfect prose: reporting is a fact-gathering and fact-disseminating rather than a creative job.

Occasionally, reporters may be on a particular story for several weeks, researching the background and/or waiting for developments. They work irregular hours, including weekends.

Specialist Reporter or Correspondent

'Hard news' is broadcast more quickly than it can be printed; to fight TV and radio competition, newspapers have developed 'interpretative' or specialist reporting. Specialists' titles and precise responsibilities and scope vary; the aim always is to interpret and explain news, and to comment on events, trends, causes and news behind the news. The number (and the expert knowledge) of specialists varies according to the type and size of newspaper. On the whole, only the nationals have specialists who concentrate entirely on one speciality; on other papers and in news agencies, reporters with a special interest in a particular field (or several) may do specialist along with general reporting. The main specializations are: Parliament and/or politics generally; industry; finance; education; foreign news; local government and/or planning; social services; sport; science and technology; agriculture and food; motoring; fashion, women's/home interests; theatre; films; broadcasting. Financial correspondents tend to be economics graduates, science correspondents are science graduates, but education correspondents are not normally teachers: there are no hard-and-fast rules about how specialists acquire their specialist knowledge (and how much they need).

News Editor

Journalists with organizing ability may become news editors, controlling reporting staffs, allocating stories to individual reporters and attending senior staff's daily editorial conferences. It is an office job and normally involves no writing. The title usually applies on daily papers; but titles and organization of work vary considerably from one paper to another.

Sub-editors

Sub-editors do the detailed editing of copy; they re-write stories to fit in with required length, re-write the beginning, and may 'slant' stories. They write headlines and, in consultation with the night or assistant editor, may do the layout of news pages. On large papers there are several specialist subs. Subbing is teamwork and entirely desk-bound; it always has to be done in a hurry.

Feature Writers

Usually experienced journalists who can write lucidly and descriptively on any topic; but specialists may also write features. Reporters may combine reporting with feature writing.

Columnist

Like feature writing, a job for experienced journalists; there are specialists, e.g. financial or consumer affairs columnists, and general columnists. The work requires a wide range of interests and contacts.

Leader-writers

Leaders may be written by the editor, or specialist correspondent, or other experienced journalists.

Editor-in-chief, Assistant Editor, Deputy Editor

Editors (including departmental editors) are coordinators, policy-makers. The number of top jobs, and the amount of writing editors do, vary greatly: some editors write leaders on specific subjects, some write in crises only; some on a variety of subjects, others not at all.

The amount of freedom an editor-in-chief has to run the paper in the way they want depends on the proprietor; policies vary enormously.

There is no set promotion structure on newspapers. Some journalists do all or several types of newspaper work in succession in preparation for senior editorial jobs (subbing is a vital step on the ladder), others become heads of departments (finance, fashion, home affairs, chief sub, etc.) fairly quickly. Many remain reporters.

Titles, functions and division of labour are not consistent throughout the industry and often change with a change of editor-in-chief or proprietor.

Freesheets

Locally distributed 'giveaway' papers are the fastest-growing advertising medium. Free newspapers vary enormously in the proportion and variety of their editorial content. A few are much like small local weekly papers; most carry very little editorial matter. Some are published by established newspaper houses, some by members of the Association of Free Newspapers, yet others are run individually from tiny offices by one or two people. Jobs on free newspapers with varied editorial content may be acceptable as traineeships (see below), but generally are unlikely to lead to jobs on national or other prestigious local newspapers.

Magazines

Broadly there are two types:

1. Professional, business to business and 'house' journals, geared to a particular profession, trade or organization.

2. 'Consumer' magazines: they cater for all types of leisure interests and include women's, teenage and hobby magazines and comics.

On (1) journalists often work closely with experts in the particular field of which they must have/develop some understanding. They write features, report developments, and re-write experts' contributions. Magazine work, however specialized, can be a way into newspaper work – especially for graduates (particularly science or technology) with writing ability. It often requires broader skills than newspaper journalism: e.g. knowing about sub-editing and layout.

Consumer magazines employ feature writers, sub-editors and departmental editors more than reporters, but organization varies enormously. Consumer magazines use freelances more than do newspapers. Editors' work includes originating feature ideas and selecting and briefing outside contributors, both freelance journalists and specialists who are not journalists.

Freelance Journalism

Freelances are either 'generalists' – feature writers who write on any subject – or specialists. On the whole, only experienced journalists with staff experience, and particularly those with specialist knowledge which is in demand (technology, consumerism, child development, education, for example), succeed.

Specialists – teachers, engineers, lawyers, with writing ability and topical ideas – also do freelance journalism as a sideline, but this is becoming more difficult.

Newspapers

Training These are the most common methods:

Direct entry traineeship: 2 years, including 6 months' probation. Acceptance depends as much on paper's policy and candidate's suitability as on academic qualifications. Competition for trainee posts at any stage is fierce. Candidates must apply direct to editors of provincial (including suburban) dailies and weeklies. The London-based nationals rarely take trainees. (Previous experience in student or freelance journalism is essential. Candidates need to submit samples of work done: an article or report specially written for the particular paper, which shows the editor that the applicant has identified the paper's style, is important, as is work done for school or university paper.)

Trainees complete a foundation distance-learning package during probation and attend a 12-week block-release course later in their training. All trainees must pass preliminary examinations in media law, public affairs (local and central government), newspaper journalism and 100 wpm shorthand and serve a 2-year period of work experience maintaining a log book of their achievement, before being allowed to sit the National Council for the Training of Journalists' National Certificate Examination (NCE). The syllabus for this includes: English usage; relevant law; public affairs; interpretative reporting (interviewing, fact-gathering methods, etc.); current affairs; sub-editing skills. Also still necessary is shorthand (100 wpm), which reporters still use alongside tape recordings to take notes.

Practical training should cover work in all departments. Quality and thoroughness of training schemes vary, so it is essential to find out as much as possible about them before accepting a traineeship. 1 or 2 groups now run their own training schemes independently of the NCTJ.

NVQs/SVQs: NVQs/SVQs are available at level 4. The NCTJ preliminary examinations can provide the necessary evidence of underpinning knowledge needed for NVQs/SVQs in Newspaper Journalism and Periodical Journalism.

1-year full-time pre-entry courses: 2 A levels required. The majority of entrants to newspaper journalism now take such courses, at colleges of further and higher education. Courses shorten subsequent traineeship by 6 months. A few candidates are sponsored by newspapers; the majority are accepted after having taken a written test and been interviewed by the NCTJ, to which applications must be made. Courses do not guarantee employment.

Post-graduate courses (18/20 weeks to 1 year): Graduates from these courses also have to start as trainees, but they take the NCE after 18 months' training.

A few national papers are taking on trainees without previous experience and putting them through the NCTJ training scheme.

NOTE: The NCTJ also runs distance-learning courses in magazine journalism and sub-editing, open to journalists and non-journalists: these can contribute towards NVQs in magazine or newspaper journalism (production).

Magazines

The Periodicals Training Council (PTC) accredits a number of vocational courses for intending periodical journalists. A full listing of those courses which have achieved PTC accreditation is available on their website at *www.ppa.co.uk/ptc*. Alternatively contact the PTC directly to obtain a copy of their careers guide.

Post Entry Training run by the Periodicals Training Council has recently been developed. The PTC Professional Certificate in Journalism combines on-the-job experience, coaching and perhaps some formal training. This certificate is for those new to journalism who want to show they have the core knowledge and skills needed to be a magazine journalist. This certificate combines on-the-job assessment with an external assessment and interview.

NOTE: First degrees in journalism are available. Although these will be very attractive to school-leavers they are unlikely to give their graduates any real advantage over entry routes outlined above for either newspaper or periodical journalism. The same applies to media studies courses. Editors may take candidates who have shown breadth of interest by studying disciplines other than journalism/communications/media. Vocational training then follows the degree.

Some 2-year, full-time Foundation degrees are now being introduced.

Magazine journalism training is much less tightly structured than newspaper training and entry is still largely with specialist knowledge (especially scientific/technical/computing, but also other expertise, from drama to sport, education to law) and with writing/ editing ability. Quite a few arts graduates are editing technical journals.

Competition for trainee posts on magazines is fierce. Previous experience in student or freelance journalism is essential. Work on a journal dealing with one particular subject, whether electronics or municipal affairs, is good experience and can be a stepping stone to more general journalism. There is some scope in broadcasting (see p. 623) for experienced reporters. Science and engineering graduates have reasonable scope on the increasing number of publications which deal with various aspects of science and technology (especially information technology/computing) and which try to attract both specialist and lay readers.

Personal attributes The different jobs demand different talents and temperaments, but all journalists need a feeling for words; the ability to express themselves lucidly and concisely; wide interests; an unbiased approach; a pleasant easy manner so that shy, inarticulate people will talk to them easily; a certain presence so that busy, important people do not feel they are wasting their time answering questions; powers of observation; ability to sift the relevant from the irrelevant; ability to absorb atmosphere and to sum up people and situations quickly; an inquiring mind; great curiosity; the ability to become temporarily interested in anything from apple-growing to Zen Buddhism; resourcefulness; resilience; tact; willingness to work very hard; punctuality; a fairly thick skin (interviewees can be rude). For *senior jobs*: organizing ability.

Late start *Newspapers*: Late entrants account for 25% of the intake and follow the normal training programme (though this is not compulsory for those aged over 30).

Magazines: Quite normal for specialists.

Work life balance Only well-above-average people who have proved their value to their paper before the break have much hope of returning after a career break. Many turn to freelancing or edit, on a freelance basis, small organizations' or professional magazines: this is almost a cottage industry and badly paid. Fewer problems for feature writers, sub-editors.

Few problems on *magazines*. Some job-sharing possibilities. Up to 80% of magazine copy may be written by freelances.

Further information NCTJ Training Ltd, Latton Bush Centre, Southern Way, Harlow, Essex CM18 7BL.
www.nctj.com
Newspaper Society, Bloomsbury House, 74–77 Great Russell Street, London WC1B 3DA.
www.newspapersoc.org.uk
The Scottish Newspaper Publishers' Association, 48 Palmerston Place, Edinburgh EH12 5DE.
www.snpa.org.uk
Periodicals Training Council, Queen's House, 55–56 Lincoln's Inn Fields, London WC2A 3LJ.
www.ppa.co.uk/ptc
Reed Business, Reed Elsevier, 25 Victoria Street, London SW1H 0EX.
www.reedbusiness.com

Related careers ADVERTISING – INFORMATION WORK – PHOTOGRAPHY – PUBLIC RELATIONS – TELEVISION, FILM AND RADIO

Landscape Architecture

Entry qualifications No set requirements but usually a course accredited by the Landscape Institute. GCSEs or A-levels (or equivalent) in subjects such as geography, art and design, geology, environmental science or ecology can be useful. See 'Training' below for more detail.

The work

Landscape architects plan, design and manage our rural and urban landscapes and the outdoor environment. They work on the spaces between buildings: streets, squares, parks, promenades, waterways, shopping centres, business parks, housing developments, roads and transport networks, and a whole range of natural and built environments. A varied profession, landscape architecture could involve large-scale landscape planning or massive design projects, regenerating a rundown inner city area, or specializing in nature conservation, dealing with conservation of historical parks and gardens, or the complexities and intimacies of domestic gardens.

Often working with architects, civil engineers and planners, landscape architects reconcile the demands made on the environment by developments such as industrial or housing schemes or new roads with aesthetic and environmental needs. Their aim is to create landscapes which are pleasing, and at the same time functional, environmentally sustainable, economic to build and manage, able to accommodate buildings, and that work with the people that use them. They must also take account of the natural environment and nature conservation. In urban areas the work is often concerned with regeneration schemes in almost any public space, including the layouts of housing schemes, roads and streets, public squares, shopping and pedestrian precincts, and urban parks and green spaces. In the countryside, landscape architects may plan how best to blend developments or industrial sites such as power stations and reservoirs into their surroundings so that they cause as little environmental and visual impact as possible. They may work on the restoration of derelict land caused by industrial processes, quarrying or mining. They may work on restoration, management, conservation or the science of rivers, canals and other waterways. They may be responsible for the long-term management of the landscape of National Parks, Areas of Outstanding Natural Beauty, World Heritage sites, or Areas of Special Scientific Interest.

Landscape architects may also specialize in landscape science. Landscape scientists investigate and explore the geology, wildlife and natural features that make up landscape. They are predominantly concerned with the physical and biological principles and processes that are basic to landscape design and management.

Landscape scientists might have specialist skills such as soil science, ecology, biology or geology. These skills are then applied to landscape design and management, for example by the ecological analysis of sites, working with the designers to ensure that land can be utilized and enjoyed by all plant and life forms now and in the future.

Once the design is agreed with the client, landscape architects invite tenders from contractors, arrange the contract and supervise the subsequent work, to ensure that it is carried out satisfactorily and within the budget. They may also be responsible for specifying the right type of plants to achieve the desired appearance at all times of the year and at all stages of growth. An increasingly important part of their work is concerned with environmental assessments. Landscape architects frequently act as expert witnesses at planning and other inquiries affecting the landscape.

About 50% of landscape architects work for private practices – many of these are large multidisciplinary companies, working alongside architects, planners or engineers. Others work for the public sector, for local authorities or government agencies such as the Environment Agency or non-government bodies such as Groundwork. There are opportunities in EU countries, the USA and the Middle East.

Training The majority of landscape architects begin their career by undertaking a course accredited by the Landscape Institute. Courses can be: undergraduate entry, often consisting of either a degree and diploma or an MA, and usually incorporating a period of work experience; post-graduate, after taking a degree in another subject. Many universities offer conversion courses to enable progression on to a post-graduate programme for those whose first degree was in a subject not specifically related to landscape.

A list of accredited courses, with further contact details, is available on the Landscape Institute website at *www.l-i.org.uk*

On successfully completing an accredited course, graduates are eligible for Associate Membership of the Landscape Institute. After at least two years' qualifying work experience candidates can sit the LI's professional Practice Examination leading towards Chartered status.

Alternative method of entry An alternative route to entering the profession may be available to those who have not undertaken a course accredited by the Landscape Institute but have a degree in an area relevant to landscape, and who have also gained relevant qualifications and experience, such as geography, geology, planning, soil science, plant sciences, environmental studies, art and design, architecture, garden design or horticulture. (See 'Horticulture', p. 66.)

Personal attributes Visual imagination: flair for or interest in design; a keen interest in the environment, ecology, human or physical geography; an appreciation of how people live in town and country-side; ease of expression, both in drawing and writing; the ability to work well in teams; a good business head (for private practice).

Late start With the right initial qualifications it should be possible to make this a second career.

Landscape Architecture

Work life balance People who have kept up with developments should have no problem taking a career break. The Landscape Institute has a reduced subscription for members temporarily unemployed.

There are reasonable opportunities for part-time employment; possibly of running small consultative practice – but part-time work likely to be sporadic rather than regular.

Further information Education and Membership Department, Landscape Institute, 6–8 Barnard Mews, London SW1 1QU.
Website: *www.l-i.org.uk*
Email: *careers@l-i.org.uk*

Related careers AGRICULTURE AND HORTICULTURE – ARCHITECTURE – ART AND DESIGN – ENGINEERING: *Civil Engineering* – TOWN AND COUNTRY PLANNING

Languages

The British notoriously lack foreign language competence and the implications are likely to grow more serious with increasing European integration. In the European market, British companies could be at a real disadvantage compared with European competitors with a polyglot workforce. As one European businessman put it, 'We are happy to sell to you in English, but we like to buy in our own language.' Individuals could also lose out as increased labour mobility within the European Union will favour those with language skills.

Nevertheless, it must still be emphasized that language skills on their own are of very little value. Saying that you can speak German or Italian is, on its own, about as useful to an employer as saying that you can speak English. What matters is the framework of technical, professional or practical skills within which you can apply your languages.

There are very few careers for which languages are the primary skill required, and even these require other skills and qualities. For a growing number of careers, however, languages are a useful, sometimes essential, secondary skill.

LANGUAGES AS A PRIMARY SKILL

Interpreting

Conference interpreters
The work At international conferences interpreters may do either 'simultaneous' (the main type) or 'consecutive' interpreting. They must be exceptionally proficient in at least 2 major languages; an

additional knowledge of 1 or more less common languages is a help. *Simultaneous interpreters* relay the meaning of a speech, often on complicated subjects, almost instantaneously. The technique can be learned, but the talent and temperament are inborn. *Consecutive interpreters* relay a speech as a whole, or in large chunks, after each speaker. This requires as much skill as simultaneous interpreting.

Conference interpreters invariably interpret into their own language.

Some interpreters are employed by international agencies; others are freelances and are booked for a particular conference. Most of the year is spent travelling to and from New York, Geneva, Strasbourg, Brussels and London, living in hotels. The life may be luxurious, but it is extremely hectic, with very long irregular hours. Most conference interpreters now are specialists.

Conference interpreting is an extremely small profession.

Business and specialist interpreters

Business organizations of many kinds may need interpreters, for example when receiving trade delegations, negotiating international contracts and at trade fairs. Some of these interpreters may need specialist knowledge (such as engineering, information technology, computing, physical science or economics). Translators, both staff and freelance, may undertake this type of work. There are also opportunities working for conference organizers.

Public service interpreters

They are employed mainly by local authority social services departments to help members of ethnic communities whose first language is not English deal with officials in departments. For example, they help them to communicate with social security and housing officials, teachers and medical staff. They may also work in the courts. Employment is usually part time.

Interpreters in the last two groups use ad hoc or liaison interpreting, in which they interpret into and out of two languages, for example in a conversation between speakers of different languages.

Translating

The work Translators must be able to translate idiomatically and to write lucidly and concisely – being bilingual is not sufficient. They translate into their mother-tongue, so the prevalence of English has increased rather than reduced work for English translators.

They need a very good education and specialist knowledge of preferably a range of related subjects, though this may be acquired on the job. Most translations have some specialist content – contracts require some legal knowledge; scientific articles some understanding of the subject matter; specifications (for construction work, of anything from ships to atomic power stations) need some technical knowledge. Translators often have to discuss phrases and technical jargon with engineers, scientists, lawyers, etc., to get the sense absolutely right; translating is therefore often team-work.

Government departments, and industrial, commercial and research organizations, often have translating departments which employ specialists in particular fields, and sometimes non-specialists, who have, for instance, Chinese or Arabic, as well as 1 or 2 of the more usual languages.

Translating agencies employ specialists, and people who have unusual languages, often on a freelance basis. They like to have on their books a large number of people with widely different specialities and languages, on whom they can call at a moment's notice. There is increasing scope in translating instruction manuals for consumer goods manufacturers.

Much is rushed deadline work, especially for freelances.

Training It is increasingly important for interpreters and translators to have formal training and qualifications. The main courses and qualifications are:

1. Post-graduate courses, usually lasting 1 year, in technical and specialized translation/interpreting. Candidates must normally have a degree in 2 languages at the same level. Different courses offer different languages; Arabic, Czech, Slovak, Danish and Norwegian are among the more unusual options.

2. A few 4-year degree courses include emphasis on translating and interpreting skills.

3. The Institute of Linguists offers examinations (but not courses) including a Diploma in Public Service Interpreting in a large number of community languages and a post-graduate Diploma in Translating. (A number of institutions offer courses; distance-learning is available through the National Extension College.)

4. An NVQ/SVQ in Interpreting is available at level 4 and a level 5 NVQ/SVQ has been introduced for those competent in a range of professional and language skills.

Personal attributes An agile mind; interest in current affairs; a knowledge of cultural and social structures not only of their own country but of any country in whose language they specialize; ability to concentrate for long stretches and to work under pressure; ability to work well with others.

Conference interpreters need a calm temperament and the ability to snatch a few hours' sleep at any time.

Teaching
(see TEACHING, p. 610, for details)

Late start Translating and teaching possibly; interpreting unlikely.

Work life balance Theoretically flexible working should be possible as translating and interpreting are so often done by freelances. However, much of the work has to be done quickly – which means it may not be regular part-time work, but could be a few days' or weeks' rushed full-time work every now and then.

LANGUAGES AS A SECONDARY SKILL

There are a number of areas in which a knowledge of a foreign language can be a requirement or an asset, though it is not the primary skill and may not be a day-to-day part of the work. They include broadcasting (see p. 620); bilingual secretarial work (see p. 550), librarianship and information work (see p. 295); the Diplomatic Service (see p. 164); travel and tourism (see p. 642); patent agents (see p. 440); banking (see p. 119); law (see p. 323). In industry and commerce languages are undoubtedly becoming more important, but it is impossible to generalize about the roles in which they are most useful. Export marketing is an obvious example, but engineers, computer staff, general managers could all, in some circumstances, need languages. Receptionists and switchboard operators are often the first point of contact with a foreign supplier or customer. You should not consider any of these careers simply as a way to 'use my languages'. Rather, you should recognize competence in a foreign language as a skill that can enhance almost any career, giving an entrée to more interesting prospects, at home and abroad.

General language training There are many ways in which people may become proficient in a foreign language. Recent education initiatives aim to give more young people at least a starting-point at school. Under the National Curriculum all pupils have to study a foreign language until the age of 16. GCSEs in languages concentrate much more on oral skills than previous courses did.

No matter which direction your education takes at this point, there will almost certainly be the chance to further develop language skills. Some people will go on to A levels and then language degrees; the options include a traditional literature-based course, an 'applied' language course with emphasis on oral fluency and the economy, institutions and social climate of the relevant countries, or a degree combining languages with another subject such as law, engineering, business studies, marketing, computer studies and so on. There are also a number of college courses for A level entrants which offer languages for business, as well as language options in Dip. HE and BTEC courses.

Examinations in languages at different levels, and for different purposes, are also offered by the Royal Society of Arts, the London Chamber of Commerce and the Institute of Linguists.

A spell abroad is an extremely useful way to refine language skills. Most schools run exchanges, and most language degree courses include a year abroad. There are also a number of European Community schemes under Socrates to encourage young people to work or study in other member states.

Further information Institute of Linguists, Saxon House, 48 Southwark Street, London SE1 1UN.
www.iol.org.uk
Institute of Translation and Interpreting, Fortune House, South Fifth Street, Milton Keynes MK9 2EU.
www.iti.org.uk
CiLT, The National Centre for Languages, 20 Bedfordbury, London WC2N 4LB.
www.cilt.org.uk

Law

Barrister (Advocate in Scotland)

Entry qualifications First or second class honours degree (any subject).

The work Barristers plead in courts and give advice on legal matters. They clarify points of law and use their critical judgement in deciding what legislation and what precedents are relevant in any particular case. Their expertise helps clients, but barristers are first and foremost concerned with points of law, not with helping individuals: their relationship with clients is far more formal than that of solicitors.

Barristers are normally consulted by solicitors on behalf of their clients and do not normally see clients without a solicitor being present. In some instances, barristers may be instructed by members of other professions, e.g. accountants, surveyors, architects and overseas lawyers.

Though it is no longer required, most barristers work from 'chambers', sharing overheads and administrative back-up with other barristers. However, each barrister is self-employed; they may not go into partnership or be employed by other barristers. Once in practice, a barrister must wait for briefs by *solicitors* or be given work by the *barristers' clerk* (see p. 328), who 'distributes' work which comes to the set of chambers rather than to a particular barrister in the chambers.

Barristers normally specialize either in *common law*, which includes criminal work (the greatest proportion: it covers any case of law-breaking, however minor the offence), divorce, family, planning, personal injuries litigation and commercial law; or in *chancery work*, a much smaller branch which covers conveyancing, trusts, estate duty, taxation, company law.

In common law the emphasis is on pleading in court ('advocacy'); in chancery on work in chambers, drafting 'opinions' and advising. Common law work appeals, therefore, more to people who enjoy verbal battles and the court's somewhat theatrical atmosphere; chancery work appeals to those who enjoy the challenge of intellectual problem-solving.

Common law barristers usually join one of the six 'circuits' into which England and Wales are divided for legal administration purposes; they may then plead in provincial courts as well as in London. About a third of barristers in independent practice work from provincial chambers.

Barristers earn very little at first and often supplement their income by coaching, or other work, unless they have enough money to live on for the first year or so. Many barristers never attempt to practise at the Bar (others try to, but cannot get into chambers or get work); instead they become legal advisers in industry, or in local or central government. Such work is usually more easily available. It is far less precarious than the Bar, and in industry and commerce can lead to board-level jobs, but the work is not as varied as, nor has it the glamour of, being at the Bar.

The *Civil Service* offers a variety of work (see p. 168). *Justices' Clerks* advise the lay justices (JPs) in magistrates' courts, and have close day-to-day contact with the public.

The *Crown Prosecution Service* is responsible for deciding whether or not to prosecute cases in the criminal court; where they decide to prosecute it is the solicitors and barristers employed at headquarters or in one of the 42 areas who conduct the case, not, as previously, the police. In Scotland, *Procurators Fiscal*, assisted by Deputes, are the public prosecutors in the sheriff courts. Legal staff at the Crown office deal with more serious crimes.

Barristers, after at least 7 years' practice, are eligible for appointment (by the Lord Chancellor) as Chairpersons of Employment Tribunals. These Tribunals deal with unfair dismissal, redundancy payments and other matters relating to employment generally. Under the Sex Discrimination Act they also hear complaints from individuals who believe they have been discriminated against in terms of equal pay, promotion, acceptance for a particular job and other employment matters. Other Tribunals involve mental health and social security. Chairpersons are appointed to regional panels and sit on Tribunals within a given area. Appointments can be full time or part time (i.e. some lawyers carry on with their practice as well).

It takes a good deal of determination, and sometimes good contacts, to succeed at the Bar.

Training Training consists of an *Academic Stage*, a *Vocational Stage* and a *Practical Stage*.

1. The *Academic Stage*: students take *either* a qualifying law degree, which is basically one that covers the foundation subjects (see 'Training', under 'Solicitor', p. 331), *or* a non-law degree followed by a 1-year course for the Common Professional Examination (the CPE) at an approved institution or an approved Post-graduate Diploma in Law (PgDL).

Law degree courses vary greatly in emphasis on particular aspects of law. Most include the core subjects, but these are not always compulsory, so students must make sure they take the appropriate subjects in order to fulfil the requirements of the Academic Stage. It is also important to relate content to one's interests and plans: for example, some courses concentrate more on international and/or EU law; some on family and welfare law; some on tax and/or company law; some are geared more to private practice, some more to public service. Consult Hobson's *Degree Course Guide*.

2. The *Vocational Stage*: this consists of a 1-year full-time or 2-year part-time Bar Vocational Course (BVC) at one of the eight BVC institutions validated by the Bar Council. The emphasis is on the practical application of knowledge and advocacy skills. Students develop skills in, for example, negotiation, legal research, problem-solving, opinion-writing, drafting documents, oral and written communication, and presentation. Assessment is continuous and takes into account practical work, tests and examinations. On successful

completion of this stage students are 'called to the Bar'. Applications for a BVC are made online at *www.bvconline.co.uk*

Before enrolling on the Bar Vocational Course all Bar students must join one of the 4 Inns of Court. By the end of the BVC year students must complete 12 qualifying sessions, including dining in the Hall of their Inn a certain number of times. The purpose of this is to make contact with practising barristers and to be initiated into the traditional ways of the Bar.

3. The *Practical Stage*: Barristers wishing to practise at the Bar (or represent business employers in court) must serve 1 year's *pupillage*. During the first 6 months the pupil takes a background role, reading papers, drafting documents, attending court, helping to prepare cases, and becoming familiar with the rules of conduct and etiquette of the Bar. During the second 6 months a pupil is awarded a provisional practising certificate and may take cases on his or her own account. All chambers must now provide an income for pupil barristers of at least £5,000 per six months.

Online applications for pupillage (OLPAS) were introduced in 2001 (see *www.olpas.co.uk*). The Bar Council has a pupillage website at *www.pupillageonline.org.uk*, where all pupillage vacancies can be found.

Scotland: Scottish barristers, called advocates, must be members of the Faculty of Advocates in order to practise at the Bar. The procedures for qualification as an advocate are currently under review but at present, candidates, known as 'intrants', qualify in 4 stages:

1. A law degree from a Scottish university, giving subject-for-subject exemptions from the Faculty examinations. (Many entrants take 1 or 2 Faculty papers because it gives them greater freedom to choose other subjects in their degree courses.)

2. A 1-year full-time course at a Scottish university for the Diploma in Legal Practice (in common with Scottish solicitors).

3. For those wishing to practise: 21 months' (reduced by 9 months in certain cases) traineeship in a solicitor's office, followed by 9 months' pupillage (known as 'devilling') with a member of the Bar.

4. Pass the Faculty examination in evidence, practice and procedure.

English barristers who have completed a full period of pupillage may be admitted on passing an Aptitude Test.

Personal attributes A confidence-inspiring personality; power of logical reasoning; gift of expression; a quick brain; capacity for very hard work; tremendous self-confidence; some acting ability, or at least a sense of drama and relish for verbal battles in front of critical audiences; physical stamina; a good voice; resilience.

Late start Only for the very determined and able. *Exceptional* non-graduates over 25 may be accepted for a special CPE route (details from the Bar Council, address below), but this is very rare. A law degree might be a better bet as it gives a degree more generally accepted in the jobs market. In Scotland, between 1988 and 2000, the average age of persons starting practice at the Bar was 34. About 75% of those admitted to the Faculty during that period had at least 2 years' experience in another career, usually as solicitors.

Work life balance The Bar Council is currently revising the Equality Code for the Bar which will now draw attention to work life balance issues and include new guidance encouraging better practice. Nearly 50% of entrants to the Bar are female but there is a disproportionate drop-out amongst women barristers after about 10 years and issues regarding their retention and progression to senior levels are now receiving attention. Barristers in chambers are self-employed and in some cases have to pay flat rate rent and expenses regardless of income, which can make part-time work financially unviable. As self-employed barristers do not get statutory maternity leave, chambers have been asked to develop maternity leave policies and most offer 3 months' leave without rent and expenses and may keep positions open for up to a year. Anyone wanting a longer break would need to keep well in touch if wishing to return. An advantage of self-employment is that barristers can accept cases to fit in with other commitments, for example only during term time. They can choose to work from home when possible and IT developments are making this easier.

The Bar Council is a joint organizer of the ongoing Women's Lawyers Forum which is considering issues surrounding flexible working.

Further information The Bar Council/General Council of the Bar of England and Wales, 2 Cursitor Street, London EC4A 1NE.
www.barcouncil.org.uk
Faculty of Advocates, Advocates Library, Parliament House, Edinburgh EH1 1RF.
www.advocates.org.uk
The Law Careers Advice Network
www.lcan.csu.ac.uk

Related careers ACCOUNTANCY – CIVIL SERVICE – *Legal Executive/Solicitor* (see below)

Barristers' Clerk (England and Wales only)

Entry qualifications 4 GCSEs (A–C), including English language and maths.

The work This small profession has changed little over the past 100 years or so. Barristers' clerks 'manage' chambers and the barristers working in them (see Barrister, p. 323). The job of senior clerk (or Clerk to Chambers) is a unique mixture of power-behind-the-throne and humdrum clerking, involving negotiating fees and other matters relating to briefs coming to chambers with solicitors (from whom the briefs come). Clerks play a particularly important role in 'building up' young barristers: many briefs come to chambers rather than to individual barristers and it is the senior clerk who decides which of the young barristers is to be given the brief.

Senior clerks usually have junior clerks who make tea, carry barristers' books and robes to court, type opinions and pleadings. There is no career structure and no hope whatever of progressing to becoming a barrister, but as senior clerks get a commission on all their chambers' barristers' earnings they often earn more than some of the barristers for whom they are clerking.

Training On the job, with lectures. Clerks can take the BTEC course recommended by the Institute of Barristers' Clerks examination, after 4 years' clerking.

Personal attributes Very great self-confidence and presence; tact; willingness to tackle any kind of menial office job; respect for tradition and the established professional and social pecking order, in which barristers are a long way above clerks; interest in the law.

Late start Upper age for starting is normally 20; people who worked as barristers' secretaries very occasionally switch to clerking at any age: i.e. barristers are not willing to train late entrants, secretaries would know what clerks' duties are.

Work life balance Return to work after a career break would be very difficult.

Limited opportunities for part-time work, and none for senior clerk.

Further information Institute of Barristers' Clerks, 2/3 Cursitor Street, London EC4A 1NE.
www.barristersclerks.com

Related careers CIVIL SERVICE – *Legal Executive* – SECRETARIAL AND CLERICAL WORK

Solicitor

Entry qualifications A degree *or* Fellowship of the Institute of Legal Executives (see p. 333) (most entrants are graduates). In Scotland non-graduates need high grades in the SCE Highers, which must include English and either maths or science or a foreign language.

The work A solicitor is a confidential adviser to whom people turn for legal advice and information in a vast variety of personal and business matters. As everyday life becomes more complex, the solicitor is increasingly asked to help in matters where common sense, wisdom and an objective approach are as important as legal knowledge. Whenever possible, solicitors try to settle matters out of court.

Solicitors have full rights to represent clients personally in magistrates' and county courts and, with additional qualification, can appear as advocates also in the Crown and High Courts (Scottish solicitors have somewhat greater rights in the equivalent courts). Increasing numbers of solicitors practise advocacy. When a barrister is briefed to appear for a client, the preparatory work and the liaison with the client is still undertaken by the solicitor.

The majority of solicitors work in private practices, ranging from large multi-partner departmentalized city firms to small general, or even sole-practitioner, firms. Work content, conditions and remuneration are correspondingly wide-ranging. A city solicitor will generally specialize immediately, working for corporate clients in mainly commercial fields such as banking, taxation, company law and property development. Solicitors in smaller practices tend to handle a wider range of tasks, usually for individual clients, but everywhere there is a trend to earlier and greater specialization. Typical areas of work in smaller firms are crime, family law, personal injuries, conveyancing, landlord and tenant matters, and smaller-scale commercial work. There are now small firms which concentrate on providing an expert streamlined service in just 1 or 2 areas, for example, medical negligence, entertainment law, immigration.

Most social welfare law, civil and human rights cases, and almost all legally aided cases, are undertaken by smaller firms and, to some extent, by publicly funded law centres, usually in inner-city areas.

Relaxation of traditional rules has enabled solicitors to become involved also in financial services and estate agency and to advertise their services. Solicitors are now required to undertake continuing professional development.

A solicitor with 3 years' experience can establish a practice but will need capital and contacts to succeed. Securer employment opportunities are available at all levels in local government and the Civil Service. For those interested exclusively in criminal work there are opportunities in the Crown Prosecution Service or the Procurator Fiscal Service in Scotland. Many commercial, industrial and other organizations employ legal advisers where the nature of the work will depend on the activities of the employer.

After substantial experience solicitors can apply to become registrars, stipendiary magistrates, recorders or circuit judges. There are also opportunities for appointments to chair industrial and other tribunals.

Training There are 3 routes to qualifying in England and Wales: .

1. The *law degree route* (the majority of solicitors qualify this way): After successfully completing a qualifying law degree (one covering the foundation subjects – obligations including restitution, contract and tort, criminal law, equity and trusts, European law, property law and public law including constitutional, administrative and human rights) graduates go on to the Legal Practice Course. This replaced the Law Society Finals Course in 1993 and lasts 1 year full time and 2 years part time. Successful completion of the Legal Practice Course is then followed by a 2-year training contract ('articles'), and a Professional Skills Course in 3 compulsory parts: advocacy and communication skills; finance and business skills; and client care and professional standards. Most people train in private practice, but there are some opportunities in the Civil Service, local government, the Crown Prosecution Service, the Magistrates' Courts Service, and industry and commerce.

2. The *non-law degree route*: Graduates take a 1-year course leading to the Common Professional Examination (CPE) or a Diploma in Law before proceeding to the Legal Practice Course and the training contract as above. Qualifying therefore takes 1 year longer than for law graduates.

3. The *non-graduate route*: Candidates first become Fellows of the Institute of Legal Executives (see p. 333). They then take the Legal Practice Course and the training contract may be waived.

NOTE: All routes are very competitive. Good grades are essential at both A level and degree stages. Relevant work experience can also be useful.

*

Routes to qualifying in Scotland:

Either an LLB degree at a Scottish university followed by a 26-week full-time course for the Diploma in Legal Practice followed by a 2-year post Diploma traineeship *or* a 3-year training contract with a firm of solicitors leading to the Law Society of Scotland's professional examinations, followed by the Diploma in Legal Practice followed by a 2-year post Diploma traineeship. The law degree route is the more popular. The traineeship is undertaken with a practising solicitor, either in private practice or a public service or other organization.

Personal attributes Capacity for absorbing facts quickly; logical reasoning; ability to see implications which are not obvious; ability to come to grips with an intricate problem; a good memory for facts and faces; tact; patience; good communication skills; sound judgement of character; an understanding of human behaviour; a personality that inspires confidence.

Late start Mature entrants are advised to take the ILEX route or take a law degree (most academic institutions make concessions for mature students).

Work life balance Some firms of solicitors are now instituting formal career break schemes. The Association of Women Solicitors runs courses for returners and is helping universities and colleges to develop courses in this area. The Association, with the Young Solicitors' Group, is also part of the Women Lawyers' Forum which is currently looking into the issues surrounding flexible working.

Part-time opportunities are improving in private practice, the Civil Service and local government. The last two also offer job-sharing, but it is very rare in private practice, where part-time work is seen to be more acceptable.

Further information The Law Society, Ipsley Court, Redditch, Worcs
B98 OTD.
www.lawsociety.org.uk
www.solicitors-online.com

Law Society of Scotland, 26 Drumsheugh Gardens, Edinburgh EH3 7YR.
www.lawscot.org.uk

Legal Executive (England and Wales only)

Entry qualifications 4 GCSEs (A–C) or equivalent, including NVQ level 3 and GNVQ Intermediate. (A level law shortens the training.)

The work Legal executives work for a solicitor in much the same way as junior executives work for a managing director. Solicitors are in overall control, make contact with clients and lay down policy. Legal executives usually specialize in one particular branch of the law – probate, conveyancing, litigation, company law, etc. Their day-to-day work will include: looking up references in law books, preparing documents, interviewing clients and witnesses and conferring with clients on points of detail. In small practices, or when managing a branch office, they may also be involved with the whole spectrum of work.

Legal executives undertake advocacy before judges in the county court and Masters of the High Court on preliminary, or interlocutory, matters. They also have some limited rights of audience in the county court, particularly on family matters.

Legal executives may become solicitors in 1 or 2 years after becoming Fellows (see p. 331).

Training On the job, together with part-time training at day-release or evening classes, or by approved distance-learning courses, for the 2-part Institute of Legal Executives' Membership Examination. The syllabus includes general legal subjects and practice and procedure, and allows for specialization in one branch of the law. Training time varies from 2 to 4 years, but each part *normally* takes 2 years. There are a small number of full-time courses for the ILEX level 3 Professional Diploma in Law. After 5 years' relevant employment (2 of which must follow the ILEX level 4 Professional Higher Diploma in Law) members can become Fellows.

Personal attributes Sufficient powers of concentration to detect relevant details in a mass of complex documentation; patience and perseverance; self-confidence and ability to discuss matters with all types of people from criminals to judges, common sense and good practical skills.

Late start Over-21s do not need specific educational qualifications: many decide to become legal executives after having worked as legal secretaries. It is possible to prepare for the ILEX professional qualification without being in relevant employment.

Work life balance Career-breaks should not be a problem for people who keep up with legislative changes.

Some opportunities exist for part-time jobs and also for training, but promotion is difficult. Job-sharing should be possible.

Further information The Institute of Legal Executives, Kempston Manor, Kempston, Bedford MK42 7AB.
www.ilex.org.uk

Related careers *Barrister/Barristers' Clerk/Solicitor* (see above)/ *Licensed Conveyancer* (see below) – CHARTERED SECRETARY AND ADMINISTRATOR

Licensed Conveyancers (England and Wales only)

Solicitors no longer have a monopoly in conveyancing property. Independent conveyancers may work on their own or in qualifying employment, i.e. licensed conveyancers, solicitors, financial institutions, local government departments, or property developers with in-house conveyancing departments.

Entrants need to have 4 GCSEs (A–C), including English. Mature students over 25 and those in qualifying employment may be accepted with relevant experience only. Training is in 2 parts:

1. Part-time study or distance-learning for the Council for Licensed

Conveyancers' Foundation and Finals examinations. Exemptions are available to those who have a recognized legal qualification.

2. 2 years' supervised full-time practical training, in qualifying employment, while studying for the examinations (can be completed on a part-time basis which extends the 2-year period). Exemptions are available for those with conveyancing experience.

Further information Information pack available from the Council for Licensed Conveyancers, 16 Glebe Road, Chelmsford, Essex CM1 1QG.
www.conveyancer.org.uk

Leisure/Recreation Management

Though we may not have become the 'leisure society' as predicted some years ago, people are spending more time and money on leisure activities. The leisure industry is enormous and at its broadest includes everything from hotels and catering to zoos and safari parks, taking in pubs, wine bars, cinemas, theme parks and heritage sites, sport and leisure centres, museums, art galleries and theatres, parks and playgrounds, even libraries. Though this may suit economists and industry analysts, it is not a practical starting-point for career-choosers. Running a pub is almost certainly not what someone turning to this chapter has in mind; nor is the average librarian likely to consider themselves as part of the leisure industry. Many people who will find themselves in this broad-sweep leisure industry are likely to have interests and motivations that lead them to other chapters in this book. Nevertheless it is helpful for people who see leisure as primarily sport and physical recreation to recognize that the opportunities are very much wider than is commonly realized.

Entry qualifications None specified. In practice professional qualification and/or administrative experience.

The work The leisure industry has developed piecemeal, but it is characterized by growth, diversity and increasing integration. It is generally recognized that leisure and recreation are an important aspect of the well-being of both individuals and the community; it is also recognized that well-run leisure facilities can be profitable. So more facilities are being developed. They are increasingly sophisticated in response to market demand. Where once you had swimming pools you now have 'leisure pools' with waves, water slides, deck-chairs and interior landscaping.

Integration occurs on several levels. Local authorities (who used to be the largest employers of leisure management staff, though they have now been outstripped by the private and voluntary sectors) have established integrated, multidisciplinary departments to cover indoor and outdoor sports, parks and countryside, the arts, community and children's play facilities, entertainments and libraries and tourism. Large-scale complexes are being developed where people can, for example, shop, eat, swim, bowl, or take in a film or concert. Increasingly, leisure facilities are a partnership of public and private sectors with, for example, an authority providing finance for a development, while a private concern manages it on a contract basis. In addition to local authority facilities there are opportunities in, for example, company sports and social clubs, countryside and theme parks, Sport England and governing bodies of individual sports, the Arts Council, arts centres, theatres and concert halls.

The work involved obviously varies a great deal and it is possible to give only a few examples. *Senior managers*, whatever their title, are responsible for financial management, marketing, promotion, and management and motivation of staff who might include administration, catering, maintenance and specialists, e.g. coaches or instructors. *Assistant managers* generally look after a particular function (bookings and administration, for example), a facility (e.g. the swimming pool and all associated activities) or a range of activities (e.g. all outdoor sports or entertainments in an authority's parks). *Supervisors* are concerned with the day-to-day running of activities and the work of staff such as poolside staff, gardeners or entertainment centre staff. There are variations on this pattern: in a smaller centre a manager will have to take on a broader range of responsibilities, while in a larger facility there may be more specialized roles. Depending on the size and nature of the organization there may also be central roles in policy formulation, budgeting and planning.

By definition 'leisure' is when you are not working, so leisure staff at operational levels must work when most other people are not working.

The leisure industry is a very broad-based pyramid with many more jobs at basic than at senior levels. Its relative lack of structure, however, makes it a fairly easy pyramid to climb for those with the right motivation and qualifications. On the other hand entrants often have to start at a level lower than their paper qualifications seem to warrant.

Some areas of this vast field are obviously more specialized. *Arts administration*, for example, has a particular character and appeal, especially for graduates. It entails enabling artistic events (plays, concerts, etc.) to take place. This may involve planning, publicity, engaging performers, booking venues, handling ticket sales, finance (often including negotiating grants and sponsorship), maintenance of buildings and general administration. The actual range of tasks will depend on the size and nature of the organization – in a small company managers might have to sell tickets at the door, at the Barbican they will not! There are a few relevant degrees and post-graduate courses, as well as options on more general leisure courses (see 'Training', below). There is still, however, a foot-in-the-door element in this field and people develop careers from spare-time activities and voluntary work.

Training It is becoming increasingly necessary to have relevant higher educational or professional qualifications. Nevertheless, particularly in commercial leisure centres, successful managers may have few qualifications but lots of flair and entrepreneurial skills. Generally speaking, however, and certainly for local authority posts, systematic training is advisable.

The Institute of Leisure and Amenity Management offers four qualifications achieved through a work-based practical research project:

1. The ILAM First Award – pre-entry requirements are 4 GCSEs (A–C) or equivalent; GNVQ/GSVQ Intermediate in Leisure and Tourism; NVQs/SVQs in appropriate leisure-related fields at Level 2; a relevant City & Guilds qualification.

2. ILAM Certificate in Leisure Operations – pre-entry requirements are 2 A levels or equivalent; NVQs/SVQs in appropriate leisure-related fields at level 3; or relevant BTEC, City & Guilds or management qualification.

3. ILAM Certificate in Leisure Management – pre-entry requirements are NVQs/SVQs in appropriate leisure fields at level 4; BTEC Continuing Education Certificate in Leisure Management or HNC/HND in Leisure Studies or other leisure-related field; relevant management qualifications; a leisure-related or business and finance degree.

4. ILAM Diploma/Advanced Diploma in Leisure Management – pre-entry requirements are the ILAM Certificate in Leisure Management; a recognized degree or post-graduate qualification.

An individual wishing to enter the ILAM Qualification Scheme who has worked in the industry but does not have the required qualifications, may apply to ILAM for recognition of their prior experience.

Personal attributes Good organizing ability; practicality; ability to make different specialists work as a team; interest in the needs of all sections of the community; confidence in dealing with members of the public (even when they are impatient or boisterous).

Late start No reason why not.

Work life balance Opportunities for career breaks and flexible working will differ depending on employer – they should be readily available if working for a local authority.

There is considerable shift-work in some jobs.

Further information Institute of Leisure and Amenity Management, ILAM House, Lower Basildon, Reading, Berks. RG8 9NE.
  www.ilam.co.uk
Institute of Sport and Recreation Management (ISRM), Sir John Beckwith Centre for Sport, Loughborough University, Loughborough LE11 3TU.
  www.isrm.co.uk
sportscotland, Caledonia House, South Gyle, Edinburgh, EH12 9DQ.
  www.sportscotland.org.uk

Leisure/Recreation Management

Related careers AGRICULTURE AND HORTICULTURE — LOCAL GOVERNMENT — MUSEUMS AND ART GALLERIES — PUBLIC RELATIONS — SPORT — TEACHING

Local Government

Local government is not a career but an employer. More precisely it is more than 400 employers throughout England, Scotland and Wales. Together they employ about 2 million people in hundreds of occupations and spend more than £70 billion every year providing services, many of which are required by law, to their local communities.

In recent years there have been great changes in the way local services are managed. Increasingly council services are subject to competition and scrutiny. Some council departments are run as external consultancies, selling their services to other departments. The idea is that the providers of the service will have to improve efficiency, while the 'purchasers' will develop a keener eye for quality of service and value for money, both of which local residents and businesses are entitled as council tax payers to expect. As in other public-sector areas, new management skills are required of those responsible for bringing a more businesslike approach to the provision of public services, e.g. contract management and quality assurance.

Entry qualifications Most local authority employees hold qualifications relevant to the work they do. Some openings for those with a good general education, usually in administrative posts.

The work This varies enormously. Local government is enabled or required by law to provide a wide range of services. The larger employers of staff include: education, which includes schools, colleges, the youth service; social services; public protection, which includes the work of the police and fire services, consumer protection and environmental health; leisure services, which can include sports and community facilities, libraries, museums, theatres and the promotion of tourism; highways, housing, buildings and planning, which ranges from strategic planning to provision and maintenance of a range of community buildings. Obviously the scope of such activities involves a large number and wide range of people doing different things!

Among the scores of careers in local government are a number which can be pursued both inside and outside of local government. These include accountancy, law, engineering, computer work, librarianship, public relations and human resources management. Local government is one option within these career areas. For another group of careers local authorities are the exclusive or major employers. These include teaching, social work, town planning, environmental health and trading standards (consumer protection). Another large group is involved in general administration, advising on policy formulation and procedures and coordinating the implementation of policies agreed by the elected councillors. Their work may include servicing committees, research and report-writing, as well as the day-to-day administration ensuring the smooth running of departments and services.

Many of the professionals employed by local authorities provide services directly to the public, e.g. teachers and librarians. Others, however, are part of the vast, essential support structure. Computing and for the most part legal services, for example, are not offered direct to the local community, but they are essential to the provision of education and social services. In fact departments and services are not self-contained and projects usually involve multidisciplinary teams. For example, the building of a new school would involve not only the education department, but architects and surveyors, lawyers, planners, finance, possibly the fire services, even the leisure department if, say, it were intended that the school's sports facilities be used by the community outside school hours.

People may be promoted within a department and authority, but it is common to move among employing authorities, and being willing and able to move can aid rapid progress. It is also becoming increasingly easy, especially for those with good management skills, to move across departments.

Training Local authorities provide extensive training for all levels of staff, with opportunities to study for appropriate qualifications in a range of areas. The entry point, length and structure of training may vary. In some cases local authorities offer graduate entrants the opportunity to gain the practical training and experience necessary for professional qualification; in others they offer A level (or equivalent) entrants sponsorship on an appropriate degree course. Other entrants may be sponsored for day-release for relevant qualifications. Among the fields in which training schemes are offered are: personnel (human resources management), IT, environmental health, town planning, trading standards, accountancy, engineering, surveying, social work, leisure management, architecture, housing management, law.

There is also a national graduate development programme (ngdp) for local government, which recruits recent graduates with the potential to become senior managers on to a 2-year management training scheme.

For individual professions: see individual entries. (Some professionals train with local authorities; others join after qualifying.)

For general administration: entry qualifications vary. An increasing number of administrative officers are *graduates*, with some authorities running special graduate-training schemes. The professional qualification for senior administrators is membership of the Institute of Chartered Secretaries and Administrators, for which day-release may be available. *A level entrants* may also study for this qualification or for a BTEC Higher award in public services. Those with 4 GCSEs (A–C) can begin work and study for BTEC National awards in public services; those who are motivated and able can continue on to a related BTEC Higher award, a degree and/or ICSA membership. (It is probably best for those who are ambitious to aim for educational qualifications that will take them to the highest entry point possible for them.)

It is difficult to draw lines about who is an administrator and who is not. Many of the professionals mentioned above are part of the administrative structure (for example, personnel), and many qualifications can lead to senior management. In some departments it is very common for the senior management to have grass-roots experience; for example, senior education administrators commonly have teaching experience.

NVQs/SVQs and/or Modern Apprenticeships are available in many occupational areas such as amenity horticulture, business administration, care, customer service, IT, sport and recreation and vehicle maintenance.

Some authorities also offer Foundation degrees in partnership with local universities in subjects such as community governance, early years care and education and housing.

Personal attributes Depends on the particular type of work, but generally interest in local affairs; good written and oral communication skills and ability to deal with people; good organization skills; ability to work as one of a team. *For senior management*, willingness to carry into effect decisions taken by councillors, whether or not one agrees with them.

Late start Good for those with relevant experience and, as seen above, so much is relevant. Authorities' policies and practices vary.

Work life balance Local authorities have been among the most forward-looking employers on flexible working arrangements. Increasingly they need to investigate different ways of working, not only to deliver more cost-effective and competitive services, but also to meet the demands of employees who want to achieve a better balance between their work and other priorities. Arrangements vary from authority to authority but among the flexible options are flexi-time, job-sharing and part-time work, term-time working, working at home, secondments and career breaks.

Further information Employers' Organisation for Local Government, Layden House, 76–86 Turnmill Street, London EC1M 5LG.
Local government careers information *www.lgcareers.com*
National graduate development programme *www.ngdp.co.uk*

Related careers CIVIL SERVICE

Logistics, Distribution and Transport Management

Entry qualifications See 'Training'.

Logistics is a term of military origin, commonly used in connection with the movement of goods and people. In industry it has a specific meaning as the management of the 'supply chain' for goods, from raw materials right through to the end user. Logistics is a vital part of manufacturing, retailing, local and central government departments and the armed forces. The final product could be anything from a loaf of bread on the breakfast table, a car in a high street showroom, military supplies in a front-line soldier's hands, a pint of beer in the pub, petrol in a car's tank, or a pair of surgical gloves in an operating theatre. Some estimates show that over a quarter of the UK population works in a logistics-related job.

There are two main reasons why logistics has become a specialist function, both concerned with giving companies a competitive edge. The first is the rapid development of computers and information technology and their applications to logistics and distribution. For example, when the checkout operator's scanner 'reads' the label on a tin of dog food, a message is sent by computer to the supplier to say that the item has been sold and needs replacing. Similar systems enable a car manufacturer to monitor the exact level of stock of components and to order more to arrive 'just in time' – storage space is costly, so this system saves money. The second is the drive to provide better customer service: customers not only want basics, such as the right amount of raw materials arriving at the right time, but may be attracted by extra services, for example after-sales support or disposal of waste products.

The aim of all those involved in logistics is to ensure that the right resource is in the right place at the right time in the right quantity, the right condition, and at the right cost. All managers need an understanding of the issues involved, but, increasingly in larger organizations, logistics specialists are employed to oversee every link in the chain. Companies and organizations may have their own logistics department or they may use outside logistics services. These services may manage the whole supply business or may deal solely with *transport* or *storage*.

Job titles in logistics and distribution management vary between employers. Logistics manager, transport manager, supply officer, operations manager, warehouse manager, materials planner, inventory controller, commodity manager are some of the most usual. Associated disciplines/functions are MARKETING AND SELLING (see p. 371), PURCHASING AND SUPPLY (see p. 506), RETAIL MANAGEMENT (see p. 512), MANAGEMENT (see p. 351) and finance.

Examples of logistics jobs

Logistics planner/strategist: Planners analyse the various links of the supply chain and try to find ways of making the whole work ever more smoothly and efficiently. The key is the flow of information at every stage and this is where sophisticated computer systems can be so effective. Planners working in logistics consultancies will work with managers in the client's organization to look at logistics issues such as warehousing, supply, materials handling, transport and IT systems.

Road transport manager (freight): The vast majority of goods in Britain (and only slightly fewer in Europe) are carried by road. Movement of goods can be carried out by suppliers/manufacturers/retailers' own transport fleets (known as 'own account' operations) or by 'third party' operations. These specialists include small local hauliers and huge national and international carriers whose lorries are a common sight on motorways and at ports. A transport manager will oversee a fleet of vehicles and their drivers, making sure that deliveries reach customers on time and in good condition. The many aspects of running a transport business include finance, purchase and maintenance of vehicles, recruitment and training of drivers, safety (both of vehicles and in the loading and unloading of dangerous substances), looking for ways of making lorries more environmentally friendly (for example by changes in design and limiting of noise and other forms of pollution). Movement of lorries needs to be planned to ensure the lowest mileage and, wherever possible, 'backloading' – collecting a load for the return journey.

Warehouse manager: Many manufacturers and retailers own and operate their own warehouses. Others use specialist distribution companies who may offer both transport and storage services. Warehouse managers may operate a warehouse dedicated to one customer's goods or provide storage, packaging and handling services to several different customers. The efficient use of space, the use of sophisticated systems for the checking in and out of goods means fewer people are employed in warehouses than in the past, but managers still have to oversee people, vehicles and systems.

Training Entry to trainee management posts is *either* with a degree/ HND in transport/logistics/distribution, *or* a degree/HND in another discipline with or without a relevant post-graduate qualification, *or* into a junior post as a school-leaver (A levels in geography or economics useful) followed by study on-the-job for professional qualifications. Many people working in this area have not gained formal qualifications, but these are becoming more important, especially where recognition by other European countries is necessary.

The main professional organization is the Institute of Logistics and Transport. It offers modular programmes leading to its Certificate, Diploma and Advanced Diploma qualifications which can be followed at an approved centre or through distance-learning. It also offers a 3-year distance-learning degree course leading to an MSc in Logistics or Passenger Transport Management, validated by Aston University.

NVQs and SVQs (see p. 10) are also available.

Third party transport providers have to have someone in control who has a Certificate of Professional Competence awarded by the OCR examining body, or an exemption certificate issued by one of the authorized professional bodies on behalf of the Department for Transport.

Personal attributes Practical, analytical mind; interest in problem-solving; ability to see the large picture as well as attending to detail; independence and willingness to take responsibility; good communication and negotiation skills; for many jobs, willingness to move from one function to another; ability to cope with pressure and frequent changes; ability to motivate and lead others.

Late start Many people have moved sideways into logistics functions or moved up from clerical or operational roles (many transport managers started as drivers). This *may* become less common as graduate entry grows, but it will depend on whether or not the candidate has relevant previous experience.

Work life balance Opportunities for career breaks and flexible working will depend on employers, but some in this sector, such as large retail companies, have a good record in this area.

RELATED SPECIALIZATIONS

Freight Forwarding

Freight forwarders: arrange transport of all types of freight to and from anywhere in the world. They search out the most efficient method or combination of methods of transport in each particular case, evaluating respectively the need for speed, security, refrigeration, the type of goods, legal and commercial constraints, etc. Goods may be sent by rail, road, air or sea, or by a combination of several modes of transport. Freight forwarders must be well acquainted with the advantages and disadvantages of the various methods of transport (which they are likely to learn by experience and from colleagues rather than from the transporters themselves), and with the intricacies of freight handling and storage and the different techniques and arrangements in the various ports and airports all over the world. They must make it their business to find out routes which, though possibly longer in mileage, may be more efficient because turn-round arrangements in some ports and airports are quicker than in others.

They are also responsible for documentation, such as Bills of Lading, import and export licences, and for specialized packing and warehousing.

Some freight forwarders specialize in certain commodities or geographical areas; others in certain methods of transport and/or types of packing or warehousing.

Training On the job with part-time or distance-learning study leading to membership of the British International Freight Association.

BIFA also offers classroom-based courses including the Multimodal Freight Training programme, at 2 levels, involving block and home study.

The BIFA also recognizes the NVQ/SVQ in International Trade and Services and in other related areas.

Shipbroking

Shipbrokers: match up empty ships with cargoes and negotiate terms on behalf of their clients. This process is known as 'fixing', and is rather like solving a giant jigsaw puzzle. Shipbrokers may use a regular cargo run or charter a ship for a single voyage or a series of voyages, or a part of a ship's freight space. They also act as agents for shipowners when their ships are in port and deal with customs formalities, loading documentation, arrangements for the crew and any problems that may crop up. Shipbrokers also buy and sell ships for their clients. Some specialize in one activity, others are involved in several.

Shipbrokers often work long and irregular hours, as they have to be in telephone contact with people all over the world during their working hours.

Training Trainee shipbrokers take a correspondence or part-time course leading to membership of the Institute of Chartered Shipbrokers. For the Foundation Diploma in Shipping they take one compulsory subject, Introduction to Shipping, and one other. For the Qualifying examinations, in addition to compulsory subjects including Shipping Business, they take 3 specialist subjects of their choice:

these include Ship Sale and Purchase, Marine Insurance, Tanker Chartering, Dry Cargo Chartering and International Through Transport. Partial exemptions may be given to entrants with relevant qualifications.

Further information Institute of Logistics and Transport, Logistics and Transport Centre, PO Box 5787, Corby, Northants NN17 4XQ.
www.iolt.org.uk
British International Freight Association, Redfern House, Browells Lane, Feltham, Middlesex TW13 7EP.
www.bifa.org
Institute of Chartered Shipbrokers, 3 St Helens Place, London EC3A 6EJ.
www.ics.org.uk

Related careers MANAGEMENT – MARKETING AND SELLING – PURCHASING AND SUPPLY – STOCK EXCHANGE AND SECURITIES INDUSTRY – TRAVEL AGENT/TOUR OPERATOR

Management

Entry qualifications Nothing specific (see 'The work' and 'Training', below), but a degree or professional qualification is advisable.

The work Management is a vast and confusing field, with vague terminology. It is not so much one structured career as an activity, the purpose of which is to make the best use of available resources – human, money, material, equipment, time – in order to achieve a given objective. It is becoming much more professionalized, with specific, though varied, theories, techniques and training leading to various qualifications (or none). It is also a 'transferable skill': managers now often take their expertise from one type of organization – say manufacturing industry – to another, say tourism. Any system which provides a product, or a service, has to be managed. Someone has to see that things actually happen and that policies are carried out effectively and economically. Traditionally, this has been implemented through a hierarchy of managers sandwiched between the policy-makers at board or equivalent level and the 'doers'. Now, however, the pattern is less one of rigid hierarchies with policy emanating from the top. Companies cannot afford to carry the costs of too many 'non-productive' managers; instead they are beginning to 'empower' staff at all levels and encourage them to create and act on their own initiative. Many companies have ripped out layers of management, flattening the hierarchy (which can be as few as 4 levels from top to bottom in a large international company) and giving managers considerable autonomy. At all levels, managers must enthuse their subordinates into doing things as efficiently as they – the managers – would wish to have done them themselves.

351

One of the most important aspects which applies to all types and levels is, therefore, communication: managers spend between 70% and 90% of their time talking to people – in conference, on the phone, in one-to-one discussion. That applies whether a manager manages a whole or part of a supermarket; an international sales force; a large export department or a small section of one; an engineering workshop; a manufacturing company.

There are basically two ways into management: *either* by first becoming a specialist in something, *or* by starting as 'management trainee' in an organization with a management training scheme. But trainee schemes which give broad-based, systematic training are not easy to get for people without qualifications, so pre-entry training for a qualification is advisable (see 'Training', below).

Levels of management: There is no clear-cut distinction between junior, middle and senior management. Designations vary between organizations. Rising from one level to another does not necessarily depend on gaining further qualifications. However, qualifications are very useful and may be essential, especially when changing employers.

Most people who choose a management career think of senior, and general, managers – but they are the smallest management section.

Junior managers are the easiest to define. They are usually responsible for controlling the work of a number of people who are all doing the same work – usually work in which the junior managers are trained (or at least which they are able to do) themselves. For example a supervisor fitter is a skilled fitter; an administrator of word-processing services is a word processor operator (see p. 556), though he/she is now often a graduate management trainee; a team leader on a factory production line has worked on the production line (though possibly as a graduate engineer gaining experience). Junior managers organize the flow of work, and sort out minor problems (often including subordinates' personal ones). In the office of, say, an export department, a junior manager might be responsible for ensuring that documentation relating to goods for one or two countries is dealt with correctly; on the shop-floor junior managers might be responsible for one or two production lines, which could mean about 100 people.

Junior managers are also the link with middle management. However, there is a slow but growing trend to 'self-managed work groups', where there is either no manager, or the management element is a small part of the job. Some companies are experimenting with the concept of teams electing their own leaders on an annual basis.

Middle managers coordinate and implement policies; increasingly they also set policies. This level of management spans a wide range of jobs and levels of responsibility. The step from junior to middle management is the most crucial on the management ladder: while junior managers are usually responsible for people all doing the same kind of work, middle managers are responsible either for the work of a number of junior managers who are all doing different jobs, or for a larger group of people in the same field. Junior managers who want promotion must therefore broaden their experience and 'move sideways' before moving up. This experience-broadening is part of 'management development' (see PERSONNEL/HUMAN RESOURCES MANAGEMENT, p. 444) and should be built into managers' training, but in very many firms young managers have to plan their own career-paths rather than rely on personnel managers to do it for them. This is partly what makes 'management' such a difficult career to plan and to describe. It is not so much qualifications as varied experience, luck, drive and initiative that matter.

The majority of managers remain middle managers always, gradually taking responsibility for a wider range of activities or for bigger departments. For example, a sales manager in charge of a regional sales force is a middle manager and remains so even when responsibility covers a larger sales force, or becomes more important in cash- terms or regions. A manager in charge of a mail order firm's dispatch department, responsible for a large sum of money and for the firm's reputation for reliability, is a middle manager, and might still be a middle manager when, say, also overseeing the dispatch and the packing departments. However, in another firm the job might be designated 'senior manager': it depends on a firm's organization, and their interpretation of what senior management is.

A vital and growing 'senior-middle management' area is 'management of change'. Typically this is the result of automation. Introduction of new technologies – whether robots in a factory or a new computer system in an office – is a 'socio-technical' problem. There is as yet no single tried and tested way of tackling this development and its implications. In some companies consultants in 'organizational change' or 'organizational behaviour' (usual backgrounds: social or behavioural science degree plus/or extensive business experience) may be called in to advise; more often managers (departmental, office, production, personnel – it varies enormously) have to cope. These managers may have to deal with employees' fears of new and unknown working practices; with the 'de-skilling' of some jobs and retraining staff for others; with 'slimming down' the workforce and with the search and training for new job opportunities for redundant employees. 'Planning for change' is evolving into a management specialism or at least a new management task (see MANAGEMENT CONSULTANCY, p. 364). Change does not result only from automation. Companies also re-examine how they do things by looking at processes (a chain of activities that delivers value to a customer) rather than functions (bits of processes that represent the way a company is typically organized). This gives much greater scope for rationalization and avoidance of duplication, as well as brand-new ways of working. This is what is usually called 'business process re-engineering or redesign'. Technology may enable this change to happen, but it is not the 'driver' and is only one component of the change. 'Planning for change' involves close cooperation with computer and other specialists.

Senior managers innovate and lead. They are concerned with strategy. They may plan far ahead and base planning and policy decisions on information and advice from specialist managers. The higher up the ladder, the more creativity, imagination and understanding of economic and social trends and the environment in which an organization operates are required. Senior managers also initiate changes in both the structure and the direction of an organization, and they are responsible for establishing effective lines of communication to ensure that policies are known and understood (and discussed) right down the line. They must also ensure that the effects of policy-implementation are monitored.

There is, however, no strict dividing line between middle and senior managers. Anyone responsible to the board is definitely a senior manager. That usually includes heads of departments – personnel, production, finance, marketing, etc. And 'general managers', who do the coordinating, are usually considered senior managers.

Some terms used in management jargon

Line management: A line manager is the manager in charge of whatever the organization's principal activity and main purpose is. In a manufacturing industry it is the production manager; in retail it is the store manager; in an air freight charter company it is the person selling aircraft space. (The term 'line' is apparently derived from 'being in the firing line' – the line manager is the one who tends to get shot at when things go wrong.)

General management: General managers coordinate the work of several specialist departments (or functions), for example personnel, production, accountancy, etc. By training they are usually specialists in one of the functions for which they are responsible, which one is immaterial.

Executives and managers: The distinction is vague. Broadly, managers are responsible for controlling other people's work, whereas executives are not necessarily: for example, a legal adviser is a senior executive, but not a manager. But middle or senior managers may also be called executives.

Managers and administrators: Again the distinction is vague. What is called management in industry is often called administration in the public sector. The terms are often interchangeable (in terms of activity), particularly in the forces, but 'administrators' are more likely to be concerned with the smooth running of a department or organization without making any changes; whereas 'managers' are expected to choose the most efficient (or 'cost-effective') of various alternative routes to achieve an objective. Management implies more decision-making. But as in the whole of the management field, different people mean different things by the same terms.

Management covers such a vast range of jobs that it is impossible to generalize about prospects. However, there is a shortage of good managers (especially with a technical background). Nevertheless, entry to management trainee jobs is very competitive. Graduate and HND candidates on the whole stand a better chance than others. Over one-third of vacancies are for 'any discipline' graduates; where the discipline is specified, engineering/technological degrees are most in demand with computing subjects and then business/management studies next. First jobs are often in large firms' *manufacturing* (see p. 227), *marketing and sales* (see p. 371), *purchasing and supply* (see p. 506) departments, and in small and medium firms where specialisms are not so clearly defined. There are numerically more openings in small and medium-sized firms than in the large, household name 'first choice' companies and all-round experience in small firms can be very good training.

Employers prefer management trainee applicants who have had some work experience – if not on a sandwich placement, then in holiday or temporary employment. Having worked abroad – in whatever capacity – can also be an advantage. It follows that it may be advisable to take almost any job even if it is not a 'management' one, to gain experience of the 'real world' work environment.

Training Paths into management and progress once in are nothing like as clear-cut as they are in established professions – because of the diversity of management tasks, environment and objectives; of levels of responsibility and of 'management styles' (and because there is no precise, universally agreed definition of 'management'). What has become clear over the last few years is that getting *in* requires a very different combination of qualities and qualifications than getting *on* afterwards. That makes description and definition of training rather difficult. However, here are some guidelines and trends:

To be considered for a management trainee job, qualifications certainly matter in the majority of cases, but they must be accompanied by the right personal qualities (which vary from one employer to another – for broad guidelines see 'Personal attributes', below). Later, the balance and combination of requirements are different. For promotion, paper qualifications are less important; track record is more important. For example, a person with a degree but unimpressive work experience has fewer promotion/job-change chances than a person who proved managerial ability in a previous job, and somehow acquired the necessary theoretical knowledge. But the relatively few organizations with elaborate management training schemes cannot train all the managers required; so for the majority of potential managers these are the usual ways of qualifying for management in industry, commerce and elsewhere:

Senior management

1. Degree in business or management studies (titles vary). Courses usually include practical experience in industry or commerce (or public authority) which gives students an insight into the real world of work. This enables those who do not enjoy the atmosphere, or find the pace too exacting, to change to some other graduate career. Employers welcome business/management studies graduates because they have had work experience, know what to expect, and have a basic understanding of business. All universities and many colleges of higher education run business/management degrees. These may be full time or sandwich (i.e. with spells of work experience). There are also part-time business/management degrees, mainly for people in relevant employment, though people who have had previous relevant experience may be accepted. These courses are useful for people who want to return to work after a break or want to switch to a business career while still in other employment. Some 'mixed mode' courses enable students to combine 1 or 2 years' full-time study with 2 or 3 years' part-time study.

Syllabuses vary. Titles vary too, and do not necessarily indicate any specific content or structure. 'Management Science' does not involve more management science than does 'Business Studies', for example. All courses contain a systematic introduction to management theories and techniques and to the various business functions; most courses specialize and many offer options in a particular branch or management function – for example, marketing or international marketing; industrial relations; export management; manpower planning; finance; organizational behaviour, etc. Some courses are more suitable for people interested in, for example, 'human resources management';

others for those interested in business economics/finance; or in transport or distribution or engineering management. Students should look carefully at course content and options before applying.

Entry requirements: Normally 3 A levels and 5 GCSEs (A–C), including English and maths. Only a few courses require A level maths; and a few (those which specialize in international marketing or European business administration) a modern language. Most courses accept good BTEC National or SQA awards (see pp. 8, 10) in lieu of A levels. Mature candidates are often accepted with experience in lieu of qualifications.

2. A degree in any discipline or specialist qualification (see 'The work', above), e.g. in accountancy (p. 41), engineering (p. 216), work study (see MANAGEMENT SERVICES, p. 367).

3. *Post-graduate or post-experience courses*. These fall into two main groups: (i) courses in general management; and (ii) courses leading to specialist qualifications such as personnel management, international marketing, transport, production, export management, etc. Both types of courses can be either full time, part time while in relevant employment, or, possibly, while preparing to go back to work after a break. The best-known courses are at the graduate business schools in London, Warwick, Cranfield and Manchester, but there are a great number of others. Most courses last 1 or 2 years full time or 2–4 years part time. Some may be suitable also for people who have been working for a few years but have no academic or professional qualifications, and for people who have been out of employment for some time (women who raised families mainly) as well as for mid-career changers.

Courses may lead to higher degrees (Master of Business Administration – MBA, M.Sc. or M.Phil.) in management sciences, administrative management, industrial management, international management, etc. Titles vary and do not necessarily indicate a particular emphasis or content. Prospective students should look at graduate study guides and carefully study course prospectuses. MBAs especially have proliferated recently.

Another type of course is the Edexcel BTEC Diploma in Management Studies (DMS). The course structure is very flexible. The DMS can take 9 months full time; but most courses take 2 or 3 years' day- or block-release or evening study. (A few DMS courses are organized to suit people with children to look after, with 10-to-3 attendance. Inquire at local further or higher education institutions about existing or planned short-day courses.) The scheme is intended primarily for people with at least 2 years' middle-management experience. Entry qualifications are *either* HND/HNC, degree, equivalent professional qualifications; and, often, minimum age 23; *or* minimum age 27 with, usually, at least 4 years' relevant experience in lieu of academic qualifications.

DMS courses update students' knowledge of management techniques and aim to improve their management skills. Most courses also specialize either in a 'management function', for example personnel; export marketing; production management; or in an 'operational area', for example recreation/leisure management; transport management; public administration; education administration.

Some business degrees, post-graduate and post-experience courses offer options in 'small business' management, mainly for people who want to set up and run their own small show (see WORKING FOR ONESELF, p. 648) and for those who particularly want to work in small firms.

Below degree-level training

BTEC/SQA (see pp. 8, 10) Higher National Diplomas and Certificates. Higher National Diploma courses are usually 2 years full time or 3 years sandwich. Higher National Certificates are usually taken by day- or block-release while in appropriate employment (see 'employers' training scheme', below).

All BTEC courses cover what are called 'central themes': (i) money – basically financial consequences and implications of decisions taken; (ii) people – how to get on with and manage them; (iii) communication – overlaps with (ii) and broadly means making sure everybody in an organization understands what others are doing and why; it involves explaining actions and proposals clearly, in writing and verbally; (iv) numeracy and application of new technology to problem-solving. This involves learning how to 'quantify' plans, problems and situations, and developing an analytical approach. BTEC's 'central themes' approach should enable students to be flexible and adapt to the different kinds of jobs everyone is likely to be doing throughout their working lives.

On top of the 'central themes', BTEC students specialize in a career group. Some of the main business-related ones are business and finance, business administration, distribution, leisure management, management services, international business, personnel management and business and management.

SQA (see p. 10) titles are similar and cover much the same ground as BTEC courses.

BTEC/SQA Higher National awards may lead to complete, and certainly lead to partial, exemption from relevant professional bodies' 'intermediate' examinations; for example, the Institute of Management recognizes certain BTEC HNC/HNDs with a management content and the CMS/DMS and NVQs levels 4 and 5 in management for guaranteed entry into membership. The BTEC Business and Finance HND leads to the Chartered Institute of Bankers' and Chartered Institute of Insurance's final examinations. Increasingly, professional bodies in the commercial field accept, or require, BTEC Higher National awards instead of their own 'stage 1' or 'intermediate' examinations. The advantage from the students' point of view is that they can postpone narrow specialization till they know more about all the related specializations, and that they can more easily switch specializations in mid-career.

Qualifications leading to junior or middle management

(i) BTEC National Diploma or BTEC National Certificate in a wide range of subjects.

(ii) BTEC Certificate in Management (Supervision and Leadership), a part-time course for middle managers and potential managers. No set requirements but candidates normally have either 5 GCSEs (A–C), an NVQ level 2 or 3, a BTEC National award, or extensive experience. Most courses are 'generalist' – but there are some specialist ones, e.g. National Health Service, Local Government, Recreation/Leisure Management. The course is intended for people who want to progress up the management ladder and have to acquire specific knowledge as well as general education/training to be able to analyse and understand changing management processes and practices.

Employers' training schemes: Many firms (mainly large ones) and public sector industries run training schemes. Entry is at various levels either for training, with day-release, for a professional qualification, or, for professionally qualified people – in whatever subject, but specially business/management, accountancy or engineering – as 'graduate trainee' or 'management trainee'. Schemes vary enormously in content, quality and usefulness to the trainee. In some firms, trainees learn only how to be of use to that particular organization – and thus their future job choice is more limited; in others they get a thorough management training. Detailed research before accepting management trainee jobs is essential. Large organizations often take only, or mainly, graduates for training schemes likely to lead to senior or even senior/middle management. Some organizations consider HND and degree holders on an equal footing. Some large companies – sometimes as part of a consortium – run in-house MBA programmes tailored to their particular needs.

Open or distance-learning (see p. 23) – primarily intended for people at work, but useful also for career-changers and returners.

The Open University Business School (see p. 16) works on similar lines. Courses include tutorials, weekend schools and are at 3 levels: Professional Certificate in Management, Professional Diploma in Management and MBA. The first two can be completed in a minimum of 1 year. There are no entry requirements for the Certificate programme but applicants for the Diploma should have already achieved the Certificate or have a relevant higher education qualification or award from a professional body. The MBA is an internationally recognized and demanding programme for practising managers and entrants are required to have at least 5 years' business experience at middle or higher level, be at least 27 years old at the start of their first year of study, and hold an honours degree, a Diploma in Management Studies or the OUBS Professional Diploma in Management. (Full details can be found at *wwwopen.ac.uk/oubs*.)

The MBA is in 2 parts: part 1 consists of either the Certificate and

Diploma or, for managers aged 27-plus with an honours degree or equivalent, a 12-month foundation course, Fundamentals of Senior Management.

Henley Management College and some other establishments are also running, or planning, distance-learning schemes.

NVQs/SVQs

These vocational qualifications are becoming established quite fast among managers. They have been developed to form a benchmark against which managers' competence can be measured at supervisor, middle and senior levels. NVQs/SVQs are offered by Awarding Bodies including Edexcel BTEC, the Chartered Management Institute, City & Guilds and SQA. Some NVQs/SVQs are delivered by centres together with taught programmes. For example, a level 4 NVQ can be delivered with a BTEC Higher National Certificate. The Chartered Management Institute's own awards – Certificate in Supervisory Management, Certificate in Management, Diploma in Management – lead to NVQs at levels 3–5.

Personal attributes Numeracy; business acumen; the ability to get on well with and be respected by people at all levels in the hierarchy; natural authority; willingness to take the blame for subordinates' misdeeds; self-confidence; unflappability in crises; organizing ability. *For senior management*: an analytical brain; creativity and imagination; ability to see implications and consequences of decisions and actions taken; ability to sift relevant facts from a mass of irrelevant information; enjoyment of power and responsibility; a fairly thick skin to cope with unavoidable clashes of temperament and opinion; resilience; courage; entrepreneurial flair; boundless ambition; ability to take snap-decisions without worrying about them afterwards; physical and mental energy.

Late start See above for post-graduate courses, DMS and open learning.

A few companies, so far mainly in retail and in catering, are encouraging women of 30-plus to become management trainees.

Candidates are expected to have a degree, or professional qualification, or relevant experience which is usually selling or secretarial; but a few companies realize that women who have managed a home, family, voluntary work and/or hobbies of some kind have in fact been 'project managers', i.e. they know how to bring different strands together.

Work life balance A survey conducted by the Chartered Management Institute of 2,400 managers across the UK at the end of 2003 found that over 55% of both male and female respondents had resolved to spend less time at their desks in 2004. Opportunities for career breaks and flexible working vary greatly depending upon the level of management and type of employer. The Civil Service and local authorities are introducing flexible work schemes including part-time work and job-sharing at lower levels of management, but a long hours culture may be the price to pay for climbing the management ladder whether in the private or the public sector.

Further information No one specific information point; see specific careers; higher education guides (see p. 36); Hobsons' *Degree Course Guides*: Edexcel, SQA.

The Chartered Management Institute, Management House, Cottingham Road, Corby, Northants NN17 1TT.

www.inst-mgt.org.uk

Women in Management, contact through Chartered Management Institute.

Related careers *Virtually every career offers management opportunities*

Management Consultancy

Entry qualifications Degree and/or professional qualification and, usually, management experience. This is essentially a 'second career'.

The work The term 'management consultants' is often used rather loosely. Some self-styled management consultants do not satisfy established practitioners' or the professional organization's standards. The Institute of Management Consultancy defines management consulting as the provision to management of objective advice and assistance relating to the strategy, structure, management and operations of an organization in pursuit of its long-term purposes and objectives. Such assistance may include the identification of options with recommendations; the provision of an additional resource and/or the implementation of solutions. To be accepted for membership, practitioners are expected to have relevant qualifications and experience.

Management consultants are called upon to improve organizations' effectiveness, diagnose faults and suggest remedies. They may, for example, be called in by a food manufacturer to investigate reasons for the company's declining market-share. Before producing a plan of action to improve matters, they thoroughly research the firm's organization, its potential and the competition. They might then suggest the company should widen, or narrow, or completely change, its product-range; or they might recommend changes in the company's marketing strategy, its management structure, its industrial relations policy, the introduction of new technology – or a combination of any of these and perhaps other strategies. But work is by no means confined to industry. Consultants are increasingly called in by, for example, charities and public authorities. A particular growth area is 'managing change' in any type of organization – i.e. helping to implement smooth transition from traditional to new working patterns – not only new technology-based ones but also such innovations as job-sharing.

Because the field is so wide and requires so many varieties of expertise, consultants tend to specialize. They may specialize in an aspect of management – for example in information technology (IT), financial, distribution, marketing, human resources (see PERSONNEL/ HUMAN RESOURCES MANAGEMENT p. 444), or information management. They may also specialize in working with one type of organization – local authorities; charities; manufacturing industry or even one type of manufacturing such as light engineering, or one type of service industry such as catering or retail. Others specialize as consultants in 'change management' (see p. 353).

Training/experience Some management consultancies recruit new graduates – usually, but not always, people with technical or business/ management degrees – and give them rigorous internal training, followed by on-the-job training while working for a client. But the vast majority of recruits have a few years' post-graduate or post-qualification experience. Many have an MBA. Consultancy firms may then provide in-house training and/or send staff on external courses. IT consultancies may be large accountancy firms or associated companies, major hardware suppliers who are taking on this role or independents. There is a trend away from big consultancies to small specialist ones.

Personal attributes Ability to work as one of a team as well as independently; ability to cope with possibly hostile attitudes on the part of staff whose work is being scrutinized; adaptability to working in different environments; great diplomatic skill to deal with people at all levels and persuade them to change their ways; self-confidence and a confidence-inspiring manner; an analytical mind; an open mind to approach each new set of circumstances on its merits; curiosity; patience; willingness to work long hours; ability to put complex matters concisely and simply.

Management Consultancy

Late start Maturity and experience are an asset.

Work life balance Career-breaks are possible but it is essential to keep up with developments and to keep the break short.

Part-time work is possible theoretically by having small work loads or job-sharing. Few consultants work part time.

The Institute of Management Consultancy has a special interest group called Women In Consulting who meet throughout the year to discuss the role of the genders within the profession and for networking opportunities.

Further information Institute of Management Consultancy, 3rd Floor, 17–18 Hayward's Place, London EC1R OEQ.
www.imc.co.uk

Related careers ACCOUNTANCY – INFORMATION TECHNOLOGY (IT)/INFORMATION SYSTEMS – MANAGEMENT – PERSONNEL/ HUMAN RESOURCES MANAGEMENT – MANAGEMENT SERVICES

Management Services

Entry qualifications For *work study* and *organization and methods*, nothing rigid, just appropriate work experience. For *operational research*, a degree, normally in a subject requiring numeracy.

The work 'Management services' is the collective term for a number of functions concerned with the application of analytical techniques to problems concerning the efficient use of manpower, equipment, machinery or processor systems. They provide objective information and analysis for improved management decision-making. The 3 core management services are work study, organization and methods (O & M) and operational research (OR), but some management services departments include other specialists such as economists (see p. 213), statisticians (see p. 535), or systems analysts (see p. 283), while some work study or O & M work might come under another department, for example human resources. Other words describing the results of management services activities are utilization, performance and productivity.

Work Study and Organization and Methods

Work study had its origins in manufacturing production, and organization and methods in the office (initially in central government), but the aims and principles are basically the same. There are 2 main aspects of the work: method study and work measurement. Method study is the analysis of how operations are carried out and how they might be improved. Work measurement means using specific techniques to measure the time and human effort involved in specific tasks so that standards of performance can be established for planning, control, payment systems and the introduction of new technologies, for example.

In addition to identifying problems, collecting the necessary data, evaluating and proposing solutions, work study and O & M practitioners often get involved in implementing the solutions, for example by training line managers or helping to design a new office layout or select new equipment. Tact, sensitivity and good communication skills are needed at every stage. People at all levels can be reluctant to admit there is a problem and can feel resentful at being 'measured' or threatened by the thought of change especially by somebody who appears 'external' to the function/activity to be reviewed. Your solutions may have to be 'sold' to a range of interested parties.

During the late 1990s and early 2000s, new application areas for management services' 'tools and techniques' were developed including such descriptions as: Business Process Re-engineering, Continuous Improvement, Stop Change Management, Lean Engineering, Process Improvement, Process Management, Business Excellence Model, Purchase Chain Management, Business Improvement, Business Performance, Six Sigma, Quality Improvement, Knowledge Sharing, 'Innovation' and Model Office.

Operational Research

Whereas work study and O&M are concerned with the detail of systems in the workplace, operational research applies scientific method to complex organizational and management problems at a broader policy or strategic level. The aim is to improve existing systems and methods of decision-making. Many opportunities are with large concerns with extremely complex problems. For example, OR is used by a utility company to develop strategies which will stand up to a range of possible future prices for energy; factors taken into account are estimates of future demand, availability, and production and freight costs. At the other end of the scale OR has been instrumental in the development of computer packages which enable schools to design a timetable which satisfies the choices of as many pupils as possible.

A key tool of OR is the 'model', a computer simulation of the system to be improved. All sorts of variable factors can be incorporated to see what would happen in given situations if different courses of action were taken. The implications of alternative decisions can then be compared. The operational researcher needs good technical and analytical skills to find the right model, method or technique to suit the problem. He or she also needs good communication skills to help define the problem in consultation with management, gather the necessary information, explain the progress, often to a non-technical audience, and promote the solution at senior levels. Numeracy is important but, unlike in OR's early days when it was very 'hard' or quantitative, there has been an increasing realization that problems often have a large non-quantitative element. When the problems are 'messy', OR needs to be 'soft'.

Most operational researchers are young; OR is a good springboard to general management and to related areas such as corporate planning, marketing, finance, distribution and production.

Training For work study and O & M, largely on the job as an assistant. Distance-learning, day-release, evening and a few full-time courses are available for the Certificate and Diploma of the Institute of Management Services. It usually takes 3 years of part-time study to reach the Diploma via the Certificate.

For operational research a post-graduate degree may be an advantage. Employers may sponsor students on these courses. On-the-job training is also provided, often supplemented by in-house or outside short courses.

Personal attributes Ability to get on with people at all levels in an organization; good communication skills; methodical approach; analytical mind; tact. *For work study and O & M*, common sense and imagination. *For OR*, ability to understand and explain complicated matters clearly.

Late start Prospects are good in work study and O & M, which are very much 'second careers', most people having gained some previous

369

work experience. In OR a late start is possible only for those with a suitable degree and industrial experience. As mentioned above, OR is largely a young person's field; it is estimated that some three-quarters of practitioners are under 40.

Work life balance A career break should be no problem for those who keep in touch. Opportunities for returners and for flexible working are better in the public sector.

Part-time work can take the form of project or consultancy work rather than reduced hours in a regular job. Opinions differ on job-sharing; keeping in touch would be vital and home computer links could help. Given the problem-solving nature of the work, the 'two minds' argument seems persuasive.

Further information Institute of Management Services, Stowe House, Netherstowe, Lichfield, Staffordshire ws13 6tj.
www.ims-productivity.com
Operational Research Society, Seymour House, 12 Edward Street, Birmingham b1 2rx.
www.orsoc.org.uk

Related careers ACTUARY – ENGINEERING – HEALTH AND SAFETY INSPECTORS – INFORMATION TECHNOLOGY (IT)/INFORMATION SYSTEMS – MANAGEMENT – SCIENCE: *Mathematical Sciences*

Marketing and Selling

Entry qualifications Nothing specific; for *Chartered Institute of Marketing's Certificates*: See Training. Considerable graduate entry.

Marketing

The work Effective marketing is the key to profitability and essential for Britain's trading position in the world economy. Marketing goods and services is as skilled an occupation, and as important, as producing them. But marketing is a rather vague term, often used loosely to cover a range of activities. Different establishments interpret the term differently, and titles include brand manager; product manager; development manager; marketing executive; marketing manager; export marketing manager, etc. Titles do not necessarily indicate any particular level of responsibility or scope.

The Chartered Institute of Marketing defines the purpose of marketing as follows: 'Marketing is the management process responsible for identifying, anticipating and satisfying customer requirements profitably' – at home and, vitally important, abroad.

Marketing people (sometimes called 'marketers') find out what customers want or, more important, can be persuaded to want, at what price, and then relate potential demand to the company's ability to produce whatever it is, get it to the 'point of sale', and do all that profitably.

Marketing involves *researching* the market and *analysing* research results – which involves devising and organizing surveys and interpreting the results; discussing results with accountants, production, distribution and advertising people. Marketers may suggest the company adapt its existing products to cope with the competition's better products, or with changes in buying habits, or they may think up a totally new product and help to develop and launch it, or they may introduce a better after-sales service.

All these activities have always been carried out in business, but as business has become more complex and professionalized, with decisions being based on researched facts and, above all, figures rather than guesswork and experience, the 'marketing function' has become a 'business profession' and even an academic subject. Its importance in business has grown enormously in recent years. Poor marketing in the past is blamed for poor business performance. This applies particularly to *international marketing*. As exporting is becoming more and more essential for economic survival, international marketing is becoming a vital function in many more businesses. Marketing people have good prospects of going to the top in general management.

Marketing is often split into *consumer goods and services marketing*; *industrial marketing*; and *international marketing* (which could refer to either, and is part of the export business).

In all these activities, marketing involves several types of work: detailed research to establish customers', and potential customers', needs and potential needs: what type of customers, where, might buy at what price, with how effective an after-sales service, etc. Whether it is yet another washing powder or, in industrial marketing, a new piece of office machinery or computer, a new magazine or a food product, the procedure is basically the same. In *industrial marketing*, an engineering or science background is useful, but people switch from one area of marketing to another. In *international marketing*, a thorough understanding of other nations' cultural as well as social and economic set-up is vital (and, of course, speaking the relevant language). Perhaps the most crucial among several other marketing activities is *sales forecasting*. How many cars with what particular features will country X be willing to buy in 2, 5, 10 years' time?

Marketing people must always base their conclusions on researched social and economic trends, which include statistics. Marketing has a glamorous image, but the basis of it is the correct interpretation of information.

Though the majority of marketing people work in large, often multinational, companies, increasingly medium and small companies are separating 'the marketing function' from general business management.

Selling

Selling is both a career in itself, and an essential part of (and sometimes the best way into) marketing. The two are closely linked: *marketing* finds out what customers want and helps to put the goods/services on the market; *selling* is concerned with finding and dealing with customers for the product/service.

There are different kinds of selling – and various ways of categorizing sales staff. A useful division is between *consumer goods selling* and *specialized selling*. In consumer goods selling (this totally excludes retail and door-to-door selling), sales representatives, or reps, sell to wholesalers and/or, more usually, to retailers. Selling to retailers involves 'merchandising', which means helping the retailer to maximize sales, by promotion campaigns, suggesting ideas for improving shop display, etc. Reps may also advise retailers on new sales techniques, etc. There is a hierarchy in consumer goods selling, with the *field sales supervisors* and *area sales managers* in charge of reps, and *sales managers* and *sales directors* at head office directing the whole sales operation.

Speciality or *technical* or *industrial selling* is usually done by staff with a technical background and perhaps production management experience (see p. 227). An engineering background is particularly useful (see ENGINEERING, p. 216). The speciality selling process differs totally from consumer goods selling: purchasing decisions are made not by shopkeepers or store buyers, but by technical and financial experts. To effect one sale may take months of negotiations, and extensive after-sales service. Speciality sales staff do not necessarily sell only standard products – whether they are large pieces of machinery or machine tools – they may agree for their company to modify a product or produce a 'one-off' piece of equipment.

Sales reps may form part of a team, or be the only rep in the firm. They may have a 'territory' in this country which may require them to be away from home for several days most weeks, or it may be a territory near home – it depends on the kind of product and on how many potential buyers there are within an area.

Exporting

A wide range of companies have export departments and some staff move into the export function from another department, most obviously from sales within the UK. However, companies frequently recruit staff from outside who have particular experience and expertise in dealing with overseas markets. Job titles and functions vary, but examples are:

Export clerk in manufacturing company: checks and acknowledges orders; liaises with production and packing departments; lets customers know of any delays; organizes necessary paperwork.

Export sales correspondent: prepares quotations, tenders and delivery schedules for customers, often within a geographical area or product range; supervises the work of the export clerk; takes part in sales promotions and deals with overseas agents.

Export area sales or *product manager*: responsible for reaching sales targets within a market or product area; visits and looks after existing customers and agents and researches openings for new business; arranges overseas promotions/exhibitions; negotiates new contracts.

Export manager/director: in charge of all aspects of export function; visits customers and agents in all the company's markets and product areas; appoints new staff; sets sales targets; liaises with UK sales and production managers.

Training There are various ways into marketing. It is possible to enter employment at any level and train while working or to transfer into marketing within an organization. Most graduates go straight into marketing as trainees on management training schemes; entry to these schemes can be extremely competitive and often requires a minimum of a 2:1 honours degree.

While working as a trainee, marketing staff can study for the Chartered Institute of Marketing's examinations. These are at 4 levels:

the Introductory Certificate in Marketing, for which candidates need to be over 17 but no experience is needed; the Certificate in Marketing, requiring 2 A levels or equivalent; the Advanced Certificate at graduate level; and the Post-graduate Diploma in Marketing for which a post-graduate degree with significant marketing content from a CIM-approved university or equivalent or at least 6 years' management experience is needed. The Advanced Certificate offers modules in research and information, planning, communications and marketing management in practice. The CIM also offers courses in arts market-ing and e-marketing.

The CIM also offers 3 levels of qualification in professional sales: Certificate, Advanced Certificate and Intensive Diploma.

Most of the CIM's courses can be studied in a variety of ways, through full-time or part-time courses, e-learning, workshops and residential training.

Pre-entry training for marketing is either by business studies degree with marketing option or by specialized marketing degree. These degrees either link marketing to a specific area such as chemicals or textiles or engineering; or concentrate on international marketing and export. An engineering or science degree is a good way into speciality selling.

There are also BTEC/SQA Higher awards (see pp. 8, 10) with marketing export options and distribution options.

For *export marketing* some trainees work for the Institute of Export's examinations, by day-release or distance-learning. The syllabus adds export procedure and principles of export management to marketing methods, principles and procedures.

The Institute's *Advanced Certificate in International Trade*, which tests knowledge of the practical aspects of international trade, is run as a first-stage professional examination. Students then go on to take the Diploma in International Trade. (People working in export departments may take the Institute of Export's Certificate in Export Office Practice before the Advanced Certificate.)

Personal attributes *Marketing*: A high degree of business acumen and of numeracy; a little risk-taking instinct; self-confidence; ability to assess the effects of economic, social or political events; ability to stand perhaps unjustified criticism when forecasts turn out wrong, due to unforeseeable causes; social awareness and interest in social and economic trends; ability to communicate easily with colleagues and clients, whatever their temperament and their degree of expertise; ability to cope with change.

Selling: Numeracy; extrovert personality; ability to establish instant rapport with people; judgement; sensitivity for gauging right approach to customers; indifference to the occasional rebuff; enjoying being alone when travelling; willingness to be away from home a lot; good listening and communication skills.

Late start People with technological or business qualifications can switch to marketing.

Work life balance In this competitive field it will not be easy for any but the best and most determined people to return after a career break to what is essentially still a young person's career. Those with technological or science degrees or experience stand the best chances in industrial marketing.

There are very few openings for part-time work, unless able to work for oneself as a consultant.

Further information Chartered Institute of Marketing, Moor Hall, Cookham, Maidenhead, Berks. SL6 9QH.
www.cim.co.uk
Institute of Export, Export House, Minerva Business Park, Lynch Wood, Peterborough PE2 6FT.
www.export.org.uk
Market Research Society, 15 Northburgh Street, London EC1V 0JR.
www.mrs.org.uk

Related careers ADVERTISING — LOGISTICS, DISTRIBUTION AND TRANSPORT MANAGEMENT — MANAGEMENT — PUBLIC RELATIONS — RETAIL MANAGEMENT

Medicine

Entry qualifications Three good A levels (or Scottish equivalent) are normally required for entry to medical school. A level chemistry is usually required and increasingly biology but some medical schools will accept 2 science AS levels, one being chemistry, in place of 1 A level. A few medical schools are now willing to consider a VCE, but in a limited number of subjects. A small number of medical schools run a 1-year foundation course for candidates without the usual science A level background. An increasing number of medical schools are offering shortened courses for graduates, including a few for graduates in arts subjects.

General Practice (Family Doctor)

General practitioners are the front line of primary health care. As self-employed practitioners, GPs are responsible for their own premises and staff and have considerable autonomy in deciding how best to provide the services to patients required under their NHS contracts. Under the recent NHS reforms GPs now work with colleagues and other health service professionals in Primary Care Trusts. In Scotland primary care is managed by NHS Boards and contracts are practice-based rather than with GPs.

All family doctors are involved in:

1. acute disease management, i.e. diagnosing, treating or referring for specialist treatment a range of ailments presented by patients;

2. preventative medicine, helping patients to understand how to prevent, look for and deal with problems;

3. counselling, i.e. dealing with patients' fears and feelings, both

those that have a medical basis and those that lead to physical symptoms.

General practitioners may also get involved in community issues through involvement in their local Primary Care Trust. There are opportunities for GPs to work in hospitals, for example as a clinical assistant.

Most family doctors work in partnership with other doctors. Some practices organize themselves along specialist lines with, perhaps, one partner particularly experienced in obstetrics and gynaecology, while another may have a special interest in stress, and another in heart disease.

A typical family doctor's day might consist of a morning surgery from, say, 8.30 a.m. until 11.00 a.m.; routine office work, dealing with telephone inquiries, signing prescriptions, reading the post, dealing with letters to and from hospital consultants; home visits; lunch; visits or clinics (e.g. antenatal, minor operations, diabetic, child development); more office work; evening surgery. Doctors within a practice or several practices may get together to provide a night and weekend emergency call rota but many practices now rely on deputizing services.

Recent years have seen enormous changes in general practice. New drugs are continually available; practices have direct access to investigation facilities and new equipment enabling them to provide care over a more interesting range of conditions; practice nurses handle routine procedures and extend health education and preventative work. Computerization is used for repeat prescription control, for the maintenance of registers (e.g. of all women due for cervical screening, or all under 5s due for immunization) and for the compilation of data that enables the doctors to measure and assess what they are doing for their patients as a whole. However, all these developments are merely aids to improve and monitor service. They do not replace the family doctor's traditional role of caring for patients largely by listening to and talking with them. There is currently a shortage of GPs and the government has introduced incentives to encourage more to work in deprived areas.

Hospital Service

All doctors start their careers in hospitals, though eventually just over half as many stay there as enter general practice. Doctors who remain in hospital medicine become specialists. There are more than 64 specialities. These fall into 4 main groups: medicine, surgery, pathology and psychiatry. Within each group are many sub-specialities ranging from general medicine and general surgery to smaller fields such as audiological medicine or paediatric surgery. Major specialities include accident and emergency, obstetrics and gynaecology, and anaesthetics.

Both the nature and pattern of work in different fields can vary considerably. For example, general medicine and surgery and obstetrics have far more emergency work than psychiatry or dermatology, while pathology has very little. The nature of the round-the-clock demands on anaesthetists means they have evolved a more predictable shift system than other doctors.

Many years of hospital doctors' careers are, though paid employment, technically training posts. As they progress through jobs as pre-registration house officer to senior house officer and registrar they take on more and more responsibility under the supervision and guidance of more senior doctors. The most junior doctors take responsibility for practical, routine day-to-day care and administration (keeping records, communicating with families and other members of the medical team), progressing to more advisory work and greater clinical responsibility. Junior doctors' hours have traditionally been long and irregular but the European Working Time Directive will apply to doctors in training from 2004 and the maximum amount of working hours will be gradually reduced to 48 per week by 2009. The more senior doctors become, the less they are likely to be called from their beds to an emergency, but the more complex the decision or procedure when they are.

At the head of hospital teams are consultants, who have continuing responsibility for patient care. It can take from 8 to 12 years of specialist training to reach this level, although recent changes are shortening this period.

Doctors' choices of speciality are determined not only by interest and inclination, but often by opportunity. Some fields are very much more popular and competitive than others, and it can take some time and experience before a final choice is made.

Research and Teaching

Research into new forms of treatments and new drugs and their effects is done in hospitals, research establishments and drug firms. Doctors can, and usually do, combine clinical and scientific work, but there are also research appointments, often including some teaching, for those who are interested in the scientific side of medicine rather than 'patient contact' (see SCIENCE, p. 520).

Training UK medical students are required to take a 5-year undergraduate course recognized by the General Medical Council leading to a Bachelor of Medicine and Surgery – depending upon the university an MBBS; MBBS/BSc; MBChB; MBBCh; BMBS – all of which are normally referred to as a 'first MB'. A few universities still offer the traditional 2-year *pre-clinical* course, including anatomy, physiology and biochemistry, consisting of lectures, laboratory work and a great deal of reading, followed by a 3-year *clinical* course, when students have contact with patients, take case histories and, under supervision, make diagnoses. However, most medical schools now offer integrated courses which combine academic study and clinical experience throughout the 5 years. This is part of the ongoing change to medical education brought about by *Tomorrow's Doctors*, the General Medical Council report published in 1993, which also recommended that courses should concentrate less on the acquisition of factual knowledge and introduce greater emphasis on, for example, communication skills and practical clinical tasks.

Medical schools have responded differently to the recommendations and as a result courses can differ greatly. It is important to look closely at their content as some still offer traditional lecture-based study while some have a more clinical setting-based approach. Some courses include study for a BSc degree while for others this is optional.

Four new medical university-based schools have opened recently, and collaboration between universities has produced additional places in existing medical schools. In addition, new accelerated courses (usually 4 years) for graduates in other subjects are being offered by some schools. Other schemes are being introduced to encourage wider access to medical training.

Before students get their registrable qualification they must spend a 'pre-registration year' as a full-time junior house officer in hospital. (At this stage they start earning.) Post-registration training is essential, very hard work, and rather haphazard. In some areas junior doctors have to arrange their own succession of hospital 'training posts', but many others have rotational training schemes which doctors slot into. Each training post has to be educationally approved by the relevant Royal College (for example, in England and Wales a training post in surgery has to be approved by the Royal College of Surgeons).

Post-registration training begins with 2–3 years as a senior house officer, during which doctors can choose to train in a range of specialities as they decide their future career path. Those wanting to continue with a hospital-based specialism then undertake 4–5 years as a specialist registrar leading to qualification as a consultant.

Doctors wishing to become *general practitioners* take a 1–2 year period of specialist training. This is usually community based and involves further exams and assessment.

At the time of writing further reforms are under consultation. The proposals are that after graduation doctors will first do a 2-year foundation programme which will include the current pre-registration year. This will develop core or generic clinical skills. During the foundation programme, doctors will have the chance to sample a range of different specialities and will then compete to enter one of eight or so broad-based, time-capped basic specialist programmes, including training for general practice.

Doctors wishing to specialize in *occupational health* or *medicine* take the examinations of the Faculty of Occupational Medicine.

Personal attributes The ability to communicate with people, take responsibility and to make vital decisions after weighing up all the relevant factors; patience with people unable to express themselves clearly; sympathy without emotional involvement; understanding of and liking for all types of people and tolerance of human weaknesses; self-confidence; conscientiousness; resourcefulness; the energy and stamina to work hard for long and often irregular periods; great powers of concentration; above-average intelligence; good health.

For research: Patience for long-term projects and an inquiring mind.

Late start Medical schools vary in their policies on accepting mature candidates, so one has to inquire from several before giving up – if determined to start; it becomes very difficult if over 30. Length of training is not reduced even for qualified nurses or people from other related professions.

Work life balance The recent reforms to the NHS have included a significant increase in the support given to doctors combining practice with caring responsibilities. The NHS Improving Working Lives standard has required all NHS employers to introduce more flexible working and childcare support and to measure their practice against set requirements. The NHS has also introduced NHS Professionals, a new national staffing agency to provide temporary staff to hospitals. Staff are employed directly by the NHS and its Flexible Careers Scheme for doctors offers hospital doctors the opportunity to work part time or for limited hours on a temporary basis, take a career break while keeping in touch, reduced hour working for those nearing retirement, and help and supervision for those returning to practice.

Further information British Medical Association, BMA House, Tavistock Square, London WC1H 9JP.

www.bma.org.uk

Books that can be recommended include:
Learning Medicine, by Peter Richards and Simon Stockill, published BMJ Books.
The Insider's Guide to Medical Schools, compiled by BMA Medical Students Committee, published by BMJ Books.

MPW Guide to Getting into Medical School by James Burnett and Joe Ruston, published by Trotman.

Curriculum 2000, A Survey of UK Medical Schools' Requirements and Selection Policies, published by UCAS.

So You Want to Be a Brain Surgeon, by Simon Eccles, published by Oxford University Press.

The Essential Guide to Becoming a Doctor, by Adrian Park, published by BMJ Books.

Related careers ANIMALS: *Veterinary Surgeon* – DENTISTRY – ENGINEERING: *Medical or Biomedical Engineering* – NURSING – OCCUPATIONAL THERAPY – OPTICAL WORK: *Optometrist; Orthoptics* – OSTEOPATHY – PHARMACY – PHYSIOTHERAPY – SCIENCE – SOCIAL WORK

NOTE ON COMPLEMENTARY MEDICINE: Complementary medicine is the general name for a number of therapeutic techniques which include acupuncture, osteopathy (see p. 438) and chiropractic (see p. 145), herbal medicine, homoeopathy and naturopathy. In recent years interest has been growing in this style of medical practice, which regards health and disease in terms of the whole person. A demand for more treatment is bound to lead to a demand for more practitioners.

With the exception of osteopathy and chiropractic, there is currently no statutory regulation for complementary medicine although the government has announced proposals to regulate herbal medicine and acupuncture practitioners. As a result training can be a minefield. Courses range from those for qualified doctors only, through 4-year degree courses, to those lasting only a few days, with, in many fields, little objective guidance as to the reputableness or otherwise of courses. 'Buyer beware' has been the rule for both prospective entrants and clients/patients. The situation is rapidly changing, however. With government approval, the Institute for Complementary Medicine has set up the British Register of Complementary Medicine. To be admitted to the Register practitioners must meet standards set by scrutiny panels. Though registration is voluntary, it is beginning to have an effect; for example, some magazines accept advertisements only from registered practitioners.

The Institute for Complementary Medicine is currently consulting on the development of National Occupational Standards with the longer-term aim of developing a career structure and mandatory continuing professional development for all registered practitioners.

Further information is available from the Institute for Complementary Medicine, PO Box 194, London SE16 1QZ.

www.icmedicine.co.uk

Merchant Navy

Entry qualifications *Undergraduate officer trainee*: A level (or equivalent) including maths and/or physics. *Graduate officer trainee*: science, technology, engineering or similar degree. *Officer cadet*: A level, including GCSEs (or equivalent) at grades A–C in mathematics, English, physics or combined science, and one other or equivalent. *Marine apprenticeship*: 4 GCSEs (or equivalent) at grades A–C including maths, English, physics or combined science. *Marine trainee*: a minimum of 3 GCSEs or equivalent.

All candidates must be in good health and pass a statutory medical examination, with a good standard of eyesight required for prospective deck personnel.

The work Ships carry over 90% of world trade and seaborne trade is forecast to increase substantially by 2015. Most British shipping is technologically advanced and committed to respecting the environment, and includes a varied range of vessels – container ships, bulk carriers, super tankers, deep sea tugs, naval support ships, ferries, marine mining vessels and cruise liners. Life on board a ship is a 24-hour-a-day operation, 7 days a week, 52 weeks a year. This work is divided into shifts – called watches, which are typically 4 hours on watch, followed by 8 hours off watch, increasing to 6 hours on watch and 6 hours off watch at busy times. Leave time is generous, to compensate for time spent on board and away from home. For example, after a voyage of around 4 months, you could get as much as 2 months or so off at home.

The Engineering Department

Engineer officers are responsible for the provision and maintenance of all technical services on board, including the propulsion and auxiliary machinery in the engine room. They are responsible for the work of engine-room staff, so managing people is part of the job, as with all ships officers. An Engineer officer may progress to Chief Engineer officer.

Engineer ratings are involved in routine maintenance, engine operation and machinery repairs.

The Deck Department

Deck officers are responsible for controlling the navigation of the ship, communications, cargo handling and ship stability. A Deck officer is a step on the way to becoming Master or Captain.

Deck ratings assist with the navigation of the ship and are involved in operating deck machinery such as winches and cranes and carrying out maintenance tasks.

There are also some dual officer roles, covering both departments.

Communications

Electro-technical officers are responsible for the maintenance and efficient operation of complex electrical, electronic and control systems on board ship.

Hotel and Entertainment Services on Cruise Ships and Ferries

This includes pursers/receptionists, restaurant and bar staff and chefs, housekeepers, cruise directors, entertainments team, etc., hairdressers, beauticians, photographers, retail staff, etc. Recruitment is usually based on those who are qualified and experienced within their own specialism.

Training Training needed for a career at sea is provided by shipping companies or group training organizations. Training usually consists of planned and progressive programmes of learning and experience based on a sandwich pattern of alternating periods at college and at sea and leading to nationally recognized qualifications and professional maritime certificates of competency.

There are 5 main entry routes, each with deck and engineering options. Each provides progression opportunities to the next stage and, through the ranks, to Master (Captain) or Chief Engineer officer, depending on ability and ambition. The routes are:

1. *Marine Traineeship*: provides structured training for seafarers employed, usually, as ratings, in the deck or engineering departments in support of the officers of the watch. Entrants must show an aptitude to succeed to at least NVQ/SVQ level 2. As a guide, they would be expected to have attained 3 GCSEs, a Foundation GNVQ, or an equivalent.

2. *Marine Apprenticeship*: provides an enhanced level of training for those employed initially as ratings in the deck or engineering departments while following a programme of learning leading to NVQ/SVQ level 3 and qualification as officer of the watch. As a guide, entrants would be expected to have attained a minimum of 4 GCSEs (or equivalent) at grades A–C, including English, mathematics and physics or combined science. It is likely to appeal to those who do not meet the qualifications needed for officer cadet.

3. *Officer Cadet*: provides structured learning for those aiming to progress to Master (Captain) or Chief Engineer officer and achieve qualifications at HND level in addition to professional certificates of competency. Knowledge and skills are developed while serving aboard ship in a supernumerary capacity under the direct supervision of qualified officers. All of the time at sea and at college ashore is devoted to training and development. Entry standards may vary from company to company. As a guide, candidates would be expected to have attained A levels (or equivalent) and possess a minimum of 4 GCSEs (or equivalent) at grades A–C, including mathematics, English and physics or combined science. Entry with GCSEs only may be possible for suitably motivated candidates.

4. *Undergraduate Officer Trainee*: designed for those who want a degree-based education and who have an interest in a seafaring or shipping industry career. Degrees are available in Merchant Ship Operations, Nautical Science or Nautical Studies linked to seafarer training for the deck department, and in Marine Engineering for the engineering department.

The training lasts approximately 4 years, of which 3 are spent at university/college. The other year enables development of seafaring skills, to complete the sea-service needed for the initial professional Certificate of Competency, and to provide shipboard experience. It can be undertaken at various stages throughout the programme, depending on the sponsoring company and the university/college, and will either be as a sandwich-based model or as the final year of a 4-year programme.

5. *Post-graduate Entry*: accelerated programmes have been developed for new entrants with suitable science, technology and engineering-based degrees, or similar. Provides a programme equivalent to cadet training but recognizes prior qualifications and maturity of applicants.

Late start Limited except for jobs requiring previous experience/training, e.g. engineering and catering/hospitality functions.

Work life balance Opportunities for career breaks are unlikely. However, seafaring skills and experience are in great demand in a wide range of jobs in the shore-based sector of the shipping industry. These include ship-management, marine superintendents, maritime surveyors, port operations.

Position of women Women officers, trainees, cadets and ratings sail on modern ships, and are currently under-represented in the workforce. Shipping companies welcome applications from women.

Further information Careers in Shipping, Carthusian Court, 12 Carthusian Street, London EC1M 6EZ (for general information on all

merchant navy careers and list of shipping companies providing sponsorship).
www.gotosea.org.uk
Individual shipping companies, see *www.mntb.org.uk* for listing.

Related careers ARMED FORCES – ENGINEERING

Meteorology

Entry qualifications *Graduate entry*: the Met Office specifies a first or upper second in a related subject.

The work The main employer in the UK is the Met Office, an executive agency within the Ministry of Defence. The Met Office employs over 2,000 people, of whom about 70% are scientists. Most Met Office employees work in Exeter, where the agency moved its HQ in 2003, but it does run forecasting stations elsewhere in the UK and has links all over the world. Since 2000 its role has changed to take in the study of the impact of the weather on the environment and environmental sciences such as hydrology and oceanography. Many of its services are customized to meet the requirements of particular industries or recipients, for example civil aviation or train operators, public services responsible for the safety of the public and the retail industry who want to know what stock to order. A recent innovation is the delivery of customized forecasts anywhere, anytime, via mobile phone. As a result the Met Office now recruits a large number of IT specialists as well as forecasters and research scientists.

Training On-the-job training is given to all staff. In addition, initial, formal residential courses are run at the Met Office College and elsewhere.

There are opportunities for staff to study for relevant higher academic qualifications.

Personal attributes Enthusiasm and genuine interest in meteorology and/or computer science; versatility and adaptability; the ability to work independently, yet be a valuable team member; good communication skills.

Late start No age limits.

Work life balance Met Office employees are civil servants (see p. 158). Some forecasting work involves shift work.

Further information Met Office, Careers Coordinator, FitzRoy Road, Exeter, Devon EX1 3PB.
www.metoffice.com

Related careers SCIENCE

Museums and Art Galleries

Entry qualifications Various (see 'Training', below); for most jobs in museums and galleries, especially at curator-level, a degree or equivalent is essential. In theory, the degree subject does not matter; however, if applicants want to specialize in a particular area – such as fine art, social history or education – it helps to have a relevant degree.

The work The scope of museum work has widened greatly in recent years. Established museums and art galleries have shed their image of solemn shrines devoted to earnest study of art, artefacts and history. They are now a part of the leisure industry, wanting to entertain as well as inform, thus attracting a wider public. The term 'museum' is now used rather loosely and covers a more varied range of establishments than it used to. The term 'heritage centre' or 'heritage site' is increasingly used instead. Museum and heritage sector establishments overlap in terms of the work, which is basically selecting and organizing exhibits and attracting and organizing visitors.

Over half of Britain's roughly 3,000 museums were started in the last 20 years, and it is these museums which have transformed the museums scene. Museums fall into 4 main groups:

1. National Museums – such as the British Museum, the National Gallery and the National Museums and Galleries on Merseyside. These establishments receive their funding directly from central government and offer the greatest scope to the traditional academic specialist type of curators who chose the job because of their interest in pursuing their specialism. These curators may or may not combine collection management with general departmental management. National museum curators are normally graduates in subjects relevant to the

department concerned. They usually start as assistant curators. Science/technology graduates are as likely to get a job as arts graduates. Competition is very keen indeed.

2. Regional and Local Museums – such as Reading Museum, Bedford Museum and Roman Baths and Pump Room, Bath. They are funded by local authorities and range from a few large and prestigious ones to hundreds of small museums of local history or industry. Employment prospects vary; few jobs are research-based; most involve coping with everything. Entry is usually with a degree or comparable qualification (which could be non-specific management experience).

3. Independent Museums – such as the Galleries of Justice, Nottingham, and Dove Cottage and the Wordsworth Museum, Grasmere. These are the largest and fastest-growing group and are self-funded, either by sponsors and entry fees or entirely by entry fees. They are 'market-led'. Their success depends on a commercially viable idea, and management, marketing and communication skills. The group also includes sophisticated tourist attractions like the Jorvik Viking Centre in York and the Museum of the Moving Image in London, as well as hundreds of small special-interest museums such as the Silk Museum in Macclesfield and the Freud Museum in London. Jobs go to applicants with commercial and communication skills; academic qualifications are not required, but as competition is very keen, academic qualifications in addition to the required skills help.

4. University Museums – such as Pitt Rivers Museum in Oxford, the Barlow Collection in Brighton and the Petrie Museum in London. This group offers a large range of size, type and function. The Ashmolean and Fitzwilliam museums are important tourist attractions for Oxford and Cambridge while the Scott Polar Museum in Cambridge is a couple of rooms in the Scott Polar Research Institute.

Both local authority and independent museums use volunteer labour fairly extensively; such volunteer experience is very useful when applying for 'real' jobs. As there are always more applicants than vacancies, applicants are unlikely to get a foot on the career ladder without some work experience. Some museums, galleries and heritage organizations have well-run volunteer programmes on offer.

There is a broad range of career opportunities in museums and galleries – the larger the museum the more specialist the role is likely to be. Large national museums have separate departments to look after marketing, personnel, finance, conservation, education work and individual collections. In smaller museums curators have to be able to undertake a variety of responsibilities. There can be a lot of crossover between other jobs too – such as education workers and outreach workers or collections managers and registrars.

Apart from traditional curators (in larger museums curators can also be called keepers), who are concerned with collection management and research, there is a broad range of many other museum jobs, including a few 'museum-specific' ones:

Exhibition designers. A growing number of museums are appointing in-house designers, but the majority are self-employed or work for exhibition design consultancies; their expertise is 'bought in' by museums. The work now often includes using audio-visual and interactive video equipment. Designers work closely with *interpreters*. Interpretation means showing objects in their context and imaginative presentation. It overlaps with *education workers* and may involve role-playing; perhaps dressing up as a 1920s chauffeur when showing transport from that period, or as a Roman shopkeeper when interpreting shopping in ancient Rome. Interpreters also help visitors use the high-tech equipment. The National Curriculum's emphasis on hands-on experience has increased the scope for museum–school collaboration. *Education workers* work with all ages – primary and secondary school groups plus adult learners and teachers – using a mix of formal and informal teaching.

Designers usually have an art-training background at Higher National award or degree level; *interpreters* and *education workers* are usually graduates (no particular discipline), and may or may not have teaching experience. However, experience of working either as a teacher, youth worker or community worker is invaluable. Many museums also employ *outreach workers* to work outside the museum with local groups and communities. Good outreach work draws on similar skills to museum education and often comes under the education department's remit.

Collection managers ensure that objects are properly cared for, often managing storage, conservation and record keeping associated with objects. They will also be involved in developing policies and standards for acquiring and disposing of objects.

Registrars usually work in national and larger regional museums. Their job is to record information about objects. This is a core activity for museums with international collections and large exhibition programmes as the movement of loans in and out of the museum needs recording. In regional museums the *registrar* can also be responsible for information about the condition of objects as well as where they are. Sophisticated information management systems mean that many regional *registrars* are IT experts as well. In smaller museums the *curator* or *collections manager* will take on the role of *registrar*.

There is often movement between independent and other staff; experience in an independent museum may lead to work in a traditional one. Work in a heritage sector establishment or even a pure tourist attraction is useful experience in exhibit and visitor management.

Conservation is a profession in its own right and is a growth area. The national and a few local authority museums and art galleries use in-house conservators, but most are self-employed or work for private firms and collectors as well as for museums and art galleries. They do not by any means deal only with paintings or other traditional exhibits; anything from agricultural machinery to dresses or first-generation computers need conserving. Conservators see their job in 3 stages: examination to assess the object's properties and need for repair; preservation to arrest or prevent deterioration; and restoration. Most conservators specialize by material and/or type of object: textiles, paintings, machinery, furniture, etc.

Other museum work, not museum-specific, includes marketing, public relations, visitors' services, shop management.

Training The route into a museum or art gallery career is primarily an academic one; however, training has now become much more flexible to take account of changes in the work. The industry's training organization is the Cultural Heritage NTO which administers NVQs at levels 2–5 and both Foundation and Advanced Modern Apprenticeships.

There are 3 main routes to Associate Membership of the Museum Association (AMA) which, in addition, require a specified period of continuous professional development over at least the following 2 years:

1. a degree or NVQ/SVQ level 3 plus 5 years' experience or a post-graduate qualification plus an NVQ/SVQ level 4 plus 3 years' experience;

2. NVQ level 4 or 5 plus 3 years' work experience (no previous qualifications required);

3. a recognized museum study qualification plus 3 years' work experience.

There are a small number of post-graduate courses available in museums studies or heritage management. These may be full or part time and lead either to a Diploma or to a Master's degree. It is also possible to include heritage management in some first degrees and Higher National Diplomas. There are also a few work-based training schemes available. The Victoria and Albert Museum runs what is effectively a graduate training programme. Recruits are taken on as assistant curators for 5 years.

On the *conservation* side, there is a variety of courses providing specialized training in a vast range of artefacts and materials, from plastics to stained glass, paper to antique clocks. Courses are at many levels from college certificate to post-graduate degree and may be full or part time. NVQs/SVQs have also been introduced.

Personal attributes Intellectual ability; commitment; a love of knowledge for its own sake; visual imagination; a lively curiosity; organizing ability; an understanding of laypeople's interests and tastes; communication skills; patience and determination in waiting for the right job and promotion.

Late start No objection in theory, but competition from young post-graduate candidates very strong.

Work life balance Career-breaks may be available. In national and local authority museums, Civil Service (see p. 158) and local government (see p. 341) conditions apply; in independent museums and the heritage sector the situation varies greatly.

Part-time work and job-sharing are beginning to be widely accepted.

Further information Cultural Heritage NTO, 1st Floor, Glyde House, Glydegate, Bradford BD5 0UP.
  www.chnto.co.uk
Association of Independent Museums, c/o London's Transport Museum, Covent Garden Piazza, London WC2E 7BB.
  www.aimus.org.uk
Museum Association, 24 Calvin Street, London E1 6NW.
  www.museumsassociation.org

Related careers ARCHAEOLOGY – ARCHIVIST – ART AND DESIGN – INFORMATION WORK

Music

Entry qualifications Acceptance at music colleges depends on performance at audition. For most performers, except for singers, intensive musical training must have started by their teens at the latest.

For teaching, see p. 610. For degree courses, at least 2 A levels and 5 GCSEs (A–C) with, usually, A level music.

The work Work with music covers a very wide field: performing, composing, recording, video-making, administration, teaching, criticism and journalism. Some of the traditional boundaries between what are loosely called 'serious' and 'pop' music and musicians are breaking down and fashions come and go as in any arts or entertainment area. In 'pop' and other 'non-traditional' music it is possible to reach the top without a proper musical training; success depends on many other factors. This section is concerned only with those parts of the profession that need formal training.

Performing

Some symphony orchestras and opera houses employ orchestral players on a full-time basis. Others, including smaller ensembles, are made up largely of regular but freelance musicians who may, or may not, work for other orchestras as well. Singers may be salaried members of a chorus or freelance.

Most freelance musicians, however devoted to serious music, are glad to work as 'session players' on TV commercials, film incidental music and other light music recording sessions, etc. A violinist may play in a concert at the Barbican on one evening and the following day in a TV jingle recording session.

A freelance musician has to fit in work as it comes. The work may fluctuate from 3 daily sessions (3 hours each) over a long period, to no work for many weeks. Long practice at home is always necessary. Live concerts or recording sessions are arranged well in advance, but some lucrative TV or film sessions are booked at short notice, and accepting bookings requires careful judgement. Once a date is booked, it is unwise to break it, even if a better engagement is offered.

The musician's work is physically exhausting, and may include travel over long distances, combined with rehearsals and nightly performances, often in cold or overheated halls. An engagement for a season with a ballet or opera company may involve 5 performances a week with as many rehearsals, and practice at home. The atmosphere amongst musicians is usually friendly, although the competition is keen.

Part-time teaching, either privately or in schools, gives many free-lance musicians a supplementary income. However, it is often difficult to fit in performing engagements with teaching.

Prospects in music have never been good and have been made harder with cutbacks in state and local authority funding. It is esti-mated that only about 1 in 10 of music students who finish their full training (itself restricted to the good students) eventually makes a living as a performer. Only 1 in as many hundreds becomes a soloist. Good luck is almost as important as talent.

Composing

Making a living from composing concert repertoire is very difficult; it takes many years for composers to have a body of their music regularly performed. They normally need another source of income, mainly within the profession, sometimes outside. Some fortunate composers make a good living from writing music for different parts of the media, for example TV, films, commercials and corporate videos.

School Teaching

As the main job this is quite a different career. Teachers are employed in primary and secondary schools. They teach music either full time in one school, possibly with a second subject, or part time in various schools and/or youth clubs and evening institutes run by the local education authority.

There is scope for imagination and initiative. Music teachers' main job is to promote interest and enthusiasm, as only a minority of pupils take music examinations. They may start a choir or an orchestra, or record evenings; organize record libraries, visits to concerts, etc.

There is currently a shortage of music teachers, particularly at primary level, now that music forms part of the National Curriculum.

Private Teaching

Many people go straight into full-time private teaching after leaving music college or university. They may prepare children, and sometimes adults, for graded examinations in an instrument. Because of its nature, this work is mostly done after school hours, in the evenings and weekends. Some teachers prefer to do this rather than work in schools, as they have more control over what they do.

Sound Engineering/Music Technology

For broadcast sound engineering see TELEVISION, FILM AND RADIO (p. 620). Sound engineers (not to be confused with professional engineers) in recording studios are responsible for the overall recording quality and for interpreting the producer's ideas. They need a grasp of basic physics and electronics in order to understand how to work their equipment, but they do not need great technical knowledge to start with (most enter as tape operators or assistant engineers). Some highly qualified and experienced sound engineers may be called *music technologists*. They apply advanced technology to the creation and reproduction of sound. They work on the design and manufacture of equipment, as well as in recording studios and broadcasting.

It is difficult to enter this area; really good engineers, however, are always in demand and a few become producers. Limited openings as yet for music technologists as this is still a relatively 'new breed'.

Musical Instrument Technology

There is some limited scope in musical instrument technology, which means making or repairing musical instruments – anything from harpsichords to clarinets, organs to synthesizers. The electronics side, involving the manufacture and repair of musical equipment, probably offers the best prospects. There is a steady demand for piano-tuners.

Performers

Training This has been gradually changing. Most courses at music colleges/conservatoires now lead to a degree, whereas in the past many led to graduate status diploma. The choice is between a 3- to 4-year full-time course at a college of music or a university based degree. Traditionally, university music degrees were largely academic and were not intended primarily for performers. Graduates who did not want to join the profession would (and still can) go on to a post-graduate performers' course at a music college. However, there are now many university courses which do emphasize performance; they may lead to a degree in music or in performing arts. There are also now a couple of degrees taught jointly by universities and conservatoires.

Degrees may last 3 or 4 years, they may lead to an ordinary or an honours degree and this may be called a BA Music or Bachelor of Music (BMus.). Where a college or university offers both degrees, the BMus. is intended for those students who want to concentrate almost entirely on performance, while the BA Music contains more academic studies.

The syllabus of any performers' course (degree or diploma) normally includes a principal subject and a second study subject. Instrumentalists may sometimes play two instruments although resources are often scarce and instrumental tuition may be limited to the first study instrument. Singers may take either an instrument as second study or they may take speech and drama. Other subjects included are aural training, theory and history of music, analysis, orchestral experience, choral and opera study, contextual studies and, often, a language. In addition many colleges offer a wide selection of specialist options, such as composition, contemporary or early music, electronic music, music therapy, music administration, aesthetics, ethnic music and conducting.

For people interested in non-classical music, there are now a number of HE courses in popular and commercial music, jazz and band studies.

Composers

The most common route is to take a music degree at university, followed by a post-graduate course in composition at either university or a conservatoire.

Teachers

Music teachers in *schools* must gain Qualified Teacher Status (see TEACHING, p. 610) by taking *either* a music degree (or graduate diploma) followed by a 1-year course of professional teacher training *or* a BEd. with music as a main subject. There is a shortened BEd. for people over 21 with music training. Teachers who give instrumental lessons in or out of school are not required to have Qualified Teacher Status. Some take education options within performers' courses, some take post-graduate teaching courses at music college (for example the Licentiateship of Trinity College London (Music Education)). A number of short or part-time courses exist for practising teachers. For example the Associated Board has a 1-year part-time Professional Development Course for Instrumental and Singing Teachers; the ISM (Incorporated Society of Musicians) has also created a distance-learning diploma for music teachers in private practice in conjunction with Reading University.

Those wishing to be listed in the ISM Register of Professional Private Music Teachers must have suitable professional qualifications and experience.

Music technology/sound engineering

Traditionally this has been on the job. Competition to get into the recording industry is now so great that some pre-entry training or experience is necessary. There are various ways to train: short introductory courses, evening courses, occasional day-release. Recording companies often look for people with some kind of technical or engineering background, not necessarily electronics. There are now a number of degrees, Foundation degrees and HNDs available with titles such as music and technology, electronic music, music acoustics, music and physics or electronics. For classical music recording sound engineers normally need a music degree.

Musical instrument technology

There are full-time (usually 2 years) courses leading to City & Guilds, as well as BTEC/SQA and degree courses. *Piano-tuners* can study full time or by day- or block-release.

Other courses

For those wanting to go into music administration or management there are one or two relevant courses. Otherwise openings tend to be for people with experience in some aspect of the music business or with specialist qualifications in, for example, accountancy or marketing.

Personal attributes *For performers*: Apart from outstanding talent, perseverance, resilience, courage and indifference to setbacks; the ability to work as one of a team; a pleasant manner; good health; very wide musical interest; good sight-reading speed; willingness to work ouside the musical field between engagements. *For teachers*: as for teaching (p. 610), plus creative imagination and initiative.

Music Therapy

This is a small but growing field. Music therapists work with children and adults with physical disabilities or learning difficulties and in the field of mental illness in both the health and the education services.

Music can contribute to the development and treatment of disabled and maladjusted people in various ways as a medium of non-verbal communication – by helping to relax their bodies and minds, as a mental stimulus, and as an emotional outlet. Autistic children, for example, and severely withdrawn adults, who do not respond to any other form of activity and cannot form relationships, often benefit greatly from listening to, and making, music.

There are 1- and 2-year full-time and part-time post-graduate courses in music therapy. Candidates must have had at least a 3-year full-time musical education and some experience of working with disabled people. Some work full time in one hospital, some do 'sessions' in several centres. The work is extremely demanding and needs maturity and sensitivity. Many find they cannot cope with full-time therapy work.

Work life balance It is unlikely that performers can resume orchestral playing after a long gap unless they keep up with serious daily practice; but there should be no problem returning to teaching after a career break.

Performing: work as freelance is possible in many areas – but work tends to be sporadic rather than regular part time. *Teaching and music therapy*: part time or job-sharing should be possible, but not necessarily exactly where one wants it.

Further information *For early training*: Local education authority music adviser.

For general information: Incorporated Society of Musicians, 10 Stratford Place, London W1C 1AA.
www.ism.org

For music courses: *Music Education Yearbook* (Rhinegold Publishing), available at most libraries.

For sound engineering and record companies: The British Phonographic Industry (BPI), Riverside Building, County Hall, Westminster Bridge Road, London SE1 7JA.
www.bpi.co.uk

For music therapy: Association of Professional Music Therapists, 26 Hamlyn Road, Glastonbury, Somerset BA6 8HT. *www.apmt.org.uk*

Related careers DANCE – LEISURE/RECREATION MANAGEMENT – TEACHING – TELEVISION, FILM AND RADIO

Nursery Nurse/Nursery Officer/ Nanny

As more mothers choose to work outside the home there has been an increasing shortfall in childcare provision. The government has responded by launching the National Childcare Strategy, and in 2002 launched a national 4-year campaign to recruit 150,000 new childcare workers. Local authorities are now required to plan local childcare services to deliver integrated early education and childcare, and the private sector is also responding, as large multi-branched agencies are moving in to provide childcare services tailored to parental need.

Entry qualifications None laid down, but most colleges demand at least 2 GCSEs (A–C); many entrants have more; a few have A levels. Private training colleges demand at least 3 GCSEs (A–C).

The work Nursery nurses look after children 8 years and under. They are primarily concerned with healthy children (they are now often called nursery officers), but, strangely, in this context 'healthy' may include children with problems and also children with physical disabilities and learning difficulties.

Nursery nurses' roles cover very much more than physical care and supervision of young children. Young children learn through play and through communicating with other children and with adults; they need adequate stimuli and individual attention to ensure their healthy intellectual, emotional and social development. When nursery nurses read to children, talk to them individually, discuss, say, their painting efforts, and generally help them to enjoy nursery activities they are, in effect, teaching.

Nursery nurses work in various settings:

1. Nursery classes and schools (for 3–5-year-olds) and infant schools (5–7-year-olds), run by local education authorities (LEAs). Nursery nurses help organize play activities, read to and play with children. Usually 1 nursery nurse is responsible for a small group of children. A qualified nursery or infant teacher (see p. 611) is normally in charge.

2. Day nurseries and family centres, run by social services departments for under-5s (mainly 3–5-year-olds) who are at risk socially, physically or emotionally; and for children where both parents have to go out to work or for other reasons cannot satisfactorily look after them during the day. There are now very few places for children whose parents merely think that nursery is a 'good thing'. A proportion of children in day nurseries have special needs, so work can be very demanding. Occasionally staff involve parents in the nursery's activities – largely to help parents understand the children's needs and development. Staff may also do unofficial 'casework' (see SOCIAL WORK, p. 562).

3. Private day nurseries, workplace nurseries and crèches: there is an increasing number of these, catering for parents who want their children to have the benefits of nursery experience, especially in areas where there are few LEA-run nursery places. Most cater for working parents by being open all day, and some are, in fact, attached to one or more companies and open only to their staff.

4. In hospital, nursery nurses help to look after babies in maternity wards, and on children's wards they play with and care for children. Actual nursing is done by registered nurses (see p. 413).

5. The largest single group work in private families as 'nannies', mainly, these days, in homes where both parents go out to work. Unlike in the past, most nannies expect to share the care of the children with the parents.

There is a variety of working patterns: some live-in nannies take charge of a young child or 2 or 3 children all day; in addition, in between the end of the school day and a parent's return from work (and perhaps during the school holidays), they may look after several schoolchildren whose parents share the nanny's salary. Other nannies work 2 days for one family, 3 days for another if the mothers concerned are themselves part-timers and need only part-week nannies. Work in a family differs from that outside the home in that nannies are on their own: nobody to ask for help in emergencies, and much of the time no other adult to talk to. The work is both more responsible and lonelier; it may also be less rigorous. Most nannies do some housework or at least cook for the children while the parents are at work.

6. A very small proportion work in hotels and holiday camps as children's hostesses. Experienced nannies can get jobs abroad.

Nursery nurses who take the Advanced Diploma courses have fair promotion prospects and may become officers in charge of nurseries of all kinds, at home and abroad. However, the ratio of senior to junior jobs is low.

Training 1. The usual method: minimum age 16. A 2-year full-time or longer part-time course at a college of further education. Students spend three-fifths of their time at college, two-fifths on 'placements' working with children. Most placements are in public sector nurseries, etc., but colleges often include days-only placements in private families considered suitable for training purposes. Students do not normally have sole charge of children or get experience of 24-hour care, and do not get the 'feel' of being a nanny where both parents work.

The syllabus includes the social, emotional, physical and intellectual development of children from 0–8; children's social, emotional and physical needs to ensure normal development; children with all kinds of special needs, including physical and mental disabilities; importance and significance of play, companionship, communication; promotion and maintenance of health (including nutrition and prevention and control of infection); organizing play activities; employment issues; patterns of family life and social institutions – and changes in both; the nanny in a private family; how the social services work; arts and crafts; early years and the National Curriculum.

In *England, Wales and Northern Ireland* courses offered by the Council for Awards in Children's Care and Education (CACHE) lead to the level 3 Diploma in Child Care and Education (DCE, formerly the National Nursery Examination Board (NNEB) Diploma in Nursery Nursing). This 2-year full-time modular course carries a maximum of 360 UCAS points (3 A levels) and may also be used as a route into general nursing training or midwifery, as long as you have a GCSE grade C or above in English and maths. Part-time courses are also available.

The CACHE Diploma can be followed by a modular course lasting about 2–5 years part time or 1-year full time, leading to the Advanced Diploma in Child Care and Education. Students have to complete 6 modules or units, and can specialize in special groups, such as children with disabilities or disturbed children, or ethnic minorities, or in nursery management. Different modules are offered by different colleges and students study by day- or block-release. This award carries 120 CATS (see p. 13) points for people applying later for a degree course.

There is also a 1-year full-time course offered by CACHE leading to the Certificate in Child Care and Education (some centres offer it part time). This can give entry into the Diploma course and in certain cases can lead to remission of teaching time for the Diploma course.

2. There are part-time or full-time courses leading to the BTEC Certificate/Diploma in Early Years.

3. 18–24 month courses at the 3 private Association of Nursery Training colleges. Students must be at least 18; to make sure they like the work, most look after children privately, in between school and college. Private colleges prepare students for the CACHE awards and for their own diplomas.

4. Work-based routes: NVQs/SVQs levels 2, 3 and 4 (see p. 10) in aspects of childcare and early education are widely available and qualify candidates to work with children in a range of situations.

Foundation and Advanced Modern Apprenticeships are available (see p. 11).

In *Scotland* the most usual route is a 1-year SQA National Certificate course followed by a 1-year SQA HNC course in Childcare and Education. Alternatively, SVQs in Early Years Care and Education can be achieved either through full-time college courses or while in employment. Both routes lead to registration by the Scottish Childcare and Education Board. Modern Apprenticeships are available (see p. 11).

Personal attributes A way with young children; patience; imagination; willingness to take responsibility and to work hard at routine chores; ability to work well in a team; interest in mental, social and physical development of children.

Late start Entry is possible at any age. There are two centres offering very intensive 1-year Fast Track courses, suitable for those with some experience.

Work life balance A career break should be no problem.

Opportunities for flexible working depend very much on type of employment. Local authorities usually have schemes in place.

Position of men Under 1% of students are men; no reason at all why this should remain so – men welcome on courses and in jobs.

Further information Council for Awards in Children's Care and Education (CACHE), 8 Chequer Street, St Albans, Herts. AL1 3XZ. *www.cache.org.uk*

Scottish Childcare and Education Board, 6 Kilnford Crescent, Dundonald, Kilmarnock, Ayrshire KA2 9DW (enclose s.a.e.).

Local authority education or social services departments.

Related careers NURSING – SOCIAL WORK – TEACHING

Nursing

This section covers *hospital* and *community nurses, health visitors* and *midwives*. Nursing and in particular nurse education has changed dramatically in recent years and continues to change, to meet the needs of people in the twenty-first century. Changes in health care and nursing philosophy affect how nursing care is delivered. For example, increasing emphasis is put on health promotion and the prevention of disease; patients are increasingly being cared for in their own homes including such services as the 'hospital at home'. With scientific and medical advancements, patients in hospitals are receiving more sophisticated and advanced treatments; this requires the nurse to be more skilled than ever. This situation is true whether a person is doing adult or children's nursing.

The changes in mental health and learning disabilities nursing have also affected where and how care is given to these client groups. The emphasis is now on giving care in the community either in the person's own home or in small group homes. People with acute mental health problems may be cared for a period of time in an acute psychiatric unit. These units are now often part of larger district general hospitals.

Nurses, no matter which branch of nursing they work in, form a crucial part of the multidisciplinary health care team. The team includes occupational therapists, physiotherapists and doctors. This closer working together includes joint decision-making about patient care. Patients and their families are also included in the decision-making; this ensures that patients receive more information about choices and have more control over the type of treatment they may be given.

Nursing

'Nursing' covers a range of jobs which vary widely in terms of levels of functions, of responsibility, professional qualifications required, and environment worked in. There is, therefore, scope for people with widely differing aims, interests and abilities.

To attract more mature students and encourage qualified nurses to return to nursing, opportunities for flexible and part-time working have increased considerably. Education is also available on a part-time, flexible basis; this makes it possible for people to qualify as a nurse who in the past may have been prevented from doing so.

There is also a need to attract more men into all areas of nursing. As nursing covers such wide-ranging client groups, the skills and attributes a person requires to be a nurse are very varied.

Nurses' work is much more difficult to define than other professionals' because there are so many, and some contradictory, facets to it.

Entry qualifications There are two main routes to becoming a registered nurse. Applicants may either apply for a diploma or a degree in nursing.

The minimum age for entry into nursing in the UK except Scotland is 17½ years. In Scotland the age is 17 years.

Currently the minimum educational requirements are 5 GCSEs grades A–C or equivalent. For midwifery applicants this must include English language or English literature, mathematics or a science subject. For degree programmes A levels or equivalents will also be required.

The Nursing and Midwifery Council (NMC) is in the process of seeking to change the above. This requires a change in the statutory instrument covering the entry requirements for nursing and midwifery. If agreement is granted, in the future, the NMC will set general guidance for universities and higher education colleges. However, each university or college will set out its individual entry criteria.

To encourage applications from a broad spectrum of society, a wider range of routes is now available into nursing and midwifery.

There is a range of access courses available for people who do not have the traditional entry requirements for either nursing or midwifery. These courses must be Quality Assurance Agency (QAA) approved. Successful completion of the course meets the entry requirements for both the degree and diploma programmes.

People working as care assistants may be able to undertake the NVQ in Care at level 3. This level can be accepted as the minimum educational requirement for the diploma programme.

Foundation degrees/programmes are being developed which on successful completion normally allow a person on to the second year of either the diploma or degree nursing programme.

BRANCHES OF NURSING

There are 4 branches of nursing: adult, children, mental health and learning disabilities. All 4 branches require different types of people to work in them. Midwifery is a separate profession. However, a registered nurse can undertake an 18-month course to become a midwife.

Registered Nurse (Adult)

This area of nursing is concerned with the care of people throughout all stages of adulthood, who are either healthy or have a wide range of health care problems.

Nurses use a systematic approach to assessing, planning and delivering patient care. Adult nursing is not just about delivering the physical care of patients; it is also about their psychological, sociological and spiritual needs. In order to do this nurses require extensive knowledge in nursing, biology, psychology, sociology, inter-personal skills, research processes and methods, information technology. Patients are treated as individuals not as conditions.

Nurses for adults work in a wide range of settings within either a hospital or in community settings. As a registered nurse they are responsible for the organization and delivery of patients' care, keeping records, listening and giving information to patients and relatives, liaising with other members of the health and social care team.

After initial Registration, all nurses have a responsibility to remain up to date in the area in which they are working. There are a large number of courses available for continuing professional development (CPD) and these can help nurses to progress their careers in specific specialities such as accident and emergency nursing or care of the elderly. Further progression can lead to a nurse becoming a specialist practitioner such as a breast care nurse or diabetic care nurse. To carry out these types of roles, the nurse will have extensive experience in the speciality and will have undertaken further studies.

Personal attributes Common sense; practical bent; empathy for all people no matter what their age, ethnicity or religion; an interest in health and health-related issues; sensitivity coupled with a certain amount of resilience so as to be able to manage in a wide range of situations; organizing ability; patience; a sense of humour to put up with the inevitable occasional short tempers and difficult people; ability to know when to be firm – and how to be firm but not rude; powers of observation; initiative; ability to assess and make decisions in the best interest of the patient.

Registered Nurse (Children)

Nursing sick children can be both more rewarding and more arduous than nursing adults. It requires a different range of skills, including the ability to work with the child's family and involve them in his or her care: mothers or fathers often stay in hospital with their young children. Many children stay only for a very short time, but may return to hospital on a regular basis for further treatment and follow-up; others stay for longer because they are very seriously ill and/or suffer from a rare condition which has to be assessed. Children's nursing is also concerned with detection and follow-up of physical and learning difficulties. Some children's nursing is highly specialized, with nurses having taken post-Registration specialist training.

Children's wards are run to resemble home conditions as much as possible. Visiting is now normally allowed at all times with facilities being available for parents and other family members to stay. Children's nursing care is increasingly being delivered in the child's own home, therefore children's nurses are also employed in the community setting.

Jobs for children's nurses are many and varied and not just in general ward areas but also in specialist units. Some children's nurses may decide to work out of the clinical environment and gain employment in schools and other areas where children may be.

Personal attributes The same as for the adult nurse plus extra patience with children. A children's nurse must be able to talk to children on their own level while relating well to parents and other family members. They form an integral part of the multidisciplinary team who care for children. Good powers of observation are essential, as small children cannot explain their ailments.

Registered Nurse (Mental Health)

These days, caring for people with mental health problems takes place more frequently in the community than in the hospital setting.

In the community

Many mental health nurses will work within the community even when they first register; if they decide to continue in this area they will be able to undertake further training to become a community psychiatric nurse (CPN). CPNs may be employed by a health care trust or social services. This is in part because people with mental health problems frequently have social problems as well.

CPNs have, therefore, great scope to develop their own ideas and initiatives. Very broadly, CPNs combine 3 main, overlapping functions:

1. They give practical help and counselling support (see 'Counselling', p. 493) to patients discharged from hospital and now having to adjust to living with their families, in hostels or on their own; also, to patients who right from the start of their illness are treated as out-patients and/or attend day hospitals.

2. CPNs provide a preventative service: they see people who may

be referred by GPs, social workers, district nurses, health visitors, even relatives or neighbours, or they could be 'self-referred', i.e. people who realize they have problems which they cannot cope with.

3. CPNs help to 'educate' the community to understand the nature of mental illness; they also help families and foster-families (even landlords) – anyone who has a patient living in their home – to cope with disturbed people's behaviour. Supporting patients' families and others is a very important part of community psychiatric nursing.

CPNs may also run clinics, do group-work (see 'Psychotherapy', p. 491) with patients and/or their families, and help run day centres. Because of the increasing numbers of patients with psychiatric problems cared for in the community, the profession is expanding greatly.

Training for community mental health nursing is not yet mandatory, but RNs (Mental Health) interested in this work are encouraged to take one of several full- or part-time specialist courses.

In hospitals

1 adult in 8 in this country at some time in his or her life needs help because of some form of mental or emotional problem. The majority do not need hospitalization, and even most of those who do stay for only a short time, probably a few weeks, and possibly return for further brief spells in hospital in between leading normal lives. Only a minority are long-stay patients. The term 'mental illness' covers a wide spectrum. In severe cases sufferers may be unable to separate fantasy from reality and react to people and situations in unreasonable, even alarming, ways. Two groups of patients have increased in recent years: people of all ages who cannot cope with the stresses and strains of modern life and old people who suffer from dementia.

Over 90% of patients are 'voluntary' or 'informal'. Many of them are able to go out to shop or visit friends or relatives, and when in hospital most are encouraged to undertake a range of activities. Occupational therapists and mental health nurses work alongside each other to assist the patient. For most patients a vital part of their treatment is the contact with a friendly, skilled nurse; the inability to communicate with other people can be in part a feature of mental illness. Nurses help a great deal towards patients' recovery by talking to them and, above all, listening therapeutically.

In most psychiatric hospitals the atmosphere is relaxed and informal. Patients and staff live in a friendly so-called 'therapeutic' community. Patients are encouraged to share with the staff responsibility for running wards and for the active social life of the hospital. The aim is always to minimize the institutional atmosphere. Most wards are in small units of general hospitals.

At informal meetings with staff the patients are encouraged to discuss and even criticize treatment, to talk about their difficulties and to help each other with their problems. At staff-only meetings, after ward meetings with the patients, all nurses have a chance to discuss patients, treatments and new methods with consultants and senior staff.

Mental health nursing can, of course, sometimes be very demanding. Nurses must always remember that their patients' behaviour is often a symptom of their illness. Teamwork among the staff helps a great deal, and during their training nurses learn to recognize and handle the emotional aspect of their work.

Personal attributes Curiosity about what makes people behave as they do; emotional stability; patience and perseverance; the ability to listen well and to be genuinely concerned without becoming emotionally involved; outside interests to keep a sense of proportion; a sense of humour; good physical and mental health.

Registered Nurse (Learning Disabilities)

In hospitals

People with learning disabilities may have been born with the disorder or acquired it after birth either through an illness or accident. Unlike mental illness, this condition is not normally curable, and some people may require residential care all their lives. However, the tendency today is to enable as many clients as at all possible to live in the community. This means that clients in hospital tend to be severely disabled, often both physically and mentally. Nurses help patients develop their potential as far as it is possible to do so. The extent of the disability in each client determines the degree of independence that can be achieved. It takes great patience and perseverance sometimes to enable a patient even to dress or feed him/herself. However, once the patient has taken even one small step towards independence, both patient and nurse feel they have achieved something. Some clients are prepared for life outside the hospital and learn to shop, use money, etc. This type of nursing is always a mixture of teaching, showing understanding, and establishing relationships of trust with patients. Nurses work in teams with doctors, psychologists, occupational therapists and physiotherapists. Like mental health nurses, these nurses attend meetings with other professionals to discuss patients and problems.

In the community
Over 60% of persons diagnosed as suffering from learning disabilities now live with their families, on their own, in shared accommodation or in group homes. Their need for continued care varies enormously from the occasional chat to regular care. A client – the term now preferred to 'patient' – may, for example, have a sleeping problem and the nurse may be able to suggest ways of improving the situation for the client and family. Follow-up would be required. The nurse may find that the extent of the client's learning difficulty is much smaller than the parents assumed. Teaching relatives how to care for clients is an important part of the nurse's work. Some clients, perhaps those only recently discharged from hospital but able to live in a shared flat, may merely have to be encouraged to increase their independence: to learn such social skills as saying 'hello' to neighbours, and such 'living skills' as doing the shopping or using public transport. The aim of nurses is always to develop clients' potential as fully as their disability allows.

Nurses also hold 'information sessions' to help other community care and health professionals, as well as the community at large, understand developments and changes in the treatment of people with learning difficulties. Most learning disabilities nurses work in the community.

Personal attributes Affectionate nature; a practical approach; teaching ability; patience; gentleness; interests unconnected with the work; ability to be genuinely concerned without becoming emotionally involved.

Training (all branches of nursing) There are 2 routes leading to qualification as a Registered Nurse (RN):

1. 3-year Diploma of Higher Education in Nursing. Students are based at a higher education institution (HEI) where they will study theory and knowledge-based elements of the course. Half of the course will be spent in supervised nursing practice in hospitals or other environments.

2. A Bachelor (Hons) degree in Nursing Studies. These are normally 3 years although a few 4-year courses are still available, depending on the number of weeks per year spent in study. Again, half the course is spent in studying theory and half in supervised nursing practice in a range of settings.

On both diploma and degree programmes, the first 12 months cover a Common Foundation Programme. The remainder of the course follows a programme in a chosen branch – adult, mental health, children or learning disability nursing.

Some NHS hospitals employ nurse cadets who are trained through practical experience and theory to be eligible for entry to a diploma course. Most HEIs now offer diploma and degree courses on a part-time basis.

All students start at the same level. Diplomates can top up their diplomas to degree level by undertaking further studies once they are registered.

In some NHS Trusts, staff employed as health care assistants may be able to work towards qualifications (e.g. NVQs) which will enable them to meet the minimum requirements for entry on to a pre-Registration course at a local HEI.

All students on the diploma course receive a non-means-tested bursary. Students on degree courses may receive a means-tested bursary, but are entitled to a student loan. Some students who have worked for the NHS may be seconded to do their training, in which case they receive a monthly sum almost equivalent to their previous NHS salary.

OTHER NURSING IN THE COMMUNITY

Nurses who work outside the hospital, where there is always someone more highly qualified to discuss problems with, have much more independence in terms of decision-making and organizing their working days. District nurses, health visitors, community psychiatric nurses (see p. 415), school nurses, practice nurses and community midwives all come under what is now often loosely called community public health nursing. They are all examples of specialized 'nurse practitioners', a term increasingly used. They are part of the multidisciplinary community care team, working closely with GPs, social workers and other colleagues from related professions. The proportion of community nurses is growing, as more and more patients live in the community but still need nursing care and support. Community nurses like their hospital colleagues are increasingly taking on more responsibilities including prescribing certain medicines.

District Nurse

District nurses undertake skilled nursing duties for patients in their home. They give acute care and ongoing care to patients. They may also help permanently disabled patients to learn to use new aids, and help relatives to learn to carry out routine nursing care. When necessary they put people in touch with social workers or with other members of the health care team. District nurses work closely with local GPs, who advise on whom to visit and, often, the treatment required. District nurses perform most of the skills that would also be performed in hospital such as changing patients' dressings and giving intravenous drugs. They also give moral support, helping patients and their relatives to come to terms with their situation. District nurses get to know their patients and families well; they also play an important role in the wider community. Experienced nurses often lead teams that include several district nurses and health care assistants. To provide a 24-hour service, nurses work shifts. Because of the close cooperation between hospital and community services, district nurses may on occasion visit their patients in hospital if they have been admitted. This means they have both the independence of community nursing and the companionship and chance to talk shop. Some district nurses specialize, e.g. in work with diabetics, the disabled, the elderly, terminal care.

Health Visitor

Health visitors are professionals in their own right. They organize their own work.

The important difference between health visitors on the one hand and nurses and social workers on the other is that the latter usually meet clients when something has gone wrong. The purpose of health visiting is the promotion of health and the prevention and early detection of physical and mental ill health. Health visitors give health care advice, identify the need for and if necessary mobilize other sources of help.

They are responsible for monitoring children's health from the time midwifery care ceases (10 days after birth usually) until the school nurse (see p. 423) takes over checking children's development. They advise mothers on childcare, health hazards and health care both by regular home visits and in clinics. Routine home visits may act as an 'early warning system', and health visitors often notice signs of stress or disorder before these develop into problems. For example, a young mother who gave up the companionship at work just before the child was born may feel lonely and guilty for not being a radiant mother; the health visitor helps by discussing her feelings and by suggesting ways of coping with the problem. Other matters which might develop into problems but for the health visitor's early advice are older children's health or behaviour, or marital difficulties.

Health visitors also play an increasingly important role in the care of the elderly, in particular in health monitoring and health education and promotion. Health visitors work very closely with other members of the health care team, in particular GPs, CPNs and social workers.

They may visit patients recently discharged from hospital; mentally ill or disabled people who are cared for at home; the elderly; anyone who may be referred to them by social workers, doctors, a neighbour even. They are very much involved with health education and may lecture in schools and other organizations.

When visiting, health visitors are concerned with the family as a whole, not only the ill or disturbed member of the family. They may be based in doctors' practices, or work from health centres.

Occupational Health Nurse

Occupational health nurses work in factories, stores and wherever else there is a large number of employees, with the aim of promoting health in the workplace. They are also involved in health screening of staff, in particular in areas where the work environment may be hazardous. The work is about health promotion as well as preventative work.

Occupational health nurses also deal with accidents and sudden illness and give minor treatments, such as injections, changing dressings. They advise both on health problems generally and on those peculiar to a particular industry, e.g. skin or respiratory diseases caused by certain types of work. They are now very much involved, at least in most large and/or progressive organizations, with research into the effects of the introduction of new technologies and/or working patterns on employees' health and on their job-satisfaction. This may involve discussing the arrangements of desks in word processing stations, or checking noise levels in tool shops, as well as shift and night work arrangements and canteen facilities. An important aspect of their work is the identification of health hazards, and initiating whatever measures are necessary to eliminate or minimize such hazards. They work closely with factory inspectors (see p. 253).

They also work closely with occupational health doctors. They usually keep medical records of all employees and assist at the medical examination of prospective employees. They often arrange for such ancillary services as chiropody, eye-testing and physiotherapy. They discuss health and safety measures on the shop-floor and in the office with management, shop stewards and factory inspectors and work closely with the personnel department. For example, if an employee's work is deteriorating, OHNs help to find the psychological or physical cause. OHNs also help to find suitable jobs for the disabled and may discuss with management measures which should be taken in special cases.

In large concerns there may be a medical department; more often there is one occupational health nurse working for the personnel director and/or the visiting medical officer.

To become an occupational health nurse further studies need to be undertaken at an HEI. Unlike other nursing jobs, normal office hours usually apply.

School Nurse

School nurses take over the monitoring of children's development where health visitors' work stops, i.e. when children reach school age. They work in the school health service and regularly visit a number of schools. Their routine checking of vision, hearing, growth, etc. is a preventative service: they hope to detect problems before they develop into serious ones and make appropriate referrals. Teachers and parents ask school nurses' advice when a child shows signs of not being quite 'up to scratch', physically or mentally. The school nurse may contact parents when that seems advisable.

School nursing varies very much from one area to another, according to local organization; how many schools one school nurse is responsible for; and also according to individual school nurses' initiative and interpretation of their role.

School nurses are also very much involved in health education. Again, the extent of involvement varies: in some areas health education officers (usually health visitors by qualification) are appointed and school nurses would work with them; in other areas health education is left to health visitors and/or school nurses. Increasingly, school nurses take part in a programme of lectures/talks both to schoolchildren and at parents' evenings/meetings, on such issues as drug abuse, AIDS, etc.

In some areas school nurses hold a kind of 'surgery' on certain days in 'their' schools, when parents, children and teachers can come and discuss any problem that bothers them. School nursing is very much less structured in terms of specific duties than most other nursing specializations.

School nurses undertake a post-qualifying 52-week course and it is one of the areas of public health nursing.

Practice Nurse

Practice nurses have worked in GPs' practices for some time, carrying out such routine procedures as taking blood samples, changing dressings, etc. However, recent NHS changes greatly increased the range of tasks GPs or their support staff are asked to undertake; practice nurses' numbers and their importance have therefore increased greatly. Most practice nurses now undertake such non-routine tasks as setting up and running health promotion and continuing care clinics (e.g. well woman, asthma, hypertension and diabetic clinics) and they may also be involved in screening: i.e. checking patients' health. All new patients who register with a GP must be offered screening, and all over-75s at least once a year. Practice nurses may do this screening and decide whether the patient needs to see the doctor. In the case of elderly patients this may involve home visits. Some practice nurses are able to prescribe a range of drugs.

Post-Registration Courses

All nurses, wherever they work, must qualify initially as a registered nurse and the additional training required for the work outside hospitals depends very much in which part of the Registration they qualified. This training is usually provided in the form of post-Registration courses offered at Higher Education Institutions (HEIs).

Midwife

Entry qualifications As for registered nurses, see p. 412.

The work Midwives look after mother and child from early pregnancy until about 4 weeks after the birth of the child (when health visitors take over). They give ante-, peri- and post-natal advice, support and instruction, taking full responsibility during the birth in straight-forward cases, and calling a doctor in case of complications. They run hospital baby units including those for premature and sick babies. They are trained to a high professional standard and work closely with doc-tors. They also run clinics for pregnant women as well as training sessions for expectant fathers and mothers. As mothers' stay in hospital is often very short, midwives' home visits are vitally important. These may involve counselling women who suffer from post-natal depression, or who need advice on coping with a new-born baby without neglecting their other children. It also often involves family planning advice.

Midwifery is a unique combination of applying complex practical and high-tech skills, teaching parent craft and counselling.

There is today much more emphasis on the psychological aspects of pregnancy, childbirth and the post-natal period and their effects on the rest of the family than there used to be. The majority of births take place in hospital but an increasing number are occurring in mothers' own homes. To ensure continuity of care from early preg-nancy until the health visitor takes over care of mother and child, the emphasis is on an integrated hospital and community midwifery service, with individual midwives working in both home and hospital. But there are also opportunities for midwives to work only in hospital or only in the community. A small number of midwives work in the private sector. There is at present a shortage of registered midwives.

Training There are 2 routes:

1. Pre-Registration midwifery programmes for Registered Nurses (adult branch) who wish to gain a midwifery qualification. These lead to either a Diploma of Higher Education or a degree. They last a minimum of 78 weeks full time.

2. Pre-Registration courses for those who want to go directly into midwifery, not nursing. Like nurses, they take a 3-year course leading to a specialist diploma or a degree. Midwives can – and are encouraged to – take various post-Registration courses.

Personal attributes As for registered nurses (see p. 414), plus, of course, special interest in babies, and self-confidence, particularly when persuading fathers to get involved in the preparation for the birth.

Late start (within nursing in general) Excellent opportunities. Mature entrants of both sexes are very welcome because they bring a wider experience to the job.

Work life balance (within nursing in general) Nurses like other NHS employees should benefit from the Government's Improving Working Lives initiative, introduced in 2002 to aid recruitment and ensure a better work life balance for NHS staff. Every NHS Trust has to demonstrate its commitment to more flexible working patterns, which may include part-time working, job-sharing and term-time working, evening and weekend work, and supporting returners after a career break. Part-time training is becoming more widely available.

Opportunities for flexible work patterns are now available much higher up the promotion ladder than they used to be. Part time is encouraged at virtually all levels, and job-sharing is also encouraged (but the initiative still often has to come from individuals).

In recent times the restructuring of the nursing career structure in all of the branches encourages practitioners to stay within clinical practice up to the point of becoming a consultant nurse. This relatively new role is for senior nurses who are involved in patient care as well as research and education.

Position of men (within nursing in general) Still only about 10% of those entering nursing are men, with far fewer entering midwifery. There has been an increase in the number of men applying for pre-Registration courses. This relatively new role is for senior nurses who are involved in patient care as well as research and education.

Further information For further information about nursing, mid-wifery, health visiting and other careers in the NHS in England, contact: NHS Careers, PO Box 376, Bristol BS99 3EY. Tel: 0845 60 60 655.
www.nhs.uk/careers
Email advice@nhscareers.nhs.uk

For information about nursing and midwifery in other countries in the UK contact the appropriate organization:
NHS Education for Scotland, Careers Information Service, 22 Queen Street, Edinburgh EH2 1NT.
www.nhs.org.uk

For Wales: Learn Direct. Tel: 0800 100 900.

Careers Advice, School of Nursing, Queen's University of Belfast, 1–3 College Park East, Belfast BT7 1NN.

Careers Advice, Department of Health Sciences, University of Ulster, Jordanstown, Newton Abbey, BT37 0QB.

Northern Ireland Practice and Education Council, Careers Advice, Centre House, 79 Chichester Street, Belfast, BT1 4JE.

Royal College of Nursing, 20 Cavendish Square, London W1G 0RN.
www.rcn.org.uk

Royal College of Midwives, 15 Mansfield Street, London W1M 0BE.
www.rcm.org.uk

Related careers MEDICINE – NURSERY NURSE – OCCUPATIONAL THERAPY – PHYSIOTHERAPY – SOCIAL WORK

NOTE: Health care assistants (HCA) are non-qualified staff who work alongside and under the supervision of nurses and other health care professionals; they receive an on-the-job training to fulfil their role. They may also have the opportunity to undertake an NVQ level 2 and level 3 in Care or Direct Care. This could then lead on to the HCA doing nurse training.

Occupational Therapy

Entry qualifications As a guide, a minimum of 240 tariff points at A level, of which 160 points should be at A2 (grade C minimum), preferably with one A level in a science subject. Other qualifications, for example access courses and GNVQ Advanced, will be assessed for their equivalence. Learning from life experiences is also taken into account. Courses may ask for more than the minimum.

The work Occupational therapists work with people of all ages who have physical, mental and/or social difficulties from birth or as the result of an accident, illness or ageing, to help them live as full a life as practicable by overcoming as much as possible the effects of their disability. This covers a very wide range of activities concerned with physical, psychological, social and economic well-being. Occupational therapists are concerned with all the things that 'occupy' patients day-in, day-out – basic everyday care, work, leisure, social interaction.

Together with other members of the health and social care team, the occupational therapist assesses the problem and devises a programme of treatment, based on the client's lifestyle and preferences, to help them retain or regain as much independence as possible. The emphasis is on clients' ability, not disability, and looking beyond the most obvious needs to aspects that could go unnoticed. Treatment might involve strengthening exercises – or shopping expeditions. Occupational therapists devise new ways for patients to perform old tasks, e.g. cooking from a wheelchair, dressing, getting in and out of bed and bath. They may take patients on a trial visit home from hospital so they can advise on how the environment may need to be adapted. The solution is sometimes as simple as rearranging a room, or as complicated as building an extension. Sometimes there is no solution but rehousing, so the occupational therapist may have to liaise with the housing department. They also assess patients for various kinds of aids and equipment, from those which open jars to sophisticated hoists.

The range of clients and complexity of their needs means the work of an occupational therapist is challenging and varied. They have one-to-one contact with their clients and also work with groups and communities. They have the opportunity to work creatively in the way they apply their knowledge and expertise. It is important to develop a good relationship with both the service user and their family/carers, who provide much of the day-to-day support and often need help themselves to come to terms with how their lives have changed.

Occupational therapists treat patients in NHS and private hospitals, local community services, schools, prisons and in their homes. The main employers are the NHS and local authority social services departments. There are also opportunities in charities and voluntary agencies, government agencies, industry and equipment suppliers, special schools, GP practices and residential homes. An increasing number of occupational therapists are in private practice. Many choose to work in a particular field of health or social care and there are excellent career opportunities in clinical, research, teaching and management posts.

Occupational therapy support workers are generally employed in health and social services departments. They work under the supervision of occupational therapists, who can provide in-service training. They can also work towards NVQ/SNQs and other awards which can lead to a degree course.

Training 1. 3-year full-time course or 4-year part-time course leading to a degree.

2. 2-year accelerated courses for graduates.

3. 4-year part-time in-service courses: some require students to be employed as occupational therapy support workers or technical

instructors, and others allow part-time study irrespective of employment status.

Degree courses are broad based and about a third of the course is spent on practice placements, getting experience in the main branches of occupational therapy, usually physical rehabilitation, learning disabilities, mental health and social care. After qualification, students may take a rotational post in a hospital where they can expand their breadth of experience working with particular groups, e.g. children, orthopaedic patients, stroke patients, alcoholics, drug abusers, older people, people with learning disabilities or mental health needs.

Personal attributes An ability to set and solve problems; creativity; sensitivity; tolerance; tenacity; good humour; the ability to work both independently and as part of a team; good powers of observation; the ability to explain things clearly to all types of patient and to others including families, employers and other professionals.

Late start Mature students are welcomed on all courses and will be considered even if they do not have the stated academic requirements. Specific entry requirements should be checked with the university concerned. Mature students are normally expected to have considerable work experience or to be able to demonstrate their ability to undertake degree level studies or have completed recent study (e.g. an A level, BTEC, NVQ/SVQ, Open University foundation course (see p. 16) or access to higher education courses (see p. 15)).

Work life balance Occupational therapists usually work a 37½-hour week if employed within the NHS. More flexible working and weekend posts are becoming available. In local authorities, terms and conditions vary significantly between employers. Refresher courses, and financial support from local Workforce Development Confederations may be available to occupational therapists wishing to return to practice after a career break.

There are good opportunities for basic-grade and senior practitioner part-time positions as well as job-sharing, but this is dependent on employer requirements.

Further information College of Occupational Therapists, 106–114 Borough High Street, London SE1 1LB.
www.cot.co.uk

Related careers NURSING – PHYSIOTHERAPY

Optical Work

Optometrist (Ophthalmic Optician)

Entry qualifications Usually 3 A levels or 5 Scottish Highers: in both cases 2 must be in mathematics or science. GCSEs (minimum grade C) to include English, maths and physics or physics with chemistry.

The work The main duties of an optometrist are examining eyes; measuring vision defects with the help of optical instruments; and working out lens-prescriptions for short- or far-sightedness and astigmatism.

Some optometrists now test sight with computerized equipment. They are also trained to dispense ophthalmic prescriptions. The training is broad based and is both scientific and medical. The work combines dealing with people and applied science; much of the work is clinically based and the optometrist has to see the patient as a human being, not simply as a pair of eyes. Optometrists are concerned with the correction and treatment of visual errors and the health of the visual system. They do not treat patients with diseased eyes. If they find any abnormality or signs of disease in the eye they refer the patient to his or her general practitioner.

Optometrists work either in general practice, doing mainly sight-testing, or in hospital, where they see more intricate eye conditions and assist ophthalmic surgeons with investigations and treatment of eye disease, and with research. In general practice it is possible to specialize in a particular field, such as children's vision, low vision or contact lenses.

General practice may mean managing and/or owning an optician's practice and doing all the dispensing work as well; frequently it means doing the ophthalmic work in a shop managed and/or owned by a firm of ophthalmic or dispensing opticians which owns several practices.

There is a steady demand for optometrists.

Training Three years for a BSc degree (in Scotland 4 years) plus 1 year's clinical experience in paid employment. The syllabus includes physical optics, optical instruments, anatomy and physiology, abnormal and pathological conditions of the eye, refraction. The British College of Optometrists is the examining body for ophthalmic optics. After passing the College's Professional Qualifying Examinations and completing a pre-Registration year, students apply for Registration with the General Optical Council. Registration is obligatory for practitioners.

Personal attributes An interest in physics and maths; patience; manual dexterity; a liking for briefly meeting a flow of new people; a confident manner especially with old people and children; good communication skills; business ability.

Late start This is a long training and courses are oversubscribed, therefore only applicants with up-to-date knowledge of science are likely to be accepted. Approximately 7% of entrants are over 30. Once trained there should be no problem getting jobs.

Work life balance If one has kept up with developments, a career break presents no problem. *Refresher* courses available for all optometrists.

There are good opportunities for part-time work at all levels. Job-sharing is possible.

Further information The College of Optometrists, 42 Craven Street, London WC2N 5NG.
www.college-optometrists.org

Dispensing Optician

Entry qualifications 5 GCSEs (A–C) including maths or physics, English, plus 1 other science subject.

The work Dispensing opticians do not do any sight-testing or other eye-examination. They interpret the prescription of the ophthalmic surgeon or ophthalmic optician using complex apparatus to measure for, fit and supply spectacles, contact lenses and artificial eyes. All such work requires calculations of distance and angles, etc. Equally important are the selling and 'cosmetic' aspects of the work. Dispensing opticians discuss with patients (a term opticians use in preference to customers) which type of frame is the most flattering in each case.

Most dispensing opticians also deal with other types of optical instruments, supplying apparatus to ophthalmic surgeons, opticians and laboratories, and selling sunglasses, opera glasses, microscopes, etc. to the general public.

Dispensing opticians can also get managerial jobs in 'prescription houses' (firms which make lenses to prescription) and in firms of dispensing opticians which manufacture optical instruments.

Dispensing opticians usually start as assistants but later may manage a shop, or practice, in which optometrists or surgeons do the eye-testing.

Training *Either*: a 2-year full-time course at an approved training institution, plus 1 year's practical experience; *or*: 3 years' work as a trainee with a dispensing optician, plus theoretical instruction, by day-release, distance-learning or block-release course (which must be approved by the General Optical Council); *or*, a 3-year full-time course in optical management leading to a degree.

All methods of training lead to the qualifying examinations for Fellowship of the Association of British Dispensing Opticians (ABDO).

The syllabus covers optical physics, the anatomy and physiology of the eye, the interpretation of ophthalmic prescriptions, the necessary measurements and adjustments for frames, and the recording of facial measurements. The full-time courses also include business practice.

ABDO now offers an access course for students without maths, English or a general science qualification (see 'Entry qualifications').

Personal attributes Some manual dexterity; interest in salesmanship and in fashion; ability and enjoyment in dealing with flow of people; good communication skills.

Late start No special problems, except for competition from young entrants. Science graduates may be exempt from part of the course.

Work life balance A career break should be no problem: *refresher* courses exist and may increase.

There are good opportunities for part-time work and job-sharing at all levels up to managing a high street shop.

Orthoptics

Entry qualifications 5 GCSEs (A–C) including English language, maths and a science subject, and 3 A levels, preferably including a science subject.

The work Orthoptists are responsible for the diagnosis, investigation, treatment and progress-monitoring of patients who have defects of binocular vision, e.g. squint, double vision or related vision conditions. The orthoptist's role is expanding. The importance of early diagnosis and treatment of children is increasingly recognized. Orthoptists therefore work on screening programmes for pre-school-age children. Special equipment and special skills enable orthoptists to assess the visual abilities of even very young children – some patients are under a year old. Orthoptists also deal with children who have reading difficulties. They must be able to build up relationships with children of all ages and with their parents.

Other patient groups include people with disabilities; people who have had accidents or strokes; multiple sclerosis sufferers; and the elderly who can be helped to achieve their maximum visual potential, for example in glaucoma clinics. The latter client group is growing in size as the proportion of elderly people in the population is increasing.

Orthoptists thus deal with a very wide age-range, with a wide range of conditions, and in a range of settings – in hospitals, schools, paediatric, geriatric and neurological clinics or departments. Patients are referred by ophthalmic surgeons, neurologists, general physicians, paediatricians and other specialists.

Equipment used for diagnosis and treatment is highly sophisticated. Its use requires great technical knowledge and skill. The need for getting clients of all ages to cooperate and do exercises – both in the clinic and at home – requires orthoptists to understand and communicate well with people of all ages and temperaments.

There are opportunities for experienced orthoptists to become clinical teachers of orthoptics, and to work in private practice. British qualifications are accepted in most countries and there is scope for orthoptists in the EU if they speak the relevant language.

Training This is via a 3-year degree course. Syllabus includes general anatomy and physiology; child development; anatomy and physiology of eye and brain; optics; diseases of the eye and the principles of eye surgery; practice of orthoptics.

Students gradually gain clinical experience working with patients of all ages.

Personal attributes A scientific bent; powers of observation, deduction and persuasion; understanding of people of all ages and temperaments; ability to work as one of a team, and also independently; communication skills.

Late start The British Orthoptic Society requires normal entry qualifications. However, determined candidates in their 20s or 30s may be admitted for training especially if they have had experience of dealing with children. Approximately 5% of entrants are mature (see 'Access to higher education courses', p. 15).

Work life balance Opportunities for return after a career break depend on (a) whether the orthoptist kept up with developments, and (b) on level of vacancies. Short 'up-dating' *refresher* courses are available.

Opportunities for job-sharing and flexible hours do arise and are negotiated locally.

Further information British Orthoptic Society, Tavistock House North, Tavistock Square, London WC1H 0HX.
www.orthoptics.org.uk

Related careers MEDICINE – SCIENCE

Osteopathy

Entry qualifications See 'Training', below.

The work An osteopath uses manipulative methods both in the diagnosis and the treatment for the correction of derangements of the bony and muscular structures of the body, and makes a special study of the spine in relation to health and disease. Osteopathy does not include the curing of organic disease but it covers the treatment of some organic functional disorders. The majority of patients need treatment because of stiff joints, slipped discs, etc. Patients are often referred to osteopaths by GPs who recognize the value of osteopathic treatment for certain disorders, but many patients come through personal recommendation.

The majority of osteopaths work in private practice, but increasingly some are working within a number of NHS settings.

Osteopathy was granted statutory recognition under the Osteopathy Act 1993. Only practitioners registered with the General Osteopathic Council are entitled to call themselves osteopaths.

The majority of new graduates tend to practise as associates with senior colleagues in order to obtain further clinical experience and support; this may be at the same time as starting their own practice, which they may eventually concentrate upon as it becomes more established. Currently more osteopaths work on their own in practice, but there is an increasing number of group practices.

Training The only means of entry into the osteopathic profession is through a recognized course, accredited by the General Osteopathic Council. Currently, the recognized schools offer a variety of full-time and part-time courses leading to a degree or an award in osteopathy. There is one course, the London College of Osteopathic Medicine, which is open only to qualified medical practitioners.

Entrance requirements vary from one institution to another, but there is generally a preference for a science background. Emphasis is also placed on individual suitability for entry into the profession drawing upon personal attributes. The average intake of students each year usually includes a mixture of school-leavers and mature students.

The syllabus for all courses includes a comprehensive grounding in the basic medical sciences, and osteopathic theory and practice, in both the lecture room and the training clinics attached to the schools.

Personal attributes Sense of responsibility at personal and community level; self-discipline; a good communicator; concern and motivation to care for others; a degree of manual dexterity and coordination.

Late start The number of mature entrants is growing. Depending on the validation arrangements with the relevant university, there may be exemption from certain elements of a course for people with relevant qualifications (e.g. physiotherapy, medicine).

Work life balance All Registered Osteopaths, both non-practising and practising, have to undertake continuing professional development activities in order to enhance their own personal level of competency. The General Osteopathic Council offers support to registered practitioners returning into practice after a period of non-practising or a career break.

Opportunities for part-time work are very good.

Further information Osteopathic Information Service, General Osteopathic Council, Osteopathy House, 176 Tower Bridge Road, London SE1 3LU.
www.osteopathy.org.uk

Related careers MEDICINE – PHYSIOTHERAPY

Patent Agent (Chartered) and Patent Examiner

Entry qualifications Minimum 2 A levels for Foundation exam, but in practice a science or engineering degree; working knowledge of French and German very desirable.

Patent Agent or Patent Attorney

The work Patent agents (now usually known as patent attorneys) work in the field of intellectual property. Put very simply, intellectual property is the right which protects a product, process, trademark, design or written material that has been invented or originated by one person from being copied or developed by another for a certain number of years. It is a mixture of legal and scientific/technological work. A patent attorney advises inventors, and others concerned with inventions, on the validity and infringement of patents at home and abroad. Until quite recently only patent attorneys registered with the Chartered Institute of Patent Agents had the right to submit patents. A change in the law means that now anyone can do the work of a patent attorney but cannot be called a 'patent agent or patent attorney' unless registered. (They may be called 'consultants'.)

Patent attorneys make 'searches' for clients to ensure that their inventions really are new, and prepare detailed specifications, descriptions and formulations of claims which 'cover' the invention. They file and negotiate the applications for patents on behalf of their clients at the Patent Office. Having assisted in the creation of a patent, they may deal with its commercial application. They deal not only with patents for processes and products, but also with 'Registered Designs', 'Registered Trade Marks' and Industrial Copyright.

The majority of patent attorneys specialize in a particular type of work, e.g. in chemical or mechanical inventions, or in electronics – a very important area – or in designs and trade marks. Many patent attorneys are also trade mark attorneys, but there are also independent trade mark attorneys.

Patent attorneys work in private practice or for industrial organizations.

Patent attorneys' work has increased in scope and complexity since the coming into force of the European Patent Convention. In addition to preparing and processing patent applications in this country and corresponding with patent agents abroad to obtain similar protection for clients' inventions there, patent attorneys who are suitably qualified draft patent applications for submission to the European Patent Office in Munich. There are reasonable opportunities for travel to Europe and other countries.

Although this is a small profession there is increasing scope.

Training The Chartered Institute of Patent Agents' examinations are at Foundation and Advanced level, with separate exams for the Patent Agents and Trade Mark Agents Registers.

There is no longer a minimum training period before passing the exams, but trainees must have 2 years' professional experience before being registered. Most are expected to go on to take the exams of the European Patent Office in order to qualify as European Patent Attorneys, eligible to submit patents to the European Patent Office.

Preparation for examinations is mainly by private study; some firms sponsor trainees on a 3-month full-time course for the Foundation stage. The Chartered Institute arranges lectures and tutorials. Some technical assistants never qualify yet nevertheless do very well, but they cannot become partners in private practice firms.

Personal attributes Curiosity; an analytical mind; a good memory; a scientific bent; the ability to assimilate facts quickly and to reason and speak clearly; ability to write clearly and unambiguously; liking for concentrated desk-work.

Late start Entrance requirements may be waived for people with relevant experience, but there are difficulties getting training vacancies due to the length of training involved.

Work life balance Return after a career break is possible only for those who have kept up with legal and technological changes/developments.

There are some part-time opportunities; it is also possible for experienced patent attorneys with good contacts to run a small private practice from home. Job-sharing should be possible.

Further information Chartered Institute of Patent Agents, 95 Chancery Lane, London WC2A 1DT.
www.cipa.org.uk

Patent Examiner

Entry qualifications First- or second-class honours degree in a scientific, engineering or mathematical subject; ability to read French and German is very important.

The work Patent examiners work in the Patent Office in Newport, South Wales, and examine applications for patents. The Patent Office is now an executive agency of the Department of Trade and Industry. An examiner's work involves detailed examination of the description of an invention; making a search through earlier specifications to ascertain the novelty of the invention; classifying and indexing the features of the invention; writing a report embodying the findings; and, if necessary, interviewing the inventor or the inventor's agent to discuss any problems. The work requires an analytical and critical mind. Each examiner works in a specialized field. Training is on the job and includes a 2-year probationary period. There are few vacancies each year.

Personal attributes As for Patent Agent.

Late start Very rare, but occasionally possible for people with relevant (technological) degrees and experience.

Work life balance Civil Service (see p. 158) conditions apply.

Further information The Patent Office, Concept House, Cardiff Road, Newport, South Wales NP10 8QQ.
www.patent.gov.uk

Related careers CIVIL SERVICE – ENGINEERING – SCIENCE

Personnel/Human Resources Management

Entry qualifications No specific requirements but most entrants are graduates. Any discipline is acceptable but business studies, the behavioural sciences and law may be particularly helpful.

The work Personnel officers are part of the management team. Titles vary and are not necessarily any indication of scope and level of responsibility. The term 'human resources manager' is now often used. Their primary aim is always the efficient use and development of people's talents. The Chartered Institute of Personnel and Development says that personnel management is not a job for people who merely want to 'work with people'. Personnel managers' main job is 'to provide the specialist knowledge or service that can assist other members of the management-team to make the most effective use of the human resources – people – of the organization'.

Personnel management used to be considered an offshoot of social work; it is certainly that no longer. The average personnel officer does not necessarily spend more time in one-to-one discussions with individuals who need advice than do, for example, solicitors or accountants. 'Personnel' is a 'management function', like buying, marketing and production. Its challenge is to interpret conflicting views and objectives to people at various levels in an organization, some of whom have divergent interests.

Personnel officers are employed not only in industry, but also in hospitals, local and central government: the efficient use of human resources is equally vital to profit-making and to non-profit-making organizations. The range of jobs is very great indeed. In a large organization, employing say 70,000 people at several sites, a personnel director may have a staff of 70, some of whom specialize in one aspect of the work; in a small organization 1 or 2 people might do everything.

Main (overlapping) personnel specializations:

Recruitment, training and management-development: Devising, monitoring and applying selection procedures, possibly selecting the most suitable of various psychological testing and assessment methods for all levels of staff; identifying individuals' potential and planning their education, training and career development. This involves reconciling individuals' needs and aims with the employer's requirements for staff with specific skills at specific levels of responsibility. It is a very important specialization now because of the emphasis in the last few years on the need for a more highly skilled workforce at all levels from operatives to management.

Management of change: Personnel people may or may not be responsible for masterminding this – see MANAGEMENT, p. 351 – but they are invariably involved. During the introduction of new technologies or structures personnel people work closely with systems analysts/designers, with, perhaps, technologists, occupational psychologists and other specialists and with union officials, ironing out problems arising when changes in traditional working patterns are proposed and implemented. This requires personnel people to have thorough understanding of individuals' present tasks, of their place in the hierarchy, and of how proposed changes will affect individuals' jobs.

Reward management: Covers job evaluation and equal pay for equal work administration. It involves systematic study of the tasks that make up individual jobs within the organization, in order to establish their gradings. Reward management sounds misleadingly like a desk-bound routine job, but it can be one of the most non-routine and controversial specializations.

Employee relations: Establishing and maintaining lines of communication between an organization's various interest groups. It involves discussing, with shop stewards and management, 'worker participation' schemes; implication of new legislation (of which there is a constant flow); mergers; implementation of new technologies; dealing with consequent redundancies, and planning reallocation of tasks and retraining schemes.

Employee services: Concerned with matters of health and safety and all welfare aspects. It may include personal counselling services (see 'Counselling', p. 493); responsibility for canteens, etc., as well as sophisticated job satisfaction improvement schemes and cooperation with manpower planning, training and other personnel specialists.

Not all personnel departments divide personnel functions in the same way; there are many variations on the 'effective use of human resources' theme.

Personnel workers who get to the top normally have had experience in several specialist fields, but there are few hard and fast rules. A specialist training officer in a large and/or progressive organization may have greater scope, responsibility and status (and salary) than a personnel director in charge of all specialist functions in another organization. It is impossible to generalize about career-paths, but it is probably best for those aiming at top jobs to get experience in large organizations, where they have the chance of working on a wide range of problems using a variety of personnel techniques.

Many organizations with establishments in different towns expect personnel officers to move around the country. It is quite usual to move from one employer to another, not necessarily remaining in the same type of organization, for example from factory to hospital, store to local government, etc. However, with the introduction of new technologies more personnel people stay either in manufacturing or in service industries.

Training The Chartered Institute of Personnel and Development's Professional Development Scheme (PDS) is divided into 4 fields: core personnel and development; core management; applied personnel and development; and specialist and generalist personnel and development. To complete the last field candidates undertake 4 modules from a choice of 15. Graduate membership of the CIPD is achieved on completion of all 4 fields. The PDS is offered at CIPD approved centres and can be studied full time, part time, or through block, flexible or open learning.

Those not qualified or experienced enough to follow the Professional Development Scheme may take one of the certificate (foundation) level courses: the Certificate in Personnel Practice, the Certificate in Training Practice or the Certificate in Recruitment and Selection. Study is part time and is suitable for students from a variety of backgrounds, including clerical, secretarial and line management, who will acquire practical personnel skills to help them in their job.

Some NVQ/SVQs in the fields of management and personnel may be recognized by CIPD for membership.

Personal attributes A flair for seeing all sides of a problem and interpreting each side's point of view to the other; a good memory for names and faces; at least an absence of dislike for figure-work, preferably a liking for it; interest in profitable management and in change; lack of prejudice; tact; detachment; an understanding of people of all types, ages, races and backgrounds, and the ability to gain their confidence and respect; organizing ability.

Late start Some opportunities for mature entrants who have had relevant experience.

Work life balance Opportunities for flexible working should not be a problem if employed within the public sector. Personnel workers taking a career break will need to keep up with changes in legislation and other developments. The CIPD offers a flexible learning option for those who need to combine study with other commitments.

Further information Chartered Institute of Personnel and Development, CIPD House, Camp Road, London sw19 4ux.
www.cipd.co.uk

Related careers CAREERS WORK − HEALTH AND SAFETY INSPECTORS − MANAGEMENT − RETAIL MANAGEMENT

Pharmacy

PHARMACIST

Entry qualifications 3 A levels including chemistry and 2 chosen from a mathematical subject, physics and a biological science. The subject not offered at A level should be offered at GCSE. In practice, English and maths GCSE (A–C) are essential. Students with alternative qualifications are advised to check with admissions tutors.

The work Pharmacists work in 3 distinct fields: *community, hospital* and *industry*. Students do not need to decide which branch of pharmacy they want to go into until after qualifying.

Community Pharmacists (usually called 'chemists' – a title pharmacists discourage)

The work Pharmacists dispense or supervise the dispensing of prescriptions. They act as a link between doctors and their patients, by explaining the effects and the correct use of medicines.

Most medicines are now available ready-made but pharmacists still make up the occasional prescription in the dispensary. They are also responsible for the safe and correct storage of a variety of medicines and some chemical substances. They are legally required to keep records such as the 'controlled drug' registers.

Pharmacists may also deal with the buying and selling of cosmetics, toiletries, etc., and the training of shop staff. In larger pharmacies, and particularly in chains of pharmacies, the pharmacist has the choice of remaining involved with the dispensing and sale of medicines, or of becoming more involved with the commercial side.

The role of pharmacists is changing. As more and more new drugs come on the market, both doctors and patients are making more use of pharmacists' thorough knowledge of the composition, action and interaction of new drugs. Many doctors ask pharmacists' advice – or at least their views – on the best way to use new drugs for particular conditions. Pharmacists have more time to keep up with pharmaceutical developments than doctors. Also, patients increasingly ask pharmacists' advice for minor ailments and their opinion on whether they should consult their doctor. Pharmacists are well qualified to know when medical advice must be sought and when a simple remedy (which may be cheaper than one on prescription) is all that the patient needs.

Increasingly pharmacists are becoming more involved with community health care and offer basic health checks, such as blood pressure monitoring. Some also serve residential homes. They may also need to visit patients in their homes to deliver oxygen equipment or fit surgical appliances.

Pharmacists are now more often managers of pharmacies or of dispensing departments than owners of their own business.

Abroad: Qualified pharmacists can practise and get jobs fairly easily in some countries of the Commonwealth; harmonization of qualifications within EU countries has been agreed.

Hospital Pharmacists

The work Particularly suitable for those interested in the science of pharmacy. Hospital pharmacists dispense – and supervise the dispensing of – prescriptions for out-patients; they advise patients on the proper use of their medicines; they issue medicines for use within the hospital and they work closely with doctors and nurses to ensure that medicines are used safely, correctly and economically. They advise on doses and side-effects of drugs and are often involved in clinical trial work on new drugs. Most medicines used in hospital are ready-made, but some preparations are made up in the hospital pharmacy.

They also have a teaching role – they assist with the training of student pharmacists and student pharmacy technicians; and they lecture to doctors and nurses.

Some hospitals offer a 24-hour pharmacy service, provided by pharmacists who live in when on duty.

Hospital pharmacists' role is also changing. Pharmacists may accompany consultants on ward rounds and may be consulted on the best drug to use in any particular case. Young doctors often ask pharmacists' advice and pharmacists may be asked to check patients' drug-charts to look for adverse reactions if patients take several different kinds of drugs; so there is more patient contact than in the past.

Hospital pharmacists have a definite career structure. There is work which involves contact with people, and backroom work. Hospital pharmacists work in a community, with the opportunity of meeting people in similar jobs.

Outside the hospital, pharmacists also advise staff and residents in residential nursing homes and local health clinics.

Industrial Pharmacists

The work They work in laboratories of pharmaceutical and related firms and on the production and development of new drugs and the improvement and quality control of existing drugs. As in other scientific work (see p. 520), pharmacists work in teams, often together with scientists from other disciplines. Some jobs involve mainly desk-work such as providing information to doctors and the preparation of data on new products for the Licensing Authority. Those with a bent for salesmanship can become representatives, visiting doctors in their surgeries and in hospital, providing information on their companies' products (and they may become marketing executives, an expanding area).

There is therefore scope for the quiet backroom type content with semi-routine work, for the team leader with a bent for pursuing new lines of thought and for those who want to go into general management, marketing and pharmaceutical sales.

Training 4-year pharmacy degree course at a school of pharmacy (offered by a number of universities). The syllabus includes *pharmaceutical chemistry* – the origin and chemistry of drugs; *pharmaceutics* – the preparation of medicines; *pharmacology* – the action and uses of drugs and medicines in living systems; *pharmacy practice* – dispensing and counselling skills, pharmacy law and ethics.

After graduating, students must complete 1 year's pre-Registration experience in pharmacy, which must include at least 6 months in community or hospital practice, and pass the Registration Examination of the Royal Pharmaceutical Society of Great Britain, before they are eligible to apply for Registration as pharmaceutical chemists.

Personal attributes *For all pharmacists*: Good communication skills; a strong scientific bent; meticulous accuracy; a strong sense of responsibility; a calm, logical mind; ability to concentrate; organizing ability; a liking for people; ability to work with semi- and untrained staff.

For community and industrial pharmacists: A flair for business; ability to deal with semi- and untrained staff; a liking for people.

For industrial pharmacists: An inquiring mind; ability to work as one of a team; infinite patience.

Late start No upper age limit for training or jobs, but there is no relaxation of entry requirements.

Work life balance Several schools of pharmacy run short *refresher* courses to help returners update their knowledge and dispensing skills. In some cases the NHS will pay costs of refresher courses. Some large multiple pharmacy groups also offer re-training. There are also some distance-learning courses.

Job-sharing and other forms of flexible working are becoming accepted in hospital and in community work.

Further information Royal Pharmaceutical Society of Great Britain, 1 Lambeth High Street, London SE1 7JN *or* 36 York Place, Edinburgh EH1 3HU.
www.rpsgb.org.uk

National Association of Women Pharmacists, c/o Office Manager, Royal Pharmaceutical Society, London address.

Related careers MEDICINE – *Pharmacy Technician* (see below) – SCIENCE: *Chemistry*; *Biochemistry*; *Biotechnology*

Pharmacy Technician

Entry qualifications There is no formal academic requirement but many employers or colleges will ask for some GCSEs, usually maths, science and English language. These qualifications are normally expected in the hospital sector.

The work This varies according to whether the job is in *community* pharmacy which includes pharmacy departments of retail chain stores, *industry* or *hospitals*. In *community*, technicians may spend time on the selling side when not assisting the pharmacist with dispensing (but they work always under the supervision of qualified pharmacists who must check prescriptions, etc.). In *hospitals* and *industry*, technicians have more chance to do responsible and varied work. They assist with experiments, with interviewing patients, and they may liaise with other departments, etc. The role of the technician in the hospitals and in industry is changing: as in other science-based jobs (see SCIENCE, p. 520) technicians now often do jobs which overlap with graduates', but there will always be a considerable difference between the project-leader type and level of work, and that of technicians who implement proven techniques. While using their judgement and expertise, they do not take ultimate responsibility or do original research.

Training Training is usually work-based with part-time or distance-learning study leading to BTEC or SQA qualifications. A level 3 NVQ/SVQ in Pharmacy Services is also available.

Personal attributes Enjoy working with people; good communication skills; meticulous accuracy; methodical; a scientific bent; number skills.

Late start Depends on local supply and demand position. Entrance requirements may be waived; but school-leavers may be given preference.

Work life balance The NHS is favourable towards career breaks and flexible working. Elsewhere opportunities may depend on supply and demand.

Further information National Pharmaceutical Association, Mallinson House, 48 Peter's Street, St Albans, Herts. AL1 3NP.
www.npa.co.uk
Edexcel BTEC, SQA (see pp. 8, 10).

Related careers RETAIL MANAGEMENT – SCIENCE: *Science Technician*

Photography

PHOTOGRAPHER

Entry qualifications No definite educational requirements for photography as such, but see individual course requirements under 'Training', below.

Photography covers over 30 specializations, but many photographers combine several of these. London photographers tend to be more specialized than those in the provinces. Many freelance photographers take on any work which is offered, in order to earn a living. 'Bread and butter' jobs can help pay for more creative, but less well-paid, assignments.

Creative Photography

General practice

The work Approximately half of all photographers work in general photographic studios. The bulk of their work consists of portraiture, group photographs and commercial services. Portrait subjects include, increasingly, pets; some photographers specialize in children.

Photographers prefer their subjects to come to the studio to be photographed, because it is easier to arrange the lighting there. However, there is an increasing demand for portraits in the home, garden or workplace, especially in the case of children's portraits. The 'natural' portrait is much more popular today than the formal one. To produce not just a good likeness, but a characteristic portrait, photographers must have considerable understanding of, and insight into, human nature; they must be able to put sitters at ease so that their expression is natural.

Weddings and other group photographs (e.g. sports and social clubs) form another important part of the work. Wedding photography now offers more scope for 'creative' pictures in a less formal style than it used to. Commercial work is mainly for publicity purposes – for local companies, estate agencies, architects, etc. who do not have enough work to employ a staff photographer.

Opportunities are reasonable. One way in for the keen amateur is to help a busy studio with Saturday weddings.

Electronic imaging, image manipulation and electronic transfer have changed the way in which photography is processed and new entrants need to be familiar with the technology.

Advertising

Very varied. Although advertising photographers are often given exact instructions about what to photograph and what effect to aim at, they are also expected to suggest their own ideas for new angles. Many advertisements are records of everyday life – whether it is of a child eating breakfast, or a woman getting out of a car – and involve both work with models, and persuading ordinary people to agree to be photographed.

Advertising photographs are taken either by the photographic departments of advertising agencies, by photographic studios (i.e. several photographers working as partners, sharing darkroom and office facilities, or salaried photographers and assistants working for an employer), or by freelance photographers. Most do some catalogue work; some studios specialize in *mail-order* photography (and may be owned by the mail-order company).

This is the best paid and hence a very competitive branch; success depends entirely on ability, efficiency and the right personality.

Fashion

Although advertising includes fashion photography, some photographers specialize in fashion. Most fashion photography is done by specialist studios or freelances who are commissioned by editors, fashion houses or advertising agencies; they usually work under the direction of a fashion expert.

This is the most sought-after branch and hence *very* difficult to enter.

Photo-journalism (feature photography), press and editorial photography

Photo-journalism is, essentially, telling a story in pictures, and therefore a journalistic sense is needed. *Feature photographers* may work with reporters as a team; they may be freelances, or work for studios. Only a tiny minority are on editorial staffs. It is very varied work, and leads to assignments at any time and in any place – photographing VIPs at home, or life in foreign parts, or schools at work – anything that makes a story. Hours are irregular.

There is more hard, hurried work than glamour in *press photography*, which consists almost entirely of single news pictures. Press photographers must be versatile in taking all kinds of subjects. They must know what makes a good news picture; be able to write accurate captions; work well with reporters; be very quick and often work under difficult conditions. Hours are irregular.

Editorial photographers work mainly for magazines, nearly always as freelances. Work can be very varied, depending on the article or report which needs illustrating. It varies from shots of a TV star at home with children/pets to a travel feature; from contestants in a cookery competition to action shots of a parachute jump.

Prospects are fair, but competition is stiff. The market for photo-journalists is small. Most work as freelances and may specialize, e.g. in travel. For press photography there are always more candidates than jobs. Some possibilities for photographers in other branches to sell work to newspapers or press agencies. Editorial photography depends on building up good contacts and a reputation for reliability.

Industrial and Scientific Photography

The work This is the most varied branch of photography and has the most openings. Clients include manufacturing companies, research organizations, government departments, higher education establishments, the police and the Armed Forces. Examples of the work: making photographic progress reports in laboratories; recording the various stages of manufacturing processes; photographing building sites. Industrial photographers also take pictures for house magazines, exhibition stands and instructional purposes. Most of these photographers are salaried employees; some work as freelances or for studios (see 'General practice', above, p. 454).

Medical Photography

The work Most teaching hospitals and medical research institutions employ medical photographers, sometimes as part of a medical illustration team with medical artists and audio-visual technicians. They make still and video records of work done in operating theatres and research laboratories, and of particular cases among patients. They also illustrate health care guides for patients and teaching material for student nurses and doctors. Medical photographers must not be squeamish.

Of all careers in photography this is the least hectic, least tough, most companionable and worst paid. There is some demand for medical photographers.

Training *All photography* Study can be part time, while working as a junior in a studio, or, increasingly, full time. The main courses recognized by the British Institute of Professional Photography are:

1. With, preferably, GCSEs (A–C) in English and maths: 2 years full time or 3 years part time for City and Guilds Photography scheme. Students are sometimes encouraged to study full time for the first year, then to work for a photographer for a year and return to college as either a full-time or a part-time student. Some centres now offer NVQs levels 3 and 4 in photography.

2. With 4 GCSEs (A–C), normally including English language, maths and/or a science: a full-time 2-year course for BTEC National Diploma in Art and Design (Photography).

3. With 1 or 2 A levels, *or* BTEC/SQA National award, *or*, in some cases, City & Guilds certificates: 2-year full-time course for BTEC/SQA Higher National award.

This can be followed by a further year leading to the BIPP's Professional Qualifying Examination (PQE).

There are a few part-time courses leading to BTEC/SQA National Certificate and Higher National Certificate.

4. With 2 A levels and 3 GCSEs (A–C), or for some courses an art and design foundation course: a degree in photography or photography, film and television or photographic science and technology. Art and design degrees (see ART AND DESIGN, p. 105) may have photography options.

Press photography
Either: 1-year pre-entry course organized by National Council for Training of Journalists (see JOURNALISM, p. 304: Entry requirements: 4 GCSEs (A–C) plus 1 A level, including English.

Or the NCTJ's traineeship (see JOURNALISM, p. 304): Entry requirements: 5 GCSEs (A–C) including English.

NVQs/SVQs have been introduced by many newspaper companies.

Medical photography
With GCSEs or preferably A levels, or after general photography course, entry as trainee in a hospital medical photography department. Then *either* private study for BIPP Professional Qualifying Examination in medical photography and the Pre-Fellowship examination in medical photography, *or* a 3-year part-time distance-learning course leading to a BSc in Medical Illustration, which has replaced the Diploma of Medical Illustration of the Institute of Medical Illustrators. There is also a Post-Experience Certificate for those who already hold a degree which leads to membership of the Institute.

Photographic Technician

The work The processing and printing of films is an extremely important aspect of photography and one in which backroom types are happiest. They may work in 'photofinishing' companies which process film taken by amateurs (e.g. holiday snapshots) or in laboratories which service professional photographers. Most work nowadays is in colour and is increasingly automated. The work requires considerable concentration and technical knowledge, especially of the complex chemistry of colour film; without these skills a photographer's assignment worth hundreds or even thousands of pounds could be ruined. Technicians may take turns at all the jobs: processing, transparency-making, enlarging, printing and mounting, or may stick to one or two. Experienced technicians can learn more specialized skills, e.g. retouching or making duplicate transparencies.

There is a shortage of good technicians; there is a greater demand for technicians than for photographers. Photofinishing offers most openings to school-leavers.

Training Usually starting as a junior or trainee in a photographic laboratory, and studying by day-release and/or evening classes for City & Guilds examinations (see p. 10). Also, some in-service courses provided by laboratories and manufacturers of photographic materials. Some large laboratories are approved assessment centres for NVQs in photographic processing.

Personal attributes *Needed by all photographers in varying degrees*: Visual imagination; eye for detail and composition; patience; perfect colour vision; artistic sensitivity; creativeness; trust in their own judgement (photographers, unlike other craftspeople and artists, do not usually know whether they have done a good job or not until it is too late); good powers of observation; ability to work quickly, under pressure, surrounded by crowds – in all kinds of unfavourable circumstances; ability to work well with others while keeping to their own individual style; originality; unusual inventiveness (for advertising and fashion photography); business sense (for arranging appointments, sending out bills, etc.), as very few can afford secretaries; willingness to 'sell' themselves; a manner which encourages people to cooperate.

Press photographers: News sense; ability to remain calm and unmoved, however tragic or unpleasant the circumstances.

Medical photographers: A scientific bent; tactful and reassuring manner; total lack of squeamishness.

Technicians: A scientific bent; manual skill; an eye for detail; patience.

Late start A number of photographers have worked in other fields before taking up photography. Some colleges waive entry requirements for mature students. The main drawbacks are intense competition from college-leavers and poor salaries of trainee or assistant photographers.

Work life balance Possibly difficult to return in the best-paid and most competitive fields, but it should be possible to return to some kind of photography and/or to do some freelance work even while raising a family. The BIPP may offer reduced subscriptions for women on a maternity break.

Further information British Institute of Professional Photography, Fox Talbot House, Ware, Herts. SG12 9HN.
www.bipp.com
City & Guilds of London Institute, 1 Giltspur Street, London EC1A 9DD.
www.city-and-guilds.co.uk
Hon. Secretary, Institute of Medical Illustrators, Bank Chambers, 48 Onslow Gardens, London SW7 3AH.
www.imi.org.uk

Related careers ART AND DESIGN – FASHION AND CLOTHING – JOURNALISM – TELEVISION, FILM AND RADIO

Physiotherapy

Entry qualifications 5 GCSEs (A–C) including maths, English and 2 science subjects taken at one sitting and 3 A2 level passes at minimum grade C; or Scottish Highers with minimum 2B and 2C grades taken at one sitting. Highers should normally include English and either maths or physics plus another science.

Alternative qualifications are BTEC National Diploma in Health Studies (Science) with distinctions/merits in all units, a Higher National Diploma, the International Baccalaureate and certain access courses.

The work Physiotherapists use exercises and movement, electrotherapy – the use of heat, high frequency currents and ultrasonics – manipulation and massage in an integrated way to optimize an individual's functional ability and potential. They are responsible for assessing and analysing patients' conditions and for planning their treatment. This involves treating patients with recovering conditions such as head injury and stroke, patients with deteriorating conditions such as Parkinson's disease, motor neurone disease, multiple sclerosis and some cancers and managing patients with stable conditions such as spinal cord injuries and lower limb amputation. They are also involved in health promotion and injury prevention. Physiotherapists operate as independent practitioners as well as members of health care teams of doctors, nurses, occupational therapists, podiatrists and social workers. They are able to act as first contact practitioners, and patients may seek direct care without referral from another health care professional.

Patients too ill to be moved are treated in bed; others, such as

461

post-operative patients, may have to be helped to walk properly again. Stroke patients are taught to make their healthy limbs or muscles do the work, as far as possible, of paralysed ones, and how to use paralysed limbs. Some patients do exercises in water and the physiotherapist works with them in heated swimming pools.

Some patients are treated in groups, but most individually. In all cases, physiotherapists must use their judgement. They must know how far to coax a patient into doing an uncomfortable exercise, and must adapt treatment to suit each patient. They use tact and encouragement together with specialist knowledge when, for example, explaining to a patient why it is important that exercises are done regularly at home, or when persuading children to cooperate, or when allaying patients' fear of treatment.

Many work in hospitals but a large number work in GP practices and treat patients in their homes. After usually about 2 years' work, gaining all-round experience, they may specialize, for example in work with the elderly; in orthopaedic, chest or neurological conditions; and, increasingly, in work with mentally and physically disabled children and/or adults. Work outside the hospital in the community is increasing. This may be giving treatments or preventative health education work; advising in factories, hospitals, etc. on how to deal with carrying heavy weights, for example. Physiotherapists also work with expectant mothers in clinics. There is also room for physiotherapists who want to do only preventative work: sports clubs employ physiotherapists (often part time) to keep their members fit, and to treat minor injuries; large industrial and commercial organizations employ physiotherapists to see that office desks are the right height for comfort, health and therefore efficiency; to show staff how to sit without risking injury; to teach sales assistants to relax while standing; to teach porters to carry without risking injury, and so on. Health farms and, sometimes, keep fit classes also employ physiotherapists.

There is a world shortage of physiotherapists, and of physiotherapy teachers and specialists. Qualifications are recognized in the EU and in many countries abroad, but in the USA and some other countries physiotherapists may have to take additional examinations. The government has recently improved the career prospects for physiotherapists in the NHS through Agenda for Change. Experienced physiotherapists often decide to set up in private practice, treating patients either in their own treatment rooms or in patients' homes. But this needs good contacts with local doctors and capital to buy equipment and see them over the first few months.

Training In order to practise as a physiotherapist it is essential to have an honours degree, or a Masters degree, in physiotherapy. Courses are based in universities working closely with areas where physiotherapists work in practice. Degree holders are eligible for membership of the Chartered Society of Physiotherapy, and for registration as a physiotherapist with the Health Professions Council which is essential for work in the National Health Service, as well as for most other jobs.

The first year is mostly pre-clinical (theoretical); subjects studied include anatomy, physiology, physics, behavioural sciences, pathology and technical treatment skills. From the second year theory is combined with working with patients.

There are a large number of post-graduate courses which enable qualified physiotherapists to specialize in a certain field.

Personal attributes The ability to cope with the academic demands of an honours degree in science and a recognition of the need for continuing professional development throughout one's career; a sympathetic yet objective approach to disability; ability to work as one of a team and to take responsibility and use initiative; enthusiasm.

Late start The profession welcomes mature students. Entry qualifications are not so rigidly enforced; applicants' work and life experience are taken into account; but for those who do not have the usual qualifications, evidence of ability to cope with degree-level study (including science) is required. An Open University Foundation course or similar post-school study is useful. (Applicants may be advised to take an A level science or access course, see p. 15, and reapply later.) See *Guidelines for Mature Entrants*, below.

Physiotherapy

Work life balance Opportunities for part-time work are excellent, increasingly even in senior jobs. Job-sharing is encouraged. Returners are welcome; *refresher* training can be arranged by hospitals or health authorities; it is essential after a break of more than 2 or 3 years.

Further information Chartered Society of Physiotherapy, 14 Bedford Row, London WC1R 4ED (*A Guide to Becoming a Chartered Physiotherapist* and *Guidelines for Mature Entrants* available free). *www.csp.org.uk*

Related careers OCCUPATIONAL THERAPY − SPEECH AND LANGUAGE THERAPISTS − TEACHING

Police

Entry qualifications Vary slightly from force to force. In general, candidates must be at least 18½ and have good health and eyesight. There are no formal educational requirements for recruitment to the police service, but applicants must take 2 written tests to ensure they have a reasonable standard of English, as well as a numeracy test. *All* applicants sit an initial recruitment test. Competition for places in all forces is fierce, therefore applicants may find it helpful to join a voluntary cadet scheme if there is one in their area. There is also graduate entry.

The work The primary purpose of the police is to protect life and property and enforce law and order. Notions of how best to serve that purpose change from time to time as society becomes more complex and its demands change. The emphasis today is on community policing, responding to the demands of the public. Surveys have shown that the public want to see their police and expect them not just to solve crime, but to prevent it. On one level this is reflected in the traditional role of the police constable on the beat, getting to know the community, keeping an eye out not only for trouble but for potential sources of trouble. But there are also broader initiatives through which the police forge links with and respond to the community. Community liaison officers, for example, might work with a range of community groups from schools to old age pensioners.

The 43 police forces in England and Wales and 8 in Scotland are run independently and their organization will vary. Within a force, too, different areas will have differing policing needs. The problems of the inner city are not the same as those of a rural area or middle-class suburb. Whatever the situation, the police need to establish channels of communication so that problems can be evaluated and means established to reduce and prevent crime. A serious drugs problem might involve links with the local youth and community workers, while tackling car theft and vandalism in a town centre car park involves liaison with town planners and other local authority officers.

Within a typical large station you might find: the uniformed officers who patrol the community, some on foot, some in patrol cars; crime prevention officers, who, for example, advise individuals on safeguarding their homes and property; community liaison officers; juvenile liaison officers, who enforce the policy on dealing with juveniles; the custody officer, responsible for ensuring that arrests are lawful; CID, who work together with uniformed officers on the detection of crime. In the control room, staff are responsible for the operation of the computerized command and control systems, sending the right officers to the right jobs. Flexible shift-working patterns enable the police to respond better to the community's needs, which are obviously not the same at 11 a.m., 11 p.m. and 4 a.m.

Other areas of specialization are *traffic*, with responsibilities ranging from planning and operating large-scale traffic control systems to dealing with major accidents, and *mounted*, *dog-handling* and *river* police, all very small. Within the CID, specializations can include fraud, special branch and serious crime. Underwater search units are vital for investigating crime and searching for missing persons, firearm units include specialist teams trained in the use of firearms and many forces have or share full-time air support. Officers in drug squads work with operational officers and other agencies to target drug dealers and to tackle the drugs problem. Police do not specialize permanently; promotion often involves a move to a new area of specialization and/or a new force. Many specialist roles require higher standards of fitness or eyesight, for example, than those needed for joining the police service.

Promotion is through the ranks. Everyone starts out as a PC, gaining experience in various areas of police work, from communicating with the public to dealing with a traffic accident, from sorting out a domestic disturbance to dealing with a riot. Even those on accelerated programmes (see 'Training', below) spend at least 2 years at this rank. Those promoted to Sergeant, after a qualifying exam and further assessment, take on a more supervisory role with responsibility for a team of PCs. An Inspector's time is divided between operational and managerial roles. Chief Inspectors, Superintendents and Assistant Chief Constables take on progressively more managerial responsibility and become more involved in strategic and policy issues. The Chief Constable's responsibilities include financial planning and budgetary control, training and recruitment policy, and development of the force within the community. Some constables choose not to go in for promotion because they enjoy grass-roots uniformed police work and the contact with the public which it involves.

Training 1. Everyone who wants to become a police officer has to complete a 2-year probationary period working on the beat as a police constable. *Probationer training* for all new recruits is provided partly at 6 regional centres and partly in-force. (The Metropolitan Police Service runs its own probationer training course at Hendon Training School.) Subjects covered include law, liaison with social services, courts and policing procedures, and crime prevention. Role-playing exercises are carried out to teach, for example, how to deal with traffic accidents, street disorder, domestic disputes, hooliganism, to improve self-awareness, and interviewing skills (for example, how to take statements from shocked suspects or rape victims). Courses also include some sociology, psychology and training in community relations to enable officers to understand the underlying causes of contemporary problems, such as racial tension and vandalism, and how to deal with them. Self-defence and physical education also play an important part in training. *Further training* is organized by forces and includes a wide range of courses on specialist subjects.

2. *Fast track* England and Wales: The *High Potential Development Scheme (HPD)* is open to all police officers who have completed their probationary period. It is not exclusively for graduates and there is no age limit. Development is tailored to individual needs. Anyone

making a success of HPD can expect to reach at least Chief Inspector, and probably beyond.

Scotland: The *Accelerated Promotion Scheme for Graduates (APSG)* provides a structured career path for the most promising and capable graduates entering the police in Scotland. A 5–7 year programme, it provides a structure that allows career development from the rank of Constable to Inspector; a number go on to hold Chief Officer rank. Some graduates are selected for APSG on entry; others join the fast stream after standard entry.

Personal attributes Maturity; honesty; courage, both physical and moral; sense of humour; flexibility; reliability; real desire to help people; resilience; an observant eye and a cool head; understanding of and sympathy with human weakness; ability to accept both authority and discipline and a high degree of personal responsibility; good health.

Late start No upper age limit although police constables and sergeants must retire at 55. Officers in higher ranks may serve for longer.

Work life balance Police officers are already able to request part-time work or job-share and to have their application seriously considered. The police force is keen to hold on to experienced officers who might otherwise have to resign because of domestic commitments. The Home Office is currently looking at the best way to implement the recommendations of a recent report *Flexible Working Practices in the Police Service*. Guidance will probably be produced on working approaches such as self-rostering, compressed hours, annualized hours, and staggered work hours within shift. However, this will involve consultation with individual forces. The British Association of Women Police is developing the Gender Agenda, and one of the issues which this is addressing is balancing work and family commitments. Police officers who have completed their probationary period may apply for a career break up to a maximum of 5 years. Refresher courses are arranged by some forces.

Further information Any police force recruiting department.
England and Wales:
Police Recruitment Line: 0845 608 3000
Police Graduate Liaison Office, Room 556, 50 Queen Anne's Gate,
London SW1H 9AT.
Recruitment website: *www.policecouldyou.co.uk*
Scotland:
Scottish Police UK website: *www.scottish.police.uk*
Scottish Police College, Tulliallan Castle, Kincardine, Alloa FK10 4BE.
www.tulliallan.police.uk

Related careers ENVIRONMENTAL HEALTH OFFICER – HEALTH
AND SAFETY INSPECTORS – PRISON SERVICE – SOCIAL WORK

Printing

Entry qualifications See 'Training', below.

The work Printing is concerned with graphic communication. It has been called the 'meeting place of art and science', but above all it is an industry. It uses a variety of technological processes to create a product of visual impact; it is always a form of communication. The product may be books, newspapers, theatre tickets, posters, packaging, stamps, circuit boards, manuals, record sleeves, credit cards, or reproductions of old masters. The printed materials include paper, card, plastic, metal, textiles. Some printing processes are centuries old, but printing technology has changed enormously in the last few years and continues to change. For example, traditional letterpress is much less common than it was, having been largely replaced by lithography, especially offset litho. Screenprinting is widely used for non-paper materials. Most text is produced by computer-aided typesetting using DTP software. This enables an operator to turn all the elements of text and graphics into complete made-up pages which are then put on film ready for the platemakers. Special typesetting programs can 'convert' different sorts of word-processing programs used by writers so they are ready for typesetting. Electronic scanners are used in the production of both black and white and coloured illustrations; and holograms can be printed on credit and identity cards. Transmission of text and illustrations by satellite for printing in another continent is now common.

(DTP software allows individuals and organizations with the right computer and a laser printer to do their own good-quality printing of 'short-runs'; alternatively, they can give the disk to a printer who can then very quickly print large quantities.)

There are several main types of printing organizations: large and small *general commercial printers*, *specialist packaging printers*, high-quality *book printers*, *magazine printers* and the high street *instant print shops*. Newspapers now form a very small part of the industry, as changing technology has reduced the numbers of jobs. The *production manager* (or *planner*) decides with the client on the most advantageous and economic method of production for each item; this means weighing up factors such as efficient use of machines, materials, speed, cost, quality, eventual use and appearance.

Training *Technologists and technicians*: While increased technology in some parts of the industry has led to the loss of some jobs, in others it has meant greater demand for highly skilled people. There is a move to increase the number of graduates in the industry. As well as a sound knowledge of chemistry and materials science, they need to know all about computer graphics, laser scanning, computer-controlled printing and converting systems. Some work in production, some move into management, others work in research and development of printed products and on new machinery, paper, inks. Although craft and technician work sometimes overlaps and it is possible to be promoted, anyone with the educational qualifications to undertake a full-time course before joining the industry would be well-advised to do so. Most common routes are:

1. With 2 or 3 A levels including at least 1 science (preferably chemistry): for example 4-year honours degree in Printing Technology *or* 3-year BSc in Printing and Photographic Technology. 2-year Foundation degrees (see p. 14) are beginning to be introduced.

2. With A level maths, physics or chemistry or equivalent: part-time or sandwich study (2–3 years) for BTEC/SQA Higher National award.

3. With (usually) 4 relevant GCSEs: full-time course for BTEC National Diploma in Printing (or SQA equivalent, see p. 10) or part-time course for National Certificate.

4. With individually specified examination passes: courses leading

to college diplomas, e.g. 2-year full-time course for London College of Printing Diploma in Graphic Communications.

5. Art school training (see ART AND DESIGN, p. 105) with specialization in *Graphic Design* or *Typography* can also lead to printing jobs.

Craft: Trainees learn one of the following recognized skilled occupations: origination (preparation for print, which includes typesetting and platemaking); machine printing; print finishing (includes operating cutting and folding machines); bookbinding; carton manufacture; or manufacturing stationery. Training may be work-based and NVQs/SVQs at levels 2 and 3 in a large number of printing skills are available; trainees work for these and/or the City & Guilds Printing and Graphic Communications Certificate. Foundation and Advanced Modern Apprenticeships have been introduced for young people over 16.

Instant print and small printing units (for example, in-house) train mainly on the job. Most recruit experienced people.

Personal attributes Depends on type and level of work, but generally some visual imagination; interest in machinery; practicality; some dexterity.

For managerial jobs: organizing ability; ability to work under pressure; being a self-starter.

Late start About 20% are late entrants. Credit given for prior learning and shorter training possible.

Work life balance Return to work is likely to be difficult because of technological changes and shortage of jobs. A few retraining courses exist.

There are few opportunities for part-time work; possibly as freelance typographer.

Further information British Printing Industries Federation, Farringdon Point, 29–35 Farringdon Road, London EC1M 3JF.
www.britishprint.com

Institute of Printing, The Mews, Hill House, Clanricarde Road, Tunbridge Wells, Kent TN1 1PJ.
www.instituteofprinting.org

Related careers ART AND DESIGN — ENGINEERING — PUBLISHING — SCIENCE

Prison Service

Entry qualifications Minimum age 18½ (20 in Scotland). No specific academic requirement except in Scotland where 5 standard grades 1–3 or equivalent or 3 years' experience of people management are required. Selection is by aptitude test and interview. Also graduate entry to Intensive Development Scheme. (Private contractors may have their own requirements.)

The work The work of a prison officer goes far beyond locking and unlocking cells and patrolling corridors. One of the responsibilities of the prison service as set out by the Prison Board is 'to provide for prisoners as full a life as possible, to care for physical and mental health, advise and help with personal problems, work, education and training, physical exercise and recreation, and an opportunity to practise their religion'. What this means in practice is maintaining a community where prisoners eat, sleep, work, train, learn, play and so on. Prison officers are concerned with care as well as control, well-being as well as security. They are also concerned at senior levels with the management of staff and resources.

Prison officers (detention custody officers with the private contractors who manage some prisons and undertake court escort services) supervise inmates in the activities mentioned above, escort them to and from courts and hospitals, accompany visitors to the visiting room, receive new prisoners. Whatever tasks they are involved in, they must try to work through cooperation with prisoners. An important part of their role is rehabilitation, helping to prepare prisoners to return to the outside community as law-abiding citizens. This involves helping them to develop skills, confidence and self-respect. Partly this is done through activities, but also through building up a relationship. Prison officers can be involved in motivating prisoners to improve their education, whether it be learning to read or studying for an Open University degree; providing a shoulder to cry on when someone gets a 'Dear John' letter; reasoning with someone threatening violence. They must recognize and know how to deal with prisoners who are having to cope with feelings of anger, anxiety or shame, with those who are troublesome and those who are extremely worried or depressed. It may be important to know how physically to restrain a violent and abusive inmate, but it is equally important to understand how such situations arise and how to re-establish communication and cooperation.

Many prisons are old and over-crowded; prisoners' frustrations can lead to tensions that sometimes explode in violence. Most prisoners reoffend. Many are unappreciative, some abusive. Prison work can be frustrating, even depressing, but it offers more scope for personal initiative, individual responsibility and the development of interpersonal skills than is commonly realized. Like social work, it can be very rewarding and is a vital service to the community.

The demands and routines of prison work will vary according to the type and size of institution. These include remand centres, which are mainly for young offenders and those awaiting trial; prisons where high-security prisoners are dispersed; open prisons for those requiring a lesser degree of security; Young Offender Institutions, which place a great emphasis on teaching inmates useful skills; local prisons, which are often multi-purpose with separate sections for different categories of prisoner. Prison officers must be prepared to serve in any kind of institution, in any part of the country, though preferences are taken into account whenever possible. 'Opposite-sex posting' (i.e. female officers in men's prisons and vice versa) is possible, though voluntary, but most officers will for the time being continue to serve in same-sex postings.

All prison officers begin 'on the landings' (the equivalent to 'on the beat' for police constables) as part of a team. On promotion, for which it is often necessary to move, officers take on increased responsibility –

for a team, a wing, a function or service (e.g. inmate activities, staff training), ultimately a whole establishment. There is an accelerated promotion scheme (see 'Training', below) for experienced officers and graduate entrants with top management potential. There are also opportunities, after basic experience, to specialize as, for example, a hospital officer, a physical education officer or a trades officer (teaching a skill or trade).

Training Training lasts about 1 year and takes place on-the-job, under supervision, and at one of the 2 Prison Service Colleges. There is an Intensive Developement Scheme for graduates and other particularly able candidates which grooms them to reach an upper middle management position in less than 5 years. Private contractors are responsible for training their staff to standards laid down by the Home Office.

Personal attributes Leadership; a sense of right and wrong, without being censorious; a genuine desire to help people in trouble and the ability to understand and sympathize with people's failings without necessarily condoning them; the ability to find the right approach to all types of people; immense patience with people at their most unbearable; interests entirely outside prison work to help keep a sense of proportion; a friendly, naturally happy disposition; sense of humour.

Late start Entry up to 57 (the maximum age for prison officers in Scotland is 57).

Work life balance Prison officers may be posted to any prison. Part-time work and job-sharing is available. In England and Wales 5% of the workforce are part time, in Scotland 2%.

Further information England and Wales: Prison Officer Recruitment Helpline: 0807 892 2289
www.hmprisonservice.gov.uk

Scotland: Scottish Prison Service Headquarters, Calton House, 5 Redheughs Rigg, Edinburgh EH12 9HW.
www.sps.gov.uk

Related careers PERSONNEL/HUMAN RESOURCES MANAGEMENT – POLICE – SOCIAL WORK

Probation Work

Entry qualifications *England and Wales* 20 years old at start of training. Candidates under 21 years – 2 passes at A level and 3 at GCSE or 3 at A level and 1 at GCSE; candidates over 21 but under 25 years – 5 passes at GCSE; candidates over 25 years may be accepted without formal qualification. In practice many candidates have a related degree but appropriate life skills are the most necessary qualification.

Scotland From 2004 the minimum qualification will be a 4-year honours degree course. All criminal justice social workers will have to register with the Scottish Social Services Council (SSSC) in order to practise in Scotland.

The work The National Probation Service (NPS) for England and Wales was established in 2001 with the aim of ensuring a national approach to reducing reoffending and protecting the public. The NPS is organized into 42 areas responsible to the Home Office via the National Probation Directorate.

Further changes to the organization will be introduced with the planned establishment in 2004 of a National Offender Management Service (NOMS), combining the work of probation and prisons. Management of the new service will be moved to a regional basis. No further details are available at the time of going to press but the role of probation officers is expected to maintain importance, with additional career opportunities becoming available in the future. For more information on the Correctional Services Review and the recommendation for NOMS visit *www.probation.homeoffice.gov.uk*.

The Criminal Justice Act introduced by Parliament at the end of

2003 makes radical changes to the structure of prison and community sentences, which will affect the work of the Prison and Probation Services at all levels. The implementation of the Act began in January 2004 and will continue through to 2008. For more information about the Act visit *www.hmso.gov.uk/acts/acts2003/20030044.htm*.

NOTE: The following information provides an overview of the current role of a probation officer, although the developments outlined above are expected to lead to some changes in function and responsibilities in the future.

A major part of the role of a *probation officer* is the continuous assessment of offenders and the management of risk to the public. Work with offenders begins before sentencing when the probation officer may be asked to prepare a report to help magistrates and judges decide on a suitable sentence. Probation officers build up a picture of individual offenders through interviews with him or her, the family, employers and so on, and try to establish any circumstances relevant to the offence, whether it might happen again, and what risks there may be to the public and the victim/s. Information is recorded on an assessment system to help with future risk management.

Currently offenders may be sentenced to a range of community-based orders. Probation staff are responsible for managing community orders, working closely with partners in the voluntary and other sectors to ensure the offender is encouraged to stay on the order and 'breached' or sent back to court or prison if they do not comply with its requirements.

Offenders whether or not they received a custodial sentence will spend some period on 'licence'. In all these cases (where the offender is 18 years old or over) probation officers supervise the offenders, making sure they understand the nature of the licence and comply with any conditions set.

All offenders sentenced to a custodial sentence are allocated a supervising officer in their home area who keeps in touch with them during their sentence and supports them in finding accommodation and training or employment on release. Some probation officers are based in prisons, working with prisoners before their release to deal with managing problems such as substance abuse.

Probation officers have a tough job to do, being firm and clear about what is expected of offenders while in probation supervision at the same time as trying to help them develop self-knowledge and self-discipline and regain self-respect. They might assist with accommodation, work, developing skills, getting treatment for a psychiatric problem or social adjustment. Some offenders welcome the attention offered by probation officers, but others are hostile to any figure of authority. Probation officers have to find the right way of gaining cooperation, but can always ultimately refer back to the courts.

The National Probation Service also employs *probation service officers* who are not qualified probation officers but run programmes for groups of ex-offenders, often out of office hours, to help them combat particular behaviour such as substance misuse or domestic violence. They may undertake programmes with individuals, for example with sex offenders, or be responsible for carrying out drug treatment and testing orders. Probation service officers also work with the victims of offenders serving more than 4 years for a sexual or violent offence, keeping them in touch with the judicial process and helping them rebuild their lives. They also keep victims of serious crime informed about the release of violent offenders and work to alleviate any fears they may have about their personal safety or revictimization.

Scotland There is no probation service in Scotland. Criminal justice social workers, employed by local authority social work departments, perform a similar role to probation officers in England and Wales.

Training *England and Wales* The qualification for probation officers is the Diploma in Probation Studies. This is a 2-year programme combining work-based training towards a level 4 NVQ in community justice with academic study for a degree in community justice and is very demanding. Many entrants have relevant degrees and all candidates go through an intensive selection process. Trainee probation officers are employees of local probation boards and are paid a training salary.

Probation service officers are accredited through the National Probation Directorate and receive extensive in-house training. They need no specific qualifications, although in practice are usually educated at least to A level standard and many have degrees. The most important requirement is relevant experience of working with people and evidence of ability to cope with challenging behaviour.

A Modern Apprenticeship in community justice is also available.

Scotland Criminal justice social workers qualify through a 4-year honours degree in social work.

Graduates with a degree in any discipline can apply to join an accelerated 16- to 24-month traineeship – combining study with practical work experience – to gain a social work degree. For further information see *www.sieswe.org*.

Personal attributes A willingness to work with people irrespective of one's own personal likes and dislikes; the ability to communicate with every level of intelligence, cultural or social background or emotional state; perseverance in the face of apparent failure when offenders show no sign of improvement or appreciation of efforts made for or on their behalf; stability; a ready understanding of other people's way of life and point of view; sympathy and tolerance of human failings; belief in individual's potential to do better; good verbal and written skills to record and report; the ability to take an interest in other people's problems without becoming emotionally involved.

Late start New entrants to the NPS over 25 may be accepted without formal qualifications but need to show evidence of ability to study, usually by provision of an assessed piece of written work.

Work life balance The National Probation Service employs many 'returners' who can work flexible hours.

Probation Work

Further information The Home Office, National Probation Directorate, Horseferry House, Dan Ryle Street, London SW1P 2AW.
www.probation.homeoffice.gov.uk
Scotland: *www.careinscotland.co.uk*

Related careers PRISON SERVICE – SOCIAL WORK – YOUTH AND
COMMUNITY WORK

Psychology

Entry qualifications 2 or 3 A levels plus 5 GCSEs including maths and English at grades A–C. Requirements are flexible, but students need to be able to handle scientific concepts, to be numerate and able to write well. Useful A levels include biological sciences, maths, English, history, economics or similar arts or social science subjects.

The work Psychology is the scientific study of how people think and act, and of the mental and emotional processes underlying behaviour. Psychologists study individuals' development and how individuals interact with one another. They use observation, experimental and other methods (e.g. surveys, intelligence tests) to assess and measure all kinds of cognitive (mental) processes, attitudes and emotions. (They must not be confused with psychiatrists, who are *medically qualified* specialists who give treatment to mentally ill patients.) Psychologists must understand the difference between 'normal' and 'abnormal' behaviour and use their knowledge and skills to solve (or alleviate) a wide range of cognitive and behavioural problems.

The British Psychological Society maintains the Register of Chartered Psychologists; people wanting to be Chartered Psychologists and who are eligible (i.e. have taken training accredited by the BPS) can belong to one of the following specialist divisions: clinical; counselling; educational; occupational; forensic; health and teaching and research.

There is a steady demand for psychologists (see 'Training', below, for need for post-graduate training for specializations). Although only a small proportion of psychology graduates become practising psychologists, a psychology degree is a useful preparation for a range of occupations including employee relations and other personnel functions and social work.

Clinical Psychology

Clinical psychologists help people come to terms with various problems. Therapeutic work is carried out with adults, young people and children in individual counselling sessions or in groups in many different settings, including hospitals, health centres and remand centres. They usually work as part of a team, for example with other medical specialists or with social workers. The wide range of problems they treat include learning disabilities, relationship problems, child development or age-related problems, phobias and serious mental illness.

Work with clients involves clinical assessment using methods including interviews, psychometric testing and observation. Treatment may involve therapy, counselling and advice or a programme of rehabilitation. This is a rapidly developing field and practice is based on and contributes to ongoing research.

Most clinical psychologists work for the National Health Service as part of a team with other health professionals though some are in private practice. There are opportunities to work as trainers and teachers and as researchers in universities.

Educational and Child Psychology

Educational psychologists advise teachers, parents, doctors and social workers on children's and young people's adjustment and learning problems. They are responsible for making formal recommendations (Records or Statements of Special Educational Needs) for the education of children with learning difficulties. Assessment may involve sessions with the child as well as, usually, its parents and teachers, and a thorough study of the individual's background and environment. Various established techniques, such as ability tests and 'personality schedules' are used. Treatment (called 'intervention') may include individual counselling sessions with child and/or parents and advice to parents and teachers on the 'management' of the problem. Apart from helping individuals when problems have arisen, educational psychologists work with 'systems' or organizations: whole schools, families, groups of teachers or social workers, school classes, youth clubs. Running in-service courses for different groups is an important part of their work. They are largely employed by local education authorities and work in school/county psychological services and child guidance clinics, while a growing number work as independent or private consultants.

Occupational Psychology

Occupational psychologists deal with people as workers. They advise on how people can both enjoy and be efficient in their work by giving vocational guidance. They set up selection procedures for employers and develop training schemes; they help in the organizing of work itself by devising new methods of doing jobs; and they advise on the design of tools and machines so that they are easy to use ('ergonomics'). They also research into and advise on psychological implications of organizational structures and proposed changes, aiming at improving both job satisfaction and the organization's effectiveness.

Occupational psychologists have developed techniques for collecting information from people about what they like doing and what they are good at, as well as what they find difficult and unpleasant. They match this information against that collected by detailed studies of the actual work involved in the jobs concerned. They are very much involved with 'managing change' of working practices in offices and manufacturing, e.g. when new technologies are introduced (see MAN-AGEMENT, p. 351).

Other occupational/social psychology specializations are concerned with retirement: pre-retirement counselling and training and generally looking into problems connected with the growing proportion of retired people in the community; with mid-career changes necessitated by changes in job opportunities; with problems connected with women's changing career patterns and aspirations; with stress management.

The main employer of occupational psychologists is the Employment Service (Jobcentres). Opportunities are increasing in industry and commerce, especially in personnel/human resources departments.

Forensic Psychology

Psychologists are employed in the Prison Service or by health authorities to work both with prisoners and with those who look after them. They work in all kinds of prisons, including institutions for mentally abnormal offenders and in regional secure units. They may run training courses for prison officers and therapy sessions for prisoners and their families, as well as carrying out case work with individuals and preparing psychological reports to help judges decide on sentencing.

Forensic psychologists often collaborate with professionals in other related areas; police officers, probation officers and lawyers are turning more and more to psychology to aid their work. Forensic psychology is also the term used to refer to investigative and criminological psychology – using psychology as an aid in solving and preventing crime.

Counselling Psychology

Counselling psychology is an increasingly developing area. Most counsellors enter formal training after a period of work in some other field such as social work, teaching, health visiting or psychiatry. Client groups are diverse: they could be young couples (as in marriage guidance), younger people who have suffered bereavement, groups such as nurses who have emotionally stressful jobs, or patients in a hospice.

Health Psychology

This is a relatively new area of applied psychology. It covers a wide range of interventions, for example preventing damaging behaviours such as drug abuse, or encouraging healthy behaviour such as exercise. Health psychologists also investigate ways in which to explain, predict and change health and illness behaviour and work with the psychological effects of illness on individuals and their families. They also consider how health care delivery can be helped by improving communication or preparation for stressful treatment. Health psychologists work in hospitals, research units, health authorities and universities. They can also work with health service managers and clinicians in putting research evidence in practice to improve services.

Neuropsychology

Neuropsychology is concerned with the relationship between the brain and neuropsychological function. Its study and practical application help with the assessment and rehabilitation of people with brain injury, stroke, neuro-degenerative or other neurological disease. Neuropsychologists may be researchers or practitioners or combine both roles. They require specialist knowledge of the neurosciences and may work with acute patients alongside neurosurgeons and neurologists or in rehabilitation centres providing assessment, training and support to prepare a patient as far as possible for return to normal life. Rehabilitation of neurological patients requires helping their families and carers, too, and neuropsychologists often lead multidisciplinary rehabilitation teams.

OTHER OPPORTUNITIES AND NEW DEVELOPMENTS

Some psychologists teach in further and higher education; a few are involved solely in research, but most research is carried out by lecturers as part of their work. Newly-appointed lecturers may be expected to take a post-graduate certificate in higher education and for research it is usually necessary to take a PhD in a specialist subject. Research may be commissioned by government departments, the police, industrial organizations, research institutes. Research fields vary widely; as well as the mainstream areas – clinical, educational, etc. – there are other specializations; for example:

Psychotherapy

This covers a variety of psychological treatment, with individuals and groups of all ages. It may involve discussion over a long period, intensive interviews or encouraging the acting out or expression of inhibited emotions. Psychotherapists usually come from a professional background in medicine or social work and have a range of experience and skills as well as a specialist qualification in psychotherapy. Those wishing to train as a psychotherapist are first advised to acquire relevant professional training in another area of applied psychology or other relevant profession.

Sports psychology

This is another developing area in which there is no approved route to qualification as a Chartered Psychologist (though qualifications are now being developed). Most psychologists who have the expertise to offer a service in sports psychology have taken a post-graduate research degree or have trained in another area of applied psychology.

Training 3-year (sometimes 4-year) degree course, accredited by the British Psychological Society (BPS). The composition of the courses varies: some lead to BA, some to BSc. Topics usually covered include: experimental study of such cognitive processes as thinking, perception, learning and memory; biological basis of behaviour; animal behaviour; individual differences; social and developmental psychology; personality and intelligence; applied and specialist areas (clinical, educational, occupational, health, etc.); statistics and research methods.

Post-graduate courses are essential: approved post-graduate training courses are listed on the BPS website (see 'Further information').

Clinical psychologists take a 3-year full-time Doctorate training course. Applications to clinical courses are centralized by the Clearing House for Postgraduate Courses in Clinical Psychology (*www.leeds.ac.uk/chpccp*).

Educational psychologists must first take a post-graduate certificate in education (PGCE) and gain at least 2 years' teaching experience (not a requirement in Scotland) as well as a degree in psychology giving the graduate basis for Registration; they then take a Masters degree course normally lasting 1 year (2 in Scotland). Alternatively, qualified teachers can become educational psychologists by taking a conversion course followed by the specialist Masters degree. There are soon to be changes to training as an educational psychologist. For further information see *www.bps.org.uk/careers/careers3.cfm educational*

Occupational psychologists take a general psychology degree followed by a 1-year full-time Masters degree and 2 years' supervised practice. Alternatively psychology graduates can take the BPS Postgraduate Certificate in Occupational Psychology as well as complete 3 years' full-time supervised practice.

Forensic psychologists need either an accredited MSc (1 year full time) in Forensic Psychology plus Stage 2 of the BPS Diploma in Forensic Psychology or Stages 1 and 2 of the BPS Diploma in Forensic Psychology. Applicants for the prison service are required to attend a national assessment centre (for further information see *www.hmprisonservice.gov.uk*).

Counselling psychologists take either an accredited MSc/Diploma/ Doctorate in Counselling Psychology (3 years full time or equivalent part time) or the BPS Diploma in Counselling Psychology (3 years full time independent study and practice).

Health psychologists need either an MSc in Health Psychology (1 year full time) plus Stage 2 of the BPS Diploma in Health Psychology or Stages 1 and 2 of the BPS Diploma in Health Psychology.

Personal attributes Interest in individuals' development and behaviour; an interest in scientific method; the ability to work well on one's own, but also to work as part of a team and to cooperate with people from different backgrounds; patience; numeracy.

Late start No problem for qualified late entrants to degree courses who have the required entry qualifications; maturity and relevant work experience can be an asset. Owing to competition, and the length of training, mature applicants without normal entry requirements may have difficulty finding a place. GCSE or equivalent in maths is essential. An Open University degree in psychology may be the best bet.

Work life balance Returners may find competition from newly qualified people (particularly for academic posts). Most psychologists manage to work full or part time while raising a family.

Some opportunities for part-time work and job-sharing.

Further information The British Psychological Society, St Andrew's House, 48 Princess Road East, Leicester LE1 7DR. *www.bps.org.uk*

Related careers NURSING: *Mental Health/Learning Disabilities* – PERSONNEL/HUMAN RESOURCES MANAGEMENT – SOCIAL WORK – SOCIOLOGY – TEACHING

Psychotherapy and Counselling

Psychotherapy and counselling are included in this guide because of the interest in and confusion about these occupational areas. The explanations given do not fit into the format used in the rest of the guide.

Psychotherapy

The term *psychotherapy* has two meanings: it is an umbrella term for various forms of treatment for patients with emotional or psychological problems through dialogue with a skilled practitioner. Its aim is to help patients change the way they manage their problems. In this context, psychotherapy covers several methods which differ in intensity and underlying philosophy. The term *psychotherapy* is also used to define an occupation, but one without agreed entry requirements, qualifications or career structure (except for *child psychotherapy*, see below). It is *never* a career option for school or college leavers but invariably a 'second' or 'late start' career for people with relevant qualifications, work and life experience.

Persons with a range of qualifications (or none) practise psychotherapy:

1. *Psychiatrists*: They are medically qualified doctors (see MEDICINE, p. 377) who have subsequently qualified for membership of the Royal College of Psychiatrists. Psychotherapy is only one of a range of treatments they use (drug therapy is another). Most psychiatrists work in the NHS, some work partly or entirely in private practice.

2. *Psychoanalysts*: They normally have a medical degree or comparable qualification (some are also qualified psychiatrists); they have undergone lengthy personal analysis and then taken an approximately

4-year (part-time but very time-consuming) training in Jungian, Freudian or similar psychoanalytical method. Although not a registrable profession, it is generally agreed that in this country only people who have qualified for membership of the Society of Analytical Psychology or the British Psychoanalytical Society are entitled to call themselves psychoanalysts or analysts. *Very* few analysts work in the NHS; most are in private practice with, possibly, some sessional work for voluntary advice centres.

Psychiatrists who practise psychotherapy, analysts and those clinical psychologists (see 'Clinical Psychology', p. 484) who do some psychotherapeutical work are all sometimes called psychotherapists – which is the reason for the confusion surrounding the term.

3. *Psychotherapists*: At present anyone, whatever their qualification (if any), may use the title 'psychotherapist', a fact which rigorously trained psychotherapists very much regret. There are so many psychotherapy organizations and philosophies that agreement on a common training or accreditation scheme is very difficult. However, there are now two self-regulatory and registration bodies: the British Confederation of Psychotherapists (BCP) and the United Kingdom Council for Psychotherapy (UKCP). Although registration has not yet been made mandatory, both bodies are in discussion with the government. The mainstream organizations, however, base their treatment on psychoanalytical methods. Their professional bodies accept for training only candidates with relevant degree or comparable qualifications and experience; require them to undergo lengthy personal analysis or therapy and then train them much as do psychoanalytical organizations. Courses last a minimum of 3 years part time. In fact, psychoanalysts' and psychotherapists' training and work shade into each other (though psychotherapists more often than analysts also treat people in groups – families, couples, fellow-sufferers such as addicts, phobics, etc.). About a dozen universities now run courses for psychotherapists. Some are broad-based; some are run in partnership with professional associations.

There are some jobs for *psychotherapists* in the NHS (particularly for *child psychotherapists*, see below); mostly they rely on private patients and – very few – voluntary organizations' clinic sessions.

Because there is a growing demand for help for people with problems, a vast number of self-styled psychotherapy organizations have sprung up over the last few years. Some are experimenting with new methods of 'alternative psychotherapy' in good faith, but the methods and the credentials of some organizations are dubious. Before signing up for training (often expensive, and/or too short and not rigorous enough to be of any value) potential psychotherapists must thoroughly check organizations' claims.

The above refers to what is called 'adult psychotherapy'. *Child psychotherapy* is a recognized profession (though a very small one). Child psychotherapists treat children for psychological disturbances of behaviour, thinking and feeling. The work is focused on the relationship established between the psychotherapist and the child, through which insight into the problem is gained. Children, adolescents and parents are seen, usually individually, sometimes in groups. Child psychotherapists work in child guidance clinics, young people's advice and treatment clinics, and in private practice. To be accepted for training with one of the four accredited organizations, candidates must have a psychology degree or comparable qualification and experience of work with normal children. Training, a mixture of theory and practice and including extensive observation of young children, takes 4–5 years. There is a growing demand for child psychotherapists in the National Health Service, especially outside London, e.g. in the Midlands, the South-West and Scotland. Full-time and sessional work is available.

Counselling

This is a much over-used and therefore vague term. It is best defined as the skill of helping normal people, through discussion, to decide how best to cope in specific situations. By listening attentively and without passing judgement the counsellor gives clients the opportunity to explore, discover and clarify how and why they feel as they do; they (the clients, not the counsellors) may then be able to make choices and decisions about their situation which they were incapable of making before.

While psychotherapists may try to change patients' personalities, or at least their attitudes, sometimes over a long period, counsellors tend to deal with immediate, often practical problems, e.g. redundancy or alcohol addiction. Yet psychotherapists' and counsellors' work may overlap, as they use similar methods. Psychotherapists more often deal with severe psychological disorders, especially if working in hospitals, but in private practice both may see patients with similar problems.

Counsellors work in many settings – schools, colleges, GP practices, clinics, counselling centres, staff welfare departments, as well as in private practice. There are counselling services that specialize in particular groups, e.g. young people or ethnic minorities, or in specific problems, such as drug addiction or AIDS. The number of full-time posts is increasing, but there are more trained counsellors than there are jobs. Many combine part-time work with social work, welfare rights work and administration.

There are a few full-time training courses for teachers, social workers and others working in the field. There are many more part-time courses leading to a certificate or diploma. These mostly expect people to have a degree or a professional qualification. The British Psychological Society now has a counselling psychology division and accredits courses (see p. 489). For people hoping to do counselling as volunteers and not looking for a vocational qualification there are part-time introductory courses, courses in counselling skills, and specialist courses in bereavement, cancer, child abuse, etc., counselling.

Although there is no legal requirement for counsellors to be properly trained, people interested in the work are advised to contact the British Association for Counselling for advice (address below).

Further information British Association of Psychotherapists, 37 Mapesbury Road, London NW2 4HJ.
www.bap-psychotherapy.org
London Centre for Psychotherapy, 32 Leighton Road, Kentish Town, London NW5 2QE.
www.lcp-psychotherapy.org.uk

Tavistock Clinic, 120 Belsize Lane, London NW3 5BA.
www.tavi-port.org
Association of Child Psychotherapists, 120 West Heath Road, London
NW3 7TU.
www.acp.uk.net
British Association for Counselling and Psychotherapy, BACP House,
35–37 Albert Street, Rugby CV21 2SG.
www.bacp.co.uk
UK Council of Psychotherapy, 167–169 Great Portland Street, London
W1N 5FB.
www.psychotherapy.org.uk
British Confederation of Psychotherapists, West Hill House, 6 Swains
Lane, London N6 6QS.
www.bcp.org.uk
Society for Analytical Psychology, 1 Daleham Gardens, London NW3
5BY.
http://jungian-analysis.org

Related careers PSYCHOLOGY – SOCIAL WORK – TEACHING

Public Relations

Entry qualifications 95% of new entrants to the Institute of Public Relations are now graduates.

The work Public relations officers advise on ways to develop relationships with sections of the public whose support and goodwill is essential for the success of an enterprise. Public relations is part of the marketing mix, but is specifically about protecting and promoting reputation. Public relations is more than a publicity tool – it is an essential part of successful management in an increasingly competitive environment. Public relations officers provide factual stories about clients or their product to newspapers, magazines and television, thus keeping the product or the service in the news and creating a 'favourable climate or image'. They answer journalists' questions about their client's product, views or services, and may take journalists to see the client's product or service. They arrange receptions, exhibitions and other projects to 'put over' a client or promote a cause, and give talks to interested groups – schools, women's organizations, etc. They deal with inquiries (and also complaints) from the public as well as working in areas such as community and stakeholder relations. In recent years they have begun to share (with human resource management professionals) and in some cases lead on internal communications.

Public relations officers work either in public relations consultancies (between 2 and 30 partners each with their own accounts and a shared office and staff), in public relations departments of advertising/multi-service agencies, or in separate press and public relations departments of individual organizations. More and more organizations employ PR specialists to advise on and put into action ways of communicating the organization's functions and activities to relevant groups. Today, local authorities, employers' federations, charities and professional organizations such as the British Medical Association employ public relations or information officers. In the Civil Service they are called information officers and work in nearly all departments, where they usually specialize in either press or publicity work. Hospitals, schools and universities increasingly make use of PR. Other important areas include financial PR and public affairs; some sporting and TV personalities also use public relations officers to help further their careers.

Entry into PR is highly competitive; far more people want to do this sort of work than there are opportunities, although really talented people are sought after. There has been a growth in the number of small, independent consultancies in the last few years.

Training Competition for jobs is such that it is now very difficult to get into PR by working oneself up from a junior position, such as secretary. The following are all possible entry routes:

1. A sideways move with a degree and work experience in a relevant discipline or industry (e.g. engineering or science). Traditionally many PR people moved sideways from journalism and this is still a possible route.

2. As a trainee with a PR firm or in a PR department with a non-specialist degree. Useful degree subjects are business studies, economics, languages, communication, but employers will take promising people from any discipline.

3. With a degree or post-graduate diploma/degree course in PR. The IPR recognizes over 20 university and college courses as leading to awards which qualify the holder for associate membership of the Institute. (A list of these courses is available on the IPR website.)

Work-based training is through part-time study or distance-learning. CAM offer an Advanced Certificate in Public Relations which can also be studied full time. Entry qualifications are 5 GCSEs at Grade C or over, but many entrants are graduates. Those progressing to a senior level can study for the CAM Higher Diploma in Public Relations.

The IPR Diploma is the major vocational qualification for membership of the Institute. New entrants to PR need to study the IPR Advanced Certificate course in order to qualify for entry into the PR Diploma. The Advanced Certificate course consists of 48 hours' teaching over 24 weeks at a number of centres around the UK and entrants must be at least 21 and hold either any UK degree or have 2 years' experience in PR or a related environment, plus 5 GCSEs.

NVQs in Public Relations are no longer available although the Marketing and Sales Sector Skills Board (MSSSB) is considering a set of new standards.

Personal attributes Ability to get on exceptionally well with people of all kinds, whether hard-hitting journalists or less confident members of the public; enterprise and initiative; good news sense; sense of salesmanship; a calm temperament; analytical powers; ability to write and speak well and persuasively; imagination; tact; ability to keep polite under provocation and/or pressure.

Late start Possible for people with special expertise/experience. Approximately a quarter of CAM students are aged 30+.

Work life balance Well-established PR professionals can work from home, perhaps having only one client for a year or so, then gradually increasing their workload.

Flexible working is usually possible in the public sector or larger companies and part-time work may be possible in small, non-commercial (i.e. usually voluntary) organizations.

Further information Institute of Public Relations, The Old Trading House, 15 Northburgh Street, London EC1V 0PR.
   www.ipr.org.uk
CAM Education Foundation, Moor Hall, Cookham, Berkshire SL6 9QH.
   www.camfoundation.com

Public Relations Consultants Association, Willow House, Willow
Place, London SW1P 1JH.
www.prca.org.uk
Scottish Public Relations Consultants Association, Barkers Scotland,
324 West George Street, Glasgow G2 4QY.

Related careers ADVERTISING – CIVIL SERVICE: *Information Officer*
– FASHION AND CLOTHING – JOURNALISM – MARKETING AND
SELLING – SECRETARIAL AND CLERICAL WORK

Publishing

Entry qualifications In practice a degree or comparable qualification and/or specialist knowledge/experience; design training for some aspects of production. In specialist publishing, such as educational, scientific or art, editorial assistants normally have a degree in a relevant subject. In general publishing, the degree subject is normally irrelevant.

The work Publishing is an industry (one of the smallest in the country), not a profession. It requires business acumen and an interest in *marketing* (see p. 502) as much as creativity and literary flair. The function of publishing has been described as extending the author's idea into a finished book and getting it into readers' hands – in other words publishing involves the organization of production, marketing and distribution as much as (and in many cases more than) literary effort.

Publishing houses vary greatly in size, from large ones with overseas branches and several 'imprints', producing hundreds of titles a year, to those run on a shoe-string with a handful of employees and a small yearly output. The trend is towards 'conglomerates' with large houses buying up smaller ones, but keeping their identities fairly separate. Many are now owned by United States companies. Some publishers specialize in educational, scientific, art books, or paperbacks. *Desk-top publishing*, in which editor, designer and production staff handle text and illustration on disk at different stages, is widely used. Many organizations use DTP to produce publications for their own use and also for books which have very limited sales. In some cases one person can carry out all the tasks from start to finish.

Publishers select and commission manuscripts, design the appearance of the books, have them printed and bound, and promote and sell the finished copies, but the internal organization of 'houses' varies. The process is usually divided into 3 main departments (apart from the usual commercial ones such as accounts). The division of work is more rigid in some houses than others; in small houses everybody may have to do anything that needs doing (a good way of learning). The increase in DTP has tended to break down demarcation barriers.

The 3 main publishing departments or 'functions' are:

Editorial

Main duties are identifying publishing opportunities and commissioning authors. Increasingly agents working for authors play a large part and fewer books are commissioned from scratch. Editors are responsible also for getting outside specialist readers' opinions; preparing typescripts (or disks) for the printer; liaising with authors, possibly suggesting changes; dealing with contracts, copyright, subsidiary rights (these may be separate departments). Editorial departments also deal with new editions of existing books.

An editorial director or chief editor (titles and responsibilities involved vary greatly in different houses) is usually in charge. Individual editors may each be responsible for books on a special subject, or for a range of subjects. They may initiate a book on a special subject, select the author and deal with the project right through. The number of books one editor deals with at any particular moment varies according to type of firm and type of book, and so does the amount of contact the editor has with the author.

Editorial assistants or 'copy-editors' deal with 'copy preparation'; checking facts and references, spelling, punctuation, and possibly doing some rewriting, proof-reading and correcting. Again, responsibilities and duties vary greatly. Increasingly this work is done by out-of-house freelances under the editor's management.

Indexing is a specialist area within publishing and many indexers work on a freelance basis. For further information contact the Society of Indexers, Blades Enterprise Centre, John Street, Sheffield s2 4su. Website: *www.socind.demon.co.uk*

Design and Production

In larger publishing houses there may be a separate art department. In others designers work in the production department. The production department receives the edited typescript and decides in consultation with designer and editor on the appearance of the book, on the shape, typeface, paper, illustrations, etc.; the production department deals with printers, paper merchants, binders etc. Staff must understand all aspects of costing and marketing and of the various types of illustration and typography. But above all they must understand the new printing and production technologies which are drastically changing established production methods. Technical and textbook publishers may employ their own illustrators, but most artwork, including illustrations and book jackets, is commissioned from freelances and outside studios.

Marketing (includes Sales)

In some ways the most important publishing activity, marketing or 'promotion' is responsible for planning, researching for and preparing review lists, sales campaigns, writing 'blurbs', and for the representatives who call on bookshops, schools, libraries, etc. to give information on forthcoming books and to collect orders. Marketing staff make representations to key accounts and there is a heavy emphasis on public relations. In addition, marketing people in many houses now often initiate projects, based on feedback gained by the sales representatives when they visit bookshops. On the basis of a 'feasibility study' – mainly researching the market and costing – it is decided whether to go ahead and, jointly with editorial, get the book commissioned, or whether to abandon the idea. This is a good department in which to learn how publishing works.

There are many more posts in non-editorial than editorial departments.

OTHER KINDS OF PUBLISHING
Book Packaging

A small, but growing development outside traditional publishing is book 'packaging'. Packagers are *marketing* people. They find an idea which is likely to be profitable, commission an author and artwork and produce a dummy copy of the book. They then offer it to publishers, usually in several countries. 'Packages' are usually highly illustrated; a 'bank' of pictures is printed separately and then over-printed with the translated text with the minimum production expense. Promotion, selling and distribution are done by the publishers who buy the packaged book.

Packagers' overheads are lower than traditional publishers' and it is therefore easier to start up as a packager than as a publisher. But good contacts, publishing experience and ideas are essential.

Electronic Publishing

This has much more in common with *information technology* (see p. 281) and with *information work* (see p. 295) than with 'literary' publishing – at least for the present. It was initially used to provide databases or 'online information services' and is in fact sometimes called 'database publishing'. It produces such services as Ceefax and individual organizations' and professions' computerized research bases/libraries. The growth area now is in multi-media publishing on CD-Rom, in which most large publishers are already, or are about to become, involved. *Computer specialists, information scientists* and *librarians,* as well as experts in the appropriate field (i.e. anyone from accountant to zoologist), might work in electronic publishing, but it is at present a very small job area. Web publishing is a rapidly developing area.

Magazine Publishing

This is quite different from book publishing. *Feature editors* need to be able to write original copy; *editorial assistants* must be able to 'sub' (reword, shorten, etc.) other people's writing. They all need to know something about layout and production, as well as to understand the business side of magazines (including advertising). Some editors started as secretaries, others as freelance or staff journalists (see JOURNALISM, p. 304.) Most magazines have a 'publisher' responsible for the business side: the usual background is in advertisement selling, but some publishers are ex-editorial staff.

There are very limited opportunities on the editorial side of publishing, which attracts the most applicants, especially in general publishing; more scope in technical, scientific, educational. First editorial job is usually as editorial assistant ('assistant editor' may mean the same thing). Opportunities are slightly better in other departments, especially in sales and marketing and production.

Training Nothing specific; degree in any subject advisable. See 'The work', above.

There are a small number of pre-entry courses, some of which are for graduates, and there are several degree courses in publishing. There are training courses in book production and design, and some art and design courses include book design and production (see ART AND DESIGN, p. 105.) Pre-entry training is recommended especially for these departments. A few firms run their own training schemes, but most rely on short in-service courses provided by, for example, the Publishing Training Centre at Book House. Some of these courses are also useful to prospective applicants. NVQs have been introduced but take-up in the industry has been very slow.

Previous bookselling or other sales experience is useful.

In the past many editors came up the secretarial ladder; this still occasionally happens, but there are far more graduate secretaries working for publishers and hoping to make the break than there are editorial jobs.

Personal attributes Creative ability; interest in social and economic as well as literary trends; ability to see books as a marketable commodity; some writing ability; critical judgement; common sense; resilience; good business sense; willingness to take responsibility and make decisions; ability to get on well with a wide variety of types of people.

Late start Difficult because of the competition from young graduates, but possible in technical and educational publishing for people with technical/scientific background.

Work life balance A career break should be possible but it is advisable not to give up completely, even temporarily.

Experienced proof-readers, copy-editors, editors may be able to do freelance work.

Further information Publishers' Association, 29B Montague Street, London WC1B 5BW.
    www.publishers.org.uk
Scottish Publishers' Association, 137 Dundee Street, Edinburgh EH11 1BG.
    www.scottishbooks.org
The Publishing Training Centre at Book House, 45 East Hill, Wandsworth, London SW18 2QZ.
    www.train4publishing.co.uk
Individual publishing houses

Related careers ART AND DESIGN – BOOKSELLING – INFORMATION WORK – JOURNALISM – PRINTING

Purchasing and Supply

Entry qualifications For professional qualification: 2 A levels, 3 GCSEs (A–C), including English language and a quantitative subject; or NVQ/SVQ level 3 or equivalent qualification. Also *graduate* entry. No specific qualifications for mature entrants with relevant work experience (see also 'Late start') but see 'Training', below.

The work A company's supply, or value, chain stretches from sourcing its raw materials, via the supply market into the organization, then out through internal customers to the end user. Purchasing and supply management is the link in that chain which manages the interface between the supply market and the organization. Its importance lies in the fact that a company can spend more than two-thirds of its revenue buying in goods and services, so even a modest percentage reduction in purchasing costs can have a significant effect on profits.

Essentially, purchasing and supply management involves working with the company's internal customers to identify their requirements and then obtaining the necessary products and services by negotiation and agreement with suppliers. The primary objective is to obtain value for money. This does not always mean achieving the very lowest price – sometimes other commercial considerations are more important.

A well-qualified purchasing professional can walk into a wide range of environments where they can use their skills to buy a whole range of products. For example, in a manufacturing environment such as a car plant, the purchaser would be directly involved in buying components such as wheels, lights and shock absorbers for the production line. In a financial services company, purchases might well be for telecommunications systems, catering services and marketing services including advertising and design. A less conventional case is retail purchasing where the role is slightly different. Here some purchasers within the organization buy goods for use by the company itself, such as office furniture, electricity, etc., whereas other buyers are more involved in merchandising because they are responsible for selecting products which are sold in the shops themselves.

The choice of jobs within purchasing and supply management is vast as it is a role which is carried out by all organizations, including central government, local councils, charities as well as commercial companies. A need to influence people and achieve targets means there is plenty of intellectual stimulation, but the working environment is highly competitive. The range of specialist areas within purchasing and supply management includes purchasing, contracts, materials management, production planning, logistics and distribution, and systems implementation.

Training The Chartered Institute of Purchasing and Supply provides a degree-level professional qualification through its Graduate Diploma. There are 2 stages to the syllabus. The Foundation Stage has 6 subjects covering the basic commercial skills required while the Professional Stage is more closely focused on purchasing and supply management itself.

It is possible to obtain exemption from some subjects depending upon previous academic record and work experience, but virtually all graduates have to sit the 4 core Professional Stage subjects; the exceptions are people who have completed one of the accredited specialist degree courses which tend to be business related.

There are various methods of studying for the Graduate Diploma, including evening classes, distance-learning through correspondence course, a self-study programme and modular training, which consists of a series of intensive tutorial days.

NVQs/SVQs in Procurement at levels 3 and 4 are also available.

Personal attributes Numeracy; organizing ability; practical approach to problem-solving; considerable business acumen; ability to establish friendly relationships quickly; judgement to gauge the right approach to individual suppliers; networking abilities; awareness of technological changes and their implications for purchasing.

Late start Good opportunities. Some 30% of CIPS students are over 30 (but not all are new entrants). People with previous work experience are welcome. Graduates and others with relevant experience are granted substantial exemption from CIPS exams.

Work life balance A career break should not present problems, but keeping in touch with world economic conditions and commercial law is vital. Short Institute courses can be used as *refreshers*. Temporarily retired individuals pay reduced Institute subscriptions.

Opportunities for part-time work are good and job-sharing is possible.

Further information The Chartered Institute of Purchasing and Supply, Easton House, Easton on the Hill, Stamford, Lincs. PE9 3NZ.
www.cips.org

Related careers LOGISTICS, DISTRIBUTION AND TRANSPORT MANAGEMENT – RETAIL MANAGEMENT – SURVEYING: *Quantity Surveyor*

Radiography

Entry qualifications Degree course requirements: 1 or even 2 sciences, at either level, may be required; BTEC/SQA awards may be accepted in lieu. It is essential to check with individual courses.

See 'Late start', below, for mature students' entry.

The work Radiography has 2 branches: *diagnostic* and *therapeutic*.

Diagnostic Radiographers

They work in diagnostic imaging teams with radiologists, who are doctors with specialist qualifications. They are involved with the whole range of imaging techniques, including the use of ionizing radiation to produce X-rays, medical ultrasound, magnetic resonance imaging, nuclear medicine and others. Radiographers have to be skilled in the operation of complex equipment. They must understand not only how to use imaging techniques, but the theory behind them. In addition, they have to produce reports on the images obtained to aid their diagnosis. Radiographers, therefore, need a considerable knowledge of anatomy, physiology, physics and radiation science.

They work in hospital X-ray departments and on occasions use mobile equipment in wards. They may also be asked to produce X-ray images during operations, when it is particularly important to obtain fast, high-quality images.

Diagnostic radiographers normally see patients only once or twice, but often in traumatic circumstances. They must, therefore, be skilled in patient care techniques, especially in gaining patients' cooperation and explaining procedures.

Therapeutic Radiographers

They are a crucial element in the cancer treatment team. They work with oncologists, doctors with specialist qualifications in the treatment of cancer. They carry out treatment by means of high energy ionizing radiation and sometimes drugs.

Treatment is often given over a long period of time. Radiographers must be expert in the giving of the treatment and also highly skilled in dealing with seriously ill and often worried patients. Cancer treatment is increasingly being seen in a 'holistic' way, i.e. as treatment of the whole person, not just the illness, and this is affecting the way radiographers work, just as it does other members of health care teams. Specialist Macmillan radiographers work with patients in their own homes and take a leading role in the patient's all-round care, with responsibility for other issues such as counselling. They need extensive knowledge of human anatomy and physiology and of radiation physics.

Exposure to X-rays can be dangerous, but X-ray departments are equipped with safeguards which ensure that operators are not harmed in any way. The controls are operated from outside the treatment rooms so that the radiographer is never exposed to radiation; treatment rooms are lined with material which the X-rays cannot penetrate.

There have been shortages of radiographers, especially therapy specialists. The majority work in hospital. There are a few posts in private practice. Radiographers can earn their living in most countries of the world, provided they speak the appropriate language. There is a considerable number of post-graduate courses and opportunities to specialize in the newer techniques of medical ultrasound, nuclear medicine and magnetic resonance imaging (used in both diagnosis and treatment of various diseases).

Training An approved 3-year (4-year in Scotland and Northern Ireland) degree at university. About 50% of the course is clinical, i.e. spent within the clinical environment working with patients. Students train as *either* diagnostic *or* therapeutic radiographers.

Personal attributes A strong scientific bent; a steady hand and a sharp observant eye; a genuine liking for people and a desire to help the sick; a cheerful, confident manner; patience; calmness; firmness; ability to take responsibility and to work well with others; good health.

Late start Upper age limit for training is 50. Mature applicants are increasing. Entry requirements are relaxed. See also 'Access to higher education courses', p. 15.

Work life balance Opportunities for returning within the NHS but retraining essential – extent depends on length of break (changes in procedures and equipment are drastic and rapid). *Refresher* courses are available.

Flexible working arrangements should be available for NHS employees.

Further information Society of Radiographers, 207 Providence Square, Mills Street, London SE1 2EW.
www.sor.org

Related careers PHOTOGRAPHY – SCIENCE: *Science Technician*; *Scientist*

Retail Management

Entry qualifications Nothing rigid; all educational levels.

The work Retailing is one of the largest industries in the UK, accounting for about 11% of employment. It is one of the few career areas where getting on does not necessarily depend on passing examinations.

The industry is constantly having to adapt to changing lifestyles and new technologies. For example, the new Sunday Trading laws have increased trading hours. Computerization and 'rationalization' (less personal service; more part-timers for peak-hour work; fewer leisure periods for full-timers) has led to a reduced total workforce but, proportionately, more management opportunities.

No industry-wide career-structure exists. Titles, and responsibilities attached to titles, vary from one company to another, and so do recruiting and promotion procedures. The main types of 'retail outlet' are *hyper- and supermarkets*; *department stores*; *chain stores*; *co-operatives*; *independents*. The categories are not as clear-cut as they used to be. Supermarkets and multiples have 'diversified', i.e. sell more than one type of merchandise; some department stores give houseroom to specialist shops – for example, photographic equipment; some independents have joined together for bulk-buying purposes; some out-of-town centres combine retailing, entertainment and leisure facilities. Out-of-town retail parks have prospered at the expense of high street shops. Internet shopping is opening up new opportunities.

A growing type of retailing is *franchising*: a group of outlets – at present mainly food and fashion – is centrally controlled and sells to 'franchisees' the right to use its name and image, and to sell its centrally bought merchandise. Within certain guidelines, franchisees then run their own shows. *Mail order* is a growth area, mainly but not only in fashion and household goods. It divides into 2 kinds: the traditional 'catalogue companies' which sell through part-time agents; and the more up-market 'direct mail', 'direct response' or 'direct marketing' companies. These sell through advertising in the press and/or through catalogues sent to likely customers. This is a sophisticated, high-risk business, more a marketing operation (see MARKETING AND SELLING, p. 371) than traditional retailing. Success depends on selecting a few sure-fire items for sale, the right advertising media and the right people to send catalogues to.

In traditional retailing, buying and selling organization varies from one company to another. For chain stores, hyper- and supermarkets buying is usually done centrally: identical merchandise is allocated to stores which are also given display and promotion guidelines. In department store groups, buying is also done centrally, but individual outlets still have their own distinctive character and do not necessarily all sell the same merchandise; they target specific customer groups, e.g. sophisticated in Knightsbridge, London, down-to-earth in small northern town.

Traditionally, most people going into retailing hoped to become buyers or store managers. While these positions are still very popular, there are now other sought-after activities in retailing such as merchandising, personnel, marketing, new product development and IT. Nearly always these require people to have A levels or a degree. Specialists, such as *fashion graduates* (see p. 248), *food technologists* (see p. 547) and *electronics experts* (see ENGINEERING, p. 216) are sometimes recruited as trainee-buyers.

Most people, however, stay in selling and store management. Whatever the eventual ambition, and whatever training scheme the new entrant is on, starting on the shop-floor – the 'sharp end' – is essential to learn about customer-relations and trading principles. There are varying hierarchies from sales assistant, shelf-filler, checkout operator, warehouse clerk, via section, department, specialist (transport, staff, distribution, etc.), deputy to store manager, and after that perhaps area manager. Job titles, and job functions, vary from one retail concern to another. Speed, and likelihood of promotion, varies from company to company, and according to age and ability.

Store managers coordinate the various retailing functions: stock control, security; staff deployment; maximizing profit per square metre of premises; dealing with customers' complaints and queries; liaising with head office, etc. Supermarket and department store work differ greatly; supermarkets are much more hectic places with emphasis on fast-moving goods; managers must make their own, quick decisions, whether they are dealing with a staff, delivery or customer problem. In department stores, managers have such 'support services' as personnel, distribution and complaints departments on the premises and there is more emphasis on personal service. Hypermarkets and chain stores again make different demands. Ideally, prospective retailers should decide which type of atmosphere and work is right for them. In practice, there may not be much job choice, but one can switch from one type of retailing to another: basic retail expertise is a 'transferable skill', although it is easier to switch from supermarkets to chain stores than the other way around.

Staff management and training may have its own hierarchy, parallel with store management, and it may be a step on the store management ladder (see PERSONNEL/HUMAN RESOURCES MANAGEMENT, p. 444).

Buying is very different from its image of spending other people's money on items one likes. Buyers work closely with *merchandisers*, who control the budget. Buying consists of selecting from suppliers' existing lines and also, jointly with manufacturers, developing new ideas, and adapting existing lines and prototypes bought or seen abroad or at a competitor's at home. Developing 'own brand' lines is expanding. Buyers work closely with marketing and production specialists and with store managers. Buying policies are based on methodical analysis and interpretation of past sales figures, on economic forecasts, on demographic trends (the present ageing population and the reduction in the number of late-teenagers have important implications for buyers); on lifestyle changes (the trend for more casual than formal clothing; the fashion to drink out of mugs rather than cups; increasingly exotic foreign travel and resultant interest in foreign food and drinks, etc.). Buying is a commercial activity and requires communication and negotiating expertise and number-crunching, as well as flair for guessing next year's preferences. It involves complex decision-making. For example, a buyer may find a very efficient and inexpensive spin-dryer with an unsatisfactory after-sales service. 'Does good performance and competitive pricing outweigh less-than-perfect after-sales service?' is the kind of decision buyers have to take – and be able to justify later, if customers complain.

Merchandisers tend to work at a policy level, forecasting departmental sales and profits and determining the budgets within which buyers operate. The work of both buyers and merchandisers involves constant decision-making and assessment of information. While merchandising is usually a senior head office job, confusingly it can mean different things in different companies. It can also describe people employed by wholesalers or manufacturers who ensure that their employer's products are adequately displayed in retail outlets. And it can describe persons who, working closely with display specialists, are responsible for the display of goods in a store.

Commodity knowledge – expertise in one type of merchandise – used to be all-important; then managerial and commercial expertise determined promotion and buyers easily switched from buying one type of merchandise to another. Now, commodity knowledge, at least in 'high-tech' consumer goods, textiles and food, again seems to matter more; but it varies from company to company.

Head office jobs include *general management* (see MANAGEMENT, p. 351); *marketing* (see p. 371); *design* (see p. 105); *food and other technologies* (see p. 547); *personnel* (see p. 444); *store planning*; and *retail analysis*: what type of shop/shopping centre is likely to be profitable in the future – where, and why? How will European competition affect our stores in the integrated European market, and what can we do to remain competitive if European retailers set up their shops in this country in greater numbers? As retailing is becoming ever more sophisticated and professionalized, new specialisms emerge, or traditional jobs are being fined down into separate functions. For example, 'transport management' may be divided into 'vehicle and depot management' and 'operations management' with responsibility for the movement of goods from supplier or port of entry to depot or store (see LOGISTICS, DISTRIBUTION AND TRANSPORT MANAGEMENT p. 345). These planning/forecasting jobs involve a mixture of crystal-ball gazing, statistics, technological and economic forecasting, psychology and sociology (and are very much a growth area for graduates from any discipline).

Retailing also offers good opportunities to systems analysts and other computer experts (see INFORMATION TECHNOLOGY (IT)/ INFORMATION SYSTEMS, p. 281) as more companies adopt computerized 'point of sale' stock-control and 'electronic fund transfer' systems and introduce computer-based armchair shopping. There are openings for computer science graduates or other computer-literate graduates able to work well in a team designing and modifying databases and making systems more user-friendly.

Fashion retailing is a specialized job for people with experience of fashion (see p. 248) as well as of general retailing. Boutiques, like other small shops, suffer during recessions, and, while popular with people with a fashion or retail background wanting to start their own business, they remain 'high risk' concerns. Food retailing has been called 'recession-proof'.

Training Training is patchy and haphazard. Some employers – including most but not all of the well-known chain and department stores – train staff systematically, using outside courses and/or their own in-house training schemes, to produce 'retail professionals' with transferable skills (i.e. trainees who can later use their training in all kinds of retail companies). Other companies give little career training, but teach people to perform specific jobs in their organization. While promotion up the retail hierarchy does not depend on having paper qualifications, the importance of expertise is growing enormously, as technological and management systems are becoming ever more sophisticated; such expertise can, in practice, only be acquired by systematic training. However, there are many ways of training. It is generally agreed that the best way of becoming a retail professional is to learn on the job, with additional off-the-job training and being assessed for NVQs/SVQs (see below). That means finding a job with day-release or similar facilities for taking courses.

The alternatives to a job-with-training are:

1. taking any job in retailing and learning by experience and possibly taking a relevant distance-learning course or evening classes or

2. taking a pre-entry course (see below).

Individual companies' training schemes vary greatly. All retailers stress the flexibility of their training schemes and emphasize that no specific qualification or training scheme automatically leads to any specific point on the retail job ladder. Individual patterns vary not only from one company to another, but also from one year to another according to company plans for expansion or consolidation/contraction or change of emphasis, and also according to current views on which type of training (length, outside or in-house course, theory-and-practice mix) is the most cost-effective. Companies may recruit young people at 16 with GCSEs, at 18 with A levels or a GNVQ, or offer graduate training schemes. Candidates are strongly advised to look at several companies' recruitment literature, to read the small print and, at interviews, ask questions about promotion prospects, etc.

Qualifications are offered at different levels. Sales staff in many companies work towards NVQs/SVQs levels 1 and 2 during their training. Levels 3 and 4 are established at supervisory and management level.

Modern Apprenticeships (see p. 11) are sometimes available for young people wishing to enter retailing straight from school.

BTEC courses in distribution and retail management are also widely available, both full time and part time, for those already working in the industry. Candidates with 4 GCSEs (A–C) can take a BTEC National Certificate (or Scottish equivalent), usually 2 years full time, or National Diploma, 2 years full time or 3 years part time, which are both recognized as an entry qualification for most junior management training schemes run by major stores. For those with the BTEC National or with an A level, BTEC/SQA offer Higher National courses in retail management for those aiming at senior-level jobs.

Degrees in retail management are available at a number of universities and are increasingly recognized and requested by large retail companies.

GCSE entrants with only good Saturday/holiday retail experience may be eligible for 2-year training schemes planned for A level entrants, which may lead to the BTEC Higher National Certificate or Scottish equivalent. Equally, A level entrants with some work experience may be eligible for graduate training schemes. Graduates are expected to be ready for their first junior management job in 9–15 months; A level entrants and others with good hands-on experience are expected to take 15–24 months. Degree subject is immaterial, and Higher National Diplomas (BTEC or Scottish equivalent) are usually considered as of equal value to degrees. Training patterns are as varied, and as confusing, as this. Company training policies and candidates' personal qualities are likely to remain more important than paper qualifications. A 16-year-old without any GCSEs but with potential (including the potential to make supervisors notice it!) can catch up with a 21-year-old graduate entrant: when the graduate starts training, the school-leaver has had 5 years' practical experience and is eligible for management training along with the graduate.

Personal attributes Numeracy; an outgoing personality; an interest in both people and things; organizing ability; communication skills; commercial sense. For *store management*: leadership qualities; ability to delegate and take decisions quickly and to keep calm in crises; physical stamina. For *buyers*: interest in social and economic trends; negotiating skills; objectivity to be able to judge the relevance of one's own taste and gauge that of customers. For *buyers* and *merchandisers*: good mathematical and analytical skills.

Late start Good opportunities. Most companies positively welcome people who have had work experience, and will train people of up to about 35 for management. BTEC/SQA courses also welcome mature students and distance-learning courses are available.

Work life balance Most companies encourage returners and provide refresher training.

There are ample opportunities for flexible working up to supervisor level, and increasingly also at management levels. With lengthening shopping hours, several managers share store management anyway, so it is quite possible to organize part time and job-sharing at management levels. Head office jobs, including buying and merchandising, can also be done at 'less than full time'.

Further information Distributive Industries Training Advisory Council (DITAC), Middleton House, 2 Main Road, Middleton, Cheney, Banbury OX17 2TN.
   www.di-net.co.uk
British Institute of Retailing, 57 Grosvenor Street, London W1X 9DA.
   www.pathfinder-one.com
Individual retailing concerns

Related careers HOTEL AND CATERING – MANAGEMENT – LOGISTICS ... MANAGEMENT – PERSONNEL/HUMAN RESOURCES MANAGEMENT

Science

Scientist

Main functions or activities: Research and development; analysis and investigation; production; technical sales and service; technical writing.

Main branches: Physics; chemistry; biological sciences; environmental sciences and conservation; cybernetics; mathematical sciences; materials science; biomedical science.

Entry qualifications Scientists and technologists normally need a degree, but the borderline between scientist, technologist and senior technician – BTEC/SQA Higher award holder (see pp. 8, 10) – is often blurred; many of the last have degrees.

Precise degree course requirements vary from one course to another. In general:

For *physics, cybernetics and applied sciences* degrees, A levels must include physics and mathematics.

For *some mathematics* degrees, A levels must include pure and applied maths.

For *chemistry* degrees, chemistry and physics and/or mathematics A levels are preferred, but other combinations may be acceptable.

For *biological sciences*, biology, a physical science – preferably chemistry – and mathematics are ideal; other combinations may be acceptable.

For *some* science degrees biology may only be accepted as a third A level: if only 2 A levels are offered they must both be in sciences more relevant to the degree subject.

The vocational A level in science (or, for some biological degrees, health and social care) is another route into higher education; students should always check its acceptability with individual institutions and departments.

For *BTEC/SQA Higher National Diploma/Certificate*: 1 or 2 A levels or equivalent, BTEC National award, Scottish Group Award.

The work All jobs are based directly or indirectly on scientific or technological developments. More to the point, all jobs are likely to be affected by today's or tomorrow's scientific developments or their exploitation. 'Scientific literacy' – an understanding of what science is about and how it affects virtually every aspect of industrial society – is an advantage in most jobs, and is essential in many, however remote from schoolroom science.

A science qualification is, of course, often a vocational qualification, but it need not be by any means. The image of the white-coated, lab-based scientist as the only, or even the main kind of, science professional, is quite out of date.

Science practitioners

Scientists can choose: they can become 'science practitioners' or 'practical scientists' and use their scientific training and education in all kinds of science jobs. In research, they can push out the frontiers of knowledge even further – in space and astronomical investigations; interaction of energy and matter in lasers; optical fibres; bioengineering, etc., there is a vast variety of research areas. Then there is work for scientists who want to solve problems thrown up by scientific developments: excessive use of energy requires alternative sources; chemical industries have led to pollution of the environment. Biotechnologists, chemists and other specialists investigate and try to alleviate undesirable but inevitable side-effects of innovation. And then there is, of course, the vast, mainly physics-based, information technology industry and its spin-offs, to give just a few examples.

The nature of practising scientists' work ranges from laboratory-centred 'boffin' research to people-centred activities like technical selling (see p. 526) or people-and-technology-centred work in manufacturing (see p. 526) or profit-centred work in marketing and other commercial functions. (See below for details of the various 'functions', and of the main science specialisms or 'branches'.)

The outlook for scientists varies considerably from one branch to another and may change from one year to the next. Physicists are In greatest demand (mainly in the electronics industry, see p. 217), but mathematicians, cyberneticians and some applied scientists (e.g. materials and polymer specialists) are also in demand, followed by chemists, biochemists and microbiologists. Botanists, zoologists and environmental science graduates have been least in demand. However, scientists can often switch to another, related field (this may involve a post-graduate course).

Prospects in the various types of work or *functions* vary mainly according to economic climate. In research and development, cutbacks tend to bite much earlier than in manufacturing and analysis and investigation. Technical writing and technical sales are expanding functions. However, scientists only specialize in a function *after* graduation. (But some degree subjects are more likely to lead to one function, some to another: for example *applied* scientists are much more likely to be in demand in manufacturing than, for example, botanists, and a broad-based integrated course is not likely to lead to research.)

Scientists often start in laboratory work (*research and development, analysis, investigation*) and then move into *manufacturing, technical sales and service,* or *writing*; or they may use their science background in *marketing* (see p. 371); in *information work* (p. 295) or in *patent agency* (p. 440) or *operational research* (p. 368). *Teachers* of mathematics and most sciences are much in demand in schools (but higher education teaching prospects are bleak).

Career prospects are generally much better for graduates who have at least a reading knowledge of a foreign language (at the moment especially German or Russian). Anyone who wants to work in EU countries must be fluent in the relevant language and/or have specific experience. Short-term contracts are possible in developing countries.

Science as a tool

Scientists can equally choose not to practise as scientists, but to use their understanding of science as a tool with which to do other kinds of jobs – in commerce, industry, the public sector – more effectively. People who have scientific curiosity but are not sure whether they want to be scientists, can choose a science qualification confident in the knowledge that their scientific background will be a door-opener into a variety of jobs in many different settings. For example, a scientist who goes into stockbroking or merchant banking is likely to become skilled at market forecasting and better able to assess a new high-technology company's chances of success, or the advantages or disadvantages of a merger between two science-based companies, than someone without a scientific background who has to go by hunch, or someone else's advice. A senior Civil Servant is better at advising ministers on, for example, the implications of rapidly changing technology when discussing the future of, say, transport, or the health service, or defence expenditure, than someone without a scientific background. In publishing, to choose a very different example, a scientist will be at an advantage over a non-scientist when judging the possibilities of electronic publishing. There are dozens of similar examples.

In industrial and commercial management (see p. 351) and in marketing (see p. 371), science graduates are welcome. Over 50% of all employers' vacancies for graduates are open to graduates from any discipline: the employers buy graduates' 'trained minds' rather than their specific knowledge. Increasingly, when recruiting any-discipline graduates, employers tend to prefer science or technology to arts graduates *provided* they have the other skills they are looking for. The former's scientific literacy is useful at a time when science and technology impinge on so many aspects of every organization. Scientists' analytical approach to problem-solving is invariably useful even when the problem is not a scientific one. Scientists with communication skills are above all badly needed to close the communication gap: to explain basic relevant scientific facts, trends and implications to their scientifically illiterate colleagues (many of them in very high places). Information work (see p. 295) has good openings for scientists. Finally, for people who want to set up in business on their own (see WORKING FOR ONESELF, p. 648), a science background is extremely useful (though it will have to be complemented with business know-how).

Practising scientists' work can be divided in two ways: by the types of activities or 'functions' and by the various 'branches' or science-specializations:

THE MAIN FUNCTIONS
Research and Development

Research is the lifeblood of science, enlarging existing knowledge and stimulating the growth of new branches. *Development* translates research findings into new – or improved – products and processes. The two overlap.

The terms 'pure' and 'applied' are often used to describe the type of research undertaken. In this context 'pure' research means increasing knowledge for its own sake and 'applied' research is 'goal-orientated' – directed towards solving technical problems, improving national defence or prestige – or 'wealth creating'. Science research is very expensive to carry out, much of it is sponsored, by industry or government, and is goal-orientated. Some university departments may fund 'pure' research from their resources or through research studentships which lead to higher research degrees (MPhil. or PhD).

Most research is teamwork, with several scientists, often from several disciplines, and technicians, working under a team-leader. The work may be divided into projects; several scientists are then responsible for their own project within the overall framework.

Personal attributes Above-average intelligence; enthusiasm; willingness to work patiently for long hours (or even months) and persevere with tricky problems; creativity; ability to work in a team and to take decisions and stand up for them if things go wrong; ability to communicate findings effectively; great powers of concentration; stubborn persistence in the face of disappointing research results.

Industrial researchers must be willing to change direction – at however interesting a point in their research – in the interests of the company's profitability.

Analysis and Investigation

Routine tests and investigations are carried out in all fields of science. In chemical research, for example, analysis of intermediate compounds enables scientists to keep track of chemical changes that are taking place. In manufacturing industry, the composition of both raw materials and products is monitored by analysing samples in *quality control* laboratories. In the food industry, regular checks are made on biological and chemical purity of foodstuffs. In pharmaceuticals the safety of drugs, beauty preparations and food additives is investigated. Before such products can be marketed, substances are tried out on experimental animals or by tissue culture to see whether there are any toxic side-effects. In the agrochemical industry, new fertilizers and pesticides are given field trials; the chemicals are used on experimental plots in various parts of the country – and sometimes overseas – so that scientists can determine how performance is affected by different soils and climates.

Many analytical techniques are automated; most routine testing is carried out by technicians (see p. 540). The professional scientist trains and supervises technicians, initiates, organizes and oversees projects and researches into new experimental methods.

Personal attributes Interest in applied science; methodical approach; patience; ability to organize other people and their work; ability to communicate effectively with highly specialized colleagues and with trainee technicians; observation to recognize the unexpected.

Manufacturing Production
(see also ENGINEERING, pp. 220, 227)

The central activity in industry is organizing production. That involves supervising the people who operate the industrial plant. Production managers (titles vary) are a vital link in the chain of command from chargehand to production director, and between production and other departments. Their main function is to see that production runs smoothly and is as efficient as possible. That means they must keep up with technological developments and arrange for and supervise the installation of new equipment as necessary. Hours can be long and irregular, and may include some shift-work – but this is by no means so in all plants. Production managers usually have a small office, but they spend little time in it. The work involves daily contact with other professionals and managers from other departments as well as with supervisors, etc.

Production professionals are equally concerned with managing people and with the exploitation of new technologies. The largest opportunities are for chemists. Production managers, or whatever the title of persons in charge, are normally graduates; technicians work under them. Production specialists can switch from one type of plant to another; and they can later go into *marketing* or *general management*.

Personal attributes Willingness to accept responsibility and take decisions; ability to keep calm in a crisis; leadership skills to motivate and organize plant operatives; practicality; ability to get on well with people at all levels in the industrial hierarchy; interest in the commercial application of science.

Technical Sales and Service

Two closely related activities: selling a science-based product and providing a technical back-up service for the customer. The product might be a sophisticated scientific instrument, an industrial chemical, a drug or a pesticide. The customer could be a research scientist, an industrial manager of a tiny or a large concern, a pharmacist or a farmer, i.e. a person with a lot of or no scientific knowledge. The technical sales executive or 'rep' needs a thorough knowledge of the product, its uses and limitations. The kind of technical service a company provides depends on the nature of its products. A technical service scientist representing a plastics manufacturer deals mainly with customers who mould plastics into containers and would investigate complaints and answer technical queries (and perhaps suggest new ways of using the material). It is part of the job to act as a link between the research laboratories and the sales staff.

Representatives for pharmaceutical firms visit doctors and pharmacists and inform them about new drugs and also provide feedback to the company on doctors' opinions of its products. In agricultural service industries reps may sell fertilizers, pesticides and animal health products to farmers and give advice about how they should be used (see AGRICULTURE AND HORTICULTURE, p. 63). Reps are usually given a 'territory'; its size depends on what they sell and whether it is a country area or town: some reps may be away from home all week; others come home every night. Many work from home and only go to the office occasionally.

Personal attributes Outgoing personality; liking for meeting a succession of people; a thick skin for the occasional rude customer; sensitivity to gauge the right approach (long-winded, brief, aloof, friendly, etc.); ability to communicate facts effectively to customers who may be much more, and may be much less, knowledgeable than the reps themselves; self-sufficiency for possibly long hours of lone travelling.

Technical Writing

A technical writer assembles a package of scientific or technical information for a particular readership. The work is often done on a contract basis; specialist firms hire out technical writers to client companies for the duration of a particular writing project. This may concern, for example, a set of handbooks and instruction manuals to accompany a complex piece of electronic equipment which is being marketed by an electronics manufacturer. Two 'packages' may have to be written: one in simple language for operatives or chargehands who have only to know how to operate the equipment; and another package aimed at technical managers who want to know more technical details and may need to be able to repair or adjust the equipment. In the pharmaceutical industry, writers prepare 'case histories' of new drugs (experiments done, etc.) for submission to the Committee on Safety of Medicines.

Technical copywriters (see ADVERTISING, p. 55) may write promotional material for science-based products. This is an expanding field, particularly in electronics, engineering generally and pharmaceuticals.

Personal attributes Wide scientific/technological interests and knowledge; an inquiring mind; ability to search out information and sift the relevant – for the particular purpose – from the irrelevant; ability to explain complex matters lucidly and concisely; a scientific grasshopper mind, to switch from one type of subject to another; liking for desk-work.

THE MAIN BRANCHES OF SCIENCE

The classification of science into content areas is constantly changing. Most people are familiar with physics, chemistry and biology but as scientific investigation gets more complex, or is applied for different purposes, so different classifications may arise: a 'subset' of one of the main disciplines may be identified for more detailed study (e.g. astronomy – the study of extra-terrestrial systems – or virology – the study of viruses). An overlapping area of two main disciplines may emerge as worth studying in its own right (e.g. biophysics, biochemistry) or an interdisciplinary area may be identified, usually problem-orientated (practical rather than academic) and develop its own concepts and methods of study (e.g. cybernetics, environmental sciences, materials science, biotechnology).

Physics

Physics – the study of matter and energy – lies at the heart of science. It is closely related to mathematics and also quite closely to chemistry; *chemical physics* – the study of materials and molecules – is a subject in its own right. *Biophysics* – the physical properties of living matter – has assumed greater importance as biological knowledge has grown. Many aspects of *engineering* and *materials science* are 'applied' aspects of physics. So the physicist, who always has a sound mathematical background, has a wide choice of occupations and settings in which to work.

Most industrial openings occur in engineering and related industries – especially in electronics, telecommunications, computing and transport; other opportunities exist in chemical and energy industries, e.g. oil, gas, electricity. In the Civil Service physicists work on problems ranging from research into navigation to recycling industrial waste. (See also 'Medical or Biomedical Engineering', p. 219.)

The work of medical physicists is increasingly important to medicine. They form part of a team of specialists concerned with the diagnosis and treatment of disease, using radiotherapy and diagnostic radiology, radioisotopes, ultrasonics and many other physical methods to help doctors cure patients. In *occupational hygiene*, physicists help prevent damage to people's health by monitoring potential hazards from radiation, noise, dust and other sources in working environments. (See also 'Environmental Sciences and Geoscience', especially *geophysics* and *meteorology*, below.) There are very limited opportunities for physicists (who may or may not have taken a degree in astronomy or astrophysics) and for mathematicians to branch out into *astronomy*. Research into such aspects of astronomy as satellite communications systems or the structure of the universe is done at government, university, and some commercial telecommunications (i.e. electronics) research laboratories. In *computer* design and manufacture, physicists play an important part.

Chemistry

Chemistry – the study of the composition of materials, their properties and how they change and react with other materials – occupies a central position in the sciences. It forms the basis of, for example, the manufacture of metals, pharmaceuticals, fertilizers, paints, synthetic fabrics, dyestuffs, plastics, paper, cosmetics, herbicides, pesticides, foodstuffs and many other products.

It has links with all the other sciences, such as physics, biology and geology and contributes to 'applied' science areas such as *food science*, *forensic science*, *materials science*, *pharmacology* and *pharmacy*, and *textile technology*. So someone with an interest in chemistry has a wide choice of employment. The big chemical manufacturers, oil, drug and cosmetic companies are the biggest employers of chemists. In the Civil Service, chemists work on road-surfaces, building materials, nutrition, pollution, and other research; others are employed as forensic scientists (see p. 166); in the general Civil Service they are welcome as Fast Stream candidates (see p. 160), using their expertise in an advisory capacity and as background knowledge. Others work in the public health field, e.g. analysing drinking water, food and drugs, and in hospital laboratories. A few chemists work on restoration and research in museums. (See also 'Biochemistry, microbiology and biotechnology', below.)

Biological Sciences

Biology can be subdivided into 4 major disciplines – the study of: plants (*botany*); animals (*zoology*); micro-organisms (*microbiology*); chemistry of living matter (*biochemistry*). However, as the interdependence of plants and animals is increasingly recognized, more emphasis is being placed on biology as an integration of botany and zoology, e.g. *ecology*. More specialized biological sciences deal with particular groups of living organisms – viruses (*virology*) and insects (*entomology*) for instance – and with particular biological processes such as the functioning of the body's organs (*physiology*) or the mechanisms of heredity and variation (*genetics*).

Botany and zoology

Most opportunities used to occur in the public sector – mainly in the Civil Service, agricultural (e.g. animal and plant breeding) and medical research, and conservation, but many of these research bodies have been privatized. The Department for Environment, Food and Rural Affairs employs marine biologists to monitor fish stocks and pollution levels. A small number of biologists work in the health service, for water authorities and museums. In industry there are limited opportunities in pharmaceuticals and agrochemicals.

The most marketable aspects of botany and zoology are those related either to medical and pharmaceutical research (such as parasitology and physiology), or to agriculture and horticulture (such as plant pathology and entomology). Opportunities in *marine* and *freshwater biology* and *general ecology* are very limited. However, concern for the environment has meant an increase in jobs in industry for 'environmental' biologists.

Biochemistry, microbiology and biotechnology

Biochemists and microbiologists have much better career prospects than botanists or zoologists; there is a steady demand from industry (mainly food, drink, pharmaceuticals and agriculture), from medical research and hospital laboratories, specialist research organizations and, to a lesser extent, the Civil Service.

A *biochemist* working for a pharmaceutical company might study the mechanism of a new drug or (helped by a microbiologist) investigate biochemical aspects of the production of antibiotics by fermentation. *Hospital biochemists* work alongside medical colleagues and technicians as members of a team: they supervise routine biochemical testing (see 'Biomedical Science', p. 537), do research into, for example, the function of hormones or the body's defence mechanisms, and may also teach clinical biochemistry to doctors and nurses. Some use biochemical analysis in clinical diagnosis or in forensic laboratories (e.g. for genetic fingerprinting).

Microbiologists often specialize in bacteriology and virology and become experts in plant or animal diseases. In the food industry and in environmental health laboratories they check samples for pathogenic microbes and investigate spoilage. In oil companies they explore ways of producing synthetic protein by feeding bacteria with the by-products of petroleum refining.

Biotechnology is fairly new as an academic discipline but covers processes which use multidisciplinary approaches to problem-solving in science-based industries. It is, very broadly, the use of living organisms to perform a useful task. The main uses are in manufacturing industry – particularly brewing and the food, fertilizer, animal feedstuffs and pharmaceutical industries – medicine, agriculture and horticulture. It has also been described as 'factory farming of bugs' or microbes – the smallest living organisms – which are then put to industrial uses.

Biotechnologists work in a vast variety of science-based jobs, for example on the development of synthetic proteins; of new strains of wheat; of hormones and drugs. They also work on pollution control (e.g. with biodegradable waste products), and on the generation of new sources of energy from such varied natural materials as plant tissue and animal waste products. The usual way into biotechnology is via a science degree – preferably chemistry, biochemistry or microbiology – followed by post-graduate study, or a biotechnology degree. Genetic engineering – the manipulation, using scientific techniques, of genes – is one aspect of biotechnology. It is increasingly used to produce varieties of crops which are especially resistant to disease or tolerant of poor weather. *Molecular biology* – the understanding of how genetic information is stored and passed on – has opened up vast new areas of research.

Environmental Sciences and Geoscience

The environmental sciences are fashionable. Concern with pollution, dwindling natural resources and threatened plant and animal species has given a fresh impetus to the scientific study of the environment. *Conservation* and *ecology* (the study of how plants and animals interact with their natural surroundings), together with *meteorology*, *oceanography*, *geology* and *geophysics*, are important environmental subjects.

Environmental science is often a *post-graduate* specialization:

scientists take a first degree in a traditional subject and then either graft on an appropriate post-graduate course or get trained by employers in environmental aspects of their subject. *Meteorologists* and *physical oceanographers* usually have degrees in physics or maths; biologists normally take a specialist course (for example, in ecology or marine biology) before becoming conservationists. *Geoscience* graduates are the exception: they can go straight into professional work without further training. But there is an increasing number of first degree courses in environmental subjects – either joint honours (such as physics and meteorology) or broad-based integrated courses in environmental sciences. The most useful of these are probably those offering a placement year in which students get 'hands-on' experience. Even graduates with an environmental science degree often need to take a more specialized post-graduate course and/or gain voluntary work experience before applying for paid jobs.

Conservation

Nature conservation used only to mean protecting unusual plants and animals and their habitats. Now, many human activities have a wider environmental impact. Crop protection chemicals, for example, can upset the balance of ecological systems. If herbicides are used to control aquatic weeds, dead plants consume oxygen while decaying. As a result, fish and other organisms may die through lack of oxygen. A pipeline or bypass laid across country may disturb plant and animal life around it; a quarry may leave a permanent scar on the countryside. Modern conservationists, recognizing the importance of protecting flora and fauna, are concerned with the wider problems of preserving the countryside as a whole.

Conservancy bodies for England, Scotland and Wales between them manage over 100 National Nature Reserves and several thousand Sites of Special Scientific Interest, and advise farmers, landowners, local authorities, industrialists and others on conservation matters. Scientists (mainly biologists, botanists, zoologists, geologists and geographers) are employed as Assistant Regional Officers. The Nature Reserves are run by Wardens (not always graduates) who are experienced conservationists. Environmental research covering land, ocean and fresh water is carried out by the many institutes which come under the aegis of the Natural Environment Research Council (NERC).

Geoscience

Geoscience covers all branches of science concerned with the structure, evolution and dynamics of the earth and with the natural mineral and energy resources that it contains. It comprises *geology, geophysics and geochemistry*. Geoscience investigates the real world beyond the laboratory and is directly relevant to the needs of society. Its study develops a wide range of skills useful in a wide range of careers, with opportunities in the UK and abroad.

Activities carried out by geoscientists include geological mapping, geophysical prospecting, geochemical sampling, borehole logging, chemical analysis of rocks and minerals, rock testing of geotechnical properties, computer processing of data, computer modelling of geological processes and of subsurface geology.

Careers tend to fall into one of the following fields:

Exploration and production: the search for natural resources such as fossil fuels, metals, construction materials and ground-water, and the geological management of their extraction.

Engineering and environmental: the investigation and monitoring of local ground conditions associated with construction, planning, land use and environmental issues.

Geological survey: the systematic collection of surface and subsurface geological information, both onshore and offshore, for the production of geological, geophysical and geochemical maps and databases.

Education and research/conservation: teaching and research posts in universities; school and college teaching; museum posts; scientific posts with nature conservancy bodies.

Meteorology and oceanography (see also METEOROLOGY, p. 390)
Meteorology and oceanography – concerned with the atmosphere and the oceans – are closely related. The physics and dynamics of atmospheric and oceanographic processes have much in common; the oceans exert a powerful influence on the weather. At honours degree level, *meteorology* and *physical oceanography* are highly math-

ematical; numerical methods are widely used in modern weather forecasting.

The Met Office also carries out research into such topics as the physics of cloud formation and energy exchange between atmosphere and oceans. Scientists are usually involved either in *forecasting* or in *research*.

Research in physical oceanography is undertaken at Southampton Oceanographic Centre (part of the Natural Environment Research Council). Topics include studies of waves, tides, currents and general circulation of ocean water. NERC also investigates the ecology of deep-water organisms, the composition of the sea-floor, *marine biology* subjects. Oceanographic work is done partly in the laboratory and partly at sea.

Mathematical Sciences

Mathematicians – pure and applied – are much in demand. They work in commerce, e.g. in finance and in actuarial work (see ACTU-ARY, p. 52), in science-based activities and in computing (see p. 281). They frequently work in teams with scientists and engineers. They may analyse data produced by scientists; they may work on translating problems into mathematical terms (making 'models'), work out solutions and then express the results in non-mathematical form. They make calculations which enable *control engineers* (see p. 218) to make adjustments to the manufacturing process. Sometimes the mathematical models are so complex that a special technique called *numerical analysis* is used to solve them. Some mathematicians specialize in numerical analysis; others become expert in *operational research* (see p. 368).

Statisticians – including mathematicians who have specialized in statistics – work in industry, medical, social and agricultural research, and in the Civil Service (Office for National Statistics and all the departments with a statistics division). They are concerned with the design of experiments, questionnaires and surveys and with the collection, analysis and interpretation of results. In a government department they provide information on which policies can be based;

for example they predict the effect of changes in the tax system or the likely demand for energy. Wherever computers are used – and that is in virtually every field of activity, see INFORMATION TECHNOLOGY (IT)/INFORMATION SYSTEMS (p. 281) – statisticians process and interpret data and help design and improve systems. There is also scope for statisticians in marketing and market research where they design surveys to establish demand for goods and services. The majority of statisticians need a scientific background; some need social science expertise (it is easier to switch with a science background to statistics in social sciences than to switch with a social science background to statistics in science).

Materials Science

Materials science is an umbrella term for sciences concerned with a variety of metallic and non-metallic materials (including *polymers*, *papers*, *ceramics*, *glass* and *textiles*). *Metallurgists* work on the extraction, refining and fabrication of ferrous and non-ferrous metals used in products ranging from aircraft bodies to electronic components. *Textile* technologists work with domestic materials, such as clothing and furnishing fabrics, and with industrial products used for a wide variety of purposes, e.g. insulation, road reinforcement and even the manufacture of artificial veins. *Polymer* scientists and technologists work on all kinds of plastics and other polymeric materials used in products ranging from picnic plates and computer keyboards to gas pipes and gear components.

It is possible to specialize early on in metallurgy, polymers, textiles or one of the other non-metallic materials, but most entrants to these industries have followed a broader course in materials science. There are good opportunities for materials scientists to use their interdisciplinary approach in these industries, as well as in the newer ones concerned with composite materials: polymers reinforced with glass or carbon fibre, for example, and others still in the experimental stage. Physics, chemistry and engineering graduates are also recruited.

Biomedical Science

Most biomedical scientists work in the NHS, where they are known as Medical Laboratory Scientific Officers (MLSOs). They are concerned with laboratory investigations for diagnosis and treatment of disease, and research into its causes and cure. Trainees work under the overall direction of senior staff who have specialized in the application of their particular discipline to medicine. Work is done in hospitals, universities, blood transfusion centres, public health laboratories, veterinary establishments and pharmaceutical firms. In hospitals there may be some contact with patients, depending on the specialization. Scientists may supervise medical laboratory assistants.

The main specializations are: *clinical chemistry*: the analysis of blood and other biological materials; *medical microbiology*: the isolation and identification of bacteria and viruses from patients with infections, or in water and foodstuffs; *haematology and serology*: the study of blood; *histopathology and cytology*: the study of tissues removed during surgical operations and at post-mortem examinations, and in investigations for the early detection of cancer.

Training (all sciences) Normally a degree. Science courses usually consist either of a detailed study of a single subject, with supporting ancillary subjects, or of a study of 2 distinct disciplines in a joint honours course, or of a cluster of several related disciplines, such as biological sciences. The question of whether a broad-based or a specialized degree leads to better prospects is impossible to answer in a general way: it depends on an individual's adaptability, motivation, specialization, on changing economic circumstances and on technological developments. There is a continuing need for specialists, but a 'generalist' scientific education possibly leads to a wider choice of jobs especially for 'non-practising' scientists; its built-in flexibility enables the scientist to change direction if, for example, that should be desirable or necessary after a career break, or because supply and demand in a specialization have changed.

For *research* a first or upper second honours degree is usually required but research assistants who work part time for a PhD are occasionally taken on with a 2.2. A first degree may have to be followed by a career-orientated post-graduate course. First-degree course emphasis varies greatly. Some courses are very much more practical and vocational in approach and structure than others, and prospective students need to do careful research before applying.

Many degrees are 4-year sandwich courses, with a year spent at work. This may be an advantage to people who want to go into industry: their experience of the work situation during their training reassures employers that the applicant at least knows what a working environment is like.

There is an increasing number of full-time undergraduate courses which are extended to 4 years and lead to a Masters degree, for example MSc, MChem, MPhys. Anyone intending to do research would be advised to choose one of these.

BTEC/SQA Higher awards (see pp. 8, 10) or Dip. HEs normally lead to senior technicians', not to professional scientists' jobs, but the distinction between scientist and technician is often blurred. Technologists may have an applied science degree or BTEC/SQA Higher award. Foundation degrees in science-related subjects are gradually being introduced, often linked to a specific area of work.

Once in a job, training, or at least learning, continues. This may or may not lead to a further qualification.

Biomedical scientists

MLSOs are state registered, and for this a degree approved by the Health Professionals Council is necessary (a list of approved courses is available on the website of the Institute of Biomedical Science – *www.ibms.org*). Before they can register, graduates undertake 1–2 years as a biomedical trainee, assessed by log book and oral examination. Those with degrees in related sciences can study for an IBMS accredited top-up certificate or diploma on day-release while training – training usually takes about 2 years.

For senior MLSO posts it is normally necessary to become a Fellow of the Institute through examination, higher degree or thesis.

Late start Degree course requirements in terms of GCSEs and A levels may be relaxed, but candidates' knowledge of maths and science has to be up to date; many late entrants first take evening classes or other preparatory courses to freshen up their school sciences, etc. Opportunities limited.

Work life balance Opportunities for flexible working and career breaks are more hopeful for those employed in the public sector as both the Civil Service and the NHS are encouraging all departmental managers to support applications for flexible working. The NHS in particular encourages returners, often providing *refresher* courses. A list of Workforce Development Confederations who can assist those wishing to return to a health care science profession is available on the NHS careers website: *www.nhscareers.nhs.uk*. For those in the private sector, it will depend very much on company policy and individual circumstances.

Further information Biochemical Society, 59 Portland Place, London W1B 1QW.
www.biochemistry.org
Royal Society of Chemistry, Burlington House, Piccadilly, London W1J 0BA.
www.rsc.org
Institute of Biology, 20–22 Queensberry Place, London SW7 2DZ.
www.iob.org
Institute of Mathematics and its Applications, 16 Nelson Street, South-end-on-Sea, Essex SS1 1EF.
www.ima.org.uk
Institute of Materials, Minerals and Mining, 1 Carlton House Terrace, London SW1Y 5DB.
www.materials.org.uk
Institute of Biomedical Science, 12 Coldbath Square, London EC1R 5HL.
www.ibms.org
Royal Statistical Society, 12 Errol Street, London EC1Y 8LX.
www.rss.org.uk

Science

Institute of Physics, 76 Portland Place, London W1B 1NT.
www.iop.org

Geological Society, Burlington House, Piccadilly, London W1J 0BG.
www.goolsoc.org.uk

Civil Service Careers, Units 2–4, Lescren Way, Avonmouth, Bristol
BS11 8DG.
www.civil-service.gov.uk

English Nature, Northminster House, Northminster, Peterborough,
PE1 1UA.
www.english-nature.org.uk

Scottish Natural Heritage, 12 Hope Terrace, Edinburgh EH9 2AS.
www.snh.org.uk

Countryside Council for Wales, Maes-y-Ffyrnon, Penrhosgarnedd,
Bangor, Gwynedd LL57 2DN.
www.ccw.gov.uk

Natural Environment Research Council, Polaris House, North Star
Avenue, Swindon, Wilts. SN2 1EU.
www.nerc.ac.uk

Edexcel and SQA (see pp. 8, 10).

Science Technician

Entry qualifications Nothing rigid. They vary according to the job's
and to colleges' requirements, from a few lower grade GCSEs with at
least 1 science to 2 science A levels or even a degree. For BTEC/SQA
awards, see pp. 8, 10.

The work *Laboratory technician, assistant, technical assistant, research
assistant, scientific assistant, technical officer, assistant scientific officer*
are all titles used to describe people who perform science-related
procedures and techniques under the overall supervision of scientists.
As scientific investigations become more complex technicians become more important and the variety of jobs is growing. They are
essential team-members, not unskilled bottle-washers: they need to
be able to use new technologies and analytical methods, rather than
rely on practical skills. Their tasks range from mundane routine

to work which overlaps very much with that of professional scientists.

They may work in any of the functions and branches described under 'Scientist' (see above).

Training – general (see also under different branches) Science technicians usually train on the job. NVQ/SVQs in laboratory skills are available at levels 2, 3 & 4 and can be worked towards as part of a Modern Apprenticeship. Some technicians work towards a BTEC National or Higher National Diploma or Certificate or a degree.

There are not a great many Foundation Degrees for science technicians yet but it seems likely they may become a primary qualifying route in the future.

In Scotland students take appropriate units leading to a Scottish Group Award (see p. 7).

There are 4 main settings: hospitals, industry, education, Civil Service.

Hospitals

Scientific technical staff

There is a wide variety of technician jobs in hospitals. Some are physics-based, others require a good knowledge of biology and chemistry. Some consist almost entirely of laboratory work, others involve occasional or regular patient-contact. Most scientific technical staff working within the National Health Service are called Medical Technical Officers. Staff working in the MTO group include clinical/medical technologists, physiological scientists, perfusionists, operating department practitioners, medical illustrators/medical photographers, pharmacy technicians and anatomical pathology technicians.

Clinical/medical technologists: Broadly deal with 'imaging' equipment – X-ray machines; scanners; ultrasound; isotopes and similar matters, and with medical electronics generally. They may administer tests, i.e. have some patient contact; or they may be wholly or largely concerned with the checking, recalibrating, maintenance, development and modification of equipment from lasers to renal dialysis machines – i.e. no or very little patient contact. The very expensive and advanced imaging equipment is available only in teaching and large district hospitals, hence few medical physics jobs. In some hospitals radiographers have taken over the radioisotopes part of the technicians' work and the maintenance side may be carried out by staff from the works department (see ENGINEERING, p. 216).

Physiological scientists: Administer a variety of diagnostic tests (i.e. it is work with constant patient-contact) and it is normal to specialize in one type of work. *Audiology* technicians test the hearing and balance of adults and children, using special instruments, and select, fit and adjust hearing aids; *neuro-physiological* technicians are concerned mainly with using EEG (electroencephalography) to record the electrical activity of a patient's brain. *Cardiology* technicians measure heart function and electrical activity using cardiograms (ECGs) and monitor pacemakers. *Respiratory* technicians administer tests on lung function to help in diagnosis and treatment of lung disease. *Gastroenterology* technicians use various instruments containing highly technical, mechanical and electronic devices to measure pressure and acidity in the alimentary canal (the passage responsible for the digestion of food).

Perfusionists work in cardiac departments, using an artificial circulatory system to reroute the blood around a particular organ in order to isolate it (necessary for bypass operations). *Operating department practitioners* are MTOs specializing in surgery. They are an important part of the operating department team, working with surgeons, anaesthetists and theatre nurses to help ensure every operation is as safe and effective as possible. The ODP's role involves the application of theory to practice in a variety of clinical settings. They are involved with the assessment, delivery and evaluation of the anaesthetic, surgical and recovery phases of surgery.

Anatomical pathology technicians assist pathologists in examining bodies to establish cause of death and deal with members of the public who come to the mortuary.

Medical illustrators/medical photographers provide essential professional and cost-effective photographic and graphic services for use in patient-care, medical education and research. They are responsible for providing photographic and other visual records of patients and pathological materials (see PHOTOGRAPHY p. 454).

Pharmacy technicians prepare and deliver drugs, store incoming drugs and make up sterile preparations.

Training Some students may be recruited into a particular department and undertake training on a part-time basis while working. The type and length of training will vary depending upon the role. Although in theory trainee technicians require only the entry qualifications for BTEC/SQA courses, in practice they often need 2–3 A levels or a BTEC/SQA Higher National award to get a hospital job. Increasingly, many MTO roles are becoming higher diploma or graduate entry and it is often possible to enter after a full-time course at a higher education institution (HEI). Examples of these include higher diplomas in operating department practice and degrees in audiology.

There are some jobs for assistant technical officers (ATOs), who help MTOs and can apply to join appropriate training schemes after gaining experience.

Industry

Very varied work most of which falls into two broad categories: *quality control*, and *research and development*.

In *quality control* ('QC'), during the production of chemicals, detergents, plastics, cosmetics and other manufactured goods and in the food processing industry, technicians test, for example, the purity and/or nutritional value of foodstuffs. In the pharmaceutical industry they help with tests on drugs and medicines. In electronics, technicians may test computer circuitry or the quality of television and radio components (their work overlaps with that of engineering technicians, see p. 231).

In *research and development* technicians assist scientists with all types of research (see p. 524). They may use new equipment and help modify it and they adapt standard procedures to suit particular experimental work.

Education Establishments

Technicians help researchers, teachers and lecturers. They work in science faculties, in research institutes and medical schools, secondary schools and colleges. They prepare work for lectures; and they help generally in the department. Technicians may prepare specimens for lectures in microbiology, histology, zoology, botany or geology, using for example techniques for culturing bacteria, or prepare thin sections of rocks or fossils for microscopical study, etc. In a chemistry faculty technicians are concerned with the assembly, care and maintenance of apparatus, and the preparation of bench reagents used for demonstration and experiment. They may, in research, use such techniques as flame photometry, spectrophotometry, chromatography, or use radioisotopes.

The job of the school or college lab technician used to be rather menial, but conditions and prospects have now improved considerably. The work combines science with dealing with children and young people; it covers preparing, setting out and maintaining demonstration materials and apparatus as well as helping students and pupils in the classroom. In smaller establishments there may only be one technician; in one day the technician could then help in and prepare for classes in physics, chemistry and biology. In large establishments several technicians work under the direction of a chief technician, and there are opportunities for progress, with training, to a more senior post, and to specialize in either biology, chemistry or physics.

Civil Service
(see CIVIL SERVICE, p. 158)

Technicians in the Civil Service work as part of a team led by a scientist engaged in research in any of the scientific disciplines.

In laboratories scientists carry out fundamental research, investigate new techniques and equipment, ensure that standards of safety are maintained. Technicians provide support to research and project teams. Their work includes making observations of experiments, logging data, summarizing results for interpretation. For example, they may measure jet-pipe temperatures of a helicopter engine; determine the nitrogen content of animal fodder; test for drugs for police investigations; make weather observations at an airport.

Openings vary according to changing situations, geographic area, area of specialization, level of qualification. Best prospects probably for well qualified physics-based technicians, e.g. in the information technology 'hardware' industries as well as elsewhere. For biology/chemistry-based technicians, fair prospects in pharmaceuticals, agricultural chemicals and similar industries and hospital medical research. People with low school-leaving qualifications but interested in the job should try and improve their qualifications if they cannot get student-technician jobs. On the whole there is a growing range of jobs which are loosely called 'science technician'.

Personal attributes generally Manipulative skill; patience; scrupulous attention to detail; a sense of responsibility; willingness to take orders; ability to work both independently and as one of a team.

Late start Not much scope in most branches, school-leavers tend to be given preference. But adults can take full-time BTEC/SQA science courses, and there is a reasonable number of late entrants to hospital technician work (see p. 541).

Work life balance As this is a rapidly changing area, only technicians who systematically keep up with developments can return after a break, but there are updating opportunities, partly through the Open University (see p. 16). The Department of Health is encouraging health authorities to offer retainer schemes to all their staff.

There are fair opportunities for part-time work and job-sharing at all levels, particularly in the public sector.

Further information on hospital technical staff NHS Careers (Tel: 0845 60 60 655; website *www.nhs.uk/careers*) or the relevant professional body for the career in which they are interested.

Institution of Physics and Engineering in Medicine, Fairmount House, 230 Tadcaster Road, York YO24 1ES.
www.ipem.org.uk

Society for Cardiological Science and Technology, 9 Fitzroy Square, London W1P 5AH.
www.scst.org.uk

British Society of Gastroenterology, 3 St Andrews Place, Regents Park, London NW1 4LB.
www.bsg.org.uk

Electrophysiological Technicians Association c/o EEG Department, Staffordshire General Hospital, Weston Road, Stafford ST16 3SA.

Society of Perfusionists of Great Britain and Ireland, Department of Clinical Perfusion, Derriford Hospital, Plymouth PL6 8HD.
www.sopgbi.org

Association for Respiratory Technology and Physiology, 202 Maney Hill Road, Sutton Coldfield B72 1JX.
www.artp.org.uk

Association of Anatomical Pathology Technologists UK, 12 Coldbath Square, London EC1R 5HL.
www.@aaptuk.org

Association of Operating Department Practitioners, Lewes Enterprise Centre, 112 Malling Street, Lewes, East Sussex BN7 2RJ.
www.aodp.org

Hon. Secretary, Institute of Medical Illustrators, Bank Chambers, 48 Onslow Gardens, London SW7 3AH.
www.imi.org.uk

Royal Pharmaceutical Society of Great Britain, 1 Lambeth High Street, London SE1 7JN.
www.rpsgb.org.uk

The Institute of Science Technology, Stowe House, Netherstowe, Lichfield, Staffs WS13 6TJ.
(This runs mainly work-based courses, including one for its own Higher Diploma.)
www.istonline.org.uk

Edexcel/BTEC (p. 8); City & Guilds (p. 10); SQA (p. 10)

Related careers ENGINEERING: *Engineering Technician* – MEDICINE – OPTICAL WORK – PHARMACY – PHYSIOTHERAPY – RADIOGRAPHY

Food Science and Technology

All educational levels, see 'Training'.

The work *Food science* is concerned with the chemical and biological nature of food and its behaviour under natural conditions, during processing and during storage. *Food technology* is the application of relevant sciences, including engineering, to the processing, preservation and development of raw materials and manufactured foods. Food scientists and technologists work in quality control, product development and production departments (see p. 526) of food manufacturers and retailers. They also work for equipment manufacturers, ingredient suppliers, public analysts, environmental health departments and the Civil Service. Some work in research and development on 'fast foods' and 'systems catering' (see HOTEL AND CATERING, p. 260), monitoring the behaviour of foods as new technologies are introduced. Some work together with *biotechnologists* (see p. 532). Some research jobs are for food *scientists*, production jobs tend to be held by *technologists*; but there is no clear-cut division between the two and both types of specialists are found in most job areas. There are jobs for technicians and for graduate scientists and technologists.

The industry is less affected than many by economic slumps. Its diversity provides opportunities to specialize. The broad-based training allows for flexibility. As in other industries, technologists now often move into top general management (see 'Line management', p. 355).

Training *Technician level*: with 4 GCSEs (A–C) including biology, chemistry, maths and English, or equivalent, BTEC award in food science or technology with various options. Courses can be part-time day-release (2 years), full time (2 years); or sandwich (3 years).

Modern Apprenticeships may be available for technicians or they may work towards a BTEC award in food science and technology or NVQs/SVQs at levels 1–4. For equivalent SQA awards, see p. 10.

Graduate level: with 2, or sometimes 3, science A levels which must include chemistry (precise requirements vary), degrees in various aspects of food science. Degrees vary in title, emphasis and content, so candidates need to study different syllabuses carefully. Some are more commercially orientated (combining food science and marketing for example); some are more science-based; others put more emphasis on relevant technologies; yet others on management.

While food science and technology degrees are strictly vocationally orientated, *science* and *engineering* graduates (see pp. 520 and 216) can also get into the food industries and then take post-graduate qualifications, either by part-time or full-time study. There are post-graduate courses in food science; food analysis and composition; food and management science; food microbiology; food engineering; biotechnology.

Personal attributes A meticulous approach to technical problems plus an interest in people as consumers and changing tastes and eating habits. For many jobs a real interest in food is desirable, as is the ability to work as part of a team. For *management careers*, ability to organize people and work, to work under pressure and to take decisions.

Late start The proportion of late entrants – 10–20% – is fairly high. Recent study of chemistry is an advantage.

Work life balance Provided people stay in touch through professional institutes a career break should be no problem. There are few opportunities for part-time working, but job-sharing of certain posts should be possible.

Further information Institute of Food Science and Technology, 5

Cambridge Court, 210 Shepherds Bush Road, London w6 7nj.
www.ifst.org

Related careers ENGINEERING: *Engineering Technician* – OPTICAL
WORK – PHARMACY – RADIOGRAPHY

Secretarial and Clerical Work

Entry qualifications Various educational levels: minimum usually 4 GCSEs (A–C), including English language; but see 'Training', below.

The work Office work consists largely of handling information – searching for, producing, passing on (verbally or in print) facts and figures, questions and answers, messages and instructions. 'Information technology' (IT), which broadly describes the equipment and systems used to process, transmit, file or otherwise handle information electronically, has changed the nature of office work. But fear of the unknown has tended to exaggerate IT's effect. The 'paperless office' has not taken over. The workforce is shrinking – especially at the lower, unskilled end where automation is drastically reducing the scope. But secretaries and people who produce and handle text are still needed even when managers have their own desk-top computers on which they can call up information and which they can use to communicate with each other, customers, clients, etc. IT also creates some new jobs.

The main jobs:

Secretary

Titles have no precise meaning: executive secretary, private secretary, personal assistant are used indiscriminately. Some of the most high-powered secretaries prefer to call themselves merely 'secretary'; some 'personal assistants' just do junior executives' typing and telephoning.

The confusion over titles arose because traditionally there was no promotion ladder and career-structure, and no precise definition of the secretary's work nor of the differences between *personal assistant*, *secretary*, *shorthand- or audio-typist*, or *word processor operator* and *clerk*. Differences between these jobs are considerable, but in employers' and employees' minds they are blurred, which leads to disappointment and frustration on both sides of the desk. However, with the wider choice of career opportunities for women, fewer able women are now willing to stay in jobs without prospects of advancement (and there are still *very* few male secretaries). Mainly for that reason some organizations are now introducing something resembling career-structures (see below). For example, the difference between 'personal assistant' and 'secretary' is now often being taken seriously. Secretaries follow their boss's instructions; when they fully understand the department's work, they become a 'personal assistant' and in that capacity make their own decisions. For example, a sales manager's secretary would, if a sales representative falls ill, ask the boss to whom the sick person's work should be allocated. A personal assistant would simply reallocate the work, without asking the boss.

Another development which is changing the secretarial scene is 'team secretaries' (in another office, they might be called 'administrative assistants'). They 'manage' a group of, say, several junior architects in an architectural partnership, or overseas marketing people in an export department. They organize appointments, travel schedules, etc. and keep track of the department's various projects and assignments. If the head of the department or partnership wants to know where X is, or how project Y is progressing, the team secretary knows the situation.

Both personal assistant and team secretary are in fact junior/middle management jobs but they are not necessarily recognized as such (see MANAGEMENT, p. 351).

The traditional secretary usually still works for one person or, increasingly, more than one. (This is of course the 'office' secretary, not the administrator in charge of an institution, learned society or similar organization (see CHARTERED SECRETARY AND ADMINIS- TRATOR, p. 139).) It is the secretary's task to husband the boss's time and energy so that he or she can concentrate on whatever the job is at that moment.

Secretaries act as buffer between the boss and callers and phone calls, and take minor decisions on her/his behalf. They must understand their boss's work well enough to know when to act on their own initiative and when to ask for instructions. This is one of the most challenging secretarial skills. Secretarial duties may also involve:

1. Acting as link between individuals and various sections in an organization; this could be departments in a university, company or store, or individuals in a management team, and may involve writing memos, ringing people up, going to see them.

2. Collecting information from a variety of printed and personal sources – this involves knowing where to go for whatever the information required, perhaps telephoning trade associations or government departments.

3. Preparing agendas for meetings and collecting documents supporting the various items, distributing the papers at the right time to the right people; taking minutes at meetings, editing them and writing them up.

4. Looking through the day's mail and deciding which letters the boss has to deal with personally and which ones to cope with independently; summarizing lengthy letters and documents; drafting replies to some letters and presenting them to the boss for approval and signature.

5. Making travel arrangements and arranging meetings, at home or abroad, for several busy people: this is a time-consuming task which requires meticulous attention to detail and may involve international calls until finally a time and place suitable to everyone has been agreed upon.

The amount of typing or word processing secretaries do varies. In large offices they may deal only with their boss's confidential correspondence, other matters being dealt with by a 'junior secretary' or someone from the typing-pool or word processing unit. Secretaries may be in charge of one or several juniors, or cope single-handedly.

The extent of automation still varies from one office to another, but it is increasing everywhere. The new technologies mean that secretaries and bosses both have access to numerous types of computerized equipment. As well as enabling bosses to do *their* job more effectively, secretaries are able to perform many administrative tasks more effectively than hitherto. They are also able to relieve their bosses of administrative tasks, and possibly take over part of the boss's main task. The availability of data processing equipment – and opportunities to use it – should, in theory, enable capable secretaries to take part in executives' decision-making tasks, e.g. financial forecasting and analysis and production progress charting; or assessing customer response. The *potential* for merging the two roles – that of the manager/executive and the secretary – now exists. How much, in practice, the secretary will be able to exploit the potential depends on the boss's willingness to let go of responsibilities, the secretary's initiative, and a host of imponderables.

Traditional secretarial tasks which are, increasingly, computerized, include arranging meetings; booking conference rooms; recording and instant dispatch of voice and text messages; maintenance of lists, e.g. personal addresses, business contacts (with background information), internal telephone directories; 'unstructured information', e.g. product descriptions; training records; filing and retrieval; travel arrangements.

Invariably, being a secretary is a self-effacing job. Good secretaries rarely get the kudos they deserve when, thanks to their efficiency, crises are avoided, but they are likely to be blamed if things go wrong – if they forget to remind their boss of an appointment which she/he too had forgotten and which is written down in the appointments diary.

There are good opportunities for 'real' secretaries. They can pick and choose the environment they want to work in, whether the City, a public institution or a professional office – say, accountants' or solicitors'. The Institute of Qualified Professional Secretaries offers continuing professional development – see *www.iqps.org*.

Promotion usually still means becoming secretary to someone higher up in the hierarchy – e.g. from secretary to sales manager to secretary to finance director to secretary to managing director to secretary to chairman. In this promotion system, expertise gained in one job tends to be fairly useless in the next, therefore the opportunities for independent work, for becoming PA (or acting as PA at least) or executive, tend to be less in the new job than they were in the previous one. Many secretaries find that the higher up in the hierarchy their boss, the less the boss is likely to delegate.

Secretaries who have word processing experience can become *supervisors/coordinators/trainers*. They are the buffer between the users ('text originators') and the operators; they schedule work as it comes in and they appease users whose text cannot be dealt with instantly. They may also diagnose and possibly deal with minor equipment faults and deal with the equipment suppliers if things go seriously wrong. This job can lead to, or be combined with, 'in-house training' – work which involves training new word-processor operators and persuading managers to learn what the equipment can and cannot do; writing manuals; advising office managers by evaluating the many different types of machines when new ones are to be bought. This type of job is still evolving. It always involves contact with a large variety of people; its exact content varies according to size, type and ideas of the employing organization.

Specialist Secretary

Though there is no need to decide on any specialization before training, there are 3 specializations for which special training is useful but not essential.

1. *Medical secretaries*: They work in hospital, for one or several consultants; in consultants' private consulting rooms; or for general practitioners. They require knowledge of medical terminology and of health and social services organization. In hospital, secretaries have less contact with patients than in consulting rooms and general practice, but they have more companionship. In GPs' group practices the work involves organizing/administration.

2. *Farm or agricultural secretaries*: They deal with the paperwork which modern farming entails. They fill in forms, keep accounts, keep and analyse records, and deal with correspondence, often on their own initiative. Only very big farms employ full-timers; most need part-time help. So farm secretaries either work as freelances, spending a number of days a month on different farms, or they are employed

by farm-secretarial agencies and are sent out to different farms. The work is varied, as it involves working on different types of farm; and it requires experience and self-confidence because farmers, unlike other employers, usually know less about the work to be done (accounts, filling in VAT and other forms) than their secretaries. Specialist training is a great advantage.

Both medical and farm secretaries now use computers; doctors' secretaries to keep patients' records; farm secretaries to record, for example, cows' milk yield in relation to expenditure on various foodstuffs.

3. *Bi- or multilingual secretaries*: They translate incoming mail; they may compose their own letters in a foreign language from notes dictated in English, but most outgoing mail is written in English. They sometimes read foreign journals and search for and translate or summarize relevant articles. Occasionally they may act as interpreter. Their scope varies: some secretaries hardly use their languages at all; others are relied upon totally by their monolingual bosses. Foreign Office secretaries must be proficient in 1 language but many never use that knowledge even when working in embassies abroad. There are commercial opportunities abroad for truly bilingual secretaries with, occasionally, the relevant shorthand. International organizations usually require previous senior secretarial experience. Overall, the greatest demand is for French/English, German/English and French/German/English, mainly in international marketing and in export. There is a small, steady demand for Spanish, for other European languages, and for Russian and a growing demand for Japanese and Arabic.

At home, foreign shorthand is rarely required; in order to master it, it is essential to be *absolutely fluent* in the language(s) concerned. For most linguist-secretary jobs a grasp of the relevant country's economic and social set-up is far more important than shorthand and 100% speaking and writing fluency.

They get jobs easily, but not necessarily with much scope for using their language proficiency. Graduates are often overqualified. GCSE or A level language plus knowing how to use a dictionary is often all that is needed, even when the job was advertised as for a linguist. There are more secretaries who want to work abroad than there are jobs available. However, good linguists with about 3 years' secretarial experience can get jobs in EU countries and elsewhere, mainly in British or multinational companies' offices.

Shorthand- and Audio-Typist/Word Processor Operator

Many so-called secretaries are really typists or word processor operators. They work for a number of people, often in a central word processing unit or 'station', and not for individuals as secretaries do. Their job is far more impersonal, concerned with producing texts efficiently and economically rather than dealing with people and all the various jobs the secretaries cope with. It is work for people who like getting on with the job without having to talk much to their bosses; but it can be a step to secretarial work too.

The demand for *shorthand-writers* is still great though diminishing. There are still executives who insist on dictating to an individual rather than into a machine.

Copy-typists have virtually disappeared. Offices now either use photocopying or similar machines or word processors (WPs).

Clerk

This may involve some typing and/or word processing and/or using computers (see INFORMATION TECHNOLOGY (IT)/INFORMATION SYSTEMS, p. 281). Clerks' work varies even more than secretarial work. Some clerks work on their own all day; others are in constant contact with colleagues and/or the public. Clerks in travel agencies may send out brochures to customers or hand them out over the counter; in a mail order firm, however computerized the system, they may check incoming orders to see whether the right postal orders are enclosed; in a hospital or commercial office a junior may do nothing but photocopy. Clerks may work in post-rooms, collecting and distributing mail from and to various departments and individuals. In personnel departments, they may work on computerized staff records, entering details about absence, wage increases, etc. In large organizations, whether town hall, store or manufacturing company, there is often a computerized filing system. In a small office a clerk may still do 'old-fashioned' filing, answer the telephone, make the tea and do some typing/word processing. The extent to which clerks' work has been affected by the introduction of computerized equipment varies enormously but job opportunities have lessened. Some offices still rely largely on the old-fashioned methods of entering and updating facts and figures, transmitting messages, collecting and distributing information but in most this is done electronically.

Clerks may also become telephonists or receptionists. The receptionist's job may be rather more complex than it appears – receptionists are expected to have a good knowledge of who does what in the organization so that they can direct callers to the right person or department. Hotel receptionists (see HOTEL AND CATERING, p. 260) may do behind-the-scenes accounts work as well as dealing face-to-face with clients and staff.

Training No set pattern. Secretaries should still learn shorthand, at least at 90–100 words per minute (and transcribe it adequately), and audio-type at 50 words per minute. They must be able to spell. They must know how to use, and where to find, sources of reference. They need a good grasp of who does what in the commercial world, in the community, in government. They must be able to draft and summarize letters, reports, etc. – both verbally and in writing.

Where, and how, they acquire the 'secretarial core skills' is totally immaterial. Certificates and diplomas awarded by colleges, OCR/ Royal Society of Arts, the London Chamber of Commerce and Industry, Pitman's, for example, and specialist ones by the Association of Medical Secretaries, Practice Managers, Administrators and Receptionists, are useful when there are more applicants than vacancies. Qualifications secure a first interview, but they count for far less than impression made at interview.

A sixth-form education, A levels in such subjects as geography, English, economics, and intensive courses in shorthand, typing and then word processing, are far more useful than leaving school at 16 and taking a 2-year secretarial course. GCSE (A–C) English language is essential: a degree is rarely an advantage. Even when an employer specifies 'graduate secretary', an intelligent, well-informed sixth-form leaver is usually acceptable. There are so many graduate secretaries simply because some arts graduates cannot think of anything else to do – not because many secretarial jobs are so intellectually demanding that only graduates could fill them. Graduate secretaries do not even have significantly greater chances of getting into management than sixth-form leavers.

Courses fall into broad categories, each with many variations; and often with various optional subjects:

1. Courses for students with 2 A levels or with degrees or comparable qualifications, lasting between 3 and 9 months; a 3-months' crash course, learning the core skills, should be sufficient.

2. 6-month to 2-year courses for students with 4 or 5 GCSEs (A–C). Unless 2-year courses include something like medical, legal, farm or linguist secretarial work, or A level study, 2 years is unnecessarily long.

3. 1- or 2-year courses for students with 3 to 5 GCSEs (A–C). They often include GCSE (or A level) study. Courses are likely to lead to clerical rather than secretarial jobs in the first instance.

4. Courses for students with 'a good general education' (no specific passes). These are not strictly speaking *secretarial* courses (whatever their title). They should last 2 years and include general educational subjects if they are eventually to lead to secretarial work.

5. 1-year courses in English, shorthand, typing, word processing, office routine, lead to *clerks'* and *typists'* or *word processors'* jobs (also applies to commercial courses at school).

6. BTEC (see p. 8) courses, part time or full time.

There are NVQs/SVQs in administration at 5 levels. These can be worked towards at work or at college. The Business Administration Modern Apprenticeship is available at Foundation and Advanced level.

However, adequate word processing is not available at all colleges. Some lack up-to-date equipment or have too little of it. Applicants with good keyboard skills can still get jobs: they may then be given in-house word processing training. However, where employers are in a buyers' market, applicants who are familiar with word processing programs are at a distinct advantage. For that reason, private word processing schools have proliferated over the last few years. Their courses vary enormously in quality; some use out-of-date equipment and/or provide insufficient 'hands on' WP experience and/or are unnecessarily long. Most good courses normally last only about 1 week full time (or longer part time/evenings only) *and they only accept students who can type*. So before signing on for a private school WP course, it is essential to make sure that it is a good one. On the whole, courses attached to well-known secretarial agencies are a wise choice. Most of them have been started to ensure the agency has a pool of well-qualified people on its books rather than to make a profit; they are run 'at cost'. Courses normally teach on the two or three types of machines in widest use. Word processor operators who then get jobs where they have to use a different type of machine, get short 'conversion training' on the job. In any case on-the-job training goes on for some time: it takes quite a few months for a word processor operator to be really proficient at the job.

Specialist training

Bi- or multilingual secretary: Entry requirements from 'good GCSE pass' or 'A level standard' in the relevant language to language degree. Most courses last 2 years. Prospective linguist-secretaries who intend to take a language degree should look out for degree courses including 'area studies' – which means the course covers the relevant country's history and social and economic institutions, etc. That type of knowledge is also very important for getting jobs abroad with commercial firms and international agencies.

Medical secretary: 1 year full-time (or longer part-time) course leading to the Intermediate Diploma in Medical Reception. With 4 GCSEs (A–C) a 1- or 2-year full-time course leading to the Advanced Diploma for Medical Secretaries. For those already working as a manager, with a level 3 standard of education or suitable management experience, part-time course leading to the Diploma in Primary Care Management. Information about these courses from the Association of Medical Secretaries, Practice Managers, Administrators and

Receptionists (AMSPAR), Tavistock House North, Tavistock Square, London WC1H 9LN; *www.amspar.co.uk*.

Farm secretary: BTEC National Certificate or National Diploma courses for farm secretaries are run at some agricultural colleges.

Personal attributes *Secretaries*: Exceptional organizing ability, self-confidence, determination and ambition, a logical brain; business acumen; willingness to take responsibility and willingness to take orders; ability to communicate easily with people at all levels of education and status in the organization; willingness to work long hours.

Personal assistants: Willingness to take responsibility must be coupled with willingness to remain in a supportive role; a sympathetic manner; a desire to be of use to others; ability to ignore getting undeserved blame when things go wrong and not getting well-deserved praise; indifference to seeing less able 'executives' have higher status and pay, and more responsibility.

Typists/word processor operators: Wanting to get on with one's work without involvement with people and in the organization's business; accuracy.

Clerks: Depends on type of job – some require a liking for quiet backroom work dealing with paperwork; others a liking for dealing with people; most require attention to detail and willingness to do as told.

Late start Secretarial work is easy to start late. While there are some employers who will not consider anyone over 35, there is a growing number of employers who prefer the over 35s. Some courses geared to mature students are available.

Work life balance A career break should be no problem for secretaries with word processor operating experience. Numerous courses are available for those wishing to update their skills.

Good part-time opportunities for word processor operators. Not quite as good for secretaries, who are expected to be available whenever the boss wants them. However, even here part-time work and job-sharing are becoming accepted, but part-timers are never likely to have as wide a choice of jobs as full-timers. The fewer the hours they are willing to work, the more restricted the choice of job.

Part time can be anything from 6 hours a week, to 4 full days; 2 or 3 full, or 3 or 4 half days are the most usual. A flexible number of hours, to suit both secretary and employers and varying week by week, is sometimes possible. There are a few jobs which can be done in term-time only, leaving mothers free during the children's holidays; and occasionally some 1 week (or fortnight) on, 1 week (or fortnight) off jobs.

Temping is a kind of part-time work. It is particularly suitable for actors, artists, models, etc., people who have to 'fill in' while waiting for their own kind of work; for mothers who cannot get a term-time-only job, and for secretaries, WP operators and typists who prefer a frequent change of environment to getting involved with one set of people and one type of work. Temps normally work for agencies who send them to employers on a weekly or daily basis; only those with very good contacts and experience can work as freelances.

Further information No central organization. Local education authority for lists of local courses (and see 'Medical secretary', p. 559).

Related careers CIVIL SERVICE – HEALTH SERVICES MANAGEMENT – HOTEL AND CATERING: *Hotel Reception* – INFORMATION TECHNOLOGY (IT)/INFORMATION SYSTEMS – LANGUAGES – MANAGEMENT – PERSONNEL/HUMAN RESOURCES MANAGEMENT – PUBLIC RELATIONS – WORKING FOR ONESELF

Social Work

Entry qualifications Recognized degree. English and maths GCSE at grade C or above or equivalent at Key Skills Level 2.

The work Social workers help people to overcome or adjust to a wide variety of social or personal problems. They work in a variety of settings: in local authority social services departments, dealing with the problems of families and children, the elderly, those with physical and mental disabilities and the homeless; in hospitals and other health settings, dealing with those who are ill and their families; in education departments, with children who are having problems which affect their education; in voluntary agencies which supplement the work of statutory services, sometimes with particular groups, e.g. the elderly or disadvantaged children.

The training of social workers is 'generic', i.e. it equips them to deal with all kinds of social problems, in various settings, with all age and client groups. Nevertheless, on graduation and after a period of practice, there is scope to specialize in work with particular client groups, e.g. children or the elderly.

Fieldwork

Field social workers generally work with people who live in their own homes, as opposed to residential care. Most local authority social services departments (social work departments in Scotland) organize their field workers into area teams, providing a full range of services across the spectrum of client groups in a given geographical area. Within the area team there may be specialist workers or teams dealing with particular groups. Organization and balance between 'generic' workers and specialists vary. Some generic workers become virtual specialists simply by the balance of their case allocation. The nature of the area also affects social workers' caseloads; problems occur in some areas (e.g. a large refugee population) which are non-existent in others.

The work is a mixture of counselling, liaison, mediating, monitoring and practical problem-solving. Some people who turn to social services for help have immediate problems which can be sorted out fairly quickly. For example, a family with a young baby might need a social worker to negotiate on their behalf with an electricity company so that their supplies are not cut off. Other problems require a longer-term relationship in which the social worker provides both practical assistance and counselling, helping individuals or families to identify both their problems, which are often complex and inter-related, and ways in which they might cope with them. The problems are very varied, from the stresses and problems of intractable poverty or long-term ill-health to the strains of caring for elderly relatives or children with disabilities.

Social work is very much more complex than simply offering a sympathetic ear and practical help. There is a great deal of legislation which gives social workers both responsibility and powers to act in cases where people are at risk. The most obvious example is child protection, which is a top priority at present and which can take up a large proportion of a social worker's time. Social workers must assess and monitor families at risk of neglecting or abusing their children, visiting regularly and giving support, keeping an eye on how they handle their children, perhaps referring them to a family centre to learn childcare skills and discuss their problems. Sometimes, of course, social workers decide that it is not in the children's best interests to remain with their families and must take the necessary action and provide the proper supervision. The mentally ill are another group over whom social workers have powers of removal if they become a nuisance or a danger to others or to themselves.

Social workers do not just sort out problems: they try to prevent them from getting worse or leading to other problems. For example, the isolation and poverty of young mothers can lead to child abuse. Social workers' preventative work can take the form of individual counselling and support, work with whole families or group work, where people with similar problems are brought together for mutual support.

The day-to-day work of a field social worker is very varied. Much time is spent visiting clients, listening to their problems, offering support and encouragement and monitoring those at risk. Most team members will have a day as duty officer, seeing clients who come into the office (e.g. seeking advice on benefits or without money to pay overdue bills) and taking calls (e.g. from a neighbour or teacher concerned about a child with unusual bruising). Time is also spent on paperwork, keeping detailed case notes, and writing reports, e.g. on a juvenile offender or for an adoption hearing. Liaison with other professionals or organizations is very important and time-consuming. For example, a social worker might have to arrange for an elderly client to have help at home, find residential accommodation for someone unable to cope alone, or track down additional complementary support from a voluntary agency.

Some field social workers within area teams specialize in, for example, adoption or child abuse cases. Others do more specialized work in a variety of other settings. *Social workers in hospitals* help with the problems that can arise through illness. For example, children might need to be looked after while their mother is in hospital; a family might need advice on financial assistance when the main breadwinner is unable to work; a pregnant teenager might need support and advice before, during and after the birth of her baby. Some social workers are attached to special units, such as clinics for the treatment of those dependent on drugs or alcohol, and some work in general practices or health centres alongside the family doctor, nurse, health visitor, community midwife and district nurse.

Social workers also work in day centres, adult training centres, social education centres, child guidance clinics and intermediate treatment, which involves working in the community with young people at risk. *Community social workers* (there is debate about to what extent they are a part of mainstream social work) work in the community to help people identify their common problems and work together to solve them, e.g. by setting up a mother and toddler group or establishing a community social centre. (With cutbacks in public expenditure this type of work has virtually disappeared in some areas.)

Social workers work with schools, dealing with the problems which prevent children benefiting fully from their education. The problems can be very wide-ranging, from inadequate transport in a country area to complex family problems leading to truancy or behaviour problems, to material or emotional deprivation. The social workers work with schools to identify the problems, establish links with the home and devise ways of overcoming the problems.

Residential Care

Some people have problems that cannot adequately be dealt with in their homes with their families, even with the other help available. These people may need residential care on a long-term or temporary basis. Residential homes vary in size, purpose and client group. They may be run by local authorities or by voluntary agencies. They may cater for the elderly, the physically or mentally disabled, single mothers or children.

The work varies greatly according to the type of home and client group. It can range from complex assessment and care in conjunction with other professionals to arranging birthday and other celebrations, to helping with basic day-to-day tasks such as dressing, feeding, shopping and so on. Counselling is also part of the job and may arise from many everyday occurrences. The aim is to help the residents to achieve as much stability and independence as possible, whether they return to their own homes or remain in care. Good residential care depends on developing good relationships with residents and effective team-work with colleagues.

Residential care workers do not necessarily need to live in, but may be required to do so on a shift basis. Even those who live on site are not required to be on call all the time. A high proportion of workers in residential care are not qualified social workers. There are NVQs/SVQs (see p. 10) available for care assistants.

Training The professional qualification for social work in England, introduced in 2003, is a 3-year honours degree course. The degree can be studied full time, part time, or through work-based, distance or open learning. Graduate entrants may achieve the qualification in a shorter timescale and in some cases this may be linked to a post-graduate award. As part of their degree students will be required to complete 200 days in practice settings to ensure they have the practical skills required of them before entering the workforce.

A non-means-tested bursary is available to students not supported through training by an employer. Some employers will fund the training, others have a traineeship scheme.

In Scotland, from 2004, the minimum qualification will be a 4-year honours degree course. Wales and Northern Ireland will be introducing their own degree level qualifications in 2004.

There are Foundation and Advanced Modern Apprenticeships in Health and Social Care and a wide range of NVQs/SVQs for social work support workers.

In England all social workers and social care workers are required to be registered with the new General Social Care Council, in Wales with the Care Council for Wales and in Scotland with the Scottish Social Services Council.

Personal attributes The desire to help people irrespective of one's own personal likes and dislikes; the ability to communicate with every level of intelligence, cultural or social background or emotional state; perseverance in the face of apparent failure when clients/groups show no sign of improvement or appreciation of efforts made for or on behalf of them; stability; a ready understanding of other people's way of life and point of view; sympathy and tolerance of human failings; belief in individuals' potential to do better; good verbal and written skills to record and report; the ability to take an interest in other people's problems without becoming emotionally involved; a sense of humour; wide interests unconnected with social work (to keep a sense of proportion); patience and empathy.

Late start Age is not necessarily important but maturity is essential.

In 2002–2003 nearly 50% of entrants to social work training were over 35. Some programmes are specially designed for those with family commitments.

Work life balance Social work returners are welcomed back. Some authorities may have formal schemes. Part-time work and job-sharing are available.

Further information England: General Social Care Council, Goldings House, Hay's Lane, London SE1 2HB.
  www.gscc.org.uk
  www.socialworkcareers.co.uk
Wales: Care Council for Wales, 6th Floor, West Wing, South Gate House, Wood Street, Cardiff CF10 1EW.
  www.ccwales.org.uk
Scotland: Scottish Social Services Council, Compass House, Discovery Quay, 11 Riverside Drive, Dundee DD1 4NY.
  www.careinscotland.co.uk

Related careers CAREERS WORK – NURSERY NURSE – NURSING – POLICE – PRISON SERVICE – TEACHING – YOUTH AND COMMUNITY WORK

Sociology

Entry qualifications 2, or more often 3, A levels and 3 GCSEs (A–C); usually maths or statistics and English at either level.

The work Sociology is sometimes confused with social work, but there is a vast difference between the two. Social work is a practical profession that deals with individuals and families, and the problems that they experience (see SOCIAL WORK, p. 562); sociology, on the other hand, is an intellectual discipline that tries to examine social life itself. Sociologists study the conditions that give rise to 'social problems' and to understand the causes that lie behind this. Sociology is not bound by a concern for such social problems, however. Its theories and concepts are concerned with building an understanding of how societies actually work and how they change over time.

Sociologists research into the social relationships from which societies are formed. They look at the interactions between individuals, between groups, and within and between whole communities. They are concerned with how all of these change or remain constant over time. For example, sociologists who are interested in education will investigate a number of different issues. They may examine interactions between teachers and pupils in different settings (in class, on the sports field, in the street), the family backgrounds of different pupils and the inequalities that these involve, the gender and ethnic composition of pupil groups and the teaching profession, the organization of schools and local authority control over them, and government policies towards education. These various investigations allow sociologists to develop an understanding of and theories about the structure of school life, its importance in society and the problems that people may experience in the educational system.

Sociology covers every area of human social activity, including race and ethnic relations, sex and gender divisions, union–management disputes, doctor–patient relationships, crime and policing, illegal drug use, class inequalities, patterns of religious belief and practice, the organization of protest movements, sexual behaviour, family relationships and kinship patterns, the nature of the mass media, life in cities and communities, and such issues as homelessness, poverty and unemployment. Sociologists examine the institutions and inequalities of a society in relation to its changing position in an increasingly globalized world.

Virtually every aspect of modern life is of interest to sociologists, and they are usually concerned with highly topical issues. In recent years these have included the impact of new information technologies, the development of genetic and reproductive medicine, child sexual abuse, the spread and treatment of AIDS, and anti-capitalist protests.

Sociological understanding can often help to avert or alleviate social problems. Advice may be offered to employers, councils and government with a view to changing the conditions responsible for these problems. Policy-makers are not always prepared to listen to sociologists or to take their advice, and many sociologists have emphasized the critical task of sociology. By exploring the conditions responsible for the problems that are experienced by people, sociologists help to raise public consciousness about wider social issues.

Sociology is an empirical discipline: its theories are guided by the collection of information. This information is collected through a variety of research methods, such as the fieldwork techniques of observation and interviewing, the social survey, and the use of published documents and statistics. Sociological observation may involve participating in the work of an institution or an organization such as a factory, a church, or a gang, or it may mean moving into an urban or rural community and joining in the life of that community. A particular study may take many months or even years. Interviewing can sometimes be combined with observation, but is often carried out independently. This will generally involve using systematically prepared sets of questions, and many interviews take the form of an in-depth interview or life history interview. Other kinds of interviewing are those that are carried out in large-scale surveys, using interview schedules or questionnaires. Many such surveys do not rely on interviews but involve the self-completion of a questionnaire. In much sociological research the data sources will be newspapers, government documents, television programmes, and other kinds of documents and media products. A great deal of research uses official statistics produced by government and other agencies.

Different kinds of study call for different styles of research, and sociological studies often combine two or more methods. After the information has been collected, it must be analysed, collated and interpreted, and it must be presented in sociological reports. Statistical methods are widely used, and computers are used extensively, but much research involves the qualitative and non-mathematical assessment of data. The development of theory and concepts through empirical research forms the starting-point for new investigations.

Sociology is closely allied to and overlaps with other social sciences, especially social anthropology, social psychology, criminology, politics and economics (p. 213).

There are far more sociology graduates than there are jobs or professional training as sociologists. Careers in research and higher education have become very scarce. However, sociology can be the basis for many other kinds of jobs, some of which involve further specific training. There are good opportunities for employment involving applied social research within health and the social services, in government departments and in voluntary agencies. Many sociology graduates go into industry, often working in *industrial relations* or other *personnel specializations* (see p. 444) and in jobs related to organizational and technological change. There are some opportunities in *market research* (see p. 57) and *marketing* (see p. 371). The *police* (see p. 465) welcome a sociological understanding of human behaviour, especially if a degree scheme has involved the study of crime and deviance.

Training Honours degree in sociology or in combination with other social sciences and humanities. There are courses that combine sociology with modern languages. On some business studies degrees sociology is a major option. There are also a few courses where sociology can be combined with physics and/or maths, engineering, education, management studies or computer studies. Modularization of degree courses gives wider scope for students of all disciplines to study some sociology.

The choice of the right course is important, and complicated: the wording used to describe courses varies, and the combination of subjects covered and the emphasis given to the different aspects of sociology cannot necessarily be deduced from the title given to a particular course. It is essential to study up-to-date prospectuses. It can be useful to go by the experience of people who read sociology very recently, but be aware that changes and innovations occur very rapidly in this field.

In some universities, students begin their specialization in their first year and study the subject almost exclusively through their degree. In other universities, the first year may involve studying a number of different social sciences (economics, politics, social and/or economic history, psychology, geography, etc.), with specialization beginning only in the second year.

Personal attributes A deep but detached interest in how people live, think and behave; a rigorous and disciplined approach to contemporary social issues, rather than a purely emotional response; an ability to recognize one's own prejudices and biases, and a willingness to control them; an analytical, logical mind; the ability to discuss and write lucidly, and some basic mathematical ability.

Late start Many mature students study sociology.

Work life balance A career break should not cause any problems as long as would-be returners keep up with developments. There are occasional part-time research assignments. Job-sharing is possible.

Sociology

Further information British Sociological Association, Units 3G/3F, Mountjoy Research Centre, Stockton Road, Durham DH1 3UR. *www.britsoc.co.uk*

Related careers ADVERTISING: *Market Research* – ECONOMICS – MANAGEMENT SERVICES: *Work Study* – NURSING: *Health Visitor* – PERSONNEL/HUMAN RESOURCES MANAGEMENT – POLICE – PSYCHOLOGY – SOCIAL WORK

Speech and Language Therapists

Entry qualifications Usually 3 A levels or equivalent. Some courses require specific GCSEs and A levels.

The work Speech and language therapists are specialists in communication disorders. They assess, diagnose and treat people with speech, language and communication problems. Around 2.5 million people in the UK have a communication disorder of some kind. Of those, 800,000 have a difficulty so severe that it is hard for anyone outside their immediate families to understand them. The aim of speech and language therapy is to help people to communicate to the best of their ability.

Speech and language therapists work with people who have difficulty producing and using speech, difficulty understanding or using language, a stammer, a voice problem, or difficulty with feeding and swallowing.

Clients may have a range of conditions including learning disabilities, physical disabilities, neurological disorders like Parkinson's disease, stroke, cancer of the mouth and throat, head injury, hearing impairment, cleft palate, dementia or psychiatric disorders. Clients can be any age, although around 60% are children. Communication problems can make people feel isolated and depressed, so empathy and support are important aspects of the job. As well as working directly with clients, speech and language therapists advise and support their families and carers.

Speech and language therapists work closely with a range of other professionals from the health, education and social care sectors including doctors, nurses, psychologists, physiotherapists, dietitians, social workers, teachers and representatives from charities and voluntary organizations.

Work locations include community health centres, hospitals (wards and outpatients), mainstream and special schools, assessment units and day centres, and clients' homes. Some travelling can be involved in seeing clients, particularly in rural areas. Most speech and language therapists are employed by the NHS, others by education services or charities, and some work privately.

Qualified speech and language therapists are in demand so employment prospects are generally very good. Most newly qualified speech and language therapists work with a general caseload of clients for at least a year with appropriate support and supervision. They may then choose to specialize in the treatment of a particular group of clients or a type of clinical work. There are also opportunities to move into research, teaching or management.

Most speech and language therapists apply for more senior positions after around 2 years' work.

Training Speech and language therapists must successfully complete a degree or post-graduate course jointly approved by the Health Professions Council and Royal College of Speech and Language Therapists (RCSLT). Courses are offered at 15 higher education establishments across the UK.

Degree courses last for 3 or 4 years. Post-graduate courses last for 2 years.

Subjects studied include language pathology and therapeutics, speech and language sciences, behavioural sciences, biomedical sciences, education, research methodology, psychology, sociology and professional issues. The practical component of the courses is very important and usually combines weekly clinical placements with periods of longer placements. These may take place in a variety of settings such as schools, hospitals and community health clinics, and are designed to develop skills in the assessment and treatment of communication disorders.

The courses are funded by the Department of Health which means that eligible students have their tuition fees paid in full by the NHS and are eligible to apply for a means-tested bursary.

Personal attributes Good communication, listening and problem-solving skills; ability to relate to people of all ages, abilities and backgrounds – clients may suffer from behavioural or emotional problems, so sensitivity and understanding are vital; a creative and flexible approach to work with individual clients. Good negotiation skills and the ability to influence others are needed as therapists may have to advise families, carers, teachers and employers to change their behaviour, and often have to represent the interests of clients who cannot speak up for themselves. Teamwork is important, but so is the ability to work and take decisions as an individual.

Late start Mature applicants to speech and language courses are welcome: evidence of recent study may be required.

Work life balance Therapists who have not practised for less than 5 years and who wish to return to work must obtain two references from RCSLT members in order to register. Returners who have not worked for 5 years must work for a period under supervision.

Opportunities for part-time work or flexible working depend on employer. Through its Improving Working Lives standard the NHS is committed to flexible working, including part time, job-sharing and term-time working, as well as evening and weekend work.

Further information The Royal College of Speech and Language Therapists, 2 White Hart Yard, London SE1 1NX.
www.rcslt.org
NHS Careers, PO Box 376, Bristol, BS99 3EY. Helpline: 0845 60 60 655.
www.nhscareers.nhs.uk

Related careers OCCUPATIONAL THERAPY – PHYSIOTHERAPY – PSYCHOLOGY – TEACHING: *Special Needs Education*

Sport

Entry qualifications No formal educational qualifications. For degree courses in sport or recreation studies: 2–3 A levels.

The work Sport can be divided into 3 main career areas, although many people combine 2 or more:

1. *Players* or *participants* who are paid professionals. This guide is concerned only with those sports in which it is possible to earn a living, but the professional/amateur distinction is frequently blurred or has disappeared altogether.

2. *Teaching* or *coaching* children or adults.

3. *Administration* (which overlaps with LEISURE/RECREATION MANAGEMENT, see p. 336).

Professional Players

In most cases those with sufficient talent will have been spotted well before they leave school. People whose job it is to find and nurture talent will have discovered potential players through schools, youth clubs, local and county teams. In general it is too late to start serious training for a sporting career after leaving school (exceptions are horse and motor racing which cannot be started while at school). For most people sport has to remain a recreation. Currently there are still more opportunities for men to participate professionally than women. However, this is gradually changing as the number of women taking part in traditionally male dominated sports, such as football and cricket, is increasing.

Football (boys only)

Training most begin at 14 (can be 13 in Scotland) as Associated Schoolboys with a professional club. At 16 they may be invited to become full-time trainees. The first year of the scheme is broad-based: on-the-job training includes football training and coaching, work experience in various aspects of running and maintaining the club. Trainees follow a day-release course at college, working towards NVQ level 2 Leisure and Tourism and following an information technology course. After the first year they are assessed: the majority stay on at the football club and continue their football training and day-release course. Others may choose to concentrate on another area of work within the club or transfer to more appropriate training. At the end of the 2 years, the club decides whether or not to offer a professional contract: the majority are not good enough and leave the game by their early 20s. There is a fast track system for 14- and 15-year-old boys of outstanding talent based at the Football Association's School of Excellence at Lilleshall. This scheme has the highest rate of success for players being signed to clubs as professionals.

As part of the Football Association's Charter for Quality programme all Premier League clubs must have academies and all Football League clubs must have Centres of Excellence. Scholarship programmes for 16–18 year olds enable trainees to allocate more time to their academic education as well as developing their technical skills.

In Scotland, professional footballers are encouraged and given financial help to continue with educational courses throughout their careers to prepare them for life after football.

Cricket (boys only)

Most county cricketers are recruited straight from school, having already played trial matches. For a few seasons they play in club and second XI matches. If they are considered to have first-team potential they may be offered a contract by the county: they agree to play exclusively for the club. The MCC runs a Young Cricketers Scheme for promising boys aged 16 to 18. Successful candidates for the scheme may choose between 2 different contracts: (1) summer only, renewable annually or (2) 3 summers of cricket and 2 winters of education.

About 50 county players each year find cricket jobs overseas during our winter, playing cricket or coaching. The rest have to find other employment in the close season (a few play professional football). Most have stopped playing by the age of 40, although top players may stay in the game as coaches, umpires or managers.

Tennis (boys and girls)

Most aspiring players will have started playing at age 7 to 9 (usually short tennis at school, club or sports centre). They progress by playing in 'starter' tournaments and other competitions at local club level and may be selected for county training. Some become full-time players by age 16–17, often joining one of the Lawn Tennis Association's national squads. A few gain scholarship to the United States at 18/19. The LTA organizes and helps finance a comprehensive national tournament programme as well as international experience for these players throughout their development.

In any one year only around a dozen men and women players make a full-time living, with those in the world's top 100 earning very large sums.

Golf (boys and girls)

There are 2 distinct kinds of golfing professional: (1) the *club professional* (belonging to the Professional Golfers' Association) and (2) the *tournament player* (belonging to the PGA European Tour and, for women, the WPGA European Tour). Although some professional golfers have become successful in both areas, this is not recommended for newcomers, since intense competition within each branch requires single-minded dedication to one only.

1. *Club professionals* (around 4,000): Work at a club, running the shop, repairing equipment and giving lessons. The job requires a high level of playing ability (they have their own tournaments organized by the PGA), business flair and organizing ability. In golf there is a very clear distinction between amateur and professional status and aspiring club pros should first seek advice from the PGA before taking the plunge and forfeiting their amateur status.

The PGA offers the Trainee Diploma Programme. Applicants

should hold a handicap of 4 or better for men and 6 or better for women and at least 4 GCSEs. A 2-day Admission Review Programme is followed by an Ability Test held over 36 holes. Before being registered as trainees, potential professionals must be 18 years old and have been working on a full-time basis with a fully qualified member of the PGA. During training they retain their amateur status and follow a 3-year planned programme (covering all aspects of the profession including coaching and managing a business) with on- and off-the-job instruction (including residential courses), leading to a final exam. Trainees must be prepared to work long hours, and earn very little while learning.

2. *Tournament players*: Aspiring professional men players have to qualify their first season for 1 of the 50 available Player's Cards by competing in a pre-qualifying school (tournament), then in the qualifying school held in Europe. To retain their Card they need to finish in the top 125 in the European tournaments that season. Only a handful of tournament players are successful enough to earn large sums through winnings and commercial sponsorship.

Women's golf is a growth area and women have their own association. Applicants for probationary membership of the WPGA European Tour must be aged 18 or over and, if amateur, have a current handicap of 1 (without star). Existing professionals may also apply, provided they are members of a recognized ladies' professional golf association tour. All applicants must be proposed and seconded by members of the tour.

Horse racing (boys and girls)

There are 2 kinds of races – flat and National Hunt (over jumps). Increasingly, training of stable staff for both kinds of racing stables is carried out at the British Racing School, Newmarket, and the Northern Racing College, Doncaster, rather than by trainers themselves. Formal qualifications are not required; the emphasis is on personal qualities of commitment, dedication, determination, alertness, a desire to work outdoors and the confidence to live away from home. School-leavers can either apply direct to the British Horse Racing Board (BHB) or to individual trainers who will then send them to a racing school after some practical experience in the stables. Pupils must be 16/17, around 9 stone or under. Previous riding experience is not essential but helps.

Basic courses at the British Racing School or the Northern Racing College last 10 weeks. The training is for stable staff, not jockeys. Boys and girls are then placed with trainers or thoroughbred stud owners as stable 'lads'. Trainees work towards an NVQ level 2 in Racehorse Care. Courses cover riding, grooming, mucking out and basic care of horses along with lectures on racing topics. Training through the racing schools is open to applicants up to the age of 25. With experience lads progress to positions with more responsibility such as travelling head lad, assistant head lad, head lad, assistant trainer or trainer. A Modern Apprenticeship is also available. A tiny minority become apprentice jockeys – the great majority remain as stable 'lads' (there are 50 'lads' for every jockey). National Hunt 'lads' are heavier (up to 9/10 stone); they need to gain experience first with a National Hunt trainer, who will send them to the British Racing School if they think they are suitable (in which case the weight restrictions are waived). A very small number become 'conditional' jockeys (the National Hunt equivalent to apprentice jockeys).

There is a clear distinction between *amateur* and *professional jockeys*, with many more races for professionals. Jockeys who race on the flat or in National Hunt races must possess a licence or permit from the Jockey Club to ride. Full professional flat jockeys are aged 25 and above and are expected to have at least 25 rides per year to renew their licence for the next season. Trainers retain some, but most are self-employed. Full professional status for jump jockeys starts at age 27. Competition among jockeys is fierce and the lifestyle demanding, with most retiring by the age of 45.

Women have done well over jumps and on the flat but their racing history is comparatively short. They have only been allowed to ride as professionals on the flat since 1975 and over jumps since 1976. The problem is that only those considered likely to ride winners are given rides; so until they have had success and proved themselves, they are unlikely to be chosen, which makes it hard for them to get started.

Teaching, Coaching/Instructing

For *PE teaching*, see TEACHING, p. 610.

Coaches and instructors in individual sports work at varying levels and in different settings, from national teams to youth clubs, from private sports clubs to local authority leisure centres. A great many coach part time and/or voluntarily, while following another paid occupation. Full-time paid coaches are nearly all ex-professionals or leading amateurs. Some combine playing with coaching. As well as having great technical expertise they need the ability to get the best from players, to know when to sympathize and when to put on pressure. The relationship between player and coach is crucial to success.

All the sports' governing bodies run courses for coaches and instructors, e.g. the LTA Training of Coaches scheme. Colleges and universities also run courses at various levels and entry is decided on the basis of ability and commitment to sport as well as academic ability. Higher education courses include degrees in sports science, coaching, movement studies or physical education. A degree in a sports-related subject can be helpful but a coaching qualification is still essential.

NVQs/SVQs and Modern Apprenticeships are available in Sport, Recreation and Allied Occupations. There is also a Community Sports Leader award scheme run by the Central Council for Physical Recreation (CCPR); although not a vocational course, it may provide a starting-point.

Sports Administration
(excluding LEISURE/RECREATION MANAGEMENT, see p. 336)

Most sports governing bodies have a very small paid staff. Apart from the usual secretarial and clerical posts, the administration of organizations such as the FA or Lawn Tennis Association is carried out by people with relevant expertise, either as former players or managers, or in business or public relations which could help to bring in sponsorship. There are occasional openings for people with degrees in sports science or recreation management.

Active sports careers are necessarily short. After this a minority manage to find work in some way connected with their sport (coaching, managing, promoting products), while the majority have to look elsewhere for employment. Therefore it is essential that those considering a sporting career should look ahead and reach as high a standard academically as possible while at school or college to enable them to take up another training later. This may mean combining a course of further or higher education with part-time playing (e.g. as some cricketers do). Skills in IT and general office procedure as well as in marketing are an advantage.

Personal attributes Total dedication and single-mindedness; strong competitive urge and will to win; high level of physical fitness and mental and physical stamina; ability to respond positively to criticism; resilience and willpower to cope with injuries and setbacks.

Late start Very few sports professionals start their career in adult life. Most professional sportsmen and women begin training extensively at an early age. Successful amateurs, however, may turn professional at any point. Some sports offer more opportunities for late entrants than others.

Position of women Sport is different from any other work area. Private clubs are excluded from the Sex Discrimination Act altogether and, as most sport is organized by clubs, those who choose to can refuse women as members. Even the outstanding girl or woman who is good enough to merit a place in a male team and who may be the best available player can be barred and so is unable to experience the highest level of competition. Girls are often automatically assumed to be worse at sport whereas certainly at primary school sex differences are negligible (and it is at this age that serious interest and training in most sports needs to start). Men's events are generally more prestigious, better sponsored and carry higher prize money than women's. Very importantly, the media often takes very little notice of women's sporting achievements, whether amateur or professional. However, the situation is improving and no potentially outstanding sportswoman should be put off. In certain sports the gap is narrowing between male and female achievements and each year sees a new 'first' for a woman. In 1997 the Football Association launched its Talent Development Plan for women's football as part of the FA's Charter for Quality, to provide a sound structure for the development of elite talent. An integral part of this plan is the establishment of a development structure for girls aged 10 to 16. Football and cricket are both examples of previously male dominated sports where women are now able to play at county and national levels. Current UK initiatives in women's sport include the launch in November 2003 of a UK coordinating group. The strategy aims to encourage the full involvement of women in every aspect of sport, focusing on participation, performance and excellence as well as on leadership.

Further information Sport England, 16 Upper Woburn Place, London WC1H 0QP.
www.sportengland.org
The Central Council of Physical Recreation (CCPR), Francis House, Francis Street, London SW1P 1DE.
www.ccpr.org.uk
Institute of Professional Sport, same address as CCPR
Women's Sport Foundation, 305–315 Hither Green Lane, Lewisham, London SE13 6TJ.
www.wsf.org.uk (produces several careers publications).
Football Association, 25 Soho Square, London W1D 4FA.
www.thefa.com
England and Wales Cricket Board, Lord's Cricket Ground, London NW8 8QN.
www.ecb.co.uk
The Lawn Tennis Association, Palliser Road, West Kensington, London W14 9EE.
www.lta.org.uk
Professional Golfers' Association, Centenary House, The De Vere Belfry, Sutton Coldfield, West Midlands B76 9PT.
www.pga.org.uk

Sport

The PGA European Tour, Wentworth Drive, Virginia Water, Surrey
GU25 4LX.
www.europeantour.com
The British Horseracing Board, 42 Portman Square, London W1H
6EN.
www.bhb.co.uk
Sports Coach UK, 114 Cardigan Road, Headingley, Leeds LS6 3BJ.
www.sportscoachuk.org
Skills Active, Castlewood House, 77–91 New Oxford Street, London
WC1A 1PX.
www.skillsactive.com

Related careers LEISURE/RECREATION MANAGEMENT – TEACHING

Stock Exchange and Securities Industry

The securities industry is the part of the UK financial services sector often referred to as 'The City' and much of it is indeed based in the City of London. London is a major world centre for the trading of domestic and international securities – stock and shares – but the securities industry is truly international, with trading a 24-hour activity.

The London Stock Exchange is the leading UK market-place through which securities are traded. To be traded on the Stock Exchange shares need to be 'listed'. In addition to the main or 'primary' market, the Stock Exchange now has two additional markets: AIM, for new company shares that fulfil most but not all of the listing requirements, and techMARK, for technology companies, such as dotcoms.

There has been enormous change in the operations of the London Stock Exchange. Trading on the market floor has been replaced by the computer screen and telephone. All buying and selling of securities is carried out by member firms. These include merchant banks, clearing banks and investment banks as well as smaller private client stockbroking and investment management firms. Since deregulation in 1986, all are broker/dealers, able to act in both capacities. Prices for securities are quoted on SETS (Stock Exchange Electronic Trading System), which is displayed in firms' offices, or via retail service providers, competing firms of market makers.

In addition, the City is home to the commodity markets, including the International Petroleum Exchange and the London Metal Exchange which still has a trading floor although the commodities market is now mainly computerized. LIFFE, the London International

Financial Futures and Options Exchange, the exchange where derivatives (options – the right (but not the obligation) to buy or sell securities at a specified price on or by a future date, and futures – a contract to buy or sell securities or other goods at a specified future date at a predetermined price) are traded, offers the widest range of derivative products in the world. The London Clearing House guarantees the integrity of these markets, keeps records of transactions and ensures the smooth transfer of the shares.

The financial rewards in the industry can be extremely high. But recent years have shown that the risks are very high as well as firms have cut down or pulled out of trading activities – and shed large numbers of highly paid staff.

In 2001 the Financial Services Authority was established to regulate the industry and this has brought about some changes to training and recruitment.

Entry qualifications Front-office roles: a degree in any subject though a finance-related subject may be an advantage. Back-office or administrative roles: no specific requirements but good GCSEs and A levels or equivalent and increasingly a degree.

The work City institutions recruit specialists from many backgrounds, including accountants and lawyers. The industry offers a mix of roles and staff tend to work either in a front-office role dealing directly with clients, or in the back office or operations area, undertaking the administration of all the front-office transactions. The number of staff in clerical and administrative roles has fallen with the introduction of computerization but there has been an increase in demand for computer-trained staff to help in the design, development and running of the various automated systems.

The main roles specific to the securities industry are:

Traders/market makers Traders buy and sell shares, bonds and derivatives. They work under a strict code of practice and may act on behalf of stockbrokers and their clients or on behalf of their own firm. For some clients they will be trying to make as much money as possible out of the transaction, for others to minimize the risk. Traders check prices on their screens, talk to other dealers, etc. on the phone and their working environment, even at quiet times, is very pressurized. Although they are fed information on which to base their decisions by researchers/analysts, it is up to them to know and make the final decision about the state of a market and to buy or sell accordingly. This is particularly true with derivatives, as traders have to predict the market at a future date.

Researchers/analysts provide the information on which to base advice to clients. They usually specialize in a particular industrial sector or group of companies. They develop a thorough understanding of their area by studying company reports, meeting managers, seeking out any information of relevance to the industry and keeping up to date on any news likely to affect it, analysing past, present and future indicators and forecasting future performance.

Brokers/dealers Stockbrokers work for member firms, which may be based anywhere in the UK. They buy and sell shares on behalf of their clients. Some deal with institutional clients, developing long-term relationships with their fund managers. Brokers dealing with private clients may have to deal with many more clients and many more securities, since small investors may be interested in a range of companies too small to be considered by the institutional investors. Some clients follow the market themselves and require only an execution service. Others require advice on investment and brokers must thoroughly understand their clients' circumstances in order to give appropriate advice.

Settlement staff process the transactions arranged by the dealers. This is done through a paperless transfer system, CREST.

An expanding area is compliance. *Compliance officers* ensure that their colleagues know the rules and regulations and keep to them. Since the Financial Services Authority was fully established in 2001, these have been increasing in complexity and compliance officers need the tact and confidence to be able to question colleagues about their practice and to investigate breaches if necessary.

Training On-the-job training has always been a feature of the securities industry and continues to be. This, however, can mean a very sophisticated graduate training programme. While training, perhaps by a 'Cook's tour' of several back-room departments, recruits who plan to deal in securities or give investment advice normally study for the Securities Institute certificates which meet the requirements of the Financial Services Authority for 'approved person' status, mandatory for those who trade or advise. Study for front-office roles is usually via intensive face-to-face tuition though there is a growing interest in courses delivered electronically. Operations staff tend to study using distance-learning or in-company tuition. These exams are tests of basic knowledge; there are more specialized exams at the level of a Masters degree leading to the Securities Institute Diploma.

Staff employed in general clerical and administrative work can work towards the Securities Institute Investment Administration Qualification.

Personal attributes For *researchers/analysts* – numeracy, ability to assess long-term trends, analytical skills; for *brokers* – affability, the ability to develop good relationships with clients and inspire confidence; for *dealers* – stamina, willingness to take risks, ability to make quick decisions, high powers of concentration, exceptional self-confidence, memory for people and figures.

Late start Opportunities mainly for those with professional qualifications in, for example, accountancy, economics, computing, general management. Analysts often have previous experience in industry. Dealing is a young person's job.

Work life balance A career as a trader or researcher is not for those for whom work life balance is important – normal hours are 7 a.m. to 5.30 p.m. or longer and unpredictable. Career-breaks may be possible and job-sharing, but not part-time work, may be accepted. Support staff from all specialisms work more regular hours. The Stock Exchange operates a flexible benefits scheme which includes access to childcare support and part-time work may be possible for administrative staff.

Further information London Stock Exchange, Broad Street, London
EC2N 1HP.

www.londonstockexchange.com

The Securities Institute, Centurion House, 24 Monument Street,
London EC3R 8AJ.

www.securities-institute,org.uk

Related careers ACCOUNTANCY — BANKING AND BUILDING
SOCIETY WORK — ECONOMICS — INSURANCE

Surveying

SURVEYOR

Entry qualifications For membership of the Royal Institution of Chartered Surveyors: enrolment on an RICS accredited degree or diploma. For many courses, specific A levels or A levels from a group of subjects are required. For example maths, or geography or economic geography or a physical science may be asked for.

The work The work is not *necessarily* mainly technical: in many surveyors' jobs the commercial element is greater than the technical; but technical expertise may be essential background knowledge. The variety of jobs is very great.

Surveying is an umbrella term for jobs which are, in varying degrees and in varying proportion, concerned with, to quote the RICS, 'the measurement, management, development and valuation' of virtually anything: oceans, rivers, harbours, earth's surface, all land, and anything that is in or on land or water, whether natural or man-made. Many surveying jobs are also concerned with protecting or improving the urban and rural environment and the efficient use of resources. However, most surveying is a commercial activity rather than an environmental subject.

The various surveying branches each involve a different mix of technical, commercial, practical and academic ingredients, and different amounts of time spent on dealing with clients, dealing with other professionals, and on office and outdoor work. Each branch, therefore, suits people with different temperaments, interests, aptitudes. For example, the urban estate agent-surveyor has little in common with the hydrographic surveyor charting oceanic depth, or with the planning surveyor doing research into shopping centres, although they do share core skills such as law, economics, valuation and management.

The professional surveying specializations are grouped into 'Divisions' by the Royal Institution of Chartered Surveyors. These are, in order of size: general practice which covers valuation, estate agency, auctioneering and urban estate/housing management; quantity surveying; building surveying; land agency and agricultural surveying; planning and development; land and hydrographic surveying; minerals surveying.

The main surveying branches:

General Practice Surveyors

Valuation surveyors (also called valuers, or simply surveyors)

They assess the value of any type of property at any particular time. It may be in connection with rating, insurance, death duty purposes, as well as for general commercial and, these days, for investment purposes. Some specialize as *investment surveyors*. There are various valuation methods; the most commonly used is the 'comparison' method. This is an intricate mixture of basing judgement on ascertainable facts – value of property in the neighbourhood or other similar property; quality, etc. – as well as on 'getting the feel'. When assessing the value of residential property, or a row of shops, for example, factors taken into account include possible future development in the area (motorways, one-way traffic schemes, housing estates, parking restrictions); amenities (open spaces; swimming baths; entertainment facilities generally); proximity to schools, shops, transport; noise; as well as type of neighbourhood and informed guesswork as to whether the area is likely to go down/come up or whether it has any feeling of community (which might affect quality of schools or be of interest to the elderly, etc.).

Valuers may also assess contents of houses. Though they may be able to tell a Rembrandt from an amateur's efforts, valuers do not normally assess the value of works of art but call on an expert in that field as necessary (who may be a colleague qualified in the chattels section of the RICS General Practice Division). If working for a property developer or local authority they may value land. They may inspect, for example, a plot of land which is up for sale, assess its potential in terms of houses, shops, flats, etc. to be built there, and do a rough 'costing' of whatever type of building is being considered. They may also value all kinds of plant and machinery.

Apart from working for estate agents, local authorities, property developers and other commercial concerns, valuation surveyors also set up in private professional practice. Work for property developers requires a certain amount of gambling instinct and very pronounced business acumen; local authority valuers' work is more concerned with valuing according to laid-down criteria.

Estate agents

Valuation surveyors (as described above) may be estate agents, but estate agents are not necessarily valuation surveyors. Within surveying, estate agency is the most commercially and least technically oriented specialization and probably the largest in terms of opportunities. There is at the moment no need for estate agents to have particular qualifications (but this may soon change). However, most firms of estate agents have at least one RICS-qualified partner. Estate agents negotiate the sale, purchase, leasing of property – not only of houses but also of industrial and commercial premises, agricultural and other land. They arrange and advise on mortgages and on implications of rent acts, and on relevant law generally. As *managing agents* they manage property for clients, which involves drawing up leases, collecting rents, responsibility for maintenance, etc.

Estate agents' clients may be property managers of vast commercial empires, or first-time house purchasers who need to be guided through the complexities of making the most expensive purchase of their lives. Estate agents may specialize in one type of property (residential, or commercial or industrial), or they may deal with a mixture of types of properties. *Negotiators*, who deal with clients, often specialize in dealing with one type of client, for example with house purchasers, helping them to sort out priorities: few can afford their dream house, i.e. what they want exactly where they want. Negotiators help weigh up advantages of, say, sunny garden or 'good neighbourhood'; solidly built but no garage; not-so-solid but near shops/school/transport/parks, etc. Or they specialize in dealing with industrial property: are there goods transport/loading facilities; planning restrictions? Is there a supply of skilled labour?

Estate agents advise vendors on the price to ask, so they have to understand something about valuation, even if they are not professionally qualified valuers. The work involves a lot of client-contact, of getting about and getting to know an area and being aware of changes in type of locality and its effect on property values.

Auctioneers

Most estate agents are also auctioneers. (Normally estate agents employ different people as negotiators and as auctioneers, but in small firms everybody might do everything.) Some firms specialize in auctioning commercial, industrial, residential or agricultural property; others specialize in furniture, machinery, works of art. (The few well-known auction rooms where paintings etc. are auctioned are staffed by art specialists, who have learnt about auctioneering, as well as by the estate agent-valuer-auctioneer.) An auctioneer outside London may well auction the contents of a house one day, cattle in the local market-place the next, and a row of shops the day after that. Work varies according to whether done in country town or big city. The actual auctioneering is only part of the work: it also involves assessing value and advising vendors on 'reserve price', and it involves detailed 'lotting up' and cataloguing items to be sold.

While some firms of auctioneers, especially in the country, engage people specially for auctioneering and teach them the necessary skills and techniques, it is advisable to train as valuer (see above) as well.

Quantity Surveyors

Quantity surveyors are also called 'building economists', 'construction cost consultants', 'building accountants'. Quantity surveyors are essential members of the design team on construction projects of any size. They translate architects' or civil engineers' designs into detailed costs – of labour, materials, overheads; and they break down all materials and processes to be used into detailed quantities and timing. They evaluate alternative processes and materials and may suggest alternative design technologies and materials to those suggested on the original design. Their thorough and up-to-date knowledge of new construction technologies and materials enables them to find ways of getting work carried out in the most speedy, economical and efficient way, without impairing the design. Calculations involved may be very complex – for example, future maintenance costs have to be considered when evaluating the use of alternative materials and processes. Calculations are usually done with computers.

Quantity surveyors are normally appointed by the designer of the project, i.e. the architect or civil engineer. Because of soaring costs and constantly changing technologies, the quantity surveyor's status in the design team has risen enormously in the last few years. Although the architect/civil engineer still has the last word, the quantity surveyor's suggestions for modifications are taken very seriously indeed.

Quantity surveyors are responsible for cost control during the whole project. They advise on cost implications of any proposed variations to the design, make interim valuations of completed work, check contractors' interim accounts and settle final accounts. They are also involved with financial administration of contracts for mechanical and electrical engineering and similar services and may be responsible for overall project management.

Quantity surveyors' work is a combination of straightforward figure work, complex calculations and negotiating skills. They must be able to deal with colleagues from other disciplines, contractors, clients. They spend more time at their desks doing calculations or writing reports and at negotiations than on the construction site, but the time spent on the various ingredients of the job varies from project to project, and according to the type of employer and method of working.

About 60% of quantity surveyors are in private professional practice; others work for contractors, consultant engineers, in government departments, local authorities, commercial and industrial firms.

Building Surveyors

Building surveyors make structural surveys of and diagnose defects of buildings of all types, for prospective purchasers, vendors, owners, building societies. They assess maintenance costs and control maintenance programmes; they prepare plans for conversion and improvements. They draw up plans and specifications, go out to tender, and may supervise contractors' work and check accounts. They advise on building, planning, health and safety regulations, and they may also be involved with restoration or maintenance of ancient monuments and historic buildings. They spend a good deal of time clambering about on buildings to check roofs, lofts, drains, fire escapes and general structural soundness, so their work requires agility.

Many work in private professional practice; others are employed by any type of organization which owns, sells, buys, builds, manages property. This includes housing associations, building societies, all types of industrial and commercial firms, local authorities and central government. This is the most practical specialization, with the least office work.

Rural Practice Surveyors (formerly Land Agents/ Agricultural Surveyors)

Terms are confusing as they have changed in recent years. Traditionally, land agents (called factors in Scotland) were (usually resident) managers of farms or other rural properties. More usually now their work is done by firms of agricultural surveyors (now called by the RICS rural practice surveyors), who manage a number of farms and estates on a contract basis. They do much the same work in rural areas as general practice surveyors do in towns. They may do valuation (including livestock and agricultural plant), estate agency, auctioneering, or they may concentrate on farm management (see AGRICULTURE AND HORTICULTURE, p. 63). Increasingly they also advise on alternative uses of land, for recreational purposes such as country parks, caravan and camping sites, country trails, long-distance footpaths, nature reserves. They would then also implement changes.

Rural practice surveyors may also conduct sales and auctions of country properties, contents of country houses, livestock, agricultural machinery, plant, forests and forest products.

Many are in private professional practice. According to the size of the practice, other specialist surveyors (valuers, building surveyors) may be employed. Rural practice surveyors sometimes now do farm business management as well, perhaps employing specialists to advise on mechanization, diversification (see alternative land use above) and other ways of improving farm profits. They are also often involved with conservation issues, trying to reconcile landowners' and conservationists' sometimes conflicting interests.

They also work for Defra (see AGRICULTURE AND HORTICULTURE, p. 63), local government, the National Trust and other bodies which own/manage land.

Rural practice surveying is an unusual combination of business, technical, environmental and agricultural work, and is one of the few professional jobs which include getting about the countryside.

Planning and Development Surveyors

The work overlaps with TOWN AND COUNTRY PLANNING (see p. 635).

Planning surveyors are concerned with the efficient allocation of resources in planning and with planning economics and planning law. The work is largely desk research (including statistics) and communicating with other specialists concerned with planning. A planning surveyor, for example, investigates the economics of a proposed shopping area. That would involve collecting facts and figures from various sources, assessing their implications and writing up the findings. Another project might mean having to find a suitable site for an industrial plant which has to be somewhere within a given area, must be near an inland waterway, near transport and must not be within an area of scenic value. That would not necessarily involve travelling, but consulting maps and relevant organizations.

The planning surveyor also advises clients on planning implications or proposals to buy and develop a property. This could involve visiting the site, taking photographs, and then appraising the proposal from a civic design point of view. They are also involved in marketing completed properties.

Planning and development surveyors work for planning consultants, local and central government, or as specialists in general practice surveying firms.

Land and Hydrographic Surveyors

Land surveyors must not be confused with land agents/agricultural surveyors. Their work is quite different and much more 'technical'. They use sophisticated technologies (including satellite positioning systems and laser alignment devices) to measure and plot the precise shape and position of natural and man-made features on land for the purpose of map-making, including large-scale maps which are used for engineering constructions. (Before motorways can be sited, for example, or bridges built, the minutest physical details of the area have to be plotted and mapped. Their expertise was essential in planning the Channel Tunnel.)

Land surveyors do not draw maps; that is done by cartographers (see p. 136). Land surveyors work in private practice, or for the government (Ordnance Survey, Ministry of Defence mainly), or for consulting engineers and big contractors. A few go into archaeological surveying (see ARCHAEOLOGY, p. 85).

Hydrographic surveyors are the smallest and most scientific branch, although the recent growth of off-shore oil and gas industries has widened their scope. They survey oceans, waterways, harbours and ports for purposes of producing nautical charts which show the precise shape, size, location of physical features of the sea bed, etc. and hazards, currents, tides, sunken wrecks. They supervise the dredging of ports and channels. The information sent by hydrographic survey ships operating in most parts of the world to the Navy's Hydrographic Department is being continuously revised. Collecting and interpreting information is done with highly sophisticated electronic equipment. British Admiralty Charts are used by seafarers all over the world, and by North Sea oil and gas engineers.

Many hydrographic surveyors are also naval officers. This is fairly tough outdoor work, combined with high technology.

Minerals and Mining Surveyors

This is the smallest specialization. Mining surveyors are responsible for mine safety and for mapping mineral deposits, and are involved with the potential use, value, properties, management and exploitation of mineral deposits, which means combining technical, scientific, managerial and commercial aspects. They are also responsible for minimizing environmental damage to the countryside where mineral deposits are mined.

In this country, mining surveyors are concerned mainly with coal mining, but minerals surveying overseas covers a variety of other minerals.

Prospects for chartered surveyors of all kinds vary according to economic conditions, but are mostly reasonable, especially as a wider range of organizations now employ surveyors, for example financial institutions; best opportunities are for general practice, quantity and building surveyors. Some opportunities in EU countries (for those who speak the relevant language fluently), especially for quantity surveyors, who are also in demand in Africa and the Middle East.

Training For membership of the Royal Institution of Chartered Surveyors (any surveying specialization) about 70% take 3-year full-time (or 4-year sandwich) degrees or diplomas in surveying; others study while in appropriate employment, which takes 5 to 6 years of part-time study (or 4 years for the distance-learning diploma course run by the College of Estate Management). Day-release is often granted in public sector employment. In the private sector, students usually have to study in their own time by correspondence course and evening classes.

Choosing a course needs careful research. Some courses allow students to choose between several allied specializations during the second year. It is essential to study the RICS up-to-date lists of accredited degrees and diploma courses in each Division. Course titles, especially for general practice, vary and are often misleading. For example there are several different titles for courses leading to General Practice Division exemptions; nor are the titles necessarily an indication of course emphasis.

Though it is usual to work initially in the specialization in which one qualified, it is quite possible to switch specializations later. In practice some specializations (such as, for example, building and quantity surveying) are more easily interchangeable than, for example, general practice and hydrographic.

General practice surveyors (i.e. valuers, estate agents, auctioneers) can train for the RICS Diploma in Valuation, usually 3–6 years, by correspondence course while in approved employment.

Graduates from any discipline may take a post-graduate conversion course. Alternatively, they may take the distance-learning diploma course (see above). Though theoretically an arts graduate could qualify in any of the specializations, most opt for the General Practice Division. Science/engineering graduates might opt for Building or Quantity Surveying RICS Divisions. Graduates with related degrees, for example in building or planning, qualify for partial exemption if they opt for the Building or the Planning and Development Divisions. There is 1 3-year Diploma in Fine Arts and Chattels Valuation for people with 2 A levels or experience in valuation.

Personal attributes Practical approach to problem-solving; ability to inspire confidence in clients; ability to take complex decisions on own initiative and work as one of a team as well; for some jobs ability to handle labour. For *consultancy* and *estate agency*: business acumen; liking for being out of doors.

Late start Possible, but requires very strong motivation. No problem getting training, but first job may be difficult for over-30s. Depends on previous experience.

Work life balance A career break should not be difficult in, for example, general practice surveying; possibly more difficult in areas where technologies change rapidly, but here keeping up with developments by reading journals and attending meetings should help.

Part-time work is not very common. No reason why established surveyors should not suggest to their employers that part time with flexible hours or job-sharing should work well.

Further information Royal Institution of Chartered Surveyors, Education and Training Department, Surveyor Court, Westwood Way, Coventry CV4 8JE.
www.rics.org
College of Estate Management, Whiteknights, Reading RG6 6AW.
www.cem.ac.uk

Related careers AGRICULTURE AND HORTICULTURE – ARCHITEC-
TURE – CARTOGRAPHY – ENGINEERING – HOUSING MANAGEMENT
– SURVEYING: *Technician* – TOWN AND COUNTRY PLANNING

SURVEYING TECHNICIANS
(includes managerial jobs in the construction industry; see
CONSTRUCTION, p. 171)

Entry qualifications *Either* 4 GCSEs (A–C) including maths, a science and a subject proving competence in the use of English for BTEC National awards (see p. 8); *or* at least 1 A level passed for direct entry to BTEC Higher National awards. For SQA equivalents see p. 10.

The work Most specializations overlap very much with supervisory and management jobs in the construction industry (see p. 171). Titles vary: the term 'technician' may not be used, even when the qualification required is a technician qualification.

Individual technicians' work varies enormously: some are deskbound draughtspersons, some are out and about; all now use computerized procedures and equipment. Some have a great deal of client-contact, some have none. Almost invariably they are part of a team.

The majority work under the overall direction of surveyors, architects, civil engineers or planners. Some of their work is indistinguishable from that done by chartered surveyors: until some years ago, chartered surveyors qualified almost exclusively by on-the-job plus part-time training, and they had only slightly higher entry qualifications than technicians often have now. While chartered surveyors' training is certainly much more demanding academically than technicians', many tasks are still the same as they always were and do not require the chartered surveyors' in-depth training. Technician-level qualifications are sufficient for the majority of those 'surveyors' who, while wanting responsibility and professional training, do not aspire to initiate and take charge of complex projects.

Surveying technician specializations:

Building Surveying Technicians
(see 'Building Surveyors', p. 595 and 'Construction Managers', p. 172)

Subdivisions cover construction and assessment of structures; administration of building regulations; preparations of plans; specification for and organization of work to be carried out by contractors; estimates of cost before projects start; dealing with tenders and contracts and checking and passing contractors' accounts; advising lay public on soundness of construction of property they consider buying (while ultimate responsibility for such advice lies with the employing chartered surveyor, the actual surveying on which surveyors' reports to clients are based is often carried out by technicians – the customer is not necessarily aware of this); advice to property owners on maintenance and repair. This may include drawing up schedules for redecoration, advice on eradication of damp, dry rot, etc.

Building surveying technicians work in a great variety of settings – and under a great variety of titles (for example *building manager*, *building surveyor*, *building inspector*). They are employed by virtually any type of organization which owns or is responsible for the building and/or maintenance of property, and by firms of consultants. When they work for building contractors, they may also be called *planning* or *contracts manager*, or *contracts surveyor*. Their work may be mainly organizational – ensuring that manpower and equipment are used efficiently; this means planning all the operations which are involved in completing a contract to build whatever it is. For example, if a firm of building contractors is engaged simultaneously on converting several houses into flats and building office blocks, the contracts planner or manager has to estimate for how long how many workers and which equipment will be required on each job and when the various specialists, such as heating engineers, plasterers, electricians, should be where.

While in the past only very large contractors had contract planners, now middle-sized firms often engage such staff (under various titles, and not necessarily only engaged on this type of planning).

Another job for building surveying technicians is as *site managers*. They are responsible for organization of the sequence and smooth working of operations on site.

Technicians who prefer desk-bound work can become draughtspersons and eventually be in charge of a drawing office. But drawing offices now have fewer vacancies as so much work is computerized and completed more quickly. Many work for estate agents, where they meet the general public (see p. 592).

Quantity Surveying Technicians
(see 'Quantity Surveyors', p. 593)

They form part of the surveying team concerned with the costing and financial management of all types of construction work. They may use computers and word processors. There are 3 main, but interrelated subdivisions (with rather quaint traditional titles).

1. *Takers off*: They abstract and measure from architect's, surveyor's or engineer's drawings every item of labour and materials to be used on a project, and list them in recognized terms. The information is needed to produce a 'cost plan' or Bill of Quantities. The job is usually office-based, and involves liaison with architects and other specialists, often as part of a technician team.

2. *Workers up*: They work out volumes, quantities and areas of all the items which have been measured by the taker off, and record them in a way which can be understood by all construction workers. These are then presented on the Bill of Quantities used by the quantity surveyor in deciding the most economical means of construction. Workers up are entirely office-based; they may be responsible for a part or whole of a project.

3. *Post-contract surveyors* and *site measurers*: They divide their time between office and site. Work includes monitoring work done so that interim payments can be made to contractors. They may discuss the implications of variations on the plans with subcontractors employed on the site and must understand contracts. Post-contract surveyors may be physically measuring work on site one day, attending a site meeting with a number of colleagues from different building-work spheres the same afternoon, and negotiating final payment with a subcontractor the next day. Usually they will have been workers up and takers off before becoming post-contract surveyors. Their job overlaps very much with that of chartered quantity surveyors.

General Practice Technicians
(see 'General Practice Surveyors', p. 591)

This division covers the work done by chartered general practice and planning surveyors. (At chartered level, there is a separate Planning and Development Division.)

General practice technicians may specialize in valuation, estate agency, estate and property management, housing management, town and country planning (see p. 635). Openings are the most varied, ranging from suburban estate agency's or international property company's *negotiator* (see p. 592) to Inland Revenue or insurance company's valuation technician. This specialization offers scope both to those who are mainly interested in meeting members of the public and to those who want to do mainly drawing or other office work and are interested in combining technical and commercial work.

Land Surveying Technicians
(see 'Land and Hydrographic Surveyors', p. 597)

These work with chartered land surveyors. The work has changed considerably in the last few years with the use of electronic distance-measuring equipment and digital coding and modelling of land shapes. There are also opportunities in photographing and tracking man-made satellites, and in aerial photography.

This is one of the most adventurous of technician specializations, with work for oil companies and air survey companies at home or abroad, including Third World countries.

Minerals Surveying Technicians
(see 'Minerals and Mining Surveyors', p. 598)

This is a small division and involves the preparation of accurate plans in connection with safety, operation and development of mines, and plans of geological formations in connection with mineral deposits. Much of the work is underground.

Hydrographic Surveying Technicians
(see 'Land and Hydrographic Surveyors', p. 597)

Making and updating charts of seas and coastlines, and profiles of sea beds; 'sign posting', on charts, of shipping lanes. This can be arduous outdoor work on survey ships and requires practical seamanship; only few draughtsmanship, office-based jobs.

Agricultural Surveying Technicians
(see 'Rural Practice Surveyors', p. 595)

This work overlaps with agriculture (see p. 63) and land agency. Main employers are local authorities and public bodies such as gas and electricity boards.

Surveying technicians generally are in demand but especially in quantity, general practice, land and building surveying where their work often overlaps with that of chartered surveyors. In these specializations there are often more opportunities for technicians than for chartered surveyors. Experienced technicians have some opportunities in EU countries if they speak the relevant language fluently.

There is a 'bridging arrangement' which enables qualified technicians to attain RICS membership and become chartered surveyors.

Training (all technicians) Students choose courses according to the type of work they are in or want to do. However, BTEC/SQA courses are flexible and, within related areas, it is usually possible to switch from one specialization or division to another; possibly adding course units.

The main surveying divisions are now covered by 2 'generic' course categories:

1. *Building Studies*: This covers *building surveying* and *quantity surveying*.

2. *Land Administration*: This covers *general practice surveying* (incorporating valuation and property management/estate agency); *land surveying* (incorporating land, sea and air surveying; cartography); *planning* (incorporating town and country and regional planning).

Then there are specialized courses: *minerals surveying* technicians take *mine and mining surveying* courses; *hydrographic surveying* technicians train either at the Royal Navy Hydrographic School, Plymouth (residential) or take special options in BTEC *land surveying* courses. There are few training vacancies (and jobs) for mining and hydrographic surveying technicians. *Agricultural surveying* technicians normally take the National Diploma in Agriculture (see AGRICULTURE AND HORTICULTURE, p. 68).

BTEC courses are normally taken *either* by day- or block-release, and last 2 years for the BTEC National Certificate and a further 2 years for the Higher National Certificate, *or* they are taken by 2-year full-time study for the BTEC National Diploma, followed by a further 2 years' full-time or 3 years' sandwich study for the Higher National Diploma. It is possible to switch from part-time National to full-time/sandwich Higher National and vice versa. (And there are plenty of opportunities, for the less ambitious, with National rather than Higher National awards.) Entrants with 1 relevant A level and another subject studied at A level can go straight into the Higher National Diploma course or into the second year of the National Certificate course. In Scotland, students take relevant SQA National Certificate modules (see p. 10) and then take the Higher National award. They can then take the Joint Test of Competence run by the RICS and the Society of Surveying Technicians (SST).

For the majority of jobs, Higher National awards are as marketable as degrees. For some jobs in the building industry they are in fact preferred because of their practical content and approach.

The Chartered Surveyors Training Trust runs a technician training scheme for school-leavers in the London area and West Midlands. Trainees are placed with employers and study part time.

The National Association of Estate Agents offers Technical Awards in Sale of Residential Property and Residential Letting and Property Management; no previous qualifications are required.

Personal attributes Some mathematical ability; interest in finding practical solutions to technical problems; liking for outdoor work; ability to work as one of a team and also to take responsibility, coupled with willingness to work for people more highly qualified than oneself; meticulous accuracy; ability to supervise construction site workers.

Late start There is no reason why people should not start in their 20s or 30s, especially if they have had some related experience or training, e.g. a geography degree or work experience in estate agency, on a construction site, with computers.

Work life balance If returners have kept up with developments, there is no reason why experienced technicians should not return to work. It would probably be easier in general practice and quantity surveying than, say, in agricultural surveying.

There is no reason why experienced technicians should not try and make their own part-time or job-share arrangements, especially in estate agency work.

Further information Edexcel BTEC and SQA (see pp. 8, 10)

Chartered Surveyors Training Trust, 9 Bentinck Street, London W1U 2EJ.

www.cstt.org.uk

National Association of Estate Agents, Arbon House, 21 Jury Street, Warwick CV34 4EH.

www.naea.co.uk

Related careers ARCHITECTURE: *Architectural Technologist – Chartered Surveyor* (above) – CONSTRUCTION – HOUSING MANAGEMENT

Tax Inspector

Entry qualifications First or second class honours or post-graduate degree in any subject or equivalent. The Civil Service sets entry requirements for their own specific courses. (Opportunities also for those starting as tax officer, see 'Junior Managers', p. 162).

The work Tax inspectors work in the Inland Revenue department of the Civil Service. Their main duty is to investigate the accounts of business concerns in order to agree the amount of profits for taxation purposes. By examining accounts and interviewing individuals they aim to spot any cases of tax evasion or fraud. They also advise taxpayers on tax and business law. Their work brings them into contact with the whole range of Britain's industry and commerce in their own district. The Inland Revenue is now also responsible for National Insurance and Tax Credits.

They deal with many kinds of people – accountants, lawyers, industrialists, farmers, small shopkeepers – by personal interview as well as by correspondence. They also represent the Crown before an independent tribunal when they and the taxpayer concerned cannot agree on the tax assessment.

There are District Offices in all areas. Promotion prospects are best for people willing to move to where there happens to be a vacancy. Opportunities also exist outside the Civil Service as tax advisers to companies and individuals.

Training Graduates are recruited through the Civil Service Fast Stream (see p. 160) and follow the Talent Recruitment Programme, a training and development programme that takes around 4 years to complete.

They are recruited into 2 key areas: leadership and management or technical and compliance. The technical and compliance stream has replaced the Inspector Training Programme.

Personal attributes Common sense; judgement; administrative ability; keen intellect; the ability to sum up people and situations; impartiality; equanimity; enjoyment of responsibility.

Late start See CIVIL SERVICE, p. 170.

Work life balance A career break scheme – up to 5 years – is open to both men and women.

The Inland Revenue operates various opportunities for part-time work to suit individual need.

Further information Inland Revenue, Human Resources, Mowbray House, Castle Meadow Road, Nottingham NG2 1BE.
www.inlandrevenue.gov.uk
www.careers.civil-service.gov.uk

Related careers ACCOUNTANCY – ACTUARY – BANKING AND BUILDING SOCIETY WORK – CIVIL SERVICE – INSURANCE

Teaching

There are more than 400,000 teachers in service in maintained (state) schools in England and Wales alone, making teacher training the biggest graduate recruiter in the UK, and teaching one of the most varied career paths. Teaching suffers from supply problems globally, and the UK is no exception. Teachers are required to work in a demanding, stressful and continually changing environment, and the image of the profession has suffered in recent years. Nevertheless, the challenges and rewards are still attracting a rising number of recruits and in 2003 there were more than 35,000 people training to be teachers, through various routes.

It is vital that first-class teachers are recruited and retained, but supply and demand does vary from subject to subject. There is great competition amongst the professions to recruit graduates with backgrounds in maths, science, technological subjects and modern languages. Various financial incentives are available. A training salary of £6,000 is paid to eligible post-graduate trainees. Additional 'Golden Hellos' are paid to those qualified to teach English (including drama), maths, design and technology, science, modern languages, ICT and Welsh at the end of their induction year. All trainees are eligible to apply for a means-tested hardship fund. Additional means-tested financial support is available for some people training to teach maths, design and technology, science, modern languages, ICT, religious education, music or geography. The demand for primary and 'early years' teachers is increasing. In particular, primary teachers with special knowledge and skills in the above areas of the National Curriculum have good prospects.

Entry qualifications All those who wish to teach in state maintained schools in England and Wales must hold Qualified Teacher Status (QTS). This is awarded to students who successfully complete an initial teacher training (ITT) programme. A degree and GCSEs (or equivalent qualifications) at grades C or above in maths and English are also required; those born on or after 1 September 1979 who wish to teach in the primary or middle phases must also hold GCSE (or equivalent qualification) grade C or above in a science subject.

Primary Schools (including Nursery)

The work Primary schools are generally organized into infant and junior schools but there are also first and middle schools for pupils of pre-secondary school age. Most children go on to secondary school at 11, but some remain at their primary/middle school until 12 or 13. Sometimes the younger and older primary children go to separate schools; in other cases a single school deals with the whole primary range. Some schools have attached nursery units, taking children at 3 or 4. (N.B. To teach in a state-maintained nursery school you must be a qualified teacher, though there may be unqualified assistants.)

The precise organization of primary education varies from one local education authority (LEA) to another. Schools also vary greatly in size, location and catchment area. Some schools will have as few as 2 teachers, others as many as 30. In the former case each teacher will teach several age groups; in the latter several teachers will share responsibility for an age group, sometimes through 'team teaching'.

Nursery and lower primary children learn largely through play and activity, which are planned and supervised by the teacher to achieve certain goals and develop children's skills. For example, a listening game might be devised to improve children's concentration skills. The teacher observes all the time to recognize which areas need working on for each child. Children of this age are extremely demanding; they are only able to work independently for very short periods of time, and demand a high level of attention, reassurance and encouragement.

The introduction of the Literacy Hour, the Numeracy Hour and end-of-key stage assessments (sometimes known as SATs) has brought a more proscribed approach to primary education. The teacher has to plan schemes of work, relating them to the age group; make sure all the necessary resources are to hand; check National Curriculum attainment targets in the appropriate subjects are met and record them; and be prepared to constantly evaluate and rethink strategies.

One of the most important skills for a primary teacher is effective classroom management. This includes timetabling, the grouping of children and the organization of the classroom. Learning time is wasted if, for example, the most boisterous child sits with those of his or her peers least able to cope, or if children involved in a messy activity need to move among children quietly engaged in other activities in order to get to their materials.

Primary teachers normally take their classes for all subjects, all day. The demands of the National Curriculum and the introduction of new subjects have led many teachers to take additional in-service specialist training to enable them to act as advisers or coordinators for a particular subject within their schools. Lesson preparation can take up a good deal of time, as can assessment and record-keeping, extra-curricular activities and maintaining good relationships with parents.

Secondary Schools

The work Usually at the age of 11, but sometimes at 12 or 13, children transfer to secondary school. Most children go to comprehensive schools, which cater for all ranges of ability. Some authorities, however, have retained a selective system where the more academically able children go to grammar schools. In some authorities children remaining in full-time education at 16+ go to sixth-form colleges, some of which offer a traditional sixth-form curriculum, while others offer a more diverse range of courses.

Unlike primary teachers, secondary teachers teach a limited number of subjects that are usually closely related to many different age and ability groups, throughout the day and week. Within the framework of their specialist knowledge, they need the teaching skills to establish working relationships with a diverse range of pupils: the unmotivated, the slow learners, the young pupils who look to the teacher for everything, the sixth-formers who test them with profound questions. They must try to stimulate the interest of all pupils and help them to achieve the best they can, whether it be 2 hard-earned GCSEs or 3 top grade A levels. This demands enthusiasm and flexibility.

Secondary teachers obviously need a good grounding in their subjects, but they do not need to know it all. Modern education is about learning how to learn, handling data and developing thinking and problem-solving skills. These are skills and challenges for teachers as well as pupils.

Secondary teachers spend a good deal of time (much of it out of school hours) on preparation and marking. They must be clear what they are going to achieve in each lesson, following the scheme of work as planned in the syllabus, and have the necessary material ready at each point, in each lesson, every day of the week. Good organization is vital. Formal assessment and recording have, in recent years, involved teachers in a good deal of additional administrative work, but assessment is also an intuitive and continuous process which occurs as teachers build relationships with their pupils.

Most teachers have responsibilities in addition to their subject teaching. Personal, social and health education, for example, is often a shared responsibility. Time is taken up in registration, form time and assemblies; administration, departmental and other meetings with colleagues; and contact with parents. Many teachers get involved in a range of extra-curricular activities, from sport to drama, chess or other special interest clubs. These can take up considerable time. Some plan and accompany children on trips. In addition, everyone on the staff shares responsibility for standards and so is effectively 'on duty' throughout the day, watching out for, preventing and dealing with problems.

Teachers can never rest on their laurels; year by year, new subjects are introduced, old subjects develop and are approached in new ways, and teaching and examining methods change. In addition, each class and each child is unique and will require different teaching methods. Good teachers need to update and evaluate their work constantly, deciding what to change and what to repeat, and finding the right method for a particular pupil or group.

Special Needs Education

Children may have special educational needs for a variety of reasons ranging from emotional or behavioural difficulties, through specific learning difficulties, to complex multiple physical and/or mental disabilities. Increasingly, such children are, whenever possible, educated in ordinary schools. Depending on circumstances, a child might be integrated into an ordinary class but receive special help, or be in a special unit or class attached to an ordinary school. Some children still need to go to special schools, sometimes for the whole of their schooling, sometimes only for short periods.

Working in special needs education is emotionally and physically demanding. The teacher is involved not only in teaching academic subjects but may also be required to help pupils manage a range of day-to-day activities such as eating and playing. The teacher needs to build up a good relationship with a child, but also with the others concerned with the child's welfare and development, such as doctors, social workers, speech and language therapists, physiotherapists and psychologists.

Apart from teachers of children with sight or hearing impairment, special needs teachers do not need additional qualifications, though they may take up in-service training courses. The usual route is to gain a teaching qualification (see below) and experience of teaching children with no special educational needs before moving into special needs work.

Independent Schools

Independent education covers a very wide range of institutions, from the renowned public schools to Montessori nursery schools. Some are based on a traditional academic approach while others are very 'progressive'. Many have outstanding records in preparing their pupils for external examinations and higher education, while others compare unfavourably with good state schools. Some pay their teachers considerably more than the scale for teachers in the maintained sector while others fall far short.

There are courses and qualifications of interest to particular sectors of independent education (e.g. Montessori and Rudolf Steiner), but these do not qualify one to teach in state schools.

Further Education

Many of the courses offered in the further education sector have a vocational bias. Some colleges are devoted to one particular field, e.g. agriculture. However, colleges also offer a broad range of other courses, from GCSEs and A levels (which many students take in conjunction with vocational studies) to leisure interests such as painting, foreign languages and keep fit. Increasing numbers of school-leavers are continuing their education in FE colleges and some local education authorities are making them the focus of 16+ provision.

Since 2001, education lecturers have been required to hold or be working towards a recognized qualification, either a PGCE specializing in FE/post-compulsory education or a university Certificate in Education. Part-time lecturers are now also required to hold or be working towards a Stage 1 or Stage 2 Teaching Certificate. Basic skills teachers are also required to have a specialist teaching qualification. Further information is available from the Further Education National Training Organisation (FENTO). Website: *www.fento.org*

HIGHER EDUCATION

In higher education, a higher degree is normally required for teaching. Academic qualifications are more important than certified teaching skills, but the Higher Education Academy set up in 2004 is taking forward the development of standards in teaching in HE (see *www. heacademy.ac.uk*). The role of higher education institutions is not merely to pass on knowledge, but to extend it, so research is an important element of work in this sector. Administration is another key task.

Training The two most popular initial teacher training routes leading to Qualified Teacher Status (QTS) are:

1. The undergraduate route. This can be a Bachelor of Education (BEd) or a BSc or BA with QTS. Most undergraduate courses require 2 A levels or equivalent (with at least 1 subject in a National Curriculum subject) and GCSEs (or equivalent qualifications) at grade C or above in maths and English language. Additionally, those born on or after 1 September 1979 who wish to teach in the primary or middle phases must also hold GCSE (or equivalent qualification) grade C or above in a science subject. Courses last for 3 or 4 years and include experience in the classroom, professional practice (such as theory of education and child development) and subject study. Students normally specialize in the teaching of particular age-ranges and subjects, but they are not restricted to those in their subsequent careers. Many primary teachers qualify by this route. Most secondary teachers qualify through the post-graduate routes described below.

2. The Post-graduate Certificate of Education (PGCE). This is the most popular route into teaching for those who have already completed their first degree. Entry qualifications are normally a degree in a related subject to the chosen teaching specialism and GCSE (or equivalent qualification) maths and English at grade C or above. Additionally, those born on or after 1 September 1979 who wish to teach in the primary or middle phases must also hold at GCSE (or equivalent qualification) grade C or above in a science subject. PGCEs can be studied as a 1-year full-time course, or over 2 years part time. Some providers now offer 2-year PGCE courses to develop subject knowledge and professional training. Courses for primary teachers must include 18 weeks of teaching practice in schools; secondary courses must include 24 weeks. Eligible post-graduate ITT trainees receive a £6,000 tax-free bursary while they train. So ITT providers offer flexible (or 'modular') training programmes which allow candidates to fit teacher training around other commitments, for example, a job or family. These flexible routes take into account any previous experience of teaching, for example, voluntary work abroad, or teaching in the private sector.

A number of other initial teacher training routes operate, including the SCITT (School-Centred Initial Teacher Training) scheme, where consortia of schools organize school-based training for graduates which leads to QTS. For those who wish to train through a paid, employment-based route, the Graduate and Registered Teacher Programmes (or GRTP) are competitive programmes which offer a number of funded places for training in schools. The Graduate Teacher Programme (GTP) offers training to graduates for up to a year (depending on previous teaching experience), which leads to QTS. Candidates must first find a school which is willing to take them on as a trainee teacher. Candidates' training needs are assessed and the training programme drawn up by a designated recommending body (DRB) or recommending body (RB). Training is mostly delivered in schools. The Registered Teacher Programme is for candidates who have completed 2 years of higher education and wish to complete their degree studies alongside teacher training in schools. The candidate's training needs are assessed and the training programme drawn up by an RB. Training programmes last up to 2 years and require a sound foundation in the chosen teaching subject for entry. The GRTP is organized by the Teacher Training Agency.

All those training to be teachers in England and Wales are required to pass skills tests in numeracy, literacy and ICT in order to gain QTS. The award of QTS is followed by a mandatory induction year. Financial incentives, in the form of 'Golden Hellos', are available to some teachers on completion of their induction year.

NOTES ON THE SCOTTISH SYSTEM: To be eligible for permanent teaching appointments in maintained schools in Scotland, teachers must be registered with the General Teaching Council for Scotland. To be eligible to register one must hold a teaching qualification, in either primary education, secondary education or further education.

The patterns of qualification are similar to those in England. Unlike in England, however, one is registered to teach a particular age range and, in the case of secondary education, a particular subject or subjects. *Primary teachers* may take *either* a 4-year BEd, for which the normal entry requirements are 3 SCE-Higher passes (one must be in English or a National Course award at Higher level at C or above in

English and Communication) and 2 Standard or O-Grade passes
(one must be maths at grade 1 or 2 or a National Course award at
Intermediate 2 level), *or* a 1-year post-graduate course for which a
degree plus H-grade English and Standard maths are required. *Secondary teachers* usually take a 1-year post-graduate course in specific
subjects following first degrees with sufficient specified achievement in
the relevant subjects. There are secondary BEds in physical education,
music and technology.

As in England, alternative equivalent qualifications may be acceptable for entry. Mature students may get some concessions, but the
requirement for maths and English must be met. Teachers who have
trained outside Scotland and who have suitable qualifications may be
admitted to the register, in some cases after additional training.

Teachers in further education do not need to be registered. The
course for registration is open only to serving teachers seconded by
their authority.

Personal attributes To be a teacher you need: to enjoy working with
children and young people; patience; a sense of humour; enthusiasm;
flexibility; fairness and consistency; confidence; optimism; good
organizational and time-management skills; sensitivity; good communication skills; and the ability to work alone and as part of a team.

Late start There are good prospects for older candidates wishing to
enter teaching, for career changers and those seeking to return to the
profession. In 2002, over 500 of those accepted on to teacher training
courses were over 45 years old. The introduction of flexible, modular
style routes and the expansion of the GTP have improved access to
ITT for candidates with life commitments such as work or a family,
which would normally preclude full-time, institution based study.

Work life balance Supply work, part time and job-sharing are all
options, dependent on local availability and practice, and subject
specialisms.

Schools and education authorities are keen to attract teachers back
from the 'PIT' (pool of inactive teachers). Initiatives include special

courses for returners and the encouragement of flexible working arrangements such as supply work, part-time work and job sharing. The Teacher Training Agency operates a 'Returning to Teach' programme (0845 6000 993) and can provide a directory of courses and other useful information for those wishing to return to teaching. Teachers who return on a regular full- or part-time basis are entitled to be paid at a point on the standard national scale no lower than the point on which they were last regularly paid. Employers can take into account any experience or qualifications gained during the break in deciding whether to appoint at a higher pay level.

Further information The Teaching Information Line offers information and advice to those interested in becoming teachers – 0845 6000 991. This service is run by the Teacher Training Agency (TTA), TTA Communication Centre, PO Box 3210, Chelmsford, Essex CM1 3WA.
www.useyourheadteach.gov.uk
Scottish Executive, Education Department, Area 2A, Victoria Quay, Edinburgh EH6 6QQ.
www.teachinginscotland.com

Related careers CAREERS WORK – NURSERY NURSE – PERSONNEL/ HUMAN RESOURCES MANAGEMENT – SOCIAL WORK – YOUTH AND COMMUNITY WORK

Television, Film and Radio

Entry qualifications Very varied but marked trend towards graduates. IT skills are almost essential.

This whole area is going through a period of unprecedented change, both technological and organizational, with a dramatic impact on career and training opportunities. Large numbers of staff have been shed as, increasingly, ITV franchise holders will buy in, rather than originate, programmes, and so have no permanent production staff or facilities. The BBC, too, has been cutting back on staff, recruitment and training. It is in the independent, non-broadcast sector that there is likely to be most growth. The whole industry relies increasingly on freelances. Most 'career' opportunities lie in management/administration/sales.

TV, FILM AND VIDEO

The industry consists mainly of the 'terrestrial' (as opposed to satellite) broadcasting companies and independent companies producing for broadcast, the corporate sector (e.g. training and corporate image promotional film and videos), commercials, music promotion and feature films. There are also production facilities in educational establishments and community-based units. Satellite and cable have gone into production in a limited way, but they still buy in most of their programmes and offer most job opportunities in sales and marketing and on the technical side. The boundaries between the sectors of the industry are becoming increasingly blurred. Independents commonly work in more than one sector, e.g. both making programmes for broadcast and doing corporate work. The broadcast companies are also diversifying into, for example, corporate work or making programmes for satellite and cable. Broadcasters are investing more in identifying audiences, and the rapid development of interactive media is increasing the feasibility of targeting ever narrower groups of viewers, opening up more opportunities for small companies. The range of jobs is wide and evolving and Skillset, the Sector Skills Council for the audio-visual industries, now does an annual census of employment within the industry (*www.skillset.org*). Terminology and job content can vary considerably. Job titles are not clear-cut. In addition, there is an industry-wide trend towards 'multi-skilling'. Sometimes this is the result of technical development when, for example, 1 piece of equipment and operator can do what previously took 2 pieces and 2 operators. Another impetus is the need for a more flexible workforce; film editors learn video editing in order to survive.

Put simply, activities can be divided into pre-production, production and post-production. Each has a range of different jobs involved, but people tend to be employed (as freelances) not until, and then only while, they are needed. Also, distinctions between jobs are blurring as people need to do more to keep employed.

Below are some of the programme-making jobs involved in broadcast TV. They are based on the BBC, but similar jobs are needed elsewhere in programme production, including the growing independent sector. Where possible indications of the kind of qualifications and training normally needed are given, but see 'Notes on entry and training', p. 632.

Production Staff

Producers/directors

The work Exact functions vary. Producers are usually responsible for initiating, budgeting, casting, and the shape or 'treatment' of programmes. Directors are responsible for interpreting the idea and actually making the programme. These top jobs are very responsible and are done by specialists in particular fields, such as current affairs, drama, education, science or technology, who have long, often technical experience in the medium. Many work on contracts for particular projects.

Production assistants

They provide organizational and secretarial support to a programme. They may do some research, make bookings, arrange meetings, sit with the producer in the gallery checking on timing, cue the inserts of film or tape and are normally responsible for continuity. They have considerable contact with people both inside and outside TV. They see to it that the right instructions about make-up, costumes, sets, rehearsal times and studio bookings go to the right people. Production assistants perform any secretarial duties including typing (and often retyping) the shooting script.

Floor managers (known as 'stage managers' in outside broadcasts)

They may be involved at the planning stage in advising on design, sound and props. During recording they control the studio floor. They are responsible for discipline on the floor and for safety of staff and artists. Duties include relaying the producer's/director's instructions to actors and presenters, using headphones to keep in touch with the gallery. They are responsible for cueing the actors, which can be a complicated task as they are often working on different sets and cannot see each other. The floor manager has to move around the sets while keeping out of camera shot. A diplomatic, pleasant personality is essential. In outside broadcasts they have to liaise with the general public.

Entry Nearly all from the ranks of assistant floor managers or other production posts.

Assistant floor manager

Similar to assistant stage manager in the theatre. Work varies according to size and type of production, but usually includes making sure that all the props are available, taking charge of the prompt book and mark-ups during rehearsals. Assistant floor managers usually start their on-the-job training with the easier talks and discussion pro-grammes before going on to drama series, etc.

Entry Candidates are expected to have experience in professional stage management, in theatre, film or TV.

Researchers

The majority of researchers are freelance. Research may be anything from looking through newspaper cuttings and finding a suitable person to be interviewed – not by researcher but by interviewer/presenter – on a news programme, to spending several months researching the background for a documentary or drama series. Researchers must be good all-rounders, able to pick out relevant facts from a mass of material. They usually write 'briefs', which may range from a few questions which an interviewer is to ask on a programme, to exhaustive background material for a documentary scriptwriter. Researchers in current affairs must also be able to think up programme ideas and to work under tremendous pressure. Specialist researchers, for example for scientific or medical programmes, are often freelances.

Entry Usually graduates and/or ex-journalists, or by promotion from within.

News staff, presenters, interviewers

Newsroom staff compile and write scripts for the *presenters*; *reporters* and *correspondents* 'get the stories' and present some themselves. The essence of broadcast news is brevity. *TV and radio journalists* (there is a trend for all journalists to have to work in both media) must be instant fact-selectors and decision-makers. They may be sent any-where at any time. *Editors* are senior staff responsible for piecing a programme together.

Entry Entrants are almost invariably graduates (any subject) with keen interest in current affairs, but 'general education' plus proven journalistic ability (i.e. good job on a good paper) can also lead in.

Design

Set designers

They are responsible for designing the sets down to the smallest accessories in accordance with the producer's concept. The producer calls in the designer when the idea is beginning to take shape. The designer's interpretation of the atmosphere the producer has in mind and their own suggestions are vitally important to the success of the production. They must have a good grasp of the technicalities of production.

Design assistants work with the designer on the technical, rather than creative, tasks. They draw ground plans and make working drawings; draw up specifications; make models of sets; and make or search for props.

Graphic designers and their *assistants* create credit titles, 'linking material', captions, maps and general illustrations. This is now frequently done using computers, but nevertheless it is still essentially creative work.

Scenic artists and *assistants* paint backcloths and decorative features such as curtains, carpets and portraits.

Visual effects designers and *assistants* devise, make and operate a wide variety of visual effects and 'illusions'.

Entry Whatever the level of entry qualifications, all first appointments are to the post of assistant. Generally speaking, progress to designer is from design assistant. All design assistants need degree level qualification in relevant art disciplines. Additionally, graphic design assistants normally need commercial art experience (e.g. advertising) following a degree or diploma; scenic artists need wide knowledge of painting, history of art and architecture, and interior design; visual effects staff need to be able to work in all kinds of materials, make models and have a basic grasp of physics. Most design is 'outsourced', that is, done by freelances or those working in facilities houses. Some companies employ designers as project managers.

Costume designers (also called 'wardrobe')

They are in charge of hiring, designing and adapting up-to-date and period costumes. They are called in on new productions at an early stage to discuss the costumes and to advise on whether to hire, make or adapt, and to arrange for this to be done. Later they liaise with other designers and make-up staff. They need a thorough knowledge of period styles, but further research is often needed to make certain of representing the exact year or season. Assistants help designers in all aspects of their work and may stand in for them, e.g. when filming on location.

Entry Preferably with a theatre or textile design degree and considerable experience in theatre or film costume. All entrants start at assistant level, from which designers are promoted. Assistants must be at least 19 with an A level standard of education and a good knowledge of costume design and history (a degree or diploma is essential for promotion to designer). Virtually all work is done on a freelance or short-contract basis.

Dressmakers make up costumes under the supervision of designers and make alterations to costumes which are hired or from stock.

Entry With BTEC/SQA Higher National Diploma in Fashion and a minimum of 2 years' experience in the theatre or with a theatrical costumier. Knowledge of history of costume an advantage.

Dressers work on last-minute ironing and maintenance of costumes and help actors to dress for performance.

Make-up artists/designers

Television make-up is highly skilled. It requires the ability to understand and defeat the camera's often unkind effects on faces. It also requires a thorough knowledge of period hairstyles. An experienced senior assistant is usually in charge of each dramatic production and makes up the star actors. Juniors see to the rest of the cast and also look after the simpler make-up required for non-dramatic productions. Tact and diplomacy are essential.

Entry Most make-up artists train privately, which is expensive.

Technical Operations

These concern the technical interpretation of the director's instructions and producing the required sound and vision effects which are finally seen and heard. Most TV programmes are pre-recorded. When recording a programme as well as during 'live' transmission, previously recorded and/or filmed material may be slotted in. The operational and technical sides of creating programmes and getting them on to TV screens are highly complex and require creativity, technical expertise and an unflappable temperament.

Camera operators help in setting up and operating electronic cameras and associated equipment in studios and on outside broadcasts. Promotion is to assistant and later cameraman/woman, vision supervisor, vision controller and ultimately possibly to technical manager responsible for lighting (various titles).

Sound assistants help in setting up and operating sound recording and reproduction equipment; they 'collect sound effects', and may eventually become sound supervisors responsible for control and balance of the various sound sources which are combined for final transmission. They are London-based in the BBC.

Audio assistants do similar work to sound assistants but they work in the regional (smaller) centres, and are also involved in the operation of radio sound equipment in joint radio/TV centres.

Recording operators control the increasingly sophisticated videotape and telecine (the film equivalent) equipment. They set up and run the recorders and must respond instantly to the producer's requirements. Recordings may be for instant replay or later transmission.

Entry and training Minimum age 18. GCSEs (A–C) in English language, maths and physics. Applicants for training courses should also have a keen interest in, and some 'hobby experience' of, hi-fidelity reproduction, tape-recording music, colour photography or lighting for amateur dramatics, and, for sound operators, ability to read a musical score. A strong interest in current affairs and IT skills are also very useful.

Vision-mixer

Up to 6 cameras may be in operation during a production. The producer in the control room decides which camera's picture to send out to the audience, and tells the vision-mixer, who switches to the selected camera as the order is given. This needs concentration and quick reflexes.

Training Mostly on the job for existing TV staff.

Engineering

Some TV engineers work in studios or outside broadcasting, coping with emergency repairs and sudden equipment failure, generally acting as technical 'back-up'. Others are responsible for operation and maintenance of equipment used to route, control and distribute signals from various sound and vision programme sources. All this work can be hectic and needs quick decision-making and a cool head. Other departments are concerned with research, development, planning, installation of a variety of complex equipment (see ENGINEERING, p. 216, for engineering functions). In a time of changing technology they must be prepared to update their knowledge and assimilate new ideas quickly. Currently, this is one of the areas being reduced, with a blurring of distinctions between traditional engineering and IT skills.

Entry and training Increasingly, employers are favouring some specialist degree courses.

Filming for TV

Film camera and sound staff are quite distinct from TV camera and sound staff. A considerable amount of television material is filmed (although most is on videotape); whole programmes are filmed, e.g. schools broadcasts, documentaries; film is also used as an important ingredient in all kinds of programmes – light entertainment, current affairs, children's programmes, plays and series. Camera crews travel a lot and at short notice. There are 3 basic jobs: *editing, camera, sound* (titles may vary).

Film editors work entirely in the cutting-room, 'editing down' material shot in the studio or on location. A great deal of their work is done on their own initiative, as directors do not have time to be with editors all day. The job is highly creative as it is the editor who shapes and fashions the final programme which audiences see, but very few editors work purely with film. Editing can lead to directing.

Film camera crews usually consist of 2–4 people. The head of the camera crew is in charge of lighting; works in close cooperation with the director; knows the script thoroughly and arranges the all-important lighting and camera angles for each individual shot, so as to achieve the atmosphere the director wants. Lighting cameraman/woman can be an important step to directing film.

Assistant camera crews load and change magazines, make sure the right equipment is available at the right time and place and in working order, and they learn how to operate cameras and lighting equipment. Promotion is pretty slow – it takes about 10 years to reach lighting cameraman/woman status.

Rostrum camera crew record on film and tape the artwork produced by the *graphic designers* (see p. 624).

Film sound recordists/sound technicians are concerned with dubbing, sound-transfer and above all with mixing sound from various sources. This may include location recordings on tape, and sounds produced by effects machines. Achieving the correct balance, controlling the 'input' from various sources, is a highly skilled job, requiring great technical skill and musical creativity.

Assistants manipulate microphones and other recording equipment and learn by watching. Far fewer apply for sound than vision jobs so chances of acceptance are better.

Projectionists (or *film assistants*) operate projection equipment and may also work on dubbing.

Entry qualifications and training Interest and 'hobby experience' are crucial. There are a number of film/TV courses at art schools, either as part of an art and design degree course, or 2–3-year BTEC Diploma courses, or at post-graduate level (for SQA equivalents see p. 10). Course emphasis (and entry requirements) vary enormously: for example on closed circuit educational television films; on feature or instructional films; with technical or creative bias, etc.

FILM AND VIDEO INDUSTRY

Recently there has been greater investment in feature film making in Britain. The future demands of cable TV and the home video market should provide greater opportunities than the recent past. However, entry into cinema film making will remain very highly competitive. The only real job prospects lie with the growing number of often very small production companies which combine TV film making and, very occasionally, cinema, with the whole range of other productions, e.g. training and advertising films.

Video recorders, while not offering the same 'creative' scope as film cameras, have very wide and growing applications: sales promotions (e.g. for pop records and at 'point of sale' in shops), training of all kinds, recording ballets for a dance company's repertoire, monitoring the performance of racehorses during meetings. Many companies use only freelance staff as and when they need them and many of these specialize, e.g. in making wildlife or travel films. Studio facilities and sophisticated equipment are often hired from 'facilities houses' which do not themselves make programmes.

Entry and training There is no essential difference between filming for TV and making non-broadcast films. Similarly, people employed in video production do much the same work as those in films.

There are no jobs which can be done straight from school. Entry is normally via one of the following:

1. TV training and experience.

2. An appropriate diploma, degree or post-graduate course at film school or art college (titles and content vary, so it is essential to study prospectuses carefully).

3. An electronic engineering course (all levels) plus in-service training.

4. The FT² scheme (supported by all sides of the film and TV industry) coordinates new entrant training in the *freelance film industry* (*www.ft2.org.uk*). Candidates are considered not only on the basis of academic qualifications, but also on a proven commitment to the industry (i.e. through amateur film and video making). The scheme lasts 2 years. It begins with an 8-month foundation period, with attachments to editing, camera, sound or art departments. Trainees then choose their specialization and spend the rest of the scheme in their chosen area.

5. Specialized knowledge leading to making videos on a particular topic.

6. Very occasionally, extensive amateur experience.

There is more scope for versatility in video than in film making: people tend to work 'cross-sectorally', that is, move from one type of work to another fairly easily. Technicians need to be able to work in both film and television. There is always room in this expanding industry for really good technical people.

RADIO

Independent radio has more than 50% of the listening audience. They therefore account for the bulk of jobs – and most of those are in sales or advertising.

Entry routes differ between BBC network, BBC local (which has made a positive decision to become journalism-based) and independent local radio. Once trained it is possible to move from one to another. Below are some examples from network radio.

PRODUCTION

Producers are responsible for initiating and developing programme ideas. They need an interest in the creative use of radio, a journalistic approach, some experience in relevant subject areas, e.g. the arts, science, medicine, social issues, drama, comedy, popular music, etc., and good technical skills. Work formerly done by studio managers is now done by producers. Producers are recruited from within the BBC – from local radio, researchers, studio managers and radio production assistants, for example; by direct advertising in the press; via the radio production trainee scheme.

Radio production assistants help producers by providing all-round administrative back-up for a programme, varying from typing scripts to helping in the studio. They are recruited from secretarial and clerical staff within the BBC or direct from outside.

Researchers work on individual programme strands. They will have specialist knowledge and skills. They may be recruited by direct advertising in the press and work mainly on short-term contracts which can vary from 1 month to 1 year.

Continuity announcers/newsreaders are recruited from existing broadcasters in local radio or from other employees with good, clear voices. They work on their own and need to be good at problem-solving. Occasionally jobs will be advertised in the press; previous broadcasting experience is generally required.

Sports assistants and correspondents often come from local radio, or have experience as sports journalists on newspapers. They need a good broadcasting style, an all-round knowledge of sport and more detailed commitment to one or more sports.

Reporters who work on all the main 'magazine' programmes from *Woman's Hour* to *Front Row* are freelances who generally started their careers on local or independent radio.

NOTES ON ENTRY AND TRAINING (TO THE INDUSTRY GENERALLY)
The uncertainty in the industry in recent years has meant that training schemes in independent television have virtually ceased. The BBC training schemes are an excellent way into the industry but they are intensely competitive. As far as the numbers entering are concerned, they have only ever been the tip of the iceberg. The BBC has about 21,000 people under contract: permanent jobs tend to be in administration, finance, law and personnel.

Currently about 200,000 people work in the industry, of whom about half are freelance. Competition to enter the industry at any level is intense. A report from the Audio Visual Industries Training Group published in 2001 acknowledged that a key issue within the industry is that it does still survive on recruiting through networking or entrants able to afford to do unpaid work experience when they first start and that this is not helpful to those unable to follow these routes. It is still very much 'a foot in the door industry'. However, a number of initiatives are being introduced to change this, for example the BBC has opened up opportunities for work experience by advertising openings on their website: *www.bbc.co.uk/jobs/workexperience*.

Clearly, the 'take-any-job-do-anything' strategy can work. But it is not easy to get these first jobs. On the operational side you need to get skills and that means you need to be enterprising. Hospital and local radio often need volunteers and can offer 'hands-on' experience. Get involved in amateur theatre or make your own videos or recordings. Watch television and become aware of companies' output.

Independent production and facilities companies, corporate in-house production units, major educational and franchise workshops are likely to be growth sectors and can provide experience that can take you into the broadcast companies as permanent staff or on a freelance basis (*all* sectors increasingly use freelances). They are also career outlets in themselves. Most are very small. Probably about three-quarters of them have 10 or fewer employees. Recruitment and training patterns are haphazard, but a small organization can often offer all-round experience. Corporate in-house production units offer employment to only a very few people, but they often have state-of-the-art equipment. Try knocking on doors – people have been known to get jobs this way, turning up just as someone was needed, or trying again and again and again *until* someone was needed. Consider taking a job as a 'runner' (most of whom are graduates in their 20s) – the person who makes the tea, does deliveries, deals with the post and answers the phone can really find out how the industry works and who does what, which is vital.

Increasing numbers entering the industry, especially on the production side, are graduates. Media studies degree courses showed the greatest increase in number of applications in 2003, but this will not necessarily give a head start. What employers are looking for is a lively interest in current affairs and broadcasting, and evidence that you have got practically involved in a way to complement your interests. Nevertheless, some courses are favoured by employers. Before taking any 'relevant' course, question in what ways it will stretch your mind and help you to develop wide interests. Ask to see details of what previous graduates have done and whether NVQs are available.

Once in, most people develop their own careers. They may pick up new skills informally, by following around someone more experienced or experienced in a different area, or formally, as through the BBC's system of 'attachments' whereby staff can try out other jobs. The industry recognizes the need for more structured training, especially for freelances. NVQs (see p. 10) cover every level up to senior technical, production and management grades.

Even when particular training is useful or essential, getting that training does not guarantee a job. Since it is recognized that the vast majority of listeners and viewers are not ABC1s, there is a trend towards recruiting from a wider background (i.e. not just middle-class Oxbridge graduates). Good team skills are essential; this is *not* an industry for prima donnas. Specific skills, for example the ability to speak Welsh or highly developed IT skills, can give you a head start. But, as ever, much depends on being the right person in the right place at the right time. The more you know about the industry, the nearer you are to being the right person – and the better able to find the right place.

Skillset is the Sector Skills Council for the audio-visual industries. It is *vital* that anyone considering working in this complex and rapidly changing field contacts them. They publish an excellent careers handbook on the shape of the industry – the employers, the jobs, the courses – with good advice on planning a strategy. They also maintain a database of training provision.

Skillset also hold an A–Z of jobs in the audio-visual industry which can be accessed through their website: *www.skillset.org*. With BECTU, the trades union for the media industry, Skillset runs a specialist media-related careers service – see *www.skillsformedia.com*.

Personal attributes Creative imagination; wide interests generally, a special interest in a particular subject; a clear, quick, logical mind; appreciation of what audiences want; a strong constitution; the ability to work as one of a team and to take responsibility; a sociable nature; a fairly thick skin; tact; calmness in crises; speed of action; self-confidence; determination and persistence; desire to communicate ideas; ability to take criticism; temperament and skills to be self-employed.

Late start Scope mainly for people with relevant experience and qualifications, especially for experienced journalists and engineers. In general, people in this insecure, heavily freelance industry are getting younger.

Work life balance In an industry dependent on freelancers and short-term contracts career breaks are often a matter of individual choice. Skillset offers a specific range of help to established freelancers, including advice and guidance on career direction and a range of short courses for those wishing to renew or expand their skills for which funding of up to 60% may be available. The BBC offers a range of flexible working arrangements, including career breaks, part-time working and term-time only contracts.

Further information Skillset, Prospect House, 80–110 New Oxford Street, London WC1A 1HB.
www.skillset.org
www.skillsformedia.com

Related careers ADVERTISING – ART AND DESIGN – DRAMA – JOURNALISM – MUSIC – PHOTOGRAPHY

Town and Country Planning

Entry qualifications Degree or post-graduate qualification accredited by the Royal Town Planning Institute (see also 'Training', below).

Town Planners

In a world of increasingly complex, interrelated and rapidly changing urban and rural environments, town and country planners play a key role in the process of promoting and guiding physical, social and economic change and in mitigating its impact. The core of the work is based on developing an understanding of the environmental, social, economic and political factors which have shaped towns, cities and the countryside, and which are prompting change in them.

Working with a wide range of associated disciplines, including architecture, landscape architecture, estates surveying, transportation, sociology and economics, planners prepare, evaluate and respond to proposals ranging from a small house extension to a new airport runway. The variety of issues with which they may be involved is such that, whilst many planners are generalists, a growing proportion specialize in particular aspects such as economic development, social regeneration, conservation and management of historic or natural environments, urban design or renewable energy and sustainable development.

Historically, most planners worked in local and central government. However, the employment picture has now become much more complex. Private practice consultancy has grown substantially and planners now act as in-house advisers to companies and agencies, including property developers, major retailers, and organizations such as the National Trust and the utility companies.

Even within local government work roles are varied and range from core activity in the statutory planning processes such as preparing structure and local plans to guide future development and the assessment of individual applications for development through to roles with chief executives and service departments contributing to advice on issues such as transportation, recreation or housing policy, and to across-the-board corporate policy.

Career paths are very varied and a high proportion of the wide range of employing organizations now recruit new graduates who do not have initial experience gained in work on statutory planning processes in local and central government.

Training *Either*: 4-year full-time, 6-year part-time or 5-year sandwich degree accredited by the Royal Town Planning Institute; *or*: a degree in any subject followed by a 2-year full-time or 3-year part-time post-graduate course accredited by the Royal Town Planning Institute (RTPI). A few schools of planning offer preparatory bridging courses for people without the normal degree or professional qualifications (e.g. linking with some BTEC Higher National awards) which then give entry on to their accredited post-graduate courses.

After 2 years' practical planning experience, candidates who have fulfilled the academic requirements of the RTPI qualify for election to membership as Chartered Town Planners.

Sociologists, geographers, economists, architects, landscape architects and other specialists concerned with the various aspects of planning also work in planning departments, particularly in counties and big cities. For work concerned with overall strategic planning issues and policy, i.e. for senior posts, however, a planning qualification is essential.

See also ARCHITECTURE, 'Training' (p. 89).

Personal attributes A keen interest in other people's priorities and way of life; social and community concerns; powers of observation; excellent communication skills at all levels; ability to differentiate different needs and demands; creative imagination; patience for painstaking research; the ability to work as one of a team as well as to take responsibility; interest in social, economic and environmental developments.

Late start Graduates with relevant degrees (geography, social science, engineering) could start post-graduate studies. There is no specific upper age limit. An RTPI accredited distance-learning course is available for people (graduates or non-graduates) who want to switch to planning from related careers (architects, geographers, engineers, etc.) in mid-career. It should also be useful for people returning after a career break.

Work life balance Local authorities and the Civil Service are introducing flexible working practices. Planning priorities and legislation change constantly, so planners taking a career break must keep up with developments. There are 'mid-career' updating courses and seminars for all planners, which could be useful as *refresher* courses (see 'Late start', above). Returners can also take additional courses, for example in transport planning or regeneration at the returning stage. Reduced RTPI subscriptions available.

Experienced planners increasingly do consultancy work. Part-time courses available (see above).

Further information The Royal Town Planning Institute, 41 Botolph Lane, London EC3R 8DL.
www.rtpi.org.uk

Planning Support Staff

Support staff carry out various technical and practical tasks. These can include drawing up of plans; preparing maps and diagrams; conducting surveys and interpreting results; dealing with inquiries from the public. They use computers for the various activities and may be in charge of a department's computer system. Planning support staff also include planning administrators and enforcement officers.

Town and Country Planning

Entry qualifications 4 GCSEs (A–C) including maths and a subject involving written English.

Training On the job with day-release for the BTEC Higher National Certificate in Planning (or SQA Certificate in Planning) (see pp. 8, 10), or full-time study for the BTEC/SQA Higher National Diploma award. A level 3 NVQ/SVQ in Town Planning Support is available. These qualifications, together with relevant experience, can lead to Technical Membership of the RTPI. It is possible to work towards professional membership of the RTPI by taking a town planning degree after the BTEC National Certificate.

Late start Few opportunities although there can be opportunities for people with relevant skills and experience to become planning enforcement officers.

Work life balance Good opportunities for flexible working in both local authorities and the Civil Service. Opportunities for part-time work are limited, but job-sharing should be possible.

Further information The Royal Town Planning Institute, 41 Botolph Lane, London EC3R 8DL.
www.rtpi.org.uk

Related careers ARCHITECTURE: *Architectural Technician* – CARTOGRAPHY – ECONOMICS – ENGINEERING – HOUSING MANAGEMENT – LANDSCAPE ARCHITECTURE – LOCAL GOVERNMENT – SURVEYING: *Auctioneers*

Trading Standards Officer

Entry qualifications For the Diploma in Trading Standards: an approved specialist degree or a degree in a relevant subject plus accredited experience and learning.

The work Trading standards officers (TSOs) are employed mainly by local authorities to ensure a fair system of trading between consumers and traders and between traders themselves. They are responsible for the enforcement of a vast array of consumer protection legislation designed to protect the consumer from, for example, unsafe electrical products or short-weight goods. At the same time they try to ensure that no other trader suffers from the effect of such unfair trading practices. TSOs are interested in subjects as wide-ranging as food safety, metrology (science of weights and measures), animal health and welfare, consumer credit, misleading advertising, counterfeit goods and sales of restricted products to under-age children.

There are two main aspects to the work. The first is routine checking and inspecting to see that, for example, the motorist gets the amount of petrol indicated on the pump, that foods are properly labelled (the actual testing of food composition is carried out by public analysts), that video films are correctly classified and labelled. Much of this is done openly, but test buying is also done. The other aspect is investigating complaints from consumers and traders. These may claim that a holiday brochure was misleading, that a 'pre-shrunk' shirt has shrunk two sizes in the wash, that a toy contained a dangerous sharp part, that the mileage on a second-hand vehicle was not what it was claimed to be, or that goods were over-priced. In each case the TSO has to gather the facts and, in the light of these, to decide whether or not the law has been broken. If it has, the TSO makes out a report and eventually decides whether to take the trader to court.

The work is diverse and mainly carried out away from the office. It also involves working some unsocial hours. TSOs meet a great variety of people and have much scope for decision-making. Most authorities offer a good career structure within the constraints of local government spending. There are now increasing opportunities for TSOs to be employed by traders to ensure that they do not inadvertently break the law.

Enforcement officers work with TSOs in the criminal enforcement aspects of the work. *Consumer advisers* give advice to the public and may pass queries to TSOs if they need investigation.

Training The Diploma in Trading Standards is a statutory requirement for TSOs responsible for overseeing weighing and measuring legislation. The syllabus includes relevant civil and criminal law, metrology, statistics, trading practice, quality assurance, enforcement and advice. To study for the DTS it is necessary to be employed by a local authority; the course takes 18 months.

There are 2 routes to the DTS:

1. An approved specialist degree course. A pass at level 2:2 or above may lead to exemption of academic elements of the DTS.

2. Accreditation of Prior Experience and Learning (APEL). In some local authorities candidates with an appropriate degree, for example in law or a science, can acquire experience through work alongside TSOs as an enforcement officer or consumer adviser, before progressing to the DTS.

The Diploma in Consumer Affairs is a recognized qualification for people not involved in weighing and measuring, but who are employed for specific enforcement roles. They may work, for example, in consumer credit (including debt counselling), animal health inspection and food safety checking. Trainees learn on the job with distance- or block-learning. They take 'core' subjects, such as law and government and consumer protection, and modules on specific subjects. They can add other modules during their career.

Personal attributes Ability to grasp a great many facts and apply them in a practical way; good communication skills, written and verbal; scrupulous attention to detail; self-confidence and ability to work on one's own unsupervised; ability to explain technical points clearly to traders and consumers; diplomacy.

Late start In theory, people with a background in business or law should have reasonable chances. In practice, when vacancies for trainees are limited, as now, young graduates are often given preference.

Work life balance Local authorities are introducing flexible working practices. A career break should be possible.

Further information The Trading Standards Institute, 3–5 Hadleigh Business Centre, 351 London Road, Hadleigh, Essex ss7 2bt (or contact the local Trading Standards Office).
www.tradingstandards.gov.uk

Related careers CONSUMER SCIENTIST/HOME ECONOMICS – ENVIRONMENTAL HEALTH OFFICER – HEALTH AND SAFETY INSPECTORS – LAW

Travel Agent/Tour Operator

Entry qualifications None specified, but entrants to travel agencies usually have several GCSEs. A vocational A level/GNVQ or Scottish equivalent (see p. 10) in travel and tourism offers a relevant option. Also increasing *graduate* entry (mainly tour operators). Foreign languages especially useful for incoming tourism.

Travel and tourism form the UK's biggest growth industry, employing 1.5 million people. It overlaps with the growing leisure industry and is essentially concerned with providing services for people who are away from home, on business or on holiday. These may be UK residents travelling within Britain or going abroad or 'incoming' tourists who make a substantial contribution to the UK economy. More people travel for necessity than for leisure – about 85% of air travel is for business – but both business and leisure travellers increasingly seek a broader range of services and more sophisticated or unusual ways of spending their time and money. The business traveller may want sports facilities and saunas. The holiday-maker may want to try hang-gliding, hill-walking, wine-tasting, bird-watching or painting. Adventure tourism is a growing specialism and there are now courses for those wanting to lead expeditions.

Many jobs in tourism are concerned with providing accommodation and food – whether for farm-based holidays or international conferences. Other jobs are in transport operations – from hire car fleets to coach companies, airline operators to Caribbean cruise ships. Others are in entertainment and visitors' attractions, tourist information services and – increasingly important – marketing and promotions. Tourist information is both general and specific, ranging from selling Britain to potential visitors all over the world to helping a family find bed-and-breakfast accommodation in Northumbria.

As the industry becomes more complex and competitive, so it needs better-trained people who are adaptable, creative and thoroughly professional.

This section deals with 2 distinct sectors of the industry: travel agencies and tour operators. A few large companies own agencies, operators and airlines.

Travel agents are the retailers. They sell tour operators' holidays, plan trips for people within the UK and abroad, and sell tickets for rail, air, ferry and coach travel. Some specialize in business travel, arranging travel and accommodation for company executives. *Tour operators* usually specialize in either incoming or outgoing operations. They put together and organize package holidays – anything from self-catering cabins in the Scottish Highlands to trekking in the Himalayas. Tour operators concentrate on planning – and selling – their holidays, with such subdivisions as British and foreign; summer and winter; business and holiday; party and individual packages. Although the bulk of the package holiday business is controlled by a few huge operators, there has been a growth in small companies catering for special interest holidays, for example cycling and art history tours.

Travel Agents

Counter work

The work This is essentially selling. Customers may know what they want and simply buy a ticket for a train journey, or book a world tour, or want some travel literature. But most have no idea of what they want. Their leisure-time tastes must be summed up and 'channelled' into what the counter-clerk thinks is the holiday they will most enjoy in a price range they can afford.

Counter-clerks usually have not been to the places they suggest – but they should know, from travel literature, from colleagues or training courses, as much about the holidays they recommend as possible. They must take trouble with each customer; their responsibility is far greater than that of most other sales assistants. Most people 'buy' only one holiday a year, and if this one is not a success, they will go to another agency next year.

Bookings are made using computerized systems and by telephone. Clerks have to make sure their customers have the necessary information and print-outs and keep them in touch if arrangements cannot be finalized immediately. Itineraries and currency conversion have to be worked out, timetables checked, car hire arranged. Minor errors can have disastrous consequences for customers' holidays and trips.

Business house clerks deal with companies making travel arrangements for their staff. Business travel agencies may offer a 24–hour service so clerks work in shifts.

Managers coordinate the work of clerks and select those tour operators' brochures which they think will offer their clients what they want. As their profit is made from selling packages, travel agents must have good knowledge of tourist areas and also know how to advertise and promote their services to existing and potential clients.

Opportunities in travel agencies have levelled out in recent years. There is a high proportion of junior to senior staff, so promotion prospects are not very good.

Tour Operators

Planning

This is done by directors or tour managers. 'Planning trips' last from 1 to 8 weeks twice a year and are exhausting. 2 or 3 resorts and perhaps 12 hotels may be investigated in a day. Local transport, garage facilities, food, amusements, beaches will be checked and local tourist officials consulted. Planning of the tour later involves checking timetables and maps, costing, and conferring with transport and accommodation services suppliers. Costing is crucial and the success of operators depends largely on ability to negotiate discounted prices with hotels, villa companies, airlines, etc. All this has to be done up to 2 years in advance, which adds to the difficulties, as the information supplied must be accurate.

Sales

Sales people visit travel agents to make sure brochures are on display. Those companies specializing in school parties (for example, to ski resorts) have a sales team which visits schools to try to win their custom.

Representatives or couriers

Many are freelance and are employed for the summer or winter season (occasionally both) by individual companies. The majority work with incoming tours, i.e. with overseas visitors to Britain. A minority work overseas, either travelling with groups from Britain to their holiday destination or based at a resort. Some may do secretarial work and/ or planning off-season. This is not a career as such but rather a pleasant change for competent secretaries/linguists or simply good organizers. Training is mainly provided by the company (although 1 or 2 private organizations run short courses for people hoping to become couriers).

Most travel staff work long hours and most Saturday mornings.

Training Training can be full or part time or by distance-learning. NVQs/SVQs are well established.

1. The 2-year Travel Training Programme, a Foundation or Advanced Modern Apprenticeship run by TTC Training, is the main way into travel work for school-leavers. There are no set entry requirements, but in practice many trainees have 3–4 GCSEs. Most openings are in travel agencies, but there are also a few in business houses, with tour operators and with airlines. Trainees study for NVQ/SVQs level 2 or 3 in travel services, customer service, telesales or business administration.

2. There are a number of other specialized courses and qualifications which can either 'stand alone' or contribute towards an NVQ/SVQ. The ABTA Certificate in Travel (Travel Agents), formerly known as ABTAC, can be studied at college or by distance-learning. It is available at 2 levels and candidates sit a written test. There is also a specialist qualification for tour operators.

3. BTEC National Certificate or Diploma (see p. 9) in Travel and Tourism (or SQA equivalent).

4. BTEC/SQA Higher National award in related subjects.

5. 'Vocational' degrees in travel and tourism, 3-year full-time or 4-year sandwich. Some other degrees, for example in tourism studies, business studies and leisure management, offer relevant options. Potential applicants should study course syllabuses carefully. Other graduate entry to the industry is possible with qualifications in, for example, marketing or accounting.

6. There are some post-graduate courses and some of these may also accept HND holders. At graduate and post-graduate level *tourism* and *hospitality management* and *leisure management* training and work may overlap.

7. The Institute of Travel and Tourism runs short courses and awards a Diploma.

8. The Guild of Business Travel Agents/City & Guilds Certificate in Business Travel is a qualification at 4 levels – introductory, consultant, supervisory and management. Programmes involve private study or attending courses or a combination of both, workplace assessment and written exams.

Personal attributes Aptitude for figure work; good judgement of people; a friendly manner; accuracy; organizing ability; common sense; a good memory; a liking for selling.

Late start Little opportunity in travel agencies, as most posts filled by school- and college-leavers. Some opportunities with tour operators.

Work life balance As in the retail industry as a whole, travel agency hours are getting longer so there may be opportunities for part-time work or job-sharing. Shift work is usual in business travel agencies. Resort workers can expect very little 'off duty' time. Opportunities for returners depend on contacts, on having kept up with changes in the industry.

Further information TTC Training, The Cornerstone, The Broadway, Woking, Surrey GU21 5AR.
www.ttctraining.co.uk

Institute of Travel and Tourism, Studio 3, Mill Studio, Crane Mead, Ware, Herts SG12 9PY (for careers brochure send s.a.e. + £5).
www.itt.co.uk

Guild of Business Travel Agents, Artillery House, Artillery Row, London SW1P 1RT.
www.gbta-guild.com

Related careers CIVIL AVIATION: *Cabin Crew*; *Ground Staff* – HOTEL AND CATERING – LANGUAGES – LEISURE/RECREATION MANAGEMENT – SECRETARIAL AND CLERICAL WORK

Working for Oneself

Creating one's own job has now established itself as an 'alternative career'. Potential entrepreneurs can get encouragement, advice, and sometimes financial help, from various sources, but their business plan has to stand up to severe scrutiny.

Entry qualifications See 'Personal attributes' and 'Training', below.

The work The variety of self-generated work is unlimited. It can be broadly divided into 3 overlapping types of activity: *providing a service*; *selling*; *making*. Most enterprises combine 2 activities, one of which is usually the crucial one. Deciding which type of enterprise to choose requires a great deal of research, because setting up a business is an uncharted area in conventional career terms. First impressions of what is involved in, say, running a sandwich delivery or motorbike messenger service, or a musical instrument repair or manufacturing workshop, tend to be misleading. They conceal any number of pitfalls – the need for unexpected areas of expertise, or for much more capital than bargained for, for example.

Providing a Service

This requires least capital, involves least risk, covers a vast range, e.g. babysitting, window or office cleaning, running a bicycle delivery service – activities based on using one's time, basic skills and possibly basic equipment; or repairing videos or motorbikes, cooking directors' lunches in offices, running a word processing or computer programming service, i.e. using specific skills plus equipment and, possibly, premises – kitchen, garden shed, living-room.

Professionals – in law, accountancy, systems analysis, etc. – with considerable experience may set up their own computerized service and sell their expertise to companies for specific projects. This is a growing option and enables professionals to be their own boss, working from home, while retaining links with previous employers and at the same time also working for new clients. Companies like it because using people who work from home saves overheads.

Selling

This usually overlaps with *providing a service* or with *making*, or it depends on 'buying-in' goods to sell (or collecting them from friends, etc.). It includes, for example, making sandwiches at home and delivering them to regular customers, or running a second-hand clothes or clutter stall. This kind of selling could be a run-up to opening a shop, restaurant, mail-order business. Selling involves more initial organization and business know-how, capital and risk than *providing a service*.

Making

This usually overlaps with *selling* and covers anything from making children's clothes to assembling car roof-racks to manufacturing high tech components for the computer industry or electric guitars. It ranges from using talent plus basic skills to using sophisticated skills acquired by a range of levels of training, from craft to degree and post-graduate course, plus equipment. It requires some capital and probably premises. But if the idea is viable (see below) and the skills are there, finance and other help is available (see below).

The Law

Far fewer formalities have to be complied with than would-be entrepreneurs tend to fear. The spirit rather than the letter of by-laws has
to be observed. It is not permissible to run a saw-mill in one's garden
because the noise would annoy the neighbours. Local authorities must
be consulted about planning, health and safety and other regulations,
but permission to go ahead is rarely 'unreasonably withheld' in the
present climate of encouragement for so called 'start-ups' – small
businesses. Even the Inland Revenue, which has to be told, advises,
informs and encourages rather than hinders. (Many people, for
example, fear they will have to cope with VAT if they want to set up
in business. In fact few people will reach the annual turnover limit
necessary for registration in the first few years. Useful leaflets can be
ordered from HM Customs and Excise website: *www.hmce.gov.uk*).

Business Format

Again, far fewer formalities have to be observed in the initial stages
than generally believed. The basic formats are (a) *Sole trader*: the
Inland Revenue merely has to be informed that the business exists;
(b) *Partnership*: if two or more people set up a business jointly, a
solicitor draws up a straightforward agreement. Both sole traders and
partnerships are liable for all the debts they incur should the business
fail; (c) *Limited company*: requires slightly more formalities, but once
set up persons involved are only liable for the money they put into
the business should things go wrong; (d) *Cooperatives*: various types;
to set one up solicitors' or special agencies' advice is essential (see
'Further information', below).

Training No formal training structure as for conventional careers
exists, but many business start-ups are based on specific skills.
Welders, beauty therapists, typographers, software engineers, electronics engineers (technicians and graduates), or whatever, must first
acquire the skill they intend to 'sell', i.e. which they want to use as the
basis for their business. (See under individual career headings how to

acquire such skills.) But to survive in the tough business world, basic business know-how is absolutely essential, too. The meaning of such terms as cash-flow, balance sheets, mark-up and, say, the difference between marketing and market research must be understood. The overall failure rate of new mini-ventures is fairly high. However, the failure rate can be linked closely to the level of research done and specialist advice/training taken prior to starting up. Statistics are misleading because there are so many variables which affect success or failure, but there is general agreement among experts that successful entrepreneurship requires several indispensable ingredients:

1. *A marketable idea*: No idea is good in a vacuum. It must fill a gap in a given market. A bike repair service in a seaside suburb mainly inhabited by retired people would fail; one on a new housing estate some miles from shops and offices, etc. stands a good chance (as long as there is no efficient competition or, if there is, the competition has more work than it can cope with and/or the local market is expanding); a mobile grocery-van on that housing estate where few shops have yet been opened sounds a good idea; a mobile grocery-van near a large shopping centre does not; a small-van removal service might flourish in bedsitter-land; it would not in a large-one-family-houses suburb. Researching the market and making a marketing plan are probably the most essential tasks when preparing to go it alone.

2. *Motivation and commitment*: The self-employed have to be willing to work harder, and more irregular hours, than employees usually do (see 'Personal attributes', below).

3. *Resources*: If the idea fills a gap in the market and the commitment is there, advice, possibly financial assistance and help with finding premises (if kitchen/garden shed/living-room are insufficient/unsuitable) are available.

Because the powers-that-be agree that in business small is beautiful (at least to start with) and that an increase in self-generated jobs will reduce unemployment, a plethora of agencies to help 'start-ups' have sprung up over the last few years. Many of these have since disappeared, but there are still several sources of help, advice and training which can help those starting a new business to avoid some of the more obvious pitfalls and to maximize their chances of success.

The main change has been the replacement of national schemes by more locally based initiatives (see 'Training', below).

The 2 main points of contact for new entrepreneurs are:

1. The *Small Business Service* can put inquirers in touch with their local Business Link office, linked through their website. The Business Links offer a range of services and access to Personal Business Advisers for small firms and anyone setting up a new business. Similar services are offered through the Small Business Gateway (*www.bgateway.com*) and Highlands and Islands Enterprise (*www.hie.co.uk*) in Scotland, Business Eye (*www.businesseye.org.uk*) in Wales, and Invest Northern Ireland (*www.investni.com*).

2. *Local Enterprise Agencies*: there are several hundreds of these, privately run. They help with information on the local business scene, with forming a business plan and with business counselling generally. They can give advice on tax, marketing, law, etc.

At the time of writing most of these services are free. Other useful organizations are:

3. The *Countryside Agency* may be able to provide helpful information to people intending to set up in business in rural areas.

4. The *Crafts Council* will advise people thinking of setting up a pottery, weaving or similar crafts workshop.

5. The *Prince's Trust* and *Livewire* advise and help young people (under-25s usually) who choose the self-employment option.

6. Some business studies degrees, post-graduate courses, BTEC and SQA awards (including BTEC Continuing Education units) have self-employment options.

7. *Some local colleges* run courses which, though not necessarily planned for potential entrepreneurs, are very useful – e.g. in book-keeping, marketing, basic computer application. Some are evening classes, others are 1 day a week.

Personal attributes Unquenchable resilience; tenacity; decisiveness; organizing ability; being a bit bossy; exceptional stamina; business acumen; enjoying risk-taking – being a bit of a gambler; ability to put up with temporary hardship; resourcefulness; self-confidence bordering on conceit; true enjoyment of hard work; ability to get on well with other people however unreasonable their requests/criticisms/impatience; imagination; ability to work under pressure; interest in economic and social trends. (Extent of these qualities depends on extent of venturesomeness of enterprise contemplated.)

Late start Age is a positive advantage in this 'alternative' career. Anyone who has had experience of the world of work scores over school/college-leavers when it comes to applying to banks, etc. for funds or to other agencies for premises or other help. Career-changers and returners are welcome on courses.

Work life balance In theory if you are your own boss you can arrange your own hours. In practice it is often customers or clients who dictate a working pattern so if the business is being considered in order to fit around family or other commitments, some thought needs to be given to priorities. For example, how will you respond if a vital call comes through just as you are dashing out to pick up the children from school? Working from home not only means you do not travel to work, it also means you are never away from work. Anyone who thinks self-employment is a synonym for part-time employment should think again. If the intention is to earn more than pin money, self-employed people on average probably work longer hours than employed people. However, with organization and contingency planning, it can work very well.

Further information Business Link: national call service: 0845 600 9006

 www.businesslink.org

Scotland: Small Business Gateway Helpline: 0845 609 6611

 www.sbgateway.com

Crafts Council, 44A Pentonville Road, London N1 9BY.

 www.craftscouncil.org.uk

Livewire: Freepost Livewire, Newcastle upon Tyne NE1 1BR.

 www.shell.livewire.org

The Prince's Trust, 18 Park Square East, London NW1 4LH.

 www.princes-trust.org.uk

Small Business Bureau, Curzon House, Church Road, Windlesham, Surrey GU20 6BH.
www.smallbusinessbureau.org.uk

National Federation of Enterprise Agencies, Trinity Gardens, 9–11 Bromham Road, Bedford MK40 2UQ.
www.nfea.com

Countryside Agency, John Dower House, Crescent Place, Cheltenham, Gloucestershire GL50 3RA.
www.countryside.gov.uk

Several high street banks have useful booklets on running your own business.

Related careers MANAGEMENT

Youth and Community Work

Entry qualifications Depend on age and experience. See 'Training', below.

The work Youth and community workers are concerned with young people aged between 11 and 25, giving priority to those between 13 and 19. Their work has elements in common with education and social work. The social education of young people is their primary concern, helping them to explore their strengths and weaknesses, develop physical, intellectual, moral, social and emotional resources, and facilitate their growth from childhood to adulthood. Recent years have seen increased 'targeting' of disadvantaged groups, but current debate sets that against the need for more mainstream work. Many young people stay at home these days in rooms full of TVs, videos, stereos and computers – all essentially passive entertainments – and miss many opportunities for social development.

Job titles vary. People with different titles can be doing substantially the same work, while the work of people with the same title can vary greatly. *Youth workers* or *youth and community workers* may be club- or centre-based, 'detached' or community-based. In a club or centre the youth worker plans activities to appeal to a wide range of ages and tastes. They give young people the means to mix socially and organize themselves, to develop confidence and skills, both practical (e.g. in sport or drama) and social (e.g. cooperating as part of a team), to channel their energies in a constructive way. Forming relationships with young people is a very important part of the work and may involve the youth worker in counselling or unofficial social work. For example, the youth worker may be the first person to recognize signs of drug abuse or the bottled-up effects of a family break-up.

In some centres activities are organized for other groups within the community, e.g. mother and toddler groups, pre-school play-groups, leisure interest classes, literacy classes or English for immigrants. Sometimes the youth and community worker is responsible for such activities; sometimes the role is one of liaison with other groups.

Many youth and community workers are 'detached', i.e. they do not work from a fixed base. Some go out into the community to make contact with young people who do not come to clubs to identify their needs and help develop community solutions. Others do project work on, for example, drug abuse, unemployment or health education. Some youth workers are attached to schools (they usually need teaching qualifications) where their work includes contributing to PSHE (personal, social and health education), citizenship and study support programmes. A number also work in social services departments with 'at risk' young people.

Youth work is very dependent on part-time, often voluntary workers. Even in a large centre there may be only 1 qualified worker, and, increasingly, qualified workers are given area responsibility for a number of clubs or centres. This means that qualified youth and community workers have less face-to-face contact with young people. Their job includes lots of administration, organizing of events and activities, recruitment, training and support of part-time workers, management of budgets and premises, liaison with the management committee and other groups, and seeking grants, sponsorship and other material support.

Youth and community workers are employed by local authorities (the Youth or Youth and Community Service is usually part of the education department, but sometimes comes under the leisure department) or by voluntary groups; it is estimated that 80% of youth work is provided by the voluntary groups (e.g. churches and organizations like Guides and Scouts). There is, however, a great deal of cooperation between the statutory and voluntary sectors.

In England, the Youth Service is a key partner in the new Connexions Service, which provides advice, guidance and personal development opportunities for all young people aged between 13 and 19. Both professional and voluntary youth workers are able to train for the new profession of Personal Advisers in the delivery of the Connexions Service (see CAREERS WORK, p. 132). Existing support services for young people are also being strengthened in Scotland, Wales and Northern Ireland. Although new professional opportunities are available for youth workers in these countries, they are not following the Connexions model.

Training This is flexible and ensures that suitable people, whatever their age and educational qualifications, have a chance of qualifying. Though applicants for courses are normally expected to have 3 GCSEs (A–C) and 2 A levels plus experience of voluntary or paid (for example, *playleader*) work with young people and/or other community work, applicants whose practical work experience has shown that they are suitable for the work may be accepted with lower educational qualifications. However, those wishing to work with young people without qualifications must commit themselves to a programme of training to achieve a qualification. Minimum entry age varies from one course to another and again depends on individuals' experience and maturity.

The National Youth Agency ensures the quality and development of youth work training at all levels in England and a list of courses is available on their website. The professional validation of courses in Northern Ireland and the Irish Republic, and in Wales, is undertaken by the Youth Council for Northern Ireland and the Wales Youth Agency respectively. There are 2 types of qualification – level 2 and 3 Vocational Qualifications and Professional Qualifications. All qualifications are based on national occupational standards for youth work, developed by the National Training Organisation for Youth Work, PAULO *www.paulo.org.uk*.

Level 2 and 3 youth work training, previously known as 'basic', 'local', 'introductory', or 'part-time' training leading to 'locally qualified' status, has undergone significant change in the last few years. Currently, each local authority and many voluntary youth services will offer a programme of basic training. Some of the training may be classroom based and some will be supported learning in the workplace.

Local authority and voluntary youth services will normally expect achievement of a level 3 NVQ.

For work at higher levels, a professional qualification is normally required. The minimum professional qualification is a Dip HE in Youth Work or a Foundation degree. There are also other types of higher education awards that count as professional qualification. A few institutions offer distance-learning programmes.

The different qualifications are:

1. Dip HE: 2 years full time and part-time equivalent, some employment based.

2. Foundation degree: 2 years full time or part-time equivalent, employment based.

3. BA (Hons): 3 years full time and part-time equivalent.

4. PGCert/PGDip: 1 year full time and part-time equivalent.

5. MA: 1 year full time and part-time equivalent.

In Scotland the minimum qualification for professionally qualified status is a degree. Programmes of study leading to professional status are validated by Community Education Validation and Endorsement or CeVe.

Personal attributes An outgoing personality; ability to communicate easily with people who may need 'drawing out'; patience; imagination to put oneself into the shoes of people who feel alienated from society; wide interests in current social and economic trends and problems; organizing ability; feeling at ease with people of all ages; creativity to think up activities (see also SOCIAL WORK, 'Personal attributes', p. 566).

Late start Mature candidates are welcome on courses. This can be a suitable 'second career' for people changing direction in their 20s or 30s, if they have relevant experience.

Work life balance Many posts require working unsociable hours. Flexible working policies are being introduced in local authorities but ample opportunities have always existed for part-time work in youth work. Job-sharing is beginning to appear. A career break should not be a problem.

Further information The National Youth Agency, 17–23 Albion Street, Leicester LE1 6GD.
www.nya.org.uk
Community Learning Scotland, Rosebery House, 9 Haymarket Terrace, Edinburgh EH12 5EZ.
www.communitylearning.org
Wales Youth Agency, Caerphilly CF83 1BQ.
www.wya.org.uk
Youth Council for Northern Ireland, Belfast BT8 4TA.
www.youthcouncil-ni.org.uk
Connexions website: *www.connexions.gov.uk*

Related careers LEISURE/RECREATION MANAGEMENT – SOCIAL WORK – SPORT – TEACHING

Index

Index

Index

Index

Index

Index

Index

Index

Index